General Principles of Law -
The Role of the Judiciary

IUS GENTIUM

COMPARATIVE PERSPECTIVES ON LAW AND JUSTICE

VOLUME 46

More information about this series at http://www.springer.com/series/7888

Laura Pineschi
Editor

General Principles of Law - The Role of the Judiciary

 Springer

Editor
Laura Pineschi
Department of Law
University of Parma
Parma
Italy

ISSN 1534-6781 ISSN 2214-9902 (electronic)
Ius Gentium: Comparative Perspectives on Law and Justice
ISBN 978-3-319-19179-9 ISBN 978-3-319-19180-5 (eBook)
DOI 10.1007/978-3-319-19180-5

Library of Congress Control Number: 2015939924

Springer Cham Heidelberg New York Dordrecht London

Printed on acid-free paper

Springer International Publishing AG Switzerland is part of Springer Science+Business Media (www.springer.com)

Foreword

The papers collected in this volume grew out of a conference on "General Principles of Law and the Judiciary" held at the University of Parma in May, 2014, at the 13th annual meeting of the European-American Consortium for Legal Education (EACLE), under the direction of Prof. Laura Pineschi.

The chapters that follow speak for themselves and are a tribute to the editor and organizers at Parma. The formal program is reflected in the table of contents. Less immediately visible, but equally valuable, were the many opportunities for serendipitous mutual enlightenment to be found the less formal interstices of a beautiful setting, among kind and generous hosts.

This recalls the broader project, of which this volume and the Parma conference are such excellent exempla—the pursuit of justice and the rule of law through transnational dialog, the exchange of insights, and the comparison of similar but differing experiences. Law often is and sometimes should be parochial in its development, but lawyers and legislators will benefit from better understanding the contingency (and frequent imperfections) of their own local practices and institutions.

Europe and the USA provide particularly useful opportunities for mutual advancement in their shared (but inevitably partial and imperfect) commitment to the liberal and republican principles of universal human dignity and equal justice for all. When shared general principles yield differing practical results, we can and should question the unstated assumptions of our parochial traditions.

Experience in every nation has shown a strong and independent judiciary to be the necessary basis for any just rule of law. Laws and their interpretation require the support and guidance of fundamental legal principles, many of which transcend local particularities and are valuable everywhere. This volume challenges our preconceptions and offers insights to improve judges and justice in any legal system that cares to serve the people that it rules. The judiciary is and always will be the last best guardian of the general and universal principles that justify and animate the law.

Baltimore, MD, USA   Mortimer N.S. Seller

Contents

Contributors

Michele Boggiani is a Ph.D. Candidate in Criminal Law at the Department of Law of the University of Parma, Parma, Italy.

Silvia Borelli is Principal Lecturer in International Law and Director of Research at the University of Bedfordshire, Bedfordshire, United Kingdom, and Visiting Professor at the Department of Law of the University of Parma, Parma, Italy.

Monica Cappelletti is a Research Fellow in Comparative Public Law at the Department of Law of the University of Parma, Parma, Italy.

Elena Carpanelli is a Ph.D. Candidate in International Law at the University of Milan-Bicocca, Milan, Italy.

Francesco De Vanna is a Ph.D. Candidate in Legal Theory at the Department of Law of the University of Parma, Parma, Italy.

Katarzyna Girdwoyń is an Assistant Professor in Criminal Law at the University of Warsaw, Poland.

Nicole Lazzerini is a Research Fellow in European Union Law at the Department of Law of the University of Parma, Parma, Italy.

Elaine Mak is a Professor of Empirical Study of Public Law at the Erasmus University Rotterdam, The Netherlands.

Leonardo Marchettoni is a Researcher in Legal Theory at the Department of Law of the University of Parma, Parma, Italy.

Francesco Mazzacuva is a Research Fellow in Criminal Law at the Department of Law of the University of Parma, Parma, Italy.

Gianluigi Palombella is a Professor of Legal Theory at the Department of Law of the University of Parma, Parma, Italy, and at Scuola Superiore Sant'Anna, Pisa, Italy.

Fabio Pantano is a Researcher in Labour Law at the Department of Law of the University of Parma, Parma, Italy.

Christopher J. Peters is a Professor of Law at the University of Baltimore, Baltimore, United States of America.

Laura Pineschi is a Professor of International Law at the Department of Law of the University of Parma, Parma, Italy.

Mortimer N.S. Sellers is Regents Professor at the University System of Maryland and Director of the Center for International and Comparative Law of the University of Baltimore, Baltimore, United States of America.

Frederic N. Smalkin is Chief United States District Judge of the District of Maryland (Ret.), and Jurist-in-Residence at the University of Baltimore, Baltimore, United States of America.

Veronica Valenti is a Researcher in Constitutional Law at the University of Parma, Parma, Italy.

Abbreviations

ACHR	American Convention on Human Rights
ACHPR	African Charter on Human and Peoples' Rights
ADA	American with Disabilities Act
ADEA	Age Discrimination in the Employment Act
BAILII	British and Irish Legal Information Institute
BVerfG	Bundesverfassunggericht
CAT	Convention against Torture
CJEU	Court of Justice of the European Union
CRA	Civil Rights Act
CTR	Claims Tribunal
DCFR	Draft Common Frame of References
DOMA	Defense of Marriage Act
EACLE	European American Consortium for Legal Education
EC	European Community
ECHR	Convention for the Protection of Human Rights and Fundamental Freedoms
ECJ	European Court of Justice
ECR	European Court Reports
ECtHR	European Court of Human Rights
EEC	European Economic Community
EPA	The Equal Pay Act
ETS	European Treaty Series
EU	European Union
EWHC	High Court of England and Wales
GC	Grand Chamber
I/ACommHR	Inter-American Commission on Human Rights
IACtHR	Inter-American Court of Human Rights
ICCPR	International Covenant on Civil and Political Rights
ICESCR	International Covenant on Economic, Social and Cultural Rights
ICJ	International Court of Justice
ICJ Rep.	International Court of Justice Reports

ICTY	International Criminal Tribunal for the Former Yugoslavia
ILC	International Law Commission
ILM	International Legal Materials
ISAF	International Security Assistance Force
ITLOS	International Tribunal of the Law of the Sea
LGBT	Lesbian, Gay, Bisexual and Transsexual
LJN	Landelijk Jurispr Nr
NWO	Netherlands Organization for Scientific Research
OAS	Organization of American States
OJ	Official Journal
OSPAR	Oslo/Paris Convention (for the Protection of the Marine Environment of the North-East Atlantic)
PCIJ	Permanent Court of International Justice
PECL	Principles of European Contract Law
QB	Queen's Bench
RBPFP	Reinstatement and the Payment of Back Pays and Front Pays
RC	Reparatory Compensation
RIAA	Reports of International Arbitral Awards
SCR	Supreme Court Reports
TEU	Treaty on European Union
TFEU	Treaty on the Functioning of the European Union
UK	United Kingdom
UKHL	United Kingdom House of Lords
UKSC	Supreme Court of the United Kingdom
UN	United Nations
UNCLOS	United Nations Convention on the Law of the Sea
UNTS	United Nations Treaty Series
UPDF	Uganda People's Defense Force
US	United States
USC	United States Code
VCLT	Vienna Convention on the Law of Treaties
WTO	World Trade Organization

Note to the Reader

- Unless otherwise stated, all internet websites cited in the book have been last accessed in March 2015.
- After the Treaty of Lisbon, the Court of Justice of the European Union (CJEU) includes the Court of Justice (ECJ), the General Court (formerly, Court of First Instance), and specialized courts (see Article 19, para. 1, TEU).

Introduction

In an increasingly complex world, the nature and function of law is rapidly changing. Arising from multiple sources and layers of regulation, legal rules progressively increase in number and tend to become more specific. The result is a fragmented legal landscape, in which contradictions are almost inevitable. Often, the task of dealing with this complexity is left to the judiciary.

Against this background, general principles of law play a prominent role in every legal system as they permeate the daily activity of domestic, regional, and international courts. Not only general principles of law (e.g., independence and impartiality) have a significant impact on the activity of the judiciary. Indeed judges have a critical role in identifying and interpreting principles, thus determining their status and, in some instances, their normative content within a given legal system. It is not uncommon for national and international tribunals to resort to general principles in their reasoning as a tool to ensure a dynamic interpretation of legal rules. General principles are used to adapt existing rules to new developments, needs, or values, to fill lacunae, and to contribute to the development of new rules. Sometimes judges "transplant" general principles from one legal system to another; frequently, international tribunals contribute to the unity of the international legal order by means of trough the application of general principles. Thus, in a world of legal pluralism and fragmented regulation, general principles often provide those bridges which are necessary to ensure that the law maintains a minimum degree of consistency and coherence.

It is beyond the scope of this book to provide a systematic and comprehensive investigation of a very broad topic. Rather, the book intends to offer some reflections, mainly in a comparative perspective and from different horizons, through the contribution of European and US scholars from various legal fields.

The volume is in four sections. In the first section, issues of legal theory are examined in light of national and international jurisprudence. The second section explores the role of general principles in selected legal systems, i.e., international law, European Union law, and common law systems. The third section features an analysis of certain general principles from a comparative perspective, with particular focus on the comparison between European and American experiences. The fourth and the last section includes chapters on the role of judges and general principles in given areas of law.

Obviously, a project of this kind risks ending up with a fragmentary set of individual studies. To avoid (or, at least, to reduce) this risk, the authors have been invited to strictly adhere to the general topic. As a result, despite an apparently patchwork format (or "impressionistic" approach), all the chapters are connected by a common thread: a reflection on how the interpretation, application, and development of general principles of law by the judiciary contribute to the evolution of legal systems, at the domestic and international levels, and further their reciprocal interactions.

A final conclusion is not feasible in view of the heterogeneous nature of general principles in different legal orders, the continuous evolution of social needs and values, and (sometimes) the ambiguous approach of certain courts and tribunals. Nevertheless, some basic considerations can be developed from the following contributions. First, all the chapters confirm the important, if not decisive, role that judges continue to play in the "shaping" of national and international law through the interpretation and application of general principles. Second, it is also evident that certain fundamental principles play a prominent role against the risk of an unfettered judicial discretion. As a result, general principles may be both a powerful tool for courts and tribunals in the exercise of a quasi-legislative power and a meaningful factor of legal certainty. Finally, as many contributions to this book show, the references by domestic courts to foreign general principles–or principles developed at the international level–are increasingly frequent. This "dialog" and interplay among courts may thus prove fruitful, by enhancing the respect of fundamental rights and values.

Some of the chapters collected in this volume were provisionally presented and discussed at the Annual Conference of the EACLE, held on 20 May 2014 at the University of Parma (Italy) and all the authors are established or early-career scholars at the law schools or faculties involved in this scientific network. The aim is to advance mutual knowledge and understanding of legal systems on both continents in accordance with EACLE's purposes and traditions.

Several institutions and persons made it possible to bring this project to its conclusion. First, I wish to thank the Department of Law of the University of Parma, which hosted the EACLE Conference and to the members of the scientific committee established in view of the Conference (Professors Alberto Cadoppi, Antonio D'Aloia and Enrico Gragnoli). I am particularly grateful to them, for their inspiring comments and suggestions, as well as to Malaika Bianchi, researcher in criminal law, and to Cesare Pitea, researcher in international law, who contributed their enthusiasm and inexhaustible energy to the success of the Conference. My deepest gratitude is due to all the scholars who generously contributed their time and intellectual resources to produce this collective work. Also on their behalf, I warmly thank Elena Carpanelli (Ph.D. candidate in international law) for having patiently and competently ensured a uniform style in the setting up of this volume. It goes without saying that any mistake or inaccuracy remains the sole responsibility of the editor.

Parma   Laura Pineschi
March 2015   Professor of International Law

Part I
General Principles and the Judiciary: Legal Theory and Courts' Interactions

Principles and Disagreements in International Law (with a View from Dworkin's Legal Theory)

Gianluigi Palombella

Abstract Principles are part of international law as much as of other legal orders. Nonetheless, beyond principles referred to the *functioning* of international law, or the sector related discipline in discrete fields, those fundamental principles identifying the *raison d'être*, purpose and value of the legal international order, as a whole, remain much disputed, to say the least. In addressing such a problem, one that deeply affects interpretation and legal adjudication, this chapter acknowledges the limits and weakness of legal positivism in making sense of the inter- and supranational legal order(s). It appraises also the novel from the late Ronald Dworkin, concerning international law, and its consequence for interpretivism in the international environment, so different from State political communities and their "integrity". Finally, some recent cases before international courts shall be considered, that expose difficulties stemming from traditional legal positivist strictures, and explain how judicial reasoning actually profits from asking further questions of principles. All the more so, if the issues at stake happen to be covered by two or more diverging legal regimes, that would, per se, lead to opposite outcomes.

1 Introduction

Despite their disputed nature, principles play a cardinal role in international law and in courts not only by filling legal gaps, but also as fundamental means for the interpretation of rules and the enhancement of legal reasoning.[1]

---

[1]Raimondo (2008).

G. Palombella (✉)
Professor of Legal Theory, University of Parma, Parma, Italy
Scuola Superiore Sant'Anna, Pisa, Italy
e-mail: gianluigi.palombella@unipr.it

© Springer International Publishing Switzerland 2015
L. Pineschi (ed.), *General Principles of Law - The Role of the Judiciary*,
Ius Gentium: Comparative Perspectives on Law and Justice 46,
DOI 10.1007/978-3-319-19180-5_1

A canonical way to see principles in international law places them among the sources of law, as stated by Article 38 (1)(c) of the Statute of the International Court of Justice (ICJ). It is to be noted, however, that they can surface within more than one source. In the context of the ICJ, from Article 38 paragraph (1)(a), or (b), i.e. in the application of conventional or customary law by which they might be generated, beyond the separate provision singling out those principles "recognized among civilized nations", in paragraph (1)(c).[2] Famously, to the latter Hersch Lauterpacht[3]—Judge in the ICJ—referred as subsidiary general principles with the special, systemic, function of banning *non liquet* from the realm of (international) law.

Taking account of that background, the issue can be raised whether some set of principles, distinctively underpinning the international legal order, is capable of shaping its *identity*: as much as in any (State) legal systems, in their constitutional and primary law, principles frame the fundamental—ethical and political—choices to be pursued. They would function as gap-filling as well as interpretive resources supporting international law as a whole.

Accordingly, they *should belong in the fundamental raison d'être of international law properly*. Besides principles of law-functioning, referring to how international law can work, like *pacta sunt servanda* or, say, *good faith*, they would be closer to the question as to *why* it is valued and *what* are being its substantive purposes.

In truth, such a question is not different from the one most recently tackled by the late Ronald Dworkin, in a posthumous article,[4] suggesting legal principles that, in his view, would frame international law, and help resolving "disagreements" in identifying positive international law norms, to be applied in adjudicative issues.

This chapter shall also consider whether an "interpretive" theory of law (renowned as one addressing the alleged weakness of strict legal positivism) can better suit the increasing appearance of principles and the current evolutionary trends of international law. To this regard, judicial cases, namely those originating from being a single issue under the reach of concurring, and often conflicting, legalities, shall be eventually examined. Among their many functions in international law, principles can help reconciling divergences stemming from the multiplicity of separate "regimes" (presently featuring in international law) that hardly would be solved by "formal" legal tools (*lex specialis*, *lex posterior*, etc.).[5]

---

[2]Ibid., p. 42.

[3]Lauterpacht (1975) [1958].

[4]Dworkin (2013), p. 1 ff.

[5]Koskenniemi, Introduction, in Conclusions of the Work of the Study Group on the Fragmentation of International Law: Difficulties arising from the Diversification and Expansion of International Law, International Law Commission, 58th session, 2006, UN Doc. A/61/10, para. 251. On the proliferation of regimes and courts, for example, Shany (2003).

2 What (and Whose) Principles?

2.1 "General principles of law recognised by civilised nations" (Article 38(1)(c)) are held to play the function of those clauses that in domestic systems refer to natural law (as in the Austrian Civil Code, Article 7) or the general principles of the legal order of the State (Italian Civil Code, preliminary Article 12). As a consequence, reference to them is mainly meant to face the issue of legal *lacunae*. It embraces the doctrine of a legal system's *completeness*, one that in turn justifies, as mentioned above, (the feasibility of) the prohibition of *non liquet*[6]: "'the principle affirming the completeness of the legal order' is to be seen as 'the positive formulation of the prohibition of *non liquet*'".[7] And both should be seen as positive rules in *customary law*.[8]

In truth, reference to principles belonging to civilised legal systems has been understood as evoking *jus gentium*, and it is contended upon, between at least two main theoretical strands. One assumes that these principles pertain to no particular system, being instead fundamental to all systems, and showing the essential unity of law, apparently as a matter of reason.[9] The other derives its rationale from comparative legal approaches: enquiry throughout various national systems shows that the widest consensus supports some legal principles that accordingly become general international law, "independently of custom or treaties".[10]

The resort of general principles, if seen through legal realist lenses, equates with an opening in favour of judicial discretion, if not judicial norm-creation. From some legal realist standpoint, general principles have been feared as the "Trojan horse" of natural law and morality into the interstices of positive norms.[11] For Julius Stone (commenting on Lauterpacht):

> Even if, for the sake of argument, we were to accept the "natural law" version most favorable to Judge Lauterpacht's position, namely, that these principles represent a kind of inexhaustible storehouse of potential law, they still would not dispense the judge from making law-creative choices.[12]

---

[6]For J. Stone: "*Non liquet* comes into argument rather when applicable rules of appropriate content and precision are simply not available for adjusting the particular clash of interests". See Stone (1959), p. 124.

[7]Lauterpacht (1975) [1958], p. 216.

[8]Ibid., p. 196.

[9]Cheng (2006) [1953], p. 24.

[10]Hearn (1990), p. 225.

[11]In different words, the door opening to (rule's) validity criteria placed outside the legal system. The duty to decide holds despite absent or conflicting rules; its feasibility is granted by recourse to principles, whose membership in the legal system—if any—would hardly prevent any reference to law of nature or of reason.

[12]Stone (1959), p. 133.

Stone stressed the point, later become largely undisputed among legal scholars, that principles might be conflicting themselves, "and, indeed, often to the same principle by reason of its ambiguity, circuity or indeterminacy" can be traced diverse outcomes.[13] Stone's early criticism notwithstanding, legal systems are undoubtedly held to include principles, whose standards, far from being a sheer appeal to vague morality or natural law, are positive law essential in the construction of present legal orders.

As I see them, and as legal theory and jurisprudence have abundantly afforded consistent evidence in that regard, principles as normative standards, regardless of their treatment in different legal theories, hold a central place as positive law. Likewise, even those most structural "general principles of law", play a fundamental function in every legal order: this is why Article 38 of the ICJ Statute upholds them as recognized among civilized nations, given their belonging to *law functioning*, as Lauterpacht would have them. Bin Cheng's analysis has recorded the general principles of law through their use by international courts and tribunals and listed several such as self-preservation, good faith (and notably *pacta sunt servanda*, as well as malicious exercise of a right), varieties of sections on the principle of responsibility (fault, causality, individual responsibility, integral reparation, among them), most principles in judicial proceedings (from those inherent in jurisdiction to the various *jura novit curia, audiatur et altera pars, nemo judex in causa propria, res judicata*, etc.).[14]

2.2 Also due to the special features of the international legal system, the capacity and latitude of fixed rules stricto sensu, in a positivist view, appears at times limited: be it a matter of completeness of the system or otherwise, there are cases where international norms have led to no answer or otherwise stated, unsatisfactory outcomes. As Jan Klabbers has recalled:

> [M]any have held that the bombing of Belgrade in 1999 was illegal, yet legitimate; the non-activity of the United Nations in Rwanda or Srebrenica, in the mid-1990s, was legally difficult to condemn, yet morally wrong.[15]

It is because of these and similar issues, that Klabbers is focusing on some "virtue ethics" that should be inherently essential for at least those that are entrusted to make the most of international law norms, and international judges among them.[16] And not by chance, among the general principles of international

---

[13]As a consequence, a "law-creating choice" shall be in place, although it shall be disguised by way of "logical deduction from the principle finally chosen" (Ibid.).

[14]Cheng (2006) [1953].

[15]Klabbers (2013), p. 430. See Simma (1999) and Robertson (2000), pp. 68–72.

[16]Some requisites of personal integrity, impartiality, honesty and the like are held for UN officials, and codes of conduct for those with special mandates as Rapporteurs. Cf. Klabbers (2013), p. 433 ff. See also Human Rights Council, Resolution 5/2, Code of Conduct for Special Procedures Mandate-Holders of the Human Rights Council, 9th session, Article 3(e), 18 June 2007.

law, *good faith* is in pride of place in measuring how should the key norm—*pacta sunt servanda*—be observed.[17]

However, aside from the prospect of a possible virtue ethics in international law, as a matter of fact those problems that stem from missing or conflicting norms—or that as such are perceived—seem to be increasingly apparent in international law context, all the more so due to the more demanding objectives of the "civilised nations" in the last sixty years. Thus, the full range of available international law principles is hardly overestimated and should better be felt as part of an ongoing constructive endeavor: it embraces certainly general principles of the law of civilized nations, principles of law-functioning, but also the principles belonging to specialized international rule-making (in, say, trade law, human rights law, environmental law, humanitarian law and the like).[18] Nonetheless, it is worth supposing that adjudicative matters would better be viewed could one be drawing on *principles bearing some substantive raison d'être* of international law as a *specific legal order.*

To such principles might lead, for example, Anne Peters "compensatory constitutionalism" as encapsulating a general rationale of current international law. It conceives international law under a specific understanding which, through evidence of what she defines micro and macro constitutionalisation trends, enhances fundamental norms that would help manage transnational level issues. Conflict-solution requires a balancing of interests in the concrete case, in the absence of abstract hierarchy. According to Peters, the international lawyer should determine "the supremacy of international law over domestic constitutional law in a non formalist way", that is, assessing the rank of the norms at stake "according to their substantial weight and significance".[19] However, fundamental norms would require some legitimacy, in the absence of a true international constitution, while State sovereignty and consent are no longer accepted as the sole source of legitimacy of international law.[20]

As I see it, the interplay between different regimes of law and separate orders in the global intercourses should be guided through mutually pondering their

---

[17]Vienna Convention on the Law of Treaties (Vienna, 23 May 1969), 1155 UNTS 331, Article 26: "Every treaty in force is binding upon the parties to it and must be performed by them in good faith".

[18]Those principles range from higher-lower levels of generality: think of the principle of non discrimination in its specific World Trade Organization (WTO) appearance as the "most favoured nation" principle, and its underlying rationale of enhancing unrestricted free trade. For example, it is maintained that: "In the current WTO, the traditional trade law principles of most favoured nation and national treatment operate against state failure in the form of protectionism. These principles are constitutive of the system of multilayered governance and thus may be considered as amounting to constitutional principles of the trading system. They constrain the WTO members and are increasingly viewed as two facets of a constitutional principle of non-discrimination ultimately benefiting the ordinary citizens (such as importers, exporters, producers, consumers and taxpayers)" (Armingeon et al. (2011), p. 76).

[19]Peters (2009), p. 348.

[20]Peters (2006).

respective fundamental principles; as they function like hermeneutic sources of interpretation of rules, it is relevant how international law rationale and legitimacy are justified and through what substantive principles.

2.3 Such a question is of a type familiar to State legal orders and to *constitutional* reasoning in the last decades. It is plain fact that substantive principles, often enshrined in our Constitutions, define scope, values, and purpose of a legal order as a whole, by channelling rules' interpretation on one side and, on the other, connecting its general coherence both to the logical consistency of its norms and to the evolving political-ethical pillars of its own community of people.

Although such a role of principles has become uncontested, it was famously made part of a self-standing theory of law, neither positivist nor naturalist, but *interpretivist*, by Ronald Dworkin: a theory that is centred explicitly upon the *adjudicative* side.[21] Each legal order is to be referred to its own community, and principles belong to or constitute a bridge toward the *integrity* of its *political morality*. In truth, an interpretivist theory of law could accordingly be extended to international law, as much as to any legal orders properly meant, provided that a general *rationale* characterising the essential principles in the political morality of an *international* system of law is found.

However, in the tradition of legal positivism, from Austin to Hart, the very foundations and the maturity of international law as a legal order were never fully recognised,[22] on the other hand, substantive principles, of an ultimate nature, sustaining international law are not easily (nor unanimously) presupposed, despite the number of supranational preambles, charters, conventions and quasi-universal convergence upon peace, security, human rights (let alone *jus cogens* and banning of war, torture, genocide, slavery). It is contentious if historical progress of international law has overcome the traditional core of a law treating bilateral interests under the dogma of States' free will; if a *super partes* law,[23] to be oriented by the interests of humanity has changed its nature[24]; if individuals have superseded States as the ultimate subjects for whose sake sovereignty itself appears now a conditional notion,[25] and so forth.

If we imagined to adopt an interpretivist approach, by Dworkin's lessons drawn on Western constitutional States, it would be arduous to argue through the key notion of *integrity*,[26] extended to international law. That concept connects coherence of a legal order with the political morality of a well-defined social polity, while inter-state arena would still lack the unity of something like a universal community.

Nonetheless, in the article of his last days,[27] eventually Dworkin tried to offer the missing template for international law, and extended his "interpretivist" theory of law to the domain of *extra*-State law, by providing some newly forged support.

---

[21] Among his many works especially Dworkin (1986).

[22] Waldron (2013a), pp. 209–223.

[23] Cassese (2005), p. 217.

[24] Teitel (2011), Cassese (2008).

[25] Slaughter (2005), pp. 619–631.

[26] Dworkin (1986), pp. 176–275.

[27] Dworkin (2013), p. 1 ff.

He did so, by spelling what he believed the fundamental principles that specifically attain to international law, those that should *justify* the existence of the international legal order. Of course, even if found controversial, still they can set the scene for a long awaited focus upon the distinctive underpinning of international law, thereby making interpretive endeavour to begin as a *principle-based exercise*.

3 The Late Dworkin's Theory of International Law

3.1 Dworkin rejects the positivist and Hartian idea[28] according to which rules are valid only depending on the criteria of recognition spelled by a fundamental secondary rule of the legal system. He refutes on one side the *conclusiveness* of such a theory as policing system's borders, on the other side, the social convention that is held to pinpoint specifically the birth and life of international law, that is, States' *consent*.

The latter remains unpersuasive: it does not establish any priority among sources, gives no clue on whose consent is ultimately relevant, or when customary rules become peremptory; and what have States consented to remains often disputed (in many cases text cannot be decisive: e.g. Article 2(4) UN Charter on prohibition of the use of force). Even more fundamentally, for States to accept something as law, "they need some other standard to decide what they should regard as law".[29] *That* more basic principle, not the fact of consent, provides "the grounds of international law": similarly, the obligating strength of promises, cannot be due to the mere *fact* of promising.[30]

Thus, being consent irredeemably flawed (and Dworkin is not alone in making that point),[31] the "sociological" and descriptive answer according to which international law is law because it is believed law by "almost everyone"[32] cannot be final.[33]

Briefly to resume, Dworkin states that it is in order to improve the legitimacy of *their* coercive strength *vis-à-vis* their citizens, that States have a duty to accept a *mitigation* of their own power and to "accept feasible and shared constraints"

---

[28]Hart (1997), Chap. X.

[29]Dworkin (2013), p. 9.

[30]Ibid., p. 10 and with reference to Chap. 14 of Dworkin (2011).

[31]For example, see Martti Koskenniemi on the vicious circle between facts and norms i.e. between States' consent and its being norm-generative (normative) upon States themselves: Koskenniemi (1990), pp. 4–32. And upon the problematic reflexivity of *pacta sunt servanda*, Fitzmaurice (1958), pp. 153–176.

[32]Dworkin (2013), p. 3.

[33]This argument is not only typical to Dworkin's criticism of legal positivism. It is an objection that can be raised against any conventionalist approach. As Cotterrell noted, accepting as law simply what "people identify and treat through their social practices as 'law'", keeps a "definitional concern with what the concept of law should cover, yet removing from the concept as defined all analytical power" (Cotterrell (2008), p. 8). The reference is to Tamanaha (2001), p. 166.

based on international law.[34] It is today adequate for the State to achieve its legitimacy only if its coercive power is "consistent with the dignity of citizens", that is, a matter of substance not of pedigree; and similarly, even the *international* order makes up for the coercive system that States impose to their citizen: for the State, "it follows that the general obligation to try to improve its political legitimacy includes an obligation to try to improve the overall international system"[35] (that means, so improving its own government legitimacy), and such an obligation includes cooperative duties, beyond a law of co-existence.[36]

The latter shall be all the more relevant in the future, if we think of those challenges to States self-referentiality stemming from climate change or other environmental interests common to all peoples.

However, of itself, such a principle of mitigation is insufficiently determinative as to different possible regimes of international law; accordingly Dworkin coins the *principle of salience*. It is a normative principle itself, and works in connection with the first. It establishes the duty *prima facie* to abide by codes and practices already agreed upon by a consistent number of States and populations. A duty that shall have an obvious "snowballing effect".[37] The moral obligation of all nations—for example, to treat UN law as law—flows from the combined sense of those two principles, and explains as well why even States' Constitutions tend to include and protect more widespread rules considered as *jus gentium* or even peremptory *jus cogens*.

3.2 Dworkin does not embrace any *cosmopolitan* view. International law principles are traced back to the rationale of the relationship between State power and its citizens, not to a global hypothetical government or to universal justice. It is a *second level order* of States, and international organisations, to matter, not a *universal community* of individuals. As far as I can see, even the "political morality" of the international system can only enjoy a second level status, that is, the integrity of its values has a derivative status not a self-standing substantive content. And in fact mitigation applies to the system of sovereigns. Therefore, even one of the fundamental canons of Dworkin's general philosophy, *equal concern and respect*[38] for

---

[34]Dworkin (2013), p. 17.

[35]Ibid.

[36]Ibid.: "Any State … improves its legitimacy when it promotes an effective international order that would prevent its own possible future degradation into tyranny" (p. 17); it does the same also when it can protect its people, on whom it has monopoly of force, from invasions of other peoples; moreover, a State fails in a further way if it discourages *cooperation* to prevent economic, commercial, medical or environmental disaster (Ibid., p. 18). As to cooperation in international law, see for example Friedmann (1964).

[37]Dworkin (2013), p. 19. As Dworkin writes: "If some humane set of principles limiting the justified occasions of war and means of waging war gains wide acceptance, for instance, then the officials of other pertinent nations have a duty to embrace and follow that set of principles" (Ibid.).

[38]"Equal concern and respect" had a pivotal role in Dworkin's (1978) philosophy since his *Taking Rights Seriously* (with a new appendix, a response to critics), Introduction, p. XII: "This most fundamental of rights is a distinct conception of the right to equality, that I call the right to equal concern and respect".

each individuals, does not feature within the scope of international law immediately. Mitigation and salience refer to *States' system* (or to powerful international organisations) premised on the general duty of States to protect the dignity of individuals. Because States shall have to respect citizens' rights, their sovereignty shall not prevent other States' intervention to stop genocide; mitigation shall ask States not to refuse cooperation in facing communal interest of humanity, be it concerning security, hunger, environmental protection. Mitigation is explained, in a nutshell, as a source of both negative and positive duties. Although Dworkin suggests, as "phantasy upon phantasy", an international court having jurisdiction "over all the nations of the world", such a thought-experiment comes with a clear statement about the domain of international law: a very distinct part of what "morality and decency require of States and other international bodies in their treatment of one another".[39] And again along these lines he asks which argument a hypothetical court should use to determine "the rights and obligations of States (and other international actors and organizations) that it would be appropriate for it to enforce coercively?".[40] So the question is defined by the borders of the Westphalian system of States and within them. States are the theoretical bridge between social communities of individuals and international law.

All in all, the "new philosophy" can be seen as an upgrade in theory, intended to explain the state of the art in international law and to validate a legal order through its own systemic principles, replacing the presumption of *consent*. But once this reconstruction of international law has been done, international law becomes suited to Dworkinian theory of law as *interpretive* (as opposed to positivist theories of law, or natural law).

4 The Features of an Interpretive (Adjudicative) Theory of Law

The features of interpretivism were spelled by Dworking in the last decades, and *not* with reference to international law. What Dworkin can contribute here, mirrors the logic of his criticism to Hartian theory in the '70s: roughly, the positivist view leaves too much to lawyers' discretion. Note that even with international law, Dworkin now warns that the recurrent appeal to morality as a direct reason for action, outside what law is held to prescribe (as Franck did in the case of NATO intervention in Kosovo)[41] would be a fatal undermining of the still fragile international law. What Dworkin is thinking about is the relocation of those choices— deemed to be morally, although not legally, mandatory—as *disagreements within* the *legal* domain. And this can be done, as we already know, by interpreting "the

---

[39]Dworkin (2013), p. 13.

[40]Ibid., p. 15.

[41]Ibid., p. 23. Dworkin mentions Franck (1999), pp. 857–860.

documents and practices picked out by the principle of salience so as to advance the imputed purpose of mitigating the flaws and dangers of the Westphalian system".[42]

However, as to the nature of law being interpretive, there is no novelty distinctive to international law. Law *is interpretive* because it postulates a practice where *participants* can *disagree* about what the practice (like international law) really requires, and assign a value and a purpose[43] to it, achieve insights about conditions of truth of particular propositions of law *under those purposes* and within the *constraints* of historical records, documents and relevant materials, sources shaping the object of that practice.[44]

It is of importance that nowhere Dworkin denies that such structures, rules, and institutions are central to the existence or identification of a legal system.[45] However, being law interpretive, a descriptive/sociological view would not be definitive or sufficiently determinative as regards the *doctrinal* questions concerning *what is the law in particular cases*. Questions about the truth of propositions of law—or about whether and how a norm (or even a judicial outcome) is "valid"— are normally traced back to the *grounds of law*,[46] that is, to the existing institutional premises (judicial precedents, legislation, procedural requirements, and the like) that "positivism" identifies by consensus. Such questions are allegedly solved, according to Hartian legal positivism, by verifying whether the required historical facts have been met (the proper procedural enactment, the "right" source etc.). Although criteria of identification are provided in the rule of recognition of a legal order, disagreement would nonetheless possibly persist. True *disagreements* are hardly revolving around what the actual *grounds of law* are, their empirical (historical) existence and pedigree. Genuine disagreements, with Dworkin (who calls them "theoretical") reach the identity (value and purpose) of the *grounds of law*, beyond their existence. Under contestation is not "what really happened", but what legal scope and import it should bear (not whether the parliament has actually legislated, but what consequence should be ascribed to that). Being not *empirical,* they involve *evaluations* of principle. Indeed, they depend on the ascription of different meaning and purpose to those *grounds of law* once factually identified. Accordingly, invoking some *different principles of political morality* (involving the identity, scope, and value of the institutional system as a whole) determines

---

[42]Dworkin (2013), p. 22.

[43]Dworkin (1986), p. 52.

[44]Dworkin (2006a), p. 140.

[45]"[H]art was right to think that the combination of first-order standards imposing duties and second-order standards regulating the creation and identification of those first-order rules is a central feature of paradigmatic legal systems. His emphasis on this structure was not itself remarkably original. ...Hart's distinctive contribution was his claim that in paradigmatic legal systems the most fundamental secondary rule or set of rules—the complex standard for identifying which other secondary and primary rules count as law—has that force only through convention". Dworkin (2006b), p. 100.

[46]Dworkin (1986), p. 4.

different interpretations of the *same* grounds of law and corresponding answers to the problem of what the law is, i.e. the truth of legal propositions.[47]

Of course, from such a perspective, the positivist assumption of consensus on the (interpretation of) *grounds of law* is untenable. Scott Shapiro has nicely summarized the positivist puzzle to this regard:

> [I]t is common ground between exclusive and inclusive legal positivists that the grounds of law are determined by convention. How can they account for disagreements about the legal bindingness of certain facts whose bindingness, by hypothesis, requires the existence of agreement on their bindingness?[48]

Accordingly, if we do *not* wish to disregard the domain of international law, as a legal one, we cannot ignore the interpretive reading.[49]

5 Multiple Legalities, Principles and Exemplary Case Law

5.1 After Dworkin's explicit contribution to international law, one further aspect, however, is to be mentioned, one that, as I shall submit, belongs to the potentialities of interpretivism within international law, although it is not either identified or elaborated upon by Dworkin himself. Because of international law being re-directed towards principles, they can also get to a function that legal positivism is hardly equipped to sustain or even admit. As I maintain, principles can be resorted to in order to explain and possibly solve disagreements on the valid rule to be applied, not only in those circumstances of routine, current in State legal orders (like gap-filling, rules interpretation, contrast among relevant principles, for example) but even, and all the more so, when divergences concern meaning, import, and scope of norms that, though controlling one single case at stake, might belong in *separate* legalities: the latter confront each other and each would lead to different legal outcomes, providing a different point of view as to validity. In other words, principles can have a further role in addressing disagreements arising from the segmented texture of supranational law and the issues covered, often divergently, by

---

[47]It goes without saying here that Dworkin can hardly be isolated or sidelined to this regard, since as he knows, the *post* Hartian decades have shown the salience of this second view, in diverse ways upheld by positivist writings, from Coleman to Waldron, MacCormick, Postema and Schauer (see Dworkin (2006a, b), p. 104). And it is rather revealing even the "nuanced difference" as to the precise role of morality *vis-à-vis* law, that Waldron has recently noticed between the late Dworkin in *Justice for Hedgehogs* and the exclusive positivism of Joseph Raz in his *Incorporation by Law*; see Raz (2004), p. 6. Cf. Waldron (2013b), p. 16 ff.

[48]Shapiro (2007), p. 38.

[49]Ironically one can say that the autonomy of the theory *vis-à-vis* empirical facts is here to be invoked not in order for them to be disregarded (recall Hegel at the news of a new planet's discovery: "*Desto schlimmer für die Tatsachen*"), but for them to be taken into account. It seems that Hegel said so when informed that a seventh planet had been discovered (by Herschel in 1781), after having based his dissertation, *De Orbitis Planetarum,* on the assumption that there could be no more than six.

different legal institutional regimes. It can be argued that, on one side, disagreements about the valid rule to be applied *cannot* be overcome by reference to the criteria in the rule of recognition controlling the jurisdictional scope of one (among the) relevant legal regime(s). On the other side, judicial decision-making has (cf. sections below) deployed a principled-based reasoning in order to address problems located at the crossroads between different legal sub-systems. This move involves the turn to an *interpretative* notion of law, one which, among the rest, adds to the received dogmas of strict legal positivism, and makes the assessment of principles to appear as the actual frontier of law-findings in international law matters.

That shall be shown by referring to some recent decisions of the European Court of Human Rights (ECtHR) (*Al-Jedda* and *Al-Dulimi*) whose reasoning treats divergence between the UN Security Council, the State involved, and the Convention for the Protection of Human Rights and Fundamental Freedoms (ECHR). For convenience we can speak of a kind of *second level* disagreements.

Proliferation of orders and regimes of law[50] generates some historical-institutional divergence, through self-referentiality, and implies that the practice of *one* rule of recognition cannot easily develop in place of the *multiplicity of relative* rules of recognition.

In the apparent inconclusiveness of "social sources based" law, divergence originates not within one single, self-contained regime, but flows from the institutional, "legally objective" otherness of one (*sub*)"legality" *vis-à-vis* the other.

Making sense of such a complex and heterogeneous setting is a constructive endeavour, ultimately prompted by the adjudicative questions: they generate, however, the need of relocating opposite claims within a kind contextual whole, as *mutually normative disagreements.*

5.2 After fragmented-law exemplary cases, like *Mox Plant* and others,[51] attention is to be brought to significant judicial decisions following some UN Security Council resolutions. Judicial cases have displayed different attitudes in a progress that goes from a self-referential, or one-sided, to a whole-related, or comprehensive legal reasoning: that is, an argument that works through bridging or integrating, for the case at hand, the normative propositions belonging to different orders involved, that would claim for divergent outcomes.

---

[50]Fears are raised that further law would only express unilateral need of the most powerful to create their own institutions, or provide leeway through multiplication of routes of non-compliance, allow for sidestepping preexisting commitments, trigger the "court choice" as a forum shopping, and so forth. For example, against constitutionalization process as an even process (or one that would freeze the existing power relations, regardless of their actual legitimacy as it would be the case of WTO multilateral trading order's absence of democratic contestability and inclusiveness), see Krisch (2005) p. 377; Howse and Nicolaidis (2003), p. 73. And for the geopolitical related analysis, Armingeo and Milewicz (2008), pp. 179–196.

[51]I recall Martti Koskenniemi, on this case—among the most debated upon some years ago—to which three different regimes were applicable: "Let me quote the Tribunal [Arbitral Tribunal at the UNCLOS]: 'even if the OSPAR Convention, the European Community Treaty and the Euratom treaty contain rights or obligations similar to or identical with the rights set out in [the

After the milestone case, *Kadi*,[52] at the European Court of Justice (ECJ), others followed at the ECtHR. In *Kadi* the Court made an argument for European primary law to prevail over the obligations stemming from international law (Article 103 of the UN Charter) to implement a resolution of the UN Security Council. The decision was widely welcomed for its defence of fundamental rights, and also criticised because of withholding the European Union from international law obligations (contrary to the advice of the Court of First Instance—now General Court—in its own *Kadi* decision),[53] thus betraying true internationalism (like the United States, in *Medellín*[54] and elsewhere): a kind of American style *exceptionalism*,[55] contradicting the original attitudes of compliance of the European Community in the '50s.[56] Actually, and beyond its many virtues (that such a criticism seems indeed to sideline), the ECJ reasoning amounted to a pronouncement shielded by self-reference to the rule of law in its own jurisdiction: accordingly, not an assessment about the infringement of fundamental rights in a supranational sphere where the two jurisdictions involved are interrelated.[57] It settled not a question of *disagreement*, but a question of *primacy*. The two things are not compatible.

A rather different approach was displayed by the ECtHR in *Al-Jedda* (2011) and in *Al-Dulimi* (2012). The ECtHR decides to exceed the latitude of its own jurisdiction as defined by the rules of recognition of the ECHR and resorts to wider principles reflecting the UN system and—as Dworkin would have put it—the deeper political morality of international law as a whole.

Footnote 51 (continued)

UNCLOS], the rights and obligations under these agreements have a separate existence from those under [the UNCLOS]'. The tribunal then held that the application of even the same rules by different institutions might be different owing to the 'differences in the respective context, object and purposed, subsequent practice of parties and *travaux préparatoires*'. It is not only that the boxes have different rules. Even if they had the same rules, they would be applied differently because each box has a different objective and a different ethos, a different structural bias". See Koskenniemi (2006), pp. 4–5. However, in the same line, there had been equally famous cases like *Swordfish* at WTO (Chile—Measures Affecting the Transit and Importation of Swordfish, Doc. WT/DS193); at the International Tribunal for the Law of the Sea, *Chile v. European Community* (15 March 2001) (suspended). See Orellana (2002), p. 55. See also *Soft Drinks* (Mexico—Tax Measures on Soft Drinks and Other Beverages, Doc. WT/DS308/R).

[52]Joined cases C-402/05 P *Yassin Abdullah Kadi and Al Barakaat International Foundation* [2008] ECR I-6351.

[53]Case T-315/01 *Kadi* [2005] ECR II-3649.

[54]*Medellín v. Texas*, 552 US 491 (2008).

[55]De Búrca (2010), pp. 1–49.

[56]De Búrca (2011), p. 649 ff.

[57]The *Kadi* decision however can also be stretched to represent a pattern of *conditional* agreement, based on mutual respect *under conditions*, which mirrors the equal protection requirement, or the Italian doctrine of "counter-limits", and similarly the *Solange* reasoning from the German Constitutional Court. See Palombella (2009), pp. 442–467.

The Grand Chamber found in *Al-Jedda v. United Kingdom*,[58] that indefinite detention without charge of Al-Jedda (dual citizen British/Iraqi) by the United Kingdom in a Basra facility controlled by British forces was unlawful and infringed his rights to liberty under Article 5 of the ECHR. The ECtHR rejected the opinion upheld by the House of Lords in the United Kingdom (before Al-Jedda's appeal to the ECtHR) that the indefinite detention of Al-Jedda flowed from compliance with the UN Security Council resolution no. 1546, as requested by Article 103 of the UN Charter.[59] That argument of conformity held by Lord Bingham does not contest the existence of human rights law, but its import within the system of international law; it amounts to a matter of hierarchy of rules in the international order.[60]

As an answer, the ECtHR walks a peculiar path: contrary to the ECJ in *Kadi*, it takes larger view than the scope of its own ECHR's regime, and even larger than the task of individual, human rights' protection. It takes into consideration the two orders' interplay and minds of the integrity of the frame of international law, where the European Convention's regime and the Security Council might sensibly concur, given general international law principles and those of the UN Charter, that is, the supranational and contextual legal setting (in which the Security Council is included). The argument does not touch the last word authority under Article 103 of the UN Charter, but first refuses to agree that the unlawful detention, without judicial review and lacking necessity, *was commanded or authorized* by the Security Council resolution. The normative context includes Article 1 of the UN Charter entrenching "respect for human rights and fundamental freedoms" and Article 24(2) requiring the Security Council to "act in accordance with the Purposes and Principles of the United Nations".[61] Within those premises, not even the imperative of peace and security can be held as unconditional.

According to the ECtHR, since there must be "a presumption that the Security Council does not intend to impose any obligation on Member States to breach fundamental principles of human rights",[62] the interpretation must be chosen that "is most in harmony with the requirements of the Convention and which avoids any

---

[58]*Al-Jedda v. The United Kingdom* (App. no. 27021/08), ECtHR, judgment of 7 July 2011.

[59]See para. 35 (Lord Bingham) of the House of Lords decision, as pasted in *Al-Jedda v. The United Kingdom* cit., para. 11: "Emphasis has often been laid on the special character of the European Convention as a human rights instrument. But the reference in Article 103 [UN] to 'any other international agreement' leaves no room for any excepted category, and such appears to be the consensus of learned opinion". The same author, Tom Bingham, though, has written the important book *The Rule of Law* (2011). Clearly, his idea of the rule of law is different from mine: cf. G. Palombella (2014).

[60]That kind of appeal to the rule of law in the international legal order, resonates in the 2005 decision of the Court of First Instance in *Kadi*.

[61]ECtHR, *Al-Jedda v. The United Kingdom*, cit., para. 102 (and the premised, para. 44).

[62]Ibid.

conflict of obligations".[63] Finally the European Court concedes that it may still be possible that the Security Council would need to impose a rupture in the fabric of UN law, but then this should result only from "clear and explicit language" (para. 102) against international human rights law. As I have submitted elsewhere,[64] such an argument hardly means that the ECtHR is ready to forfeit its content based logic, and surrender to hierarchy; it hardly means that a "clear and explicit language" would turn legitimate by source what is not (the violation of human rights conventions, outside state of necessity) in the integrity frame that the European Court itself has aptly drawn. In this picture, the ECtHR has built on a notion of legality that is complex enough to ask that whatever "clear and explicit language", a *proposition of law* be "true" under an interpretation of the *grounds of law* that grants equal weight to human rights in the pursuit of the fundamental objectives of the UN.

It is a subsequent decision, namely, *Al-Dulimi*, to confirm that this interpretation of the import of *Al-Jedda* is correct. The question would be, in fact, what should happen in case of "clear and explicit language" against human rights law? The European Court has answered that question, overcoming the kind of acoustic separation between the involved legalities sharing a common terrain, upon which to settle a potential disagreement.

The ECtHR[65] deals—indirectly—with UN Security Council resolution no. 1483 (2003), which in "clear and explicit language" imposes to Switzerland, allowing to the State no discretion,[66] the freezing of the assets of Al-Dulimi, one of those blacklisted as suspected terrorist, who had been denied any rights to defence. Since Switzerland[67] had rejected Al-Dulimi's complaints and resolved to confiscate his assets, the ECtHR decides that violation of Article 6 of the ECHR (access to justice) has taken place on behalf of the State, and that consequent responsibility falls on it as a member to the European Convention, regardless of the duty to implement sanctions from the Security Council, and even in absence of any State's discretionary power. In the reasoning of the European Court, judicial review was not granted either at the UN or in the domestic procedure. Denial of access to justice, even in pursuing the legitimate ends of peace and security, is deemed *disproportionate* to achieve those objectives.

---

[63]Ibid.

[64]Cf. Palombella (2014).

[65]*Al-Dulimi and Montana Management Inc. v. Switzerland* (App. no. 5809/08), ECtHR, judgment of 26 November 2013.

[66]The Court had already decided the *Nada* case where discretion was deemed existent. *Nada v. Switzerland* (App. no. 10593/08), ECtHR [GC], judgment of 12 September 2012.

[67]The Swiss Federal Tribunal (BGE 2A.783/784/785/2006; all of 23 January 2008) had maintained that it was not entitled to revise the legality of Security Council resolutions except in the event (that was not) of violation of a *jus cogens* rule (as in the reasoning of the Court of First Instance of the European Union in *Kadi*). After allowing Al-Dulimi more time for a (unsuccessful) further appeal to that Committee, the Tribunal concluded that Switzerland's behavior was legitimate, and did not violate either domestic constitutional norms or Articles 6 and 13 of the ECHR.

It is important that the ECtHR, in the same vein as in *Al-Jedda*, does not take a merely external attitude toward the normative corpus of the UN, assuming instead that it should be taken into consideration qua *normative* in its scope, meaning and aims. Accordingly, its reasoning is not shielded in a self-referential closure, but pursues a comprehensive assessment. This is why it believes that apparently conflicting obligations from the UN Charter and the ECHR must be at their best harmonized and reconciled (Article 31(3)(c), Vienna Convention on the Law of Treaties) (para. 112). The presumption according to which the Security Council does not in principle mean to impose obligations contradicting international laws of human rights (formulated in its *Al-Jedda* decision) is defeated. But it follows that, however commanded by the highest source in UN security purposes, not every behaviour can be deemed legitimate, just for that. The European Court engages in a *proportionality* judgment, that is, a contextual evaluation between two divergent rules-principles, one that might exceed the strict limits of its own jurisdiction (such a judgment implies a revision of the legality of the Security Council resolution, that other courts in the European Union case had considered themselves not competent to pursue).

But such an assessment can only flow from taking the participant's point of view[68] in the interconnection of diverse international law regimes, prompted by the case under scrutiny. It requires bridging the gap that separates the two orders, that is, a deeper self-understanding of one regime's role as an *agent of international law as a whole*, and a further insight into the purposes and meaning concerning the "grounds" of those laws, the mutual relation between institutions, and the founding ideals of the diverse orders in their integrity. No place the ECtHR merely resorts to "formal" tools.

It has been from such an approach that the European Court has chosen (right or wrong) to hold the State "responsible", putting the State "caught between the obligation to carry out Security Council decisions under Article 25 of the UN Charter and the obligation to respect international or regional human rights guarantees".[69] It is however preeminent point here that its reasoning implies a value choice, one that would be itself arbitrary, according to a positivist construction of the international system under a UN supremacy clause; this value choice opposes the assumption that absolute supremacy of Security Council would always fulfil its substantive *raison d'être*. The interplay between security and rights, viewed under a proportionality judgment, can basically depend on a further principle underlying the purpose of the international system. One could even submit that the argument

---

[68]Recall the opening of Dworkin's *Law's Empire* (1986) (being the role of "participant" a premise to interpretive endeavour).

[69]So writes Anne Peters. See Peters (2013). See the dissenting opinion of Judge Sajó: the complaint should have been dismissed, as "irrecevable" (inadmissible) *ratione personae*, because the State is not acting of its own but clearly under the order of the Security Council, which gave it no leeway. But he did join the majority in deciding that a violation of human rights *occurred* due to the insufficient guarantees provided by the UN sanctions system. See *Al-Dulimi and Montana Management Inc. v. Switzerland* cit., *in coda*.

here could easily conform to a general principle of power *mitigation*: in the sense that it both justifies the role of the Security Council *vis-à-vis* States arbitrary power and at the same time limits the Security Council itself in pursuing its tasks.

6 As a Conclusion

The cases recalled above from *Kadi* to *Al-Jedda* and *Al-Dulimi* should also be taken to show that in the relations between separate regimes of law, and in the relations between State legal orders and international law, the "plain fact view" and the only reference to the historical, social facts of rules-production by predefined sources, leave inevitably, outside the State, a very ample room for disagreement: one that does not in fact concern the existence of documents, institutions and orders, but the import and meaning that should be ascribed to them either in isolation or *in the mutual relations* among legalities. Genuine disagreement originates here despite the very fact that no contestation arises as regards the sources of the relevant rules (say, Article 103 of the UN Charter, or any of the Security Council resolutions). This not "empirical" disagreement exceeds the range of control conceived through "normal" legal positivism. Disagreements that Dworkin saw "theoretical" are essentially involving different interpretations-understanding of the fundamental principles, in the political-moral sense, that institutions of law are meant to be *premised on*.

The key vault in the relations among mutually *external (or self-contained) legalities*, is the recognition of their being both relevant and thus equally *internal* to the case at stake. In such a context, different interpretations of respective *grounds of law* need to be further elaborated in the interplay among legalities (that actually escape a clear hierarchical systematization) endowed, in the global space, with distinctive rules of recognition. Given the angle of the case, the ECtHR's reasoning might on one side be viewed as interpreting the rules and principles of each involved legal regimes, and on the other side arbitrating their interplay on a *proportionality* assessment. One possible argument to justify this latter move, that is, a kind of "jurisdiction overstepping", requires appeal to further principle premised to supranational law, beyond States. A plausible candidate might be the Dworkinian principle of *mitigation* of States' power and of international organisations, one that justifies both positive and negative duties. It turns to the political morality of social communities under States purview. It substantively refers to the essential concern and respect for the *dignity* of citizens, asking that the exercise of power, from whichever actors, can only be legitimate under the limitations that such respect imposes to each concurring regime of law on a case by case basis. From the foregoing, the role and potential of "principles" in the different guises and levels analysed in this chapter, can all the more be seen at the forefront of international law adjudication.

References

Armingeon, Klaus, and Karolina Milewicz. 2008. Compensatory Constitutionalism: A Comparative Perspective. *Global Society* 22: 179–96.

Armingeon, Klaus, Karolina Milewicz, Simone Peter, and Anne Peters. 2011. The Constitutionalisation of International Trade Law. In *The Prospects of International Trade Regulation: From Fragmentation to Coherence,* eds. Thomas Cottier and Panagiotis Delimatsis, 69-102. Cambridge: Cambridge University Press.

Bingham, Tom. 2011. *The Rule of Law*. London: Penguin.

Cassese, Antonio. 2005. *International Law.* II ed. Oxford: Oxford University Press.

Cassese, Antonio. 2008. *The Human Dimension of International Law. Selected Papers of A. Cassese.* Oxford: Oxford University Press.

Cheng, Bin. 2006 [1953]. *General Principles of Law as Applied by International Courts and Tribunals.* Cambridge: Cambridge University Press.

Cotterrell, Roger. 2008. Transnational Communities and the Concept of Law. *Ratio Juris* 21/1: 1-18.

De Búrca, Grainne. 2010. The European Court of Justice and the International Legal Order After Kadi. *Harvard International Law Journal* 51/1: 1-49.

De Búrca, Grainne. 2011. The Road Not Taken: The EU as a Global Human Rights Actor. *American Journal of International Law* 105: 649-694.

Dworkin, Ronald M. 1978. *Taking Rights Seriously*. Cambridge: Harvard University Press.

Dworkin, Ronald M. 1986. *Law's Empire.* Cambridge: Harvard University Press; London: Fontana Press.

Dworkin, Ronald M. 2006a. *Justice in Robes*. Cambridge: Harvard University Press.

Dworkin, Ronald M. 2006b. Hart and the Concepts of Law. *Harvard Law Review Forum* 119: 95-104.

Dworkin, Ronald M. 2011. *Justice for Hedgehogs*. Cambridge: Harvard University Press.

Dworkin, Ronald M. 2013. A New Philosophy of International Law. *Philosophy & Public Affairs* 41: 2-30.

Fitzmaurice, Gerald. 1958. Some Problems Regarding the Formal Sources of International Law. In *Symbolae Verzijl*, eds. Willem Jan Hendrik and Frederik Mari van Asbeck, 153-176. The Hague: Martinus Nijhoff.

Franck, Thomas M. 1999. Lessons of Kosovo. *American Journal of International Law* 93: 857–60.

Friedmann, Wolfgang. 1964. *The Changing Structure of International Law*. New York: Columbia University Press.

Hart, Herbert L. A (ed. Penelope A. Bulloch and Joseph Raz). 1997. *The Concept of Law* (with a *Postscript*). II ed. Oxford: Oxford University Press.

Hearn, William R. 1990. The International Legal Regime Regulating Nuclear Deterrence Warfare. *British Year Book of International Law* 61: 199-248.

Howse, Robert and Kalypso Nicolaidis. 2003. Enhancing WTO Legitimacy: Constitutionalism of Global Subsidiarity? *Governance: An International Journal of Policy, Administration, and Institutions* 16: 73-94.

Klabbers, Jan. 2013. Towards a Culture of Formalism? Martti Koskenniemi and the Virtues. *Temple International & Comparative Law Journal* 27: 417-435.

Koskenniemi, Martti. 1990. The Politics of International Law. *European Journal of International Law* 1/1: 4-32.

Koskenniemi, Martti. 2006. *International Law: Between Fragmentation and Constitutionalism.* http://www.helsinki.fi/eci/Publications/Koskenniemi/MCanberra-06c.pdf.

Krisch, Nico. 2005. International Law in Times of Hegemony: Unequal Power and the Shaping of the International Legal Order. *European Journal of International Law* 16: 369-408.

Lauterpacht, Hersch. 1975. Some Observations on the Prohibition of *Non Liquet* and the Completeness of the Legal Order. In *International Law. Collected Papers,* ed. Hersch Lauterpacht, 213-237. Cambridge: Cambridge University Press.

Orellana, Marcos. 2002. The Swordfish Dispute between the EU and Chile at the ITLOS and the WTO. *Nordic Journal of International Law* 71/1: 55-81.

Palombella, Gianluigi. 2009. The Rule of Law beyond the State: Failures, Promises, and Theory. *International Journal of Constitutional Law* 7/3: 442-467.

Palombella, Gianluigi. 2014. The Measure of Law. Domestic to International Law (and from Hamdan to Al-Jedda). In *Legal Doctrines of the Rule of Law and the Legal State*, eds. James R. Silkenat, James E. Hickey, Peter D. Barenboim, 129-143. Leiden: Brill.

Peters, Anne. 2006. Compensatory Constitutionalism: The Function and Potential of Fundamental International Norms and Structures. *Leiden Journal of International Law* 19: 579-610.

Peters, Anne. 2009. Conclusions. In *The Constitutionalization of International Law,* eds. Jan Klabbers, Anne Peters and Geir Ulfstein. Oxford: Oxford University Press.

Peters, Anne. 2013. Targeted Sanctions after Affaire *Al-Dulimi et Montana Management Inc. c. Suisse*: Is There a Way Out of the Catch-22 for UN Members? *EJIL Talk.* http://www.ejiltalk. org/author/anne-peters/.

Raimondo, Fabián O. 2008. *General Principles of Law in the Decisions of International Criminal Courts and Tribunals.* Leiden: Brill.

Raz, Joseph. 2004. Incorporation by Law. *Legal Theory* 10: 1-17.

Robertson, Geoffrey. 2000. *Crimes Against Humanity: The Struggle for Global Justice.* London: Penguin.

Shany, Yuval. 2003. *The Competing Jurisdictions of International Courts and Tribunals.* Oxford: Oxford University Press.

Shapiro, Scott. 2007. The Hart-Dworkin Debate: A Short Guide for the Perplexed, Working Paper no. 77. Michigan University, Public Law and Legal theory Working Papers Series.

Simma, Bruno. 1999. NATO, the UN, and the Use of Force: Legal Aspects. *European Journal of International Law* 10: 1-22.

Slaughter, Anne-Marie. 2005. Security, Solidarity, and Sovereignty: The Grand Themes of UN Reform. *The American Journal of International Law* 99/3: 619-631.

Stone, Julius. 1959. *Non Liquet* and the Function of Law in the International Community. *British Year Book of International Law* 35: 124-161.

Tamanaha, Brian. 2001. *A General Jurisprudence of Law and Society.* Oxford: Oxford University Press.

Teitel, Ruti. 2011. *Humanity's Law.* Oxford: Oxford University Press.

Waldron, Jeremy. 2013a. International Law: "A Relatively Small and Unimportant" Part of Jurisprudence? Working Paper no. 427. New York University Public Law and Legal Theory Working Papers. http://lsr.nellco.org/nyu_plltwp/427J.

Waldron, Jeremy. 2013b. Jurisprudence for Hedgehogs. Working Paper no. 13-45. New York University Public Law and Legal Theory Research Paper Series.

Legal Formalism, Procedural Principles, and Judicial Constraint in American Adjudication

Christopher J. Peters

Abstract American proponents of legal formalism, such as Supreme Court Justice Antonin Scalia, worry (quite reasonably) that unfettered judicial discretion poses a threat to democratic legitimacy, and they offer formalism—the mechanical implementation of determinate legal rules—as a solution to this threat. I argue here, however, that formalist interpretive techniques are neither sufficient nor necessary to impose meaningful constraint on judges. Both the text and the "original meaning" of legal rules are endemically under-determinate, leaving much room for judicial discretion in the decision of cases. But meaningful judicial constraint can and does flow from other sources in American adjudication. Judges are constrained by the dispute-resolving posture of their task, which requires that they be impartial as between the litigants and responsive to the litigants' participatory efforts. And they are constrained by the need to be faithful to the substantive principles that justify legal rules, even when those rules themselves are indeterminate. Judicial constraint in the American system thus stems not primarily from formalist interpretative methods, but rather from largely unwritten procedural principles of judicial impartiality, responsiveness, and faithfulness.

> Now the main danger in judicial interpretation of the Constitution – or, for that matter, in judicial interpretation of any law – is that judges will mistake their own predilections for the law. ... Originalism does not aggravate the principal weakness of the system, for it establishes a historical criterion that is conceptually quite separate from the preferences of the judge himself.[1]
> Hon. Antonin Scalia
> Associate Justice, United States Supreme Court

---

[1]Scalia (1989a), pp. 863–864.

C.J. Peters (✉)
Professor of Law, University of Baltimore School of Law, Baltimore, USA
e-mail: cpeters@ubalt.edu

© Springer International Publishing Switzerland 2015   23
L. Pineschi (ed.), *General Principles of Law - The Role of the Judiciary*,
Ius Gentium: Comparative Perspectives on Law and Justice 46,
DOI 10.1007/978-3-319-19180-5_2

1 "The Main Danger": Legal Formalism and Judicial Constraint

The quotation above from Justice Scalia, perhaps the most prominent proponent of legal formalism in the United States, articulates an intuitive connection between formalism and judicial constraint: to the extent judges are limited to the rote application of existing rules, they are prevented from deciding cases according to "their own predilections" or "preferences". Justice Scalia's approach implies that formalist principles are both sufficient and necessary to limit judicial discretion. In this chapter, I argue that they are neither.

For the purposes of this chapter, we can understand legal formalism as the idea that judges and other decisionmakers should decide particular cases, to the extent possible, by the mechanical application of existing legal rules. Those existing rules might come from constitutional provisions, from statutes, from treaties, from administrative regulations, or from the decisions of prior courts. To the extent a judge's decision of a case is dictated solely by the content of an existing rule, that decision is not determined by anything else, including the values or beliefs or preferences of the judge herself. There is, then, a quite literal relationship of semantic or logical entailment between pure legal formalism and judicial constraint. A purely formalist decision is an entirely constrained one—a decision constrained completely by the content of the existing rule being applied.

Why might constraining judges and other point-of-application decisionmakers be a good idea? Judges constrained by formalism will not always produce the best possible decisions; sometimes the rule being applied will be a bad rule, and sometimes even the application of generally good rules will produce bad results, as Aristotle understood.[2] There may nonetheless be strong reasons of rule-consequentialism to require judges to apply existing rules even where the judge believes the result would be bad.[3] No doubt there also are "rule of law" reasons such as predictability and consistency.[4] In this chapter, however, I want to focus on the sorts of reasons to which Justice Scalia primarily appeals in his defense of legal formalism: reasons of *democratic legitimacy*.

As Cass Sunstain has written:

> Justice Scalia is a democrat in the sense that much of his jurisprudence is designed to ensure that judgments are made by those with a superior democratic pedigree. Above all,

---

[2]In the *Nicomachean Ethics*, Aristotle (1941) wrote: "[A]ll law is universal but about some things it is not possible to make a universal statement which shall be correct. In those cases, then, in which it is necessary to speak universally, but not possible to do so correctly, the law takes the usual case, though it is not ignorant of the possibility of error. And it is none the less correct; for the error is not in the law nor in the legislator but in the nature of the thing, since the matter of practical affairs is of this kind from the start" (p. 1020).

[3]For an argument to this effect, focused on judicial application of rules gleaned from precedent, see Hellman (2014).

[4]See, for example, Scalia (1989b), p. 1179.

he seeks to develop rules of interpretation that will limit the policymaking authority and decisional discretion of the judiciary, the least accountable branch of government.[5]

The American judiciary—in particular, the federal judiciary—is "the least accountable branch of government" in Justice Scalia's view because its members serve during "good behavior" (that is, in most cases, for life or until they choose to retire),[6] thus insulating their decisions from electoral accountability. For Justice Scalia, it is significant that the American judiciary appears to be saliently less accountable, politically speaking, than most of the institutions whose rules it is charged with interpreting and applying: the legislature, state or federal (whose members are directly elected by the voters); the administrative bodies whose chief policymakers typically are appointed and confirmed by elected officials; and the constitutional framers, whose efforts were channeled through an extraordinarily deliberative and participatory political process.[7]

If we take democratic accountability as a standard of political legitimacy, as Justice Scalia does, then the judicial deficit in accountability as compared to these other decisionmakers renders judicial decisions less legitimate than political decisions, all else being equal. To be precise, it renders decisions based on judicial *discretion*—departing from the law or creating new law as opposed to simply applying existing law—less legitimate than the discretionary decisions of politically accountable actors. To hold judges strictly to an application of the rules created by these more-accountable decisionmakers thus is, for Justice Scalia, to allocate lawmaking authority to democratically superior institutions (legislatures, constitutional framers) as opposed to democratically inferior ones (courts). Legal formalism promotes democratic legitimacy.

The view that Justice Scalia represents therefore implies judicial constraint from legal formalism and democratic legitimacy from judicial constraint. For purposes of my arguments here, I will grant the premise that some meaningful degree

---

[5]Sunstein (1997), p. 530.

[6]See United States Constitution, Article III(1): "The Judges, both of the supreme and inferior Courts, shall hold their Offices during good Behaviour, and shall, at stated Times, receive for their Services a Compensation, which shall not be diminished during their Continuance in Office".

[7]The obvious apparent exception is the prior judges whose decisions often are applied as precedents by current judges. Where these precedents interpret the work of institutions that are politically accountable to current majorities—statutes enacted by legislatures and regulations adopted by administrative agencies—their continued existence might be seen as implicit acquiescence in their substance by these accountable institutions (the legislature could simply overturn incorrect interpretations of its statutes by amending the statute in question). On this theory, respect for prior judicial decisions might be understood as a form of subservience to democratically more-accountable institutions. Matters are more obscure where the judicial precedent interprets a constitutional provision and thus is very difficult to correct by means of constitutional amendment. Many formalists thus distrust the presumptive American practice of adhering to constitutional precedent (see Peters (2014), pp. 189–198), although Justice Scalia himself professes to accept the practice (see Scalia (1989a), p. 861): "[A]lmost every originalist would adulterate [originalism] with the doctrine of *stare decisis*".

of constraint upon judicial discretion is necessary for the proper functioning of democratic governance. But I will contend that the most important sources of this constraint lie in principles other than those urged by legal formalists.

2 "A … Criterion … Quite Separate from the Preferences of the Judge", Part I: The Endemic Indeterminacy of Text

In order for legal formalism to work as advertised—to constrain judges—it must be capable of doing so. Judges must actually be able to decide most or all cases primarily or exclusively by the mechanical application of existing legal rules. And whether or not judges are deciding cases in this way must be transparent to others—to the litigants, to superior judges (if any) in the hierarchy, to policymakers, to lawyers, to legal academics, perhaps to the media and to the public—if the constraint imposed by legal rules is to be real rather than merely professed. If it is not clear in most cases whether judges are in fact simply applying existing rules, then judges often will be able to avoid detection in not doing so, thus substantially reducing their incentive to simply apply existing rules.

The constraining function of formalism therefore depends on the existence of a system of legal rules that is *determinate*—capable of conclusively resolving all legal issues in a particular case—and whose determinacy is transparent. Most legal rules are communicated in textual form, so it makes sense to ask whether the text of legal rules is capable, by itself, of conferring this sort of systemic determinacy. For a familiar set of reasons, the answer is no.

We can illustrate why using an example that will be familiar to students of Anglo-American jurisprudence, arising as it does from a well-known mid-twentieth-century debate between the English legal positivist H.L.A. Hart and the American "Legal Process" theorist Lon Fuller.[8] Suppose a city ordinance prohibits "vehicles" in the public park. A group of war veterans wants to erect a monument in the park featuring a now-inoperative truck once used in combat. Would this violate the ordinance?

Note, first of all, that the applicable text of the ordinance—banning "vehicles" from the park—will not, standing alone, answer this question. As Hart saw it, any word has both "a core of settled meaning" and "a penumbra of debatable cases in which [the word is] neither obviously applicable nor obviously ruled out".[9] For the latter category, Hart had in mind examples like whether "bicycles, roller skates, or toy automobiles" qualified as "vehicles" under the ordinance.[10] Fuller, for his part,

---

[8]See Hart (1958), p. 607 and Fuller (1958), pp. 662–663.
[9]Hart (1958), p. 607.
[10]Ibid.

was skeptical of the existence even of "a core of settled meaning"; he used the war-monument example to suggest that even something we normally would call a "vehicle" without a second thought can, in some instances, fall within Hart's "penumbra" of ambiguity.[11] Both theorists understood, however, that there will be many cases in which the proper application of a rule's text to the facts of a particular case will be uncertain. As Hart put it, "the toy automobile" (or for that matter the inoperative combat truck) "cannot speak up and say, 'I am a vehicle for the purpose of this legal rule'".[12]

The hypothetical "no vehicles in the park" ordinance thus is an example of an under-determinate textual expression of a legal rule. Based upon the text alone, a judge faced with a case involving the war-monument combat truck could reasonably reach either alternative conclusion about the meaning of the ordinance: that the truck *is* a "vehicle" and thus is barred from the park, or that the truck is *not* a "vehicle" and thus is permitted. Neither interpretation would clearly be an unfaithful application of the text of the rule. And thus the judge is not constrained by the text alone to reach one interpretation rather than the other.

Nor is the "vehicles" example anomalous as a representation of textual indeterminacy in American law (or, I suspect, in the law of any reasonably complex legal system). In the context that most concerns Justice Scalia—American constitutional law—vague or ambiguous text is more the rule (as it were) than the exception. The "penumbras" of terms like "the equal protection of the laws" in the Fourteenth Amendment, "liberty" and "due process of law" in the Fifth and Fourteenth Amendments, and "the freedom of speech" in the First Amendment are considerably larger than that of the word "vehicles" in Hart's hypothetical ordinance.

Even relatively determinate legal texts have instances of indeterminacy. Justice Scalia himself[13] discusses an example of this (although he denies that it is an example): a federal statute mandating increased jail time for a defendant who "uses … a firearm" "during and in relation to… [a] drug trafficking crime".[14] Suppose a defendant offers to trade an unloaded gun for drugs; has he "use[d] … a firearm" in the sense meant by the statute? In *Smith v. United States*, the Supreme Court answered yes; Justice Scalia dissented on the ground that the decision was inconsistent with the "ordinary meaning" of the phrase "uses a firearm".[15] The Justice won two other votes with his dissent; a six-Justice majority disagreed with his interpretation of the statute's text. That the text was susceptible to at least two reasonable, and mutually exclusive, interpretations seems obvious from the nonunanimous vote.

Add to this the fact that legal rules rarely stand alone in any legal system. Often they interact with other legal rules that apply in particular cases. For example, in a

---

[11]Fuller (1958), p. 663.

[12]Hart (1958), p. 607.

[13]Scalia (1997), pp. 23–24.

[14]18 USC § 924(c) (1).

[15]508 US 223, 241, 242 (1993) (Scalia, J., dissenting).

recent lawsuit challenging the validity of a federal law refusing recognition to same-sex marriages, the Supreme Court had to interpret not only the statute being challenged, but also the Equal Protection Clause of the federal Constitution, the Due Process Clause of that Constitution, and many prior judicial decisions applying those clauses.[16] And it is virtually always true that legal rules are situated within a larger matrix of rules that, while not directly applicable to the case at hand, nonetheless may influence which interpretations of the applicable rule are most reasonable. Calling an inoperative war-memorial truck a prohibited "vehicle" will seem more or less reasonable to the extent it is consistent or inconsistent with, for example, the use of the word "vehicle" in other ordinances, or with a separate ordinance promoting "natural" uses of the park. A judge applying the indeterminate text of any given legal rule therefore often must also apply the indeterminate text of other rules and determine how the rules interact with each other.

So, in many cases within a complex legal system like that in the United States, the text of legal rules standing alone will be indeterminate, or at least will not be transparently determinate. Judges will be able to reach more than one reasonable result that is consistent with the text. This is not to say that text does not constrain at all in such cases; often there will be many applications of the text clearly within (or outside) its "core of settled meaning". An operative combat truck driven through the park clearly would violate the "no vehicles" ordinance; a toddler's small wooden pull-toy clearly would not. Nor is it to deny that some textual expressions of rules will be more determinate than others, or even that some will be determinate in every or nearly every case (consider a law setting the speed limit at 65 mph, or the provision of the US Constitution composing the Senate of "two Senators from each State"). The point is only that there will be a great many cases in which the text does not completely constrain judges. In many cases, the formalist search for a criterion of decision "quite separate from the preferences of the judge himself" (in Scalia's words) will have to extend beyond the text.

3 "A ... Criterion ... Quite Separate from the Preferences of the Judge", Part II: The Endemic Indeterminacy of Originalism

If text alone rarely can underwrite formalism, then what? Among American legal formalists, the answer is almost always some form of *originalism*. Originalists seek to supplement indeterminate legal texts with empirical facts about the process of the text's adoption: the "intent" of the authors or ratifiers of the text, or—in the currently dominant form of originalism—the "meaning" that would have been attributed to the text by a reasonable member of the public at the time of its adoption as law. Justice Scalia, a leading originalist, was an early proponent of the

---

[16]The decision in question is *United States v. Windsor,* 133 S. Ct. 2675 (2013).

latter approach.[17] This "original meaning" or "original public meaning" original-ism superseded its "original intent" progenitor in part because the former was exposed as highly indeterminate,[18] and so I will focus on the supposedly more-determinate recent version here.

For formalists, the point of a search for "original meaning" is to iden-tify some factual determinant of legal meaning that is independent of a judge's own values or desires. If, as a matter of historical linguistics, there is an "orig-inal public meaning" of, say, the Free Speech Clause of the Constitution's First Amendment—"Congress shall make no law ... abridging the freedom of speech"—then a judge can apply that original meaning without relying on her own preferences. And if the original public meaning is relatively accessible and trans-parent, then the judge can be *seen* to be applying that meaning without relying on her preferences—or not to be doing so. The original public meaning thus promises to constrain judges.

The problems with this aspiration, however, are threefold. Often an original public meaning will not exist, at least not at the level required to decide a concrete case. Sometimes, to the contrary, there will be multiple inconsistent original public meanings. And locating a single original meaning, assuming it exists, frequently will be difficult or impossible, especially for judges, who are not in fact linguistic historians.

Often an original public meaning will not exist in the required sense because, at the time the text was adopted as law, nobody considered what that text might mean in a given circumstance. Sometimes nobody at the time of adoption *could* have considered the question. For example, when the Free Speech Clause became part of the Constitution in 1791, no one could have thought about its potential application to campaign-finance laws in the late-twentieth and early twenty-first centuries. It would have been impossible to anticipate what American political campaigns would look like two centuries later—the existence of television and the Internet, the dominance of two entrenched political parties, the system of primary elections, the importance of independent "political action committees", the rise of for-profit corporations. To ask a reasonable and well-informed citizen in 1791 whether restrictions on so-called "issue advertisements" funded by corporations or unions would "abridge[e] the freedom of speech" would be to ask a nonsensical question. The words of the Free Speech Clause simply *have* no "original meaning" with respect to that question.

On the other hand, sometimes the evidence will suggest contradictory original meanings. Within a few years after ratification of the Bill of Rights, the Federalist Congress enacted the Sedition Act, which made it a federal crime to "write, print, utter, or publish ... any false, scandalous and malicious writing or writings against

---

[17]Scalia (1989a; 1997).

[18]For an originalist's account of the general rejection, among originalists, of "original intent" originalism in favor of "original public meaning" originalism, see Solum (2011), pp. 6–17. For influential critiques of "original intent" originalism as indeterminate, see Brest (1980); Dworkin (1985), pp. 34–57.

the government of the United States ... with intent to defame the said government ... or to bring [it] ... into contempt or disrepute".[19] Many citizens at the time— among them James Madison, a key delegate at the 1787 Constitutional Convention and the principal author of the Bill of Rights—argued that the Sedition Act was unconstitutional, either as a violation of the Free Speech Clause of the First Amendment or as an encroachment on the powers of the State governments.[20] Other members of the founding generation, including Alexander Hamilton and, quite obviously, a majority of the Congress that passed the Sedition Act, disagreed (though Hamilton himself did so halfheartedly).[21] What then was the "original meaning" of the Free Speech Clause with respect to "defamation" of the govern- ment, or the original meaning of the Tenth Amendment, which "reserved to the States" all powers not "delegated" by the Constitution to the federal government? The answer depends on whether one credits the stated views of the (mostly Federalist) supporters of the Sedition Act or those of its (mostly Republican) opponents. Here also, it is far too simplistic to assign a single "original meaning" to these provisions, which by all evidence were contested from the moment of their origin.

Finally, consider the practical difficulties facing the judge seeking to identify original meaning even where it exists. The judge must, first, locate relevant histori- cal evidence regarding what the appropriate collection of people thought the text meant (and in so doing must decide what evidence is relevant, which collection of people is appropriate, and what understandings or beliefs or other mental states of those people matter). She must then determine whether some of the relevant men- tal states of some of the people in question are in conflict and, if so, how to resolve that conflict. And she must, finally, figure out how to apply those historical mental states to the potentially very different and unforeseen facts as they exist today. As Justice Scalia himself puts it:

> [I]t is often exceedingly difficult to plumb the original understanding of an ancient text. Properly done, the task requires the consideration of an enormous mass of material ... Even beyond that, it requires an evaluation of the reliability of that material ... And fur- ther still, it requires immersing oneself in the political and intellectual atmosphere of the time – somehow placing out of mind knowledge that we have which an earlier age did not, and putting on beliefs, attitudes, philosophies, prejudices and loyalties that are not those of our day. It is, in short, a task sometimes better suited to the historian than the lawyer.[22]

All of which raises the obvious question: are we really constraining judges—who typically are not, after all, historians—in any meaningful way by asking them to search for original meaning in deciding contemporary cases? Many originalist theorists have been forced to admit that the answer is no. Randy Barnett and Lawrence Solum, two leading contemporary originalists, thus endorse what they

---

[19]See Urofsky and Finkelman (2011), pp. 201–205.

[20]Ibid., p. 204. See also Ellis (2001), pp. 198–201.

[21]Ellis (2001), p. 191.

[22]Scalia (1989a), pp. 856–857.

call "constitutional construction"—essentially, discretionary judicial lawmaking—
as a means of filling the many gaps in originalist interpretation.[23] In Barnett's
words:

> For better or worse, ... the US Constitution requires more than originalist interpretation to
> be applied to cases and controversies. Owing to the vagueness of language and the limits
> of historical inquiry, originalist interpretation may not result in a unique rule of law to be
> applied to a particular case or controversy.[24]

Original meaning, like the text, is endemically under-determinate. And while the
problem may be most egregious in the context of constitutional provisions, which
typically "use general concepts and abstract principles in place of specific rules",[25]
it will appear to some extent in the interpretation of any legal text.

4 "The Principal Weakness of the System": Participatory Adjudication and Judicial Constraint

The assumption that formalist techniques can meaningfully constrain judges is
therefore deeply problematic. In this and the following two sections, I argue that
this is not a great cause for concern—because the assumption that formalism is
necessary to meaningfully constrain judges also is flawed. American judges are
not constrained by the formalistic interpretation of legal rules. But they are constrained by the internal dynamics of the adversary system of adjudication; and
they are constrained by the need to keep faith with substantive legal principles,
even when those principles are not reducible to formalistic rules. I discuss the former source of constraint in this section and the latter in Sect. 5.[26]

In the United States, as in most legal systems influenced heavily by the British,
adjudication follows an "adversary" model: primary responsibility for initiat-
ing court cases, framing the factual and legal issues, investigating and proving
the relevant facts, advancing the legal arguments, and shaping the remedies lies
with the affected parties and their attorneys, not with the court itself (I will focus
the discussion here on civil disputes rather than criminal prosecutions, but most
of the same party-driven dynamics apply in criminal cases—often to an even
greater degree—although of course one of the parties to a criminal case is the
government).

---

[23]See Barnett (2004), pp. 118–130 and Solum (2010).

[24]Barnett (2004), p. 121.

[25]Ibid., p. 120.

[26]The discussion in this section is drawn from Peters (2011), pp. 155–160 and 310–328; see also
Peters (1997), pp. 347–60.

In American civil adjudication:

- The disputing parties, not the court, choose whether and when to adjudicate a dispute. In the federal courts, moreover, disputes cannot be adjudicated unless the party seeking the court's intervention can show that it has suffered an "injury in fact", that its injury is "fairly traceable" to unlawful conduct by the defending party, and that a court order is "likely" to redress that injury. The mere existence of unlawful conduct, or of some general societal harm flowing from that conduct, is not enough to trigger adjudication.[27]
- The disputing parties (typically through their attorneys), not the court, determine which factual issues will be decided in resolving the dispute. The litigants investigate the relevant facts, assemble them in forms suitable for proof, and (within limits imposed by evidentiary rules) decide whether and how to present them to the trier of fact. Expert witnesses, where required, typically are retained and compensated by the litigants themselves, not by the court.
- The disputing parties also are chiefly or solely responsible for identifying the legal issues and developing the legal arguments relevant to the dispute. With few exceptions (most of which go to the court's jurisdiction to hear the dispute in the first place), strong norms of judicial practice prevent judges from deciding cases based on legal grounds not argued by the parties.
- In many cases, the disputing parties have a substantial role in deciding who will make findings based on the proofs—whether it will be a judge or a jury, and in jury cases, who will sit on the jury.[28] The jury option is itself a significant constraint on the judge's authority that is not available in civil adjudication in most legal systems outside the United States.
- The disputing parties typically decide whether to settle their dispute (and thus terminate the adjudication) without need for court approval.[29]
- The disputing parties propose and argue the merits of remedies, such as compensatory damages or injunctive relief. While judges typically have substantial influence in the shaping of "specific" (injunctive) remedies, they generally

---

[27]See, e.g., *Lujan v. Defenders of Wildlife*, 504 US 555 (1992); *Allen v. Wright*, 468 US 737 (1984).

[28]The Seventh Amendment to the federal Constitution guarantees the right to a jury trial in many civil cases in federal court, but this right may be waived by the parties. In both federal and State courts, the litigants typically participate in the process of choosing jurors, known as *voir dire*, by asking questions of prospective jurors (either directly or by submitting them to the judge), by moving to exclude prospective jurors "for cause", and by exercising "peremptory challenges" to strike a certain number of jurors without cause.

[29]In fact, procedural rules and statutes in the United States increasingly encourage out-of-court settlement of disputes, and far more cases "settle" than go to trial in American courts. See Galanter and Cahill (1994). There are exceptions, however, to the baseline principle that judicial approval is not required for settlement, such as class-action lawsuits, where judicial approval is required in order to protect the interests of absent class members. See Federal Rule of Civil Procedure 23. And while the terms of settlements rarely require judicial approval, it is commonplace that judges use various means to encourage the litigants to settle. See Galanter and Cahill (1994).

cannot grant such remedies without being asked by the litigants to do so, and the form of specific remedies is determined by the proofs and arguments of the parties.

- The disputing parties, not the trial judge or appellate judges, decide whether to appeal the trial court's decision to a higher court and how to argue the appeal once it is taken. In the federal system, most appeals cannot be taken until there is a final judgment in the trial court, and only a party that is aggrieved by the trial court's decision has standing to appeal it. No appellate court will review an issue—no matter how publicly important that issue may be—unless an aggrieved party seeks review of that issue.[30]
- Strong norms of judicial practice, and in some cases formal rules,[31] require judges to issue written opinions explaining how their dispositive rulings are justified by the facts and the law and responding to the litigants' arguments.

These prominent elements of litigant participation can and do exert meaningful constraint on the discretion of judges. American judges, unlike American legislators, cannot take action simply because they see a problem that needs solving. They must wait for that problem to generate a dispute between parties who stand to gain or lose something real and concrete from the resolution of that dispute. Judges then must act within the confines of that dispute as defined by the parties—deciding those legal and factual issues (and *only* those legal and factual issues) identified as important by the litigants, refraining from decision if the litigants choose to settle their dispute, and explaining and justifying their decision in terms that respond saliently to the litigants' proofs and arguments. American judges are, in a very real sense, prisoners of the disputes they must resolve.[32]

This is true even in the context of important public-law litigation (which tends to be the focus of formalist concerns), although in that context the scope of the

---

[30]In the federal court system, the requirement of a final judgment as a condition of appeal is codified in 28 USC § 1291. There are a number of exceptions to this requirement, one of which allows the trial judge, of her own accord, to "certify" certain issues for immediate appeal. See 28 USC § 1292(b). The "final judgment" requirement for appeal is less stringent in many State court systems. In the federal courts, the requirement that an appeal from a final judgment may be taken only by an aggrieved party has been held to be at least partly constitutional in stature, flowing from Article III's grant of the federal judicial power to decide only "cases" and "controversies". See *Hollingsworth v. Perry*, 133 S. Ct. 2652 (2013); *United States v. Windsor*, 133 S. Ct. 2675, 2684-2689 (2013).

[31]Such as Federal Rule of Civil Procedure 52, which requires federal judges who serve as triers of fact to write opinions justifying their decisions on both factual and legal grounds.

[32]Formalists often recognize the practical constraint imposed by the American adversary model of adjudication. Justice Scalia, for example, advocates strict adherence to justiciability requirements as a way to limit judicial power. See *United States v. Windsor* cit. (Scalia, J., dissenting) (criticizing the majority's willingness to recognize standing to appeal in the case as reflecting "an exalted conception of the role of [the Supreme Court] in America"). This recognition sits somewhat uneasily alongside the professed belief that formalist interpretive techniques can meaningfully constrain judges. If formalism imposes significant constraint, it is unclear why the additional measure of strict justiciability limitations is necessary.

dispute, and thus of litigant participation, often is expanded. Consider the following example taken from a significant and relatively recent Supreme Court adjudication.

In 2003, the Court decided the cases *Grutter v. Bollinger* and *Gratz v. Bollinger*.[33] In *Grutter*, a white plaintiff who had been denied admission to the prestigious University of Michigan Law School sued the University to challenge, as a violation of the Fourteenth Amendment's Equal Protection Clause,[34] the Law School's "affirmative action" admissions policy, which gave a preference to members of certain racial minority groups. In *Gratz*, two white plaintiffs denied admission to the University's undergraduate program brought a similar challenge. By a 5-4 vote, the Court upheld the race-conscious Law School policy in *Grutter*; by a 6-3 vote, it struck down the crucially different undergraduate policy in *Gratz*.

One notable thing about the *Grutter* and *Gratz* decisions was their relative narrowness—a feature that was at least in part a function of the dispute-resolving constraints faced by the Court. In the lower courts, the litigants in each case had developed a substantial factual record regarding the particular details and effects of each affirmative-action policy at issue. The subtle differences between the Law School's policy and the undergraduate policy ended up determining the results: Justices Sandra Day O'Connor (who wrote the Court's opinion in *Grutter*) and Stephen Breyer voted to uphold the Law School's policy but to invalidate the undergraduate policy, on the ground that the former was "narrowly tailored" to achieve racial diversity while the latter was not. The decisions thus were neither broad endorsements nor broad condemnations of the use of race-conscious admissions in higher education. Instead they were relatively fact-specific rulings, capable of providing guidance to litigants and judges (and to universities seeking to avoid becoming litigants) in future similar cases, but not of conclusively resolving subsequent disputes with materially dissimilar facts.

Just how fact-specific the rulings were become evident a few years later, in *Parents Involved v. Seattle School District No. 1*, when the Court (after a crucial change in membership) invalidated race-conscious policies used to assign students to public schools.[35] The litigants challenging these policies in *Parents Involved* were able to successfully distinguish that case from *Grutter*, convincing the Court that the particular policies in question, like that in the *Gratz* case, were not sufficiently "narrowly tailored" to serve the diversity objective. The reach of the *Grutter* and *Gratz* decisions thus was confined to the facts of the disputes that produced them, with subsequent litigants left free to argue for different results based

---

[33]*Grutter v. Bollinger*, 539 US 306 (2003); *Gratz v. Bollinger*, 539 US 244 (2003).

[34]"No State shall … deny to any person within its jurisdiction the equal protection of the laws".

[35]*See Parents Involved in Community Schools v. Seattle School District No. 1*, 555 US 701 (2007). Between 2003 (when *Grutter* and *Gratz* were decided) and 2007, Justice O'Connor had left the Court, replaced by the more-conservative Justice Samuel Alito (who voted with the majority in *Parents Involved*). In addition, Chief Justice Rehnquist had died and been replaced by John Roberts, but that change did not affect the Court's attitude toward race-conscious affirmative action, which both Rehnquist and Roberts opposed.

on the differing facts of those subsequent disputes. This relatively narrow, common-law style of case-by-case adjudication in effect makes each new set of litigants the authors, in part, of the legal rules that will end up binding them.

This is not to deny that relatively broad principles can be gleaned from *Grutter* and *Gratz*, as they can from most Supreme Court decisions. Those cases did establish as a general matter that the interest of racial diversity in higher education is sufficiently "compelling" to justify race-consciousness in admissions, provided the use of race is closely tailored to achieving that objective. But even this principle has proven vulnerable to the vagaries of particular disputes. In *Parents Involved*, for example, Chief Justice Roberts, writing for a plurality of four Justices, suggested that the diversity rationale might not apply in the context of elementary and secondary education (as opposed to higher education as in *Grutter*).[36] The scope of the principles established by a decision is, to a great extent, in the hands of subsequent courts, and thus is subject to the arguments of subsequent litigants.

The holdings of prior cases can be just as indeterminate as the text or the original understanding of the legal rules those cases interpret; the idea of absolute constraint by precedent is another formalist myth. The real constraining effect of precedent derives from the fact that litigants, in a common-law system like the American one, must use precedent as a basis for their legal arguments. Precedent affects the decisions of which cases to litigate and of how to litigate them. And these factors in turn constrain the judges charged with deciding litigated cases. Once a case is properly before a court, judges will have substantial (though far from unlimited) discretion in interpreting the applicable precedents and other sources of legal norms. But which cases come before a court, and which precedents and other norms apply to them, are to a large extent outside the judges' control.

The *Grutter* and *Gratz* decisions illustrate the influence of litigant participation, not just in the relative fact-specificity of their rulings, but also in the overt responsiveness of those decisions to the participants' arguments. In the trial courts, where factfinding occurs in the American system, the judges in these cases wrote lengthy opinions recounting in meticulous detail the parties' arguments and proofs; the trial judge's opinion in *Grutter* consumes fifty-two pages of the *Federal Supplement Second* reporter, twenty-three of which are devoted to a detailed, nonevaluative statement of the facts proved at trial.[37] At the Supreme Court level, the grounds of the Court's decisions, and indeed of the opinions of the concurring and dissenting Justices, could be traced almost without exception to arguments made by one of the parties or by other litigants participating as *amici curiae*. The sole exception appeared in Justice John Paul Stevens's dissent in *Gratz*, which opined that the plaintiffs in that case lacked standing to seek

---

[36]*See Parents Involved* cit., at 723 ("In upholding the admissions plan in *Grutter*, ... this Court relied upon considerations unique to institutions of higher education ...").

[37]*Grutter v. Bollinger*, 127 F. Supp. 2d 821 (E.D. Mich. 2001). Federal district (trial) court judges are required by rule to expressly state the findings of fact and the rulings of law upon which their final judgments are based. See Federal Rule of Civil Procedure 52.

injunctive relief, an argument not made by the University or any of its allies.[38] This is an exception that proves the rule: ensuring that litigants have standing to sue—that they have something concrete to win or lose in a court case—is a way to preserve the dispute-resolving posture of American adjudication and thus to limit the scope of judicial authority.

None of this is to deny that American judges, particularly Supreme Court Justices, often retain considerable legal discretion to choose from multiple possible outcomes within the confines of a particular case, or that this choice often will be driven by extra-legal factors. The point is simply that the dispute-resolving structure of American adjudication imposes real constraints on the content (and, just as importantly, the occasions) of judicial decisions. Strong procedural norms require American judges to decide in ways that are responsive, and that are seen to be responsive, to the proofs and arguments made by disputing parties. Substantial judicial constraint is an important practical effect of these norms.

5 "A … Criterion … Quite Separate from the Preferences of the Judge", Part III: Judicial Constraint and Substantive Legal Principles

In addition to being practically constrained by the dynamics of dispute resolution, American judges are constrained by the obligation to enforce substantive legal principles, even when the otherwise-applicable legal rules are indeterminate. By "substantive legal principles", I mean legal norms that lack the all-or-nothing quality of rules. Ronald Dworkin influentially distinguished between rules and principles in this way.[39] Dworkin noted that rules "are applicable in an all-or-nothing fashion. If the facts a rule stipulates are given, then either the rule is valid, in which case the answer it supplies must be accepted, or it is not, in which case it contributes nothing to the decision".[40] If a valid legal rule states "Vehicles are not allowed in the public park", and we are given that Jones's pickup truck is a "vehicle" and that Jones has driven his vehicle into the public park, then we know that Jones has violated the law.

Principles, in contrast, "stat[e] a reason that argues in one direction, but d[o] not necessitate a particular decision".[41] Dworkin cites the example of the principle "No man shall profit from his own wrong".[42] If we are given that Smith has profited from his own wrong—by, for example, publishing a best-selling book detailing his criminal exploits—we do not (by virtue of this) know for sure that Smith

---

[38]*Gratz v. Bollinger* cit., 282 (Stevens, J., dissenting).

[39]Dworkin (1978), pp. 22–28.

[40]Ibid., p. 24.

[41]Ibid., p. 26.

[42]Ibid.

has violated the law. The principle in question "argues in [that] direction", but it may, in any given case, be outweighed by competing principles (such as a principle limiting punishments for criminal acts to those expressly provided by the legislature) or by applicable rules (such as the guarantee of "the freedom of speech" in the Constitution's First Amendment).

Dworkin also uses the concept of "legal principles" in a more specific sense, to identify non-rule-like norms flowing from "requirement[s] of justice or fairness or some other dimension of morality", as opposed to "policies", which are non-rule-like norms that "se[t] out a [social] goal to be reached".[43] I want to put this distinction to one side, however, and use the terminology of "legal principles" in its more general sense, to refer to legal norms that are not reducible to all-or-nothing rules. "Principles" in this sense might include what Dworkin calls "policies". In fact, principles in this sense might themselves be derived from all-or-nothing legal rules. And this possibility allows for the further possibility of judicial constraint in the following of rules, even when the rules themselves are indeterminate.[44]

To illustrate what I mean, suppose a judge must decide whether the inclusion of an inoperative combat truck as part of a war memorial violates the "no vehicles in the public park" ordinance. Neither the ordinance's text alone nor the "original meaning" of that text provides a clear resolution of the issue. But text and original meaning do not exhaust the possible sources of the law's content.

Suppose that although the judge is unsure whether the combat truck is a "vehicle" within the meaning of the ordinance, she can readily conjure objects that clearly fall within Hart's "core of settled meaning" of that word:[45] a working combat truck, for example, or a passenger car, or a motorcycle. Clearly the ordinance would apply to bar these objects from the park; and thus the judge can use these clear instances (we might call them *positive paradigms*) as clues to the *justification* of the ordinance—the best understanding of why the lawmaker created the ordinance and used certain language to express it. The question for the judge would be: what it is about these quintessential "vehicles" that might explain the legislature's decision to ban them from the park? If there is some property or collection of properties that obvious vehicles possess and that justifies their exclusion from a public park, then the judge might be able to resolve the case at hand by asking whether the war-memorial truck also possesses that property or collection of properties (and thus also should be excluded from the park).[46]

Suppose the judge notices a number of properties that these quintessential "vehicles" have in common: they are loud; they produce noxious fumes; they pose a danger to pedestrians in the park; they are made largely of metal; they carry one

---

[43]Ibid., p. 22.

[44]The discussion that follows is drawn from Peters (2011), pp. 176–181.

[45]Hart (1958), p. 607.

[46]Cf. Hart and Sacks (1994), p. 1378: "Why would reasonable men, confronted with the law as it was, have enacted this new law to replace it? The most reliable guides to an answer will be found in the instances of unquestioned application of the statute".

or more people from place to place; they must be driven or piloted by someone; they are relatively expensive. Some of these properties (the first three) might reasonably justify a statute banning "vehicles" from the public park. Parks are places people go, often with children, to play and relax; excessive noise, noxious fumes, and large speeding objects frequently will interfere with that function. On the other hand, it is difficult to construct a reasonable argument why other properties (the last four) would justify excluding vehicles from the park: nothing in particular about objects that are made of metal, or that carry people from place to place, or that require a driver, or that cost a lot of money is likely to interfere with the function of a public park. So the judge might hypothesize, based on these positive paradigms, that the justification of the "no vehicles" ordinance is to prevent excessive noise, noxious fumes, and danger to pedestrians in the park.

The judge might also notice that some objects that clearly are *not* vehicles— that is, cases that are *negative* paradigms—also possess one or more of these properties. Fireworks, for instance, produce lots of noise, noxious smoke, and danger to bystanders; and yet they clearly are not banned by the "no vehicles" ordinance. But this does not mean that the judge's hypothesized justification of the ordinance (preventing noise, fumes, and danger) is wrong. Legislatures have limited time and resources, and often they will address only the most salient or usual manifestations of a problem (vehicles, which are common, but not fireworks, which are less so). Moreover, sometimes the reason for regulating one type of activity will, if applied to similar types of activity, be outweighed by countervailing reasons against regulation (banning fireworks from the park, for example, would ruin the city's annual Independence Day celebration). So the judge will be cautious about reading too much into the existence of a few negative paradigms. But the existence of a great many negative paradigms—lots of loud, smelly, dangerous things that clearly aren't banned from the park—should cause the judge to rethink her hypothetical justification of the ordinance.

Relatedly, the judge is likely to consider the body of law apart from the ordinance in question, and to ask what understanding of the ordinance's impact on that body of law makes the most sense. Suppose that the park independently is subject to a noise ordinance that prohibits sounds in excess of a certain decibel level. This would militate against an interpretation of the ordinance as justified in part by concerns about excessive noise; such an interpretation would render the ordinance partially redundant. Suppose, on the other hand, that the city allows organized soccer matches to be held in the park in front of loud groups of spectators; this too would militate against the "no excessive noise" justification of the ordinance, not because it would render the ordinance redundant, but rather because it would render it useless. A focus on the state of the law absent the ordinance also suggests a complementary inquiry into the particular problems or events that led the legislature to enact the ordinance. Perhaps the city council adopted the law immediately after a pedestrian was struck and killed by a car in the park; that would suggest that the ordinance is justified at least in part by the goal of preventing such accidents.

What the judge is looking for here—what I have called the "justification" of the ordinance—is a species of "principle" in the general sense in which that concept was employed by Dworkin.[47] To conclude that the justification of the ordinance is to prevent excessive noise, noxious fumes, and danger to pedestrians in the park is not to conclude that there is a legal *rule* against these phenomena in the park. The applicable legal *rule*, after all, prohibits only one source of these harms ("vehicles"), not all instances of them. And as I have suggested, the limited scope of the rule might be explained by countervailing considerations, such as the independent benefits of allowing some non-vehicular sources of noise, fumes, and danger into the park. The justification of the ordinance is an example of Dworkin's "principle" because it "argues in one direction"[48]—the direction of banning noisy, smelly, dangerous items from the park—but might be outweighed by countervailing principles or rules.

And yet the justification of a statute, or of any legal rule, differs from Dworkin's freestanding "principles" because it is *attached* to a legal rule: it exists solely as a means of interpreting and applying that rule in cases where the rule otherwise is indeterminate. Banning loud, smelly, dangerous objects from the park might generally be a good idea, but the judge would not be authorized to do so based solely on the "principle" that it is a good idea; she may do so only as part of her task of interpreting and applying the legal rule that prohibits "vehicles" from the park. The judge's authority for applying the principle that justifies the rule stems from her authority to apply the rule itself. In applying the justificatory principle, the judge just *is* applying the rule.

And this, finally, is the point: legal rules might be *applied* to particular cases in a meaningful sense—even when they are indeterminate in such cases according to formalist methods—through the use of *principles* (justifications, reasons, purposes, goals) that explain the existence of those rules and thus are embodied in them. Judges, then, can be constrained even by indeterminate legal rules—constrained to apply those rules in the way that best serves the justifications of them.

It is true that the search for justificatory principles behind legal rules unavoidably has a normative component. The judge looks, not just for anything that might explain a statute, but for a normatively attractive explanation, a *justification*. In the "no vehicles" case, for example, the judge will reject "preventing objects made of metal in the park" as a justification for the ordinance on purely normative grounds: that justification would be normatively unreasonable. Different judges may reach different conclusions regarding which potential justifications are normatively reasonable, or more normatively reasonable than others. So the search for justificatory principles is far from absolutely constraining; the possibility (many formalists would say the danger) that the case will turn on judicial discretion remains.

---

[47]Dworkin probably would refer to it more specifically as a "policy"—"a kind of standard that sets out a goal to be reached, generally an improvement in some economic, political, or social feature of the community". See Dworkin (1978), p. 22. Or it might be called the "purpose" behind the ordinance: "the set of reasons for making those words a fixed part of the body of the law". See Wellman (1987), p. 463.

[48]Dworkin (1978), p. 26.

Still, it is fair to say that the search for justification, if it is done in good faith, imposes meaningful though not complete constraint on the party doing the searching. To attempt to apply a legal rule consistently with its justification is a very different task than to engage in unfettered, all-things-considered moral reasoning. A judge might, in good faith, determine that the inoperative combat truck is not covered by the justification of the "no vehicles" ordinance and thus is not banned from the park, even if the judge herself finds the truck unsightly, or thinks it is morally offensive to celebrate war, and thus would have banned it from the park had she been the legislator. To apply a statute in a way consistent with its justification is to apply the statute, and to apply a statute is emphatically *not* to create law from whole cloth.

6 "A … Criterion … Quite Separate from the Preferences of the Judge", Part IV: Judicial Constraint and Procedural Legal Principles

In the preceding two sections, I argued that American judges deciding cases are meaningfully constrained, despite the frequent failure of formalist techniques to provide determinate legal rules that they must follow. Judges are constrained by the dispute-resolving character of the adjudicative enterprise in which they are engaged: they can render decisions only in response to disputes that are initiated and argued by affected parties. And they are constrained by the need to interpret indeterminate rules in light of the principles that justify those rules.

Each of these sources of constraint, however, depends for its existence on judges' willingness to honor a different sort of legal principle: not substantive legal principles but *procedural* ones. The foregoing discussion suggests the presence of three fundamental procedural principles capable of generating judicial constraint in American adjudication. They are principles of *impartiality*, of *responsiveness*, and of *faithfulness*.

Impartiality is the absence from a dispute-resolving procedure of extrinsic factors favoring one side of the dispute over another. Elsewhere I have explained at length why impartiality is a necessary ingredient of an acceptable dispute-resolving process.[49] Here it will suffice to state the fairly obvious proposition that the losing party to a dispute is unlikely to willingly accept the result if she believes the process that generated it was arbitrarily biased against her. The dispute-resolving structure of American adjudication thus presupposes a reasonably impartial judge or panel of judges.

This norm of judicial impartiality often finds expression in rules of procedure or judicial ethics, such as the statute requiring disqualification of federal judges "in any proceeding in which [their] impartiality might reasonably be questioned".[50]

---

[49]See Peters (2011), pp. 78–81.
[50]28 USC § 455(a).

But, as the open-ended normative language of this rule suggests, the norm itself is best thought of as a principle in the Dworkinian sense, albeit one that emanates chiefly or entirely from the constitutional requirement of "due process of law". Nominees for federal judgeships, during Senate confirmation hearings, typically decline to state their views on active legal issues on the ground that the issue "might come before the court" should they be fortunate enough to serve on it. When they do so, it is not because some legal rule requires them to; the disqualification statutes and rules of judicial conduct have not been read so broadly and in any event do not apply to persons who are not yet judges.[51] Rather, it is because the nominees feel the strong pull of an unwritten principle of impartiality, one that requires them to avoid precommitment to particular resolutions of disputes.

This unwritten principle has real consequences for how judges decide cases. For a judge, to be impartial is, again, to avoid to the greatest extent possible the influence of extrinsic factors favoring one party over the other; and judicial predispositions and biases are such extrinsic factors. Judicial impartiality therefore requires what, in the words of the Supreme Court, "might be described as open-mindedness":

> This quality in a judge demands, not that he have no preconceptions on legal issues, but that he be willing to consider views that oppose his preconceptions, and remain open to persuasion, when the issues arise in a pending case. This sort of impartiality seeks to guarantee each litigant, not an *equal* chance to win the legal points in the case, but at least *some* chance of doing so.[52]

Impartiality doesn't guarantee that each litigant has "an *equal* chance to win", because in most instances one litigant's case, taking only the *relevant* or intrinsic factors into account, will be stronger than the other's. But it does guarantee, so far as possible, that each litigant's chance to win will not be distorted by irrelevant factors, including the judge's own preexisting biases. The principle of judicial impartiality thus requires judges to take the proofs and arguments of both sides seriously, refraining from deciding the outcome until all the evidence is in. Somewhat more obviously, impartiality requires reasonable equity in the opportunity to present these proofs and arguments, preventing the judge from denying to one litigant the procedural opportunities granted to another. If honored in good faith, then, the principle of judicial impartiality imposes real constraint.

Responsiveness is the requirement that judicial decisions be grounded in the proofs and arguments offered by the disputing litigants.[53] Lon Fuller described

---

[51]A ban on comment about active legal issues imposed on judicial nominees or candidates might run afoul of the Free Speech Clause of the First Amendment. The Supreme Court has invalidated on First Amendment grounds a state law forbidding an elective judicial candidate to "announce his or her views on disputed legal or political issues". See *Republican Party of Minnesota v. White*, 536 US 765 (2002).

[52]Ibid., at 778 (emphases in original). The Court in *White* acknowledged that preserving judicial impartiality in this sense might be a compelling state interest, but it nonetheless invalidated the limitation on judicial-candidate speech in that case on the ground that it was not in fact intended to serve that interest.

[53]See Peters (2001), pp. 25–27.

this requirement as one of "congruence" between the litigants' efforts and the judge's decision: "if this congruence is utterly absent ... then the adjudicative process has become a sham, for the parties' participation in the decision has lost all meaning".[54] For better or worse, the American litigant-driven model of adjudication reflects a more-general populist political commitment to bottom-up decision-procedures reflecting the views and interests of the affected persons, as opposed to top-down procedures embodying the supposed wisdom of professional experts.[55] American judges must be impartial, but they must be impartial in choosing from among competing proofs and arguments presented by the litigants themselves, not in choosing more generally from among all the possible proofs and arguments out there in the world, or from among those that would be made by ideally competent litigants.

This norm of responsiveness sometimes appears in procedural rules, like the federal-court rule requiring judges to "stat[e] on the record ... or ... in an opinion or memorandum" their factual findings and legal conclusions at the close of a bench trial.[56] But it mostly operates, like the impartiality norm, as an unwritten background principle. American judges typically write opinions justifying their decisions, even if no legal rule requires them to; they typically explain in those opinions why they are choosing one litigant's proofs or arguments over the other's; and (as I mentioned in discussing the *Grutter* and *Gratz* decisions) they typically avoid deciding cases on grounds not argued by the litigants. The responsiveness principle, like the impartiality principle, thus imposes meaningful constraint on judges, for it limits the bases of their decision to those the litigants choose to put forward.

Finally, *faithfulness* is the requirement that a judge seek to conform her decision to the law, even where no legal rule provides a determinate resolution of the issue. In American adjudication, as presumably in other legal systems, virtually everyone agrees with the formalists that judges (barring extraordinary circumstances) must apply existing legal rules where those rules dictate determinate outcomes. Following Dworkin and others, however, I have suggested here that judicial faithfulness requires more than the mechanical implementation of determinate legal rules. It also requires an effort to decide in accordance with the principles that justify legal rules, even when the rules themselves are indeterminate.

That this is in fact how American judges are expected to behave has I think been demonstrated by Dworkin.[57] And that it is how American judges actually do behave, or at least present themselves (and, one suspects, see themselves) as behaving,[58] is evident from any judicial decision not clearly preordained by the

---

[54]Fuller (1978), p. 388.

[55]Damaška (1986); Peters (1997), p. 349.

[56]Federal Rule of Civil Procedure 52(a).

[57]Dworkin (1978; 1986).

[58]There is of course much writing by American judges themselves regarding how they understand their duties. For a classic judicial statement of this understanding that accords with the principle of faithfulness, see Cardozo (1921).

text of a legal rule—which is to say, nearly any judicial decision, as cases with clearly preordained results rarely see the inside of a courtroom. The Supreme Court in the *Grutter* and *Gratz* cases did not throw up its collective hands in despair that the text of the legal rule at issue—the vague guarantee of "the equal protection of the laws" in the Constitution's Fourteenth Amendment—did not determinately resolve the question at hand; nor did it simply declare that, absent a clear command of the text or of "original understanding", its members would decide the issue by voting their own unfettered moral preferences. Instead, the Court decided the issue, or at least purported to decide it, in a way that was faithful to the Fourteenth Amendment without being clearly dictated by it. The fact that the members of the Court disagreed about what this duty of faithfulness required does not mean the duty did not exist or that they ignored that duty; it means only that they held differing views about how best to fulfill it.

Together these procedural principles—impartiality, responsiveness, faithfulness—can assert significant constraint on the discretion of American judges. That is, judges are constrained to the extent they honor these procedural principles. But what requires them to honor these principles?

Sometimes the answer is a written legal rule, like the one requiring judicial recusal in cases of questionable impartiality. Most of the time, though, the answer is much less concrete, and perhaps much less *legal*. It lies in expectations regarding the professional role of the judge, in longstanding practice, in legal training, in the peer pressure of lawyers and colleagues, in innate notions of justice and fairness. But these principles are no less real for lack of authoritative enactment as part of some legal code. After all, the requirements urged by legal formalists like Justice Scalia—attention to text, obeisance to "original meaning"—are themselves merely unwritten principles in this sense. A judge's obligation to obey them ultimately depends on whether they work in practice—whether they serve the normative goals that judges believe themselves committed to.

My argument here has been that the worthy normative goals of democratic governance, and thus of judicial constraint in service of democracy, can and are served at least as well by adherence to the foundational principles of impartiality, responsiveness, and faithfulness as by reflexive allegiance to legal formalism.

References

Aristotle. 1941. Nicomachean Ethics. In *The Basic Works of Aristotle*, ed. Richard McKeon, 927-1112. New York: Random House.

Barnett, Randy E. 2004. *Restoring the Lost Constitution: The Presumption of Liberty*. Princeton: Princeton University Press.

Brest, Paul. 1980. The Misconceived Quest for the Original Understanding. *Boston University Law Review* 60: 204-238.

Cardozo, Benjamin N. 1921. *The Nature of the Judicial Process*. New Haven: Yale University Press.

Damaška, Mirjan R. 1986. *The Faces of Justice and State Authority: A Comparative Approach to the Legal Process*. New Haven: Yale University Press.

Dworkin, Ronald M. 1978. *Taking Rights Seriously*. Cambridge: Harvard University Press.
Dworkin, Ronald M. 1985. *A Matter of Principle*. Cambridge: Harvard University Press.
Dworkin, Ronald M. 1986. *Law's Empire*. Cambridge: The Belknap Press of Harvard University Press.
Ellis, Joseph J. 2001. *Founding Brothers: The Revolutionary Generation*. New York: Alfred A. Knopf.
Fuller, Lon L. 1958. Positivism and Fidelity to Law – A Reply to Professor Hart. *Harvard Law Review* 71: 630-672.
Fuller, Lon L. 1978. The Forms and Limits of Adjudication. *Harvard Law Review* 92: 353-409.
Galanter, Marc, and Mia Cahill. 1994. 'Most Cases Settle': Judicial Promotion and Regulation of Settlement. *Stanford Law Review* 46: 1339-1392.
Hart, Herbert L. A. 1958. Positivism and the Separation of Law and Morals. *Harvard Law Review* 71: 593-629.
Hart, Henry M., Jr., and Albert Sacks. 1994. *The Legal Process: Basic Problems in the Making and Application of Law*, eds. William N. Eskridge, Jr. and Philip P. Frickey. Westbury: Foundation Press.
Hellman, Deborah. 2014. An Epistemic Defense of Precedent. In *Precedent in the United States Supreme Court*, ed. Christopher J. Peters, 189-226. New York: Springer.
Peters, Christopher J. 1997. Adjudication as Representation. *Columbia Law Review* 97: 312-436.
Peters, Christopher J. 2001, Persuasion: A Model of Majoritarianism as Adjudication. *Northwestern University Law Review* 96: 1-37.
Peters, Christopher J. 2011. *A Matter of Dispute: Morality, Democracy, and Law*. New York: Oxford University Press.
Peters, Christopher J. 2014. Originalism, Stare Decisis, and Constitutional Authority. In *Precedent in the United States Supreme Court*, ed. Christopher J. Peters, 189-226. New York: Springer.
Scalia, Antonin G. 1989a. Originalism: The Lesser Evil. *University of Cincinnati Law Review* 57: 849-865.
Scalia, Antonin G. 1989b. The Rule of Law as a Law of Rules. *University of Chicago Law Review* 56: 1175-1188.
Scalia, Antonin G. 1997. Common-Law Courts in a Civil-Law System: The Role of United States Federal Courts in Interpreting the Constitution and Laws. In *A Matter of Interpretation: Federal Courts and the Law*, ed. Amy Gutmann, 3-47. Princeton: Princeton University Press.
Solum, Lawrence B. 2011. What Is Originalism? The Evolution of Contemporary Originalist Theory. http://ssrn.com/abstract=1825543.
Solum, Lawrence B. 2010. The Interpretation-Construction Distinction. *Constitutional Commentary* 27: 95-118.
Sunstein, Cass. 1997. Justice Scalia's Democratic Formalism. *Yale Law Journal* 107: 529-68.
Urofsky, Melvin, and Paul Finkelman. 2011. *A March of Liberty: A Constitutional History of the United States, Volume I, From the Founding to 1900*. New York: Oxford University Press.
Wellman, Vincent. 1987. Dworkin and the Legal Process Tradition: The Legacy of Hart and Sacks. *Arizona Law Review* 29: 413-474.

General Principles of Law and Transnational Judicial Communication

Elaine Mak

Abstract In the globalised legal context, the national courts in Western legal systems increasingly interact with each other as well as with courts at the regional and international levels. Judges exchange views and experiences in networks and through visits and conferences and they consult international, European and foreign legal materials when deciding domestic cases. Which role do general principles of law play in this developing transnational judicial communication? This chapter investigates this question on the basis of a comparative and socio-legal analysis of five legal systems (Canada, United States, United Kingdom, France, Netherlands), drawing information from constitutional theory and from interviews with judges in the highest courts of the selected systems. The analysis reveals that the use of foreign legal sources by the examined courts has become a common practice in the daily business of judging cases. The examples given by the interviewed judges provide illustrations of the specific practices of each court, highlighting a relatively high number of cases in which general principles of law played a role. The legal-theoretical analysis clarifies that the added value of the developed practices of the courts is nuanced by the legal factors of authority of legal sources, legal tradition and the particularities of national legal systems. Moreover, contextual factors related to individual judicial approaches and concerns of effective and efficient judicial decision-making influence the reference that is made to comparative law, including foreign general principles of law.

E. Mak (✉)
Professor of Empirical Study of Public Law,
Erasmus University Rotterdam, Rotterdam, The Netherlands
e-mail: mak@law.eur.nl

© Springer International Publishing Switzerland 2015   45
L. Pineschi (ed.), *General Principles of Law - The Role of the Judiciary*,
Ius Gentium: Comparative Perspectives on Law and Justice 46,
DOI 10.1007/978-3-319-19180-5_3

1 Introduction

In the globalised legal context, the national courts in Western legal systems increasingly interact with each other as well as with courts at the regional and international levels.[1] Judges, in particular at the level of the highest courts, exchange views and experiences in networks and through visits and conferences and they consult binding and non-binding foreign legal sources[2] when deciding domestic cases.[3] For judges engaging in transnational communication, general principles of law might be an interesting source of information regarding shared concepts. These principles can be understood as expressing the "fundamental notions" of a legal system or more precisely "the essential characteristics of the system, its way of being and appearing, its physiognomy, its soul or spirit".[4] Western States are often considered to share a set of values, which address the public institutions as well as individuals in the national societies.[5] Courts might look to the elaboration of a certain general principle of law by foreign courts in order to improve the quality of their own judgments or to determine their position with regard to trends concerning the development of the law in the Western legal context.[6]

However, the judicial reference to general principles of law elaborated in other legal systems seems to be subject to legal and contextual possibilities and constraints. Questions which arise in this regard concern the authority of foreign legal sources in the decision-making in domestic cases as well as the usefulness of references to specific sources. Concerning authority, the judicial use of non-binding foreign law in deliberations and the reasoning of judgments might lead to criticism in light of the democratic justification of judgments. After all, these foreign sources have not been accepted as sources of national law through a procedure involving the national government and parliament. Concerning usefulness, factors such as legal culture (common law or civil law), the characteristics of national

---

[1]From a legal perspective, "globalisation" can be defined as the trend toward world domination of specific regimes; see Glenn (2007), p. 49. The emergence of transnational connections between courts has been referred to under many different names. In Muller and Richards (2010), the term "judicial internationalisation" is used to capture the increased exchange of legal ideas and experiences between judges in different legal systems, a trend also referred to as "'transjudicialism', judicial dialogue, judicial cosmopolitanism, judicial globalisation, the migration of legal ideas, legal transplants"; see the Introduction by the editors, at 4.

[2]In this chapter, "foreign law" is used as a general term to refer to legal sources which originated outside of a specific national legal system. In this sense, this qualification also applies to sources which have acquired the status of national law but originate at the international or supranational level, such as implemented treaty provisions.

[3]See Mak (2013).

[4]Alpa (1994), p. 2. See further below, Sect. 2.

[5]Ibid., p. 5.

[6]Hol (2012), p. 2.

laws in specific areas, and the effectiveness and efficiency of judicial decision-making might limit the possibility for judges to find helpful guidance regarding the elaboration of general principles of law.

In light of these concerns, this chapter addresses the following question: to what extent can foreign general principles of law be used as legal sources in the decision-making of Western highest courts? This question is analysed on the basis of a comparative and socio-legal analysis of five legal systems: Canada, the United States, the United Kingdom, France and the Netherlands. The chapter analyses the reference to foreign general principles of law in the judgments of the highest courts in these selected common law and civil law systems, drawing additional information from constitutional theory and from interviews conducted with judges in the selected highest courts.[7] Through this comparative and empirical approach, the chapter aims to clarify the added value of the judicial reference to foreign general principles of law in the decision-making of highest national courts, taking into account legal and contextual possibilities and constraints.

Section 2, firstly, examines selected examples from case law, which are indicative of the developed practices of highest courts concerning the reference to general principles of law elaborated at the international or supranational level or in other national jurisdictions. Next, Sect. 3 analyses the constitutional-theoretical aspects of these practices, focusing on the possibilities and constraints regarding the judicial reference to foreign general principles of law. Concluding remarks are presented in Sect. 4.

2 Judicial References to Foreign General Principles of Law: Selected Examples from Case Law

Shared values in the Western legal context regarding the public sphere include: reciprocal respect, expressed in the values of democratic government and the protection of individual rights and freedoms; the value of security; and the limitation of the exercise of public power by the "rule of law", guaranteed by the possibility of review by an independent judiciary. Values regarding the private sphere include: the responsibility for contractual fulfillment, taking into account the principles of contractual autonomy, equivalence and good faith; and the civil responsibility for wrongful acts.[8] General principles of law, related to these values, have been developed in different legal systems and are sometimes used as a non-binding source of reference by courts in other jurisdictions.

Examples from case law, of which the background was explained in the interviews with judges, clarify that the judicial reference to foreign general principles of

---

[7]For more information and an explanation of the comparative and empirical research methodology, see Mak (2013), Chap. 3.

[8]Alpa (1994), pp. 5–6, citing Stein and Shand (1984); and the work of Karl Larenz.

law can concern both values connected to the public sphere and to the private sphere. References to such principles have occurred in particular in cases concerning the protection of human rights and in cases in the field of contract law. This section presents pertinent examples from the five selected legal systems mentioned above, highlighting the developed judicial practices and the motives of the highest courts regarding the use of foreign general principles of law in judicial deliberations and judgments.

2.1 UK Supreme Court

British judges who were interviewed considered that citations of foreign law, including general principles of law, mostly occur in human rights cases and in private law cases. The use of foreign law is less frequent in criminal cases. In human rights cases, the British judges hope to find guidance in case law concerning the interpretation of the Convention for the Protection of Human Rights and Fundamental Freedoms (ECHR) or concerning comparable instruments for human rights protection. In contract and tort cases, the judges consider that the shared background with other common law legal systems makes legal comparison often useful.

Concerning principles related to the protection of human rights, a British judge remembered having looked at French case law in a case which concerned the balancing of the anonymity of parties and the interest of media coverage in the light of the right to a fair trial and the principle of open justice. Another judge, speaking about the same legal question, mentioned having searched German law and having made inquiries with personal contacts in Germany in order to find useful information, which then might give rise to a question to counsel to base arguments on this information. In the decision given on 27 January 2010, Lord Rodger, who delivered the unanimous judgment, remarked that:

> Unfortunately, no real additional help with the question of anonymity orders can be obtained from examining the practices of courts in Europe when issuing judgments. In all the principal systems, at least, steps can apparently now be taken, where appropriate, to anonymise reports of matrimonial disputes and disputes relating to children. Apart from that, however, what is striking is the variety of approaches.[9]

This observation was followed by an overview of French, Italian and German case law.[10] The responses of the interviewed judges and the reasoning in the judgment suggest that the comparative analysis in this case was carried out with the aim to get a clearer insight into the state of the domestic law. The observed variety of approaches can be considered a justifying argument for the decision taken, which stays very close to the facts of this specific case. Furthermore, the foreign case law

---

[9]*Guardian News and Media Ltd and others, Re HM Treasury v. Ahmed and others,* 1 UKSC 2 WLR 325 (2010), para. 53.

[10]Ibid., paras. 54–57. The judgment also contains a careful analysis of relevant ECtHR case law concerning Articles 8 and 10 of the ECHR; see ibid., paras. 22–52.

gives an indication of factors to be taken into account when balancing the right of privacy against the rights of the press. In this way, the knowledge of the practices in other legal systems seems to have helped the judges to mark out the relevant questions during the process of discovery.

Concerning the reference to foreign principles in private law cases, judges sometimes take account of "soft law" instruments which are considered to have a certain prestige. References to the Principles of European Contract Law (PECL), developed by the Lando Commission,[11] can be found in a small number of judgments of the Law Lords and the UK Supreme Court. A search of BAILII yielded five judgments given between 2001 and 2009.[12] However, these references appear to have no impact on the interpretation of domestic law. They are used as guidance for the interpretation of European law, such as the directive on unfair terms in consumer contracts,[13] or to highlight the differences between the UK and the continental legal traditions. This latter argument transpires, for example, from the opinion of Lord Hoffmann in *Chartbrook Ltd v. Persimmon Homes Ltd*, in which the judge observed that the PECL and related instruments "reflect the French philosophy of contractual interpretation, which is altogether different from that of English law".[14] An interviewed judge further considered that taking into account the PECL or the Draft Common Frame of Reference (DCFR) developed at the initiative of the European Commission would not make sense, because this source is too vague and academic in comparison with the domestic law. This judge considered that the DCFR might develop into an optional system in Europe "as an ever closer union".[15] However, it is this judge's belief that practical hindrances to commerce will remain as a result of efficiency considerations and costliness. The judge therefore considered that the DCFR can be no more than an inspiration for the UK Supreme Court.

2.2 Supreme Court of Canada

An example from the Supreme Court of Canada's case law concerns the interpretation of domestic legal norms in light of international law, in this case customary international law. In *Suresh v. Canada (Minister of Citizenship and Immigration)*,[16] the Canadian authorities wanted to extradite a Sri Lankan immigrant who allegedly

---

[11]The Commission on European contract law, chaired by the Professor Ole Lando, was established in 1982 to explore the possibilities of developing a European code of contract law. The Commission published the PECL in three parts. See Lando et al. (2000–2003).

[12]See http://www.bailii.org (search term "Principles of European contract law").

[13]Directive 93/13/EEC of 5 April 1993, *OJ* L 095, 21 April 1993, which was interpreted in *Director General of Fair Trading v. First National Bank*, 52 UKHL 2 All ER (Comm.) 1000 (2001), paras. 36–37 and 45.

[14]*Chartbrook Ltd v. Persimmon Homes Ltd and others*, 38 UKHL 4 All ER 677 (2009), para. 39.

[15]Preambles to the European Community Treaty and the Treaty on European Union.

[16]*Suresh v. Canada (Minister of Citizenship and Immigration)*, 1 SCR 3 (2002). See also LeBel and Gonsalves (2006), pp. 13–14.

posed a security risk. However, when sent back to Sri Lanka, this person would run the risk of being tortured. The Supreme Court considered the following with regard to the role of the international perspective:

> We have examined the argument that from the perspective of Canadian law to deport a Convention refugee to torture violates the principles of fundamental justice. However, that does not end the inquiry. The provisions of the Immigration Act dealing with deportation must be considered in their international context: *Pushpanathan*, cit.. Similarly, the principles of fundamental justice expressed in s 7 of the Charter and the limits on rights that may be justified under s 1 of the Charter cannot be considered in isolation from the international norms which they reflect. A complete understanding of the Act and the Charter requires consideration of the international perspective. International treaty norms are not, strictly speaking, binding in Canada unless they have been incorporated into Canadian law by enactment. However, in seeking the meaning of the Canadian Constitution, the courts may be informed by international law. Our concern is not with Canada's international obligations qua obligations; rather, our concern is with the principles of fundamental justice. We look to international law as evidence of these principles and not as controlling in itself.[17]

The Supreme Court of Canada then investigated whether the prohibition of torture is a peremptory norm or *ius cogens*, an argument which was advanced by the intervener, Amnesty International. On this point, the Court made the following observation:

> Although this Court is not being asked to pronounce on the status of the prohibition on torture in international law, the fact that such a principle is included in numerous multilateral instruments, that it does not form part of any known domestic administrative practice, and that it is considered by many academics to be an emerging, if not established peremptory norm, suggests that it cannot be easily derogated from.[18]

The Court continued with the interpretation of the conflicting international legal instruments which were at issue in this case, namely, the International Covenant on Civil and Political Rights (ICCPR), the United Nations Convention Against Torture (CAT) and the Refugee Convention. Furthermore, the Court took into account the position taken by the United Nations Committee Against Torture, and relevant judgments of the Supreme Court of Israel (sitting as the High Court of Justice) and the House of Lords rejecting the use of torture as a legitimate tool in the fight against terrorism. The Supreme Court concluded:

> That the better view is that international law rejects deportation to torture, even where national security interests are at stake. This is the norm which best informs the content of the principles of fundamental justice under s 7 of the Charter.[19]

In applying this view to the Immigration Act, the Supreme Court cited the opinions of Lord Hoffmann and Lord Slynn in the British *Rehman* case, which concerned a similar legal question.[20] Balancing all arguments thus collected, the

---

[17]1 SCR 3 (2002), paras. 59–60.

[18]Ibid., para. 65.

[19]Ibid., para. 75.

[20]Ibid., paras. 76–77 and 87. See *Secretary of State for the Home Department v. Rehman*, 47 UKHL 3 WLR 877 (2001).

Supreme Court of Canada pronounced as its judgment that torture constitutes a violation of the Charter, but that an exceptional case might occur in which extradition of an individual to a Country where this person faces the risk of torture could be allowed under section 53(1)(b) of the Immigration Act.[21]

It seems that international and comparative law were used in this case in order to clarify the possible meanings of the domestic law. The study of the relevant international legal norms also enabled the Court to ensure the consistency of Canadian practice with international law, and in this way to confirm the respect of the Canadian authorities for international law.[22] The acknowledgment of the possible occurrence of exceptional cases in the future fits the common law tradition of leaving space for the further development of the law.

The motives of the highest courts when selecting specific foreign legal sources often seem to come down to the emphasising of unity of values with other liberal-democratic regimes, such as the ECHR. However, comparative law is sometimes used in another way as well. An example is the Supreme Court of Canada's judgment in the case of *United States v. Burns*. In this case, the Supreme Court decided that it was unconstitutional under the Charter to extradite two Canadian citizens, suspected of criminal acts, to the United States if no assurances were given that the death sentence would not be imposed or carried out.[23] This decision overturned earlier judgments of the Court, in which the extradition of US residents was not prevented.[24] The Court's reasoning contained a reference to international experience and a comparison with other Countries and with the US legal system:

> International experience … confirms the validity of concerns expressed in the Canadian Parliament about capital punishment. It also shows that a rule requiring that assurances be obtained prior to extradition in death penalty cases not only accords with Canada's principled advocacy on the international level, but is also consistent with the practice of other Countries with whom Canada generally invites comparison, apart from the retentionist jurisdictions in the United States.[25]

By emphasising the exceptional position of the US with regard to the death penalty, the Supreme Court of Canada justified its refusal to allow the extradition to the United States. The Court backed up its judgment further by citing supporting case law of the European Court of Human Rights (ECtHR; *Soering v. United Kingdom*), the South African Constitutional Court (*S. v. Makwanyane*), and the English Court of Appeal.[26] In this way, the Supreme Court of Canada used the argument of almost universal consensus to enhance the legitimacy of a judgment

---

[21] Ibid., para. 131.

[22] See in this respect also *Mugesera v. Canada (Minister of Citizenship and Integration)*, 2 SCR 100 (2005), discussed by LeBel and Gonsalves (2006), pp. 12–13.

[23] *United States v. Burns*, 1 SCR 283 (2001), paras. 143–44.

[24] *Kindler v. Canada (Minister of Justice)*, 2 SCR 779 (1991); *Reference re Ng Extradition (Canada)*, 2 SCR 858 (1991).

[25] 1 SCR 283 (2001), paras. 127–128.

[26] Ibid., paras. 53, 67, 112–16, 119 and 137.

which departed from the Court's previous case law and to set itself apart from the other legal system (that of the United States) involved in this case.

Interestingly, foreign factual experience concerning potential wrongful convictions was invoked in the *Burns* judgment as one of the arguments justifying the Court's reversal of its *Kindler* and *Ng* jurisprudence. The assessment of facts in light of the principles of fundamental justice, underlying the Canadian legal system, led to a different balancing of outcomes:

> The outcome of this appeal turns on an appreciation of the principles of fundamental justice, which in turn are derived from the basic tenets of our legal system. These basic tenets have not changed since 1991 when *Kindler* and *Ng* were decided, but their application in particular cases (the "balancing process") must take note of factual developments in Canada and in relevant foreign jurisdictions. When principles of fundamental justice as established and understood in Canada are applied to these factual developments, many of which are of far-reaching importance in death penalty cases, a balance which tilted in favour of extradition without assurances in *Kindler* and *Ng* now tilts against the constitutionality of such an outcome. For these reasons, the appeal is dismissed.[27]

2.3 US Supreme Court

An example from the United States concerned the interpretation of domestic law implementing international treaty norms. This topic was addressed by the Supreme Court in a case concerning the envisaged extradition of a person to Ethiopia. It had to be decided whether this alien, who had assisted or participated in persecution under duress, could be eligible for asylum in the United States.[28] The petitioner referred among other things to "concepts of international law" to argue that the notion of "persecution" used in the Immigration and Nationality Act included the requirement of "moral blameworthiness".[29] In the discussion of the arguments put forward by both sides, Justice Kennedy, writing for the majority in the US Supreme Court, considered:

> The persecutor bar in this case... was enacted as part of the Refugee Act of 1980. Unlike the [Displaced Persons Act of 1948], which was enacted to address not just the post war refugee problem but also the Holocaust and its horror, the Refugee Act was designed to provide a general rule for the ongoing treatment of all refugees and displaced persons. As this Court has twice recognized, "'one of Congress' primary purposes' in passing the Refugee Act was to implement the principles agreed to in the 1967 United Nations Protocol Relating to the Status of Refugees, Jan 31, 1967, 19 UST 6224, TIA S 6577 (1968)", as well as the "United Nations Convention Relating to the Status of Refugees, 189 UNTS 150 (July 28, 1951), reprinted in 19 UST 6259" (Aguirre-Aguirre, 526 US, at 427, quoting Cardoza-Fonseca, 480 US, at 436–437).[30]

---

[27]Ibid., para. 144.

[28]*Negusie v. Holder,* 555 US 511 (2009).

[29]Ibid., para. II-B.

[30]Ibid.

This consideration reflects an effort to interpret the domestic law in conformity with international legal norms. The Supreme Court considered that the Board of Immigration Appeals had misapplied an earlier precedent of the Court and because of this mistaken application had not taken into account the alien's motivation and intent when determining whether the alien had assisted in persecution.[31] The case was remanded for further proceedings.

As another example, an interviewed judge mentioned that foreign references played a role in cases judged by the Supreme Court in the 1970s concerning women's rights. This judge mentioned the case of *Reed v. Reed*, which concerned the contestation by the mother of a deceased child of a statute preferring males over females in the administration of an estate.[32] Counsel in this case cited case law of the German *Bundesverfassungsgericht* to support its argument that the Equal Protection Clause of the Fourteenth Amendment to the United States Constitution had been violated. The Supreme Court ruled in favour of the petitioner, in this way acknowledging the constitutional basis for the protection of individuals against discrimination based on gender.

International opinion and the practices of other States, in particular the United Kingdom, were also taken into account by the US Supreme Court in the case of *Roper v. Simmons* to support the judgment of unconstitutionality of the juvenile death penalty.[33] In the majority judgment delivered by Justice Kennedy, the Supreme Court found support for its judgment in "the overwhelming weight of international opinion against the juvenile death penalty", which "while not controlling [the Court's] outcome, does provide respected and significant confirmation for [the Court's] conclusions".[34] In a dissenting opinion, Justice Scalia criticised the majority's argument, stating that:

> The Court thus proclaims itself sole arbiter of our Nation's moral standards–and in the course of discharging that awesome responsibility purports to take guidance from the views of foreign courts and legislatures.[35]

The disagreement in the *Roper* case is illustrative of the controversy which has developed in legal and academic debate in the United States in the last decades regarding the reference to non-binding foreign law. Justice Scalia is an important contributor to this debate. He has argued that international law which has not been integrated into the national legal system should not be used as an interpretive tool, since this practice would mean bypassing the normal process of integration of international law in the domestic legal system. Justice Scalia has further argued that there is no useful purpose to the use of comparative law or international opinion in the process of interpreting one's national law.[36]

---

[31]Ibid.

[32]*Reed v Reed*, 404 US 71 (1971).

[33]*Roper v Simmons*, 543 US 551 (2005).

[34]Ibid., opinion of the Court, para. 24.

[35]Ibid., dissenting opinion of Justice Scalia, para. 2.

[36]Scalia (1997).

2.4 French Highest Courts

In France, the *Cour de cassation* is the supreme judge in civil and criminal cases and the *Conseil d'État* is the supreme administrative judge. The *Conseil constitutionnel*, since the introduction of a posteriori review of legislation in 2009, has acquired the status of a true constitutional judge, able to protect the rights of citizens in concrete cases.

Concerning the reference to general principles of law, in particular in human rights cases, an analysis of the practice of the *Conseil constitutionnel* reveals an interesting development. In its case law, the *Conseil constitutionnel* has established that its competence is limited to the review of parliamentary acts in the light of the Constitution. The conformity of these acts to international treaty law formally is not tested.[37] However, an interviewed judge indicated that, notwithstanding this case law, the members of the Council have developed the practice to check their interpretation of fundamental constitutional rights in light of the interpretation given by the ECtHR to human rights protected by the ECHR. The reasons for the change of practice of the *Conseil constitutionnel* are of a mixed legal and political nature. In order to prevent cases from going up to Strasbourg, the members of the *Conseil constitutionnel* consider it desirable that legislation is checked for its conformity to the European Convention. Moreover, this review benefits the guarantee of the unity of the law and legal certainty in the French legal system, in which the other highest courts and the trial courts, in relevant cases, consider the conformity of legal provisions to the ECHR.[38]

According to the interviewed French judge, in principle there is no reason to give a different interpretation from the ECtHR as concerns the meaning of fundamental rights. Therefore, if the national judge wants to adopt a different solution, he should justify this. Such a justification might be found in the specificity of the national legal system, for example, as concerns the right to religious freedom and the French principle of "*laïcité*" (secularism). In this light, mention can be made of the high-profile case concerning the constitutionality of a legislative act prohibiting the concealment of one's face in public. This law was aimed in particular at the prohibition of the burqa, a garment worn by certain Muslim women. The awareness of the members of the *Conseil constitutionnel* of the ECtHR's case law can be deduced from the presentation of relevant materials in the "*dossier documentaire*" which is prepared by the Council's documentation service. In the aforementioned case, this file contained extracts from four judgments of the European Court.[39] The idea of coherence of transnational judicial interpretations thus has induced an "enrichment" of the deliberations of the constitutional judge. However,

---

[37] *Conseil constitutionnel*, decision no. 74-54 (*Loi relative à l'interruption volontaire de la grossesse*), 15 January 1975, *Recueil* 19.

[38] Steinmetz (2009). See also Dutheillet de Lamothe (2005), p. 550.

[39] *Conseil constitutionnel*, decision no. 2010-613 (*Loi interdisant la dissimulation du visage dans l'espace public*), 7 October 2010, available at: http://www.conseil-constitutionnel.fr/conseil-constitutionnel/root/bank/download/2010-613DC-doc.pdf.

this awareness is not shown in the reasoning of the Council's decisions, which will only contain the result of the conformed interpretation. In case of the predominance of a specific French constitutional principle, such as the principle of "*laïcité*", the Council only presents an argument based on this principle. Indeed, the aforementioned decision did not explicitly address the interpretation given by the ECtHR regarding the right of religious freedom.

Besides reference to the ECHR, comparisons with the law of other national legal systems are regularly used in the deliberations of the *Conseil constitutionnel* as well. However, following the French tradition of judicial reasoning, no citations of foreign law and foreign judgments feature in the decisions of the Council. In a published conference contribution, the then-member of the *Conseil constitutionnel* Olivier Dutheillet de Lamothe gave three examples of cases in which foreign legal sources had informed the Council's decision-making. In a case concerning the constitutionality of legislation on abortion the Council considered case law from the United States, Germany, Italy and the ECtHR.[40] Case law of the German *Bundesverfassungsgericht* was also taken into account in a case concerning the independence of university professors.[41] Finally, judgments of the European Court of Justice (ECJ) and the German, Spanish, Italian and US highest courts were examined in a case addressing the interpretation of the principle of equality.[42] An interviewed member of the Council observed that a useful comparative analysis is possible only when the legal systems which are compared share the same principles, and when they are at the same stage of legal development.[43] The French judge considered that a basis for comparison exists, particularly in cases involving human rights, because of the supposed universal element in these rights.

In the decision-making of the *Cour de cassation* and the *Conseil d'État* , too, the use of comparative law is related to the subject matter of cases. A judge pointed out that the Third Civil Law Chamber of the *Cour de cassation*, for example, deals with environmental law and other issues which do not specifically have a relation with comparative law. The judge considered that comparative legal analysis is reserved for important cases where it is useful to look at foreign law for the decision of the case. An example concerns the deciding of cases about the "*grands sujets*" (big topics) of the French society, such as same-sex marriage, the adoption of a child by same-sex partners, or the compensation of asbestos victims. As an example, in 2006 the *Cour de cassation* commissioned comparative research regarding the scope of *res judicata*. UK, German, Italian and Spanish legal sources

---

[40]*Conseil constitutionnel*, decision no. 2001-446, 27 June 2001, *Recueil* 74; Dutheillet de Lamothe (2005), p. 553.

[41]*Conseil constitutionnel*, decision no. 83-165, 20 January 1984, *Recueil* 30; Dutheillet de Lamothe (2005), p. 554.

[42]*Conseil constitutionnel*, decision no. 2003-489, 29 December 2003, *Recueil* 480; Dutheillet de Lamothe (2005), p. 554.

[43]See in this regard also Barak (2006), pp. 197–204.

were consulted to inform the Court's decision.[44] The *Cour de cassation* overturned a decision of 1994, in this way aligning itself with the UK and Spanish case law but diverging from the German and Italian case law.[45]

Comparative law sometimes plays a role in the decision-making in administrative cases as well. An honorary member of the *Conseil d'État* has observed that comparative law is used by the highest administrative court in four main areas, namely, liability, aliens' law, civil liberties and the relationship between domestic and international law.[46] Examples include the discussion by the *commissaire du gouvernement* of UK and US case law with regard to a wrongful life claim, and of English, US and Canadian case law with regard to the claim for compensation of moral loss on the grounds of the disrespect of a patient's expressed will not to receive a blood transfusion.[47] Explicit references to judgments of foreign courts in principle do not occur in the decisions of the *Cour de cassation* and the *Conseil d'État* , as this would not fit the style of reasoning of French courts.

2.5 Dutch Highest Courts

The Dutch judicial system was modeled on the French system, which was introduced during the Napoleonic occupation between 1795 and 1813. The system features the *Hoge Raad der Nederlanden* (Supreme Court of the Netherlands) as the final judge in civil, criminal and tax law cases and the *Afdeling bestuursrechtspraak van de Raad van State* (Administrative Jurisdiction Division of the Council of State) as the supreme administrative court with general jurisdiction. Because of the absence of citations of non-binding foreign law in published judgments, it is difficult to assess the impact of comparative law on the decisions taken by the Dutch highest courts. However, the interviews yielded more insight into the developed practices of the examined courts.

Judges confirmed that, as in the United Kingdom and in France, the judicial engagement with international legal sources concerns mostly EU law and the European Convention. The case law of the ECtHR and ECJ is usually followed by the Dutch highest courts. As an example, several judges of the *Hoge Raad* mentioned the implementation of the Strasbourg Court's *Salduz* judgment in the Dutch law.[48] This judgment, given by the ECtHR in a case against Turkey, concerned the

---

[44]Institut de Droit Comparé Edouard Lambert, *L'étendue de l'autorité de la chose jugée en droit comparé*, available at: http://www.courdecassation.fr/IMG/File/Plen-06-07-07-0410672-rapport-definitif-anonymise-annexe-2.pdf; cited by Ferrand (2012), who was one of the researchers who conducted this comparative study.

[45]Ferrand (2012), p. 355.

[46]Errera (2004), p. 156.

[47]Ibid., pp. 157–158.

[48]*Salduz plea,* HR 30 June 2009, NJ 2009, paras. 349, 350 and 351.

right of a defendant to have access to a lawyer when subjected to police interroga-
tions.[49] References to the case law of the ECtHR occur regularly in the judgments
of the *Raad van State* as well. An example is the *Jezus redt* case, which concerned
the appeal against an injunction to remove white tiles from a house, which
together formed the words "Jesus saves".[50] The appellant argued that the injunction constituted a violation of Articles 9 and 10 of the ECHR, concerning the right
to freedom of religion and the right to freedom of expression, and Articles 6 and 7
of the Dutch Constitution, concerning the same rights. In its decision on the justified limitations to the right protected by Article 9 of the ECHR, the *Raad van State*
cited the ECtHR's judgment in *Vergos v. Greece*.[51] The administrative judge used
this judgment, as well as its own case law, to support its decision that a limitation
of the protected right was justified in the case at hand when balanced against the
interests of protecting the public order and the rights and freedoms of others.[52]

Interestingly, references to specific foreign principles have occurred regularly
with regard to the defendant's rights in criminal cases. These references seem to
have for an aim to better identify the current state of the domestic law. Examples
which were mentioned concern the comparison with German law regarding the
absoluteness of the attorney-client privilege in criminal cases;[53] the explanation on
rights of appeal ("*Rechtsmittelbelehrung*"); and the interpretation of the concept of
self-defence ("*noodweer*").[54] In a case concerning the insulting of a group
("*groepsbelediging*"), *extra* literature and case law was added to the judges' file by
the reporting judge, and on the suggestion of another judge a judgment of the
British Law Lords was used in the deliberations in chambers. Concerning the right
to a fair trial, US law is considered instructive in addition to the ECHR.

In the field of private law, the Civil Law Chamber of the *Hoge Raad* sometimes
uses the PECL as a source of reference, in a similar manner as the UK Supreme
Court.[55] A search of the published judgments of the *Hoge Raad* yielded 23 judgments of the Civil Law Chamber, given between 2002 and 2012, in which reference was made to the PECL or commentaries of these Principles. All references
are to be found in the opinions of the Advocates-General.[56] The interviewed

---

[49]*Salduz v. Turkey* (App. no. 36391/02), ECtHR, judgment of 27 November 2008. The European
Court clarified this judgment in *Panovits v. Cyprus* (App. no. 4268/04), ECtHR, judgment of 11
December 2008.

[50]*Afdeling bestuursrechtspraak van de Raad van State, Jezus redt,* LJN BN1135, 14 July 2010.

[51]*Vergos v. Greece* (App. no. 65501/01), ECtHR, judgment of 24 September 2004.

[52]*Afdeling bestuursrechtspraak van de Raad van State,* LJN BN1135, 14 July 2010, para. 2.12.4.

[53]See, e.g., *Hoge Raad,* LJN BN0526, 12 October 2010 (opinion of Advocate-General Jörg),
para. 90, citing German, French, Swiss and US legal sources which define the scope of the right
of non-disclosure.

[54]See, e.g., *Hoge Raad,* LJN BO4475, 4 January 2011 (opinion of Advocate-General Silvis),
para. 10, citing German doctrine and the case law of the *Bundesgerichtshof* as sources which
confirm the case law of the *Hoge Raad.*

[55]See above, Sect. 2.1.

[56]See http://www.rechtspraak.nl (search term "Principles of European contract law").

judges and Advocates-General asserted that the PECL are used for guidance only. An Advocate-General mentioned the example of assessing the termination of a breach of contract, taking account of fundamental interests of the parties. The analysed case law of the *Hoge Raad* corroborates this view. In a case concerning the interpretation of the termination clause included in a contract of employment, Advocate-General Huydecoper observed that two kinds of interpretation identified in the Dutch academic literature in some foreign legal doctrines are considered to be identical.[57] In a footnote to this observation, he remarked that:

> Notwithstanding many differences, the sources of law for our neighbouring Countries indicate a remarkable unanimity as regards the idea a) that contracts are to be interpreted in the first place on the basis of the intentions of the parties, which unless proved otherwise have to be interpreted in light of the standard of the "reasonable man"; and b) that an addition to what was agreed upon in the absence of proved or reasonably assumed intentions of the parties has to take place with reference to what reasonably judging parties in the given case would have assumed.[58]

The influence of these observations on the deliberations and the decision of the *Hoge Raad* is not evident from the judgment, since the judgment was given with the shortened reasoning allowed by section 81 of the Judicial Organisation Act.[59]

This overview of the role of general principles of law in the case law of the selected national courts can be better understood on the basis of a theoretical analysis regarding the development of judicial decision-making in the globalised legal context. The next section will outline the factors which influence the use of transnational sources, including general principles of law, by the highest courts in specific legal systems.

3 Legal and Contextual Parameters of the Judicial Reference to Foreign General Principles of Law

The increasingly important role of foreign law in national legal systems seems to have brought about a fundamental normative change, which concerns the judicial interest to engage in processes of transnational legal exchange or even convergence.[60] The defining parameters regarding the practices of highest national courts are of a twofold nature. Firstly, these factors concern the authority of legal norms

---

[57]*Hoge Raad*, LJN BJ8724, 13 November 2009 (opinion of Advocate-General Huydecoper), para. 20.

[58]Ibid., note 18 (my translation).

[59]Based on this provision, the *Hoge Raad* has the possibility to dismiss appeals with a shortened reasoning if it considers that there are no grounds for cassation and the case does not raise any legal questions which should be answered in the interest of legal uniformity or the development of the law.

[60]See Jackson (2009).

in the globalised context. Secondly, contextual factors relate to the individual approaches of judges and concerns regarding the effectiveness and efficiency of judicial decision-making.

3.1 The Authority of Legal Norms in the Globalised Context

The authority of general principles of law in transnational judicial decision-making is connected with several aspects. These include: (i) the increased emphasis on persuasiveness as a basis for authority of legal sources; (ii) the influence of legal tradition on the authority of legal sources; and (iii) the particularities of national legal systems in which general principles of law have been elaborated. These aspects will be analysed next.

3.1.1 Authority versus Persuasiveness

Concerning the characteristics of a legal system, the research clarifies that the existence of a monist or a dualist mechanism for the implementation of international law influences the use of international and comparative law to a lesser extent than might have been expected on the basis of the traditional distinction between binding and non-binding sources of law in national legal systems. Indeed, the question of the authority of sources for judicial decision-making is more complicated than the positivist distinction between sources which *have* and sources which *have not* been approved as binding sources of domestic law by the competent national authorities.

In the globalised legal context, legal regimes are increasingly intertwined, leading to overlap between the content of legal norms of different origins—international, supranational and national. In this context, many of the interviewed judges consider that the reference to legal sources in judicial decision-making should focus on the substance of these sources and on the persuasive arguments which can be found in these sources for the deciding of the case at hand.[61] In other words, the usefulness of comparative legal research and the engagement in a transnational judicial enterprise of uniform application of shared legal rules are underlined. This approach supports the idea of increasing convergence between legal orders and therewith the idea of shared general principles of law. Furthermore, this approach fits the idea that the authority of legal sources is connected to the development of the use of these sources. In an informal and incremental process, a source will become less or more binding in proportion to the frequency with which use is made of this source in the deciding of cases.[62]

---

[61] See also Breyer, "The Supreme Court and the New International Law" (American Society of International Law, Washington, DC, 4 April 2003).

[62] Adams (2012), p. 534. See also Schauer (2008), p. 1931.

3.1.2 The Influence of Legal Tradition

Concerning legal tradition, it seems that the doctrine of precedent, which is typical for the common law tradition but not for the civil law tradition,[63] has only a limited influence on judicial practices regarding the reference to non-binding foreign case law. Indeed, as demonstrated by the presented examples from the case law of the selected national courts, the authority of legal sources in their decision-making does not depend so much on the formally binding or non-binding nature of these sources.

Yet, a relevant difference between the examined Anglo-Saxon courts and continental-European courts relates to the style of judicial reasoning. The interviewed French and Dutch judges pointed out that the citation of case law as such is rare in the judgments of their highest courts. For reasons of tradition and the requirement of a unanimous decision, judgments in these civil law systems tend to be relatively short. In this light, the citation of foreign law would be exceptional. Indeed, some interviewed judges felt that the reasoning of a judgment might be weakened because of possible criticism of the highest court's use of foreign law, for example, with regard to the scope and relevance of the legal comparison with other jurisdictions. The citation of foreign legal materials is more easily accepted in the Anglo-Saxon courts, which stand in the tradition of law development through case law and which permit individual judges to issue their own opinion on cases. A question of concern amongst judges in these courts is the question of whether a presentation of foreign law in the court's reasoning should consist of a "full" discussion of all materials found or whether the court is allowed to mention only those foreign references which support its own decision. British judges have indicated that they do not find the latter approach problematic, while some American judges have criticised the use of foreign law if it consists of "cherry picking".[64] Still, these judges seem to agree on the point that the discussion of foreign law in the judicial deliberations should be as comprehensive as possible.

Finally, legal tradition plays a role in the selection of non-binding foreign legal materials for comparison by a specific highest national court. The genealogical relation between the legal systems of the United Kingdom, Canada and the United States makes it more natural for the highest courts in these systems to look to each other for inspiration than to legal systems which do not share this British origin. The exchange between courts in these jurisdictions, furthermore, is made easier by their shared language. The French and Dutch highest courts, by contrast, most often study foreign sources which originated in other civil law jurisdictions. The Dutch courts consider that the French and German influences in the Dutch legal system provide reasons for looking to these systems first when engaging in a comparative legal study. Besides language, all interviewed judges also take into account the prestige of specific foreign courts when selecting case law for a legal comparison.

---

[63]Schauer (2012). See also Mattei (1988), MacCormick and Summers (1997).

[64]See, e.g., "Judge John Roberts Confirmation Hearings", available at: http://theusconstitution.org.

3.1.3 Particularities of National Legal Systems

The relevance of foreign general principles of law in the decision-making of highest courts might be influenced by the particularities of national legal systems and of the values which underlie these systems.

In the interviews, the judges confirmed that they do not look at foreign sources for solutions, but for ideas. They considered that the transplanting of solutions from one legal system into another one is often not possible because of differences between the designs of the national legal systems. A judge illustrated this with regard to the topic of access to legal advice. In the United States, the test for granting legal advice only comes up when a person is detained. Before detention, there is no right to counsel. In Canada, however, this difference does not exist. Therefore, one should be careful to transplant the US test as such into Canadian law. After all, a consequence might be, for example, that the right to counsel should be granted to any Canadian who is stopped by the police for speeding.[65]

A further reservation, which is also pertinent with regard to the reference to foreign general principles of law, relates to the differences between moral and social values of national societies. An interviewed Canadian judge expressed hesitation concerning the use of foreign legal sources in cases which touch upon moral values. In this respect, the judge agreed with US Supreme Court Justice Scalia's argument that different societies hold different moral values. The judge expressed the opinion that the Supreme Court of Canada should be reluctant to cite other Countries, for example in abortion cases, as comparative sources would have less persuasive weight in this context. As an example, the *Morgentaler* case was mentioned, which concerned the constitutionality of provincial legislation concerning the prohibition of the performance of abortions outside hospitals.[66] The judge observed that the use of comparative law is more appropriate in cases where social values rather than moral values are at stake. For example, in cases concerning the freedom of expression it can be useful to learn about the way in which social values on this issue were assessed by the courts in other jurisdictions.

Besides the discussed legal aspects, the judicial practices regarding the reference to foreign legal sources, including foreign general principles of law, are influenced by contextual factors.

3.2 The Influence of Contextual Factors

The "openness" of courts to the use of arguments from foreign law seems to be informed by the views of individual judges concerning the scope of judicial

---

[65]See also LeBel and Gonsalves (2006), p. 20.

[66]*R v. Morgentaler,* 3 SCR 463 (1993).

discretion in the decision-making in difficult cases[67] and concerning the usefulness of referring to non-binding foreign law in terms of effectiveness and efficiency of judicial decision-making.[68] These two factors will be analysed next.

3.2.1 "Globalist" and "Localist" Judicial Approaches

Individual judicial approaches to judging are shaped on the basis of the legal education and professional and personal experiences of judges. These approaches are closely connected with national legal culture. In the Canadian legal system, which contains English as well as French influences, an open approach to foreign law is natural. The same is true for the Dutch legal system, which has been influenced by French and German law. Moreover, the legal culture of a Country with a smaller population, such as Canada and the Netherlands, appears to contain more openness to foreign law than the legal culture of Countries with a bigger population, such as the United Kingdom, the United States and France. Indeed, judges in the big legal systems traditionally consider that they have a role in informing legal development in other legal systems rather than an interest in taking inspiration from these foreign legal systems. Still, the judicial approaches can vary between judges of the same highest court. Differences between judges in the same Country relate to: (i) professional experiences with foreign cultures and foreign languages, for example, through studying or working abroad; and (ii) personal experiences with foreign cultures and foreign languages, for example, through family relations.

Vicki Jackson's classification of judicial postures of resistance, convergence and engagement provides a framework for assessing the motives which underlie a judge's choice for either an open or a more reserved view regarding the use of comparative law in judicial decision-making.[69] The research presented above reveals that only a few judges in the examined highest courts are absolutely against the study of non-binding foreign law. Indeed, the arguments of judges with a reserved or "localist" view differ. Judges who take an absolutely *resistant* posture oppose the use of non-binding foreign legal sources on the basis of the absence of formal authority of these sources within the jurisdiction of their highest court. US Supreme Court Justice Scalia, who has expressed his views in dissenting opinions, speeches and publications, is perhaps the most well-known proponent of this view. He has argued that the citation of foreign law in judicial reasoning cannot be considered to be merely of a supportive nature besides the reasoning based on the national law. In his view, if the Supreme Court acknowledges foreign support for a specific interpretation of the law, it grants to the foreign law the value of an authoritative source for its decision-making.[70] Other localist judges do not con-

---

[67]Barak (2006), p. 118. See also Dworkin (1998) [1986].

[68]See in this regard Ng (2007), Mak (2007), Piana (2010).

[69]Jackson (2009).

[70]See cit., Sect. 2.3.

test the use of foreign law in judicial deliberations as such. However, they are doubtful about the guidance which might be derived from the study of foreign law. These judges emphasise that judgments handed down in foreign jurisdictions cannot provide specific solutions for domestic cases, because of the differences between legal systems based on the national legal culture.[71] In this respect, the time-consuming nature of comparative legal research might be an additional reason for abstaining from an inquiry into foreign legal sources.

Judges with an open attitude towards the reference to foreign law, who can be called "globalist" judges, appear in two types. Most of the judges included in the current study are not absolutely in favour of striving for *convergence* with the laws of other Countries or with international law. Indeed, and befitting the balanced nature of the judicial function, the majority of the judges have a nuanced approach regarding the use of non-binding foreign law in judicial decision-making. These judges fit the posture of *engagement* with foreign law. Still, the judges expressed different degrees of willingness to engage with global influences. This willingness seems to be related to the perceived usefulness of comparative legal sources in the decision-making in concrete cases. The mentioned limitations of comparative legal research for the judgment of concrete cases echo the criticism expressed by localist judges. However, globalist judges underline the inspiration which foreign concepts and solutions can bring for the decision-making in difficult cases and cases of public importance. The yardstick or example provided by foreign case law can help judges to find a solution or support for their decision. The globalist judges feel that this can strengthen the judicial reasoning and enhance the public trust in the court's judgment. Moreover, these judges are of the opinion that the study of non-binding foreign law can assist them in making sure that their standards for decision-making are of the same quality as those of their foreign peers. Finally, the study of non-binding foreign law for comparative purposes is considered useful for assessing whether a domestic judgment would be following general trends in the development of the law in other Western legal systems.

3.2.2 Effectiveness and Efficiency of Judicial Decision-Making

The interviews revealed that judges take into account the costs, in terms of time spent on the research and study of foreign legal materials, and the benefits of this exercise, in terms of useful concepts and arguments for their decision in a domestic case. The research provides helpful information to add further nuance to this conclusion.

The costs of the comparative exercise, first, vary for judges depending on: (i) the assistance which they can make use of for this research; (ii) their personal affinity with and ability to conduct comparative legal research; and (iii) the accessibility of foreign legal sources, for example, through databases, judicial networks

---

[71]Ibid.

and personal contacts. The availability of judicial assistance differs between the examined highest courts, as do the possibilities of commissioning universities to carry out comparative legal research.[72] An important distinction exists between the proceedings before the Anglo-Saxon courts, in which the legal counsel of a party has an important responsibility in bringing the relevant legal sources to the attention of the court, and the proceedings before the highest courts of France and the Netherlands, in which the judges themselves and Advocates-General or *commissaires du gouvernement* have a role in the research of relevant legal materials for the deciding of the case. The ability of judges to conduct comparative research, and the accessibility of sources, are related to the legal training and experience of the judges as well as to their involvement in transnational judicial exchanges. In sum, both organisational and personal factors in highest courts have an influence on the costs of using comparative law in judicial decision-making.

Concerning the benefits of the study of non-binding foreign law, a clear relation exists with the postures of judges concerning the role of their highest court in the globalised legal context. Globalist judges consider the study of foreign law to be more useful for their court's decision-making than localist judges. For this reason, depending on personal affinity and ability, globalist judges will engage in the study of foreign law more readily than their localist counterparts. Interestingly, the approaches of judges of a similar mind but working in different highest courts might be closer to each other than the approaches of two judges on the same highest court but holding opposite views on the usefulness of the study of foreign law.

In connection with these factors, the methodology regarding the use of foreign law might be criticised as being based on "cherry picking", that is: the approach of arguing that consensus exists by referring only to the foreign judgments which support the desired outcome in the domestic case.[73] Judges who are in favour of using comparative law seem to prefer using a vague standard for assessing the usefulness of reference to foreign legal sources in specific cases. Two interviewed Justices of the US Supreme Court indicated that non-binding foreign law can be taken into account when it seems appropriate to do so. Keeping in mind the current controversy in the United States regarding the use of foreign law, this standard might be too vague to counter the criticism expressed by opponents of the use of comparative law in judicial argumentation, such as Justice Scalia.

Other methodological challenges can be detected as well. The search for consensus with a foreign legal system can be obstructed by differences between the framed legal questions on human rights issues.[74] By contrast, some argumentative aspects make it easier for courts to engage in comparative exercises. For example,

---

[72]See the examples presented cit., Sect. 2.

[73]See cit., Sect. 3.1.

[74]See, e.g., the Canadian Justice Binnie's example of the "sniffer dog" cases, in which the Supreme Court of Canada could not make a valuable comparison with the case law of the US Supreme Court because of the different legal implications connected with the search and seizure issue in the US when compared to Canada; Binnie, "Foreign Sources: Searching for Enlightenment or a Fig Leaf?" (London, July 2010).

a perceived similarity in methods of decision-making with a prestigious foreign court can be a stimulus for judges to engage in comparative legal research. Canadian and US judges observed in this respect that the Supreme Court of Canada and the US Supreme Court balance rights in a similar way as the ECtHR does in its decision-making.

4 Conclusion

The analysis in this chapter reveals that the use of foreign legal sources by the highest courts in selected common law and civil law systems has become a common practice in the daily business of judging cases. The examples given by the interviewed judges provide illustrations of the specific practices of each court, highlighting a relatively high number of cases in which general principles of law played a role.

It appears that the reference to foreign general principles of law occurs mostly in support of the judgment in a domestic case or as a means of emphasising the particularity of the national principle which requires interpretation. The judicial recourse to foreign law often concerns principles related to the public sphere, in particular the protection of human rights. However, references also occur in cases concerning private interaction, such as the principle of "good faith" in the field of contract law. More generally, the views and recounted experiences of the judges reveal awareness of the increasingly global context of the functioning of highest courts, and of the implications of this trend for the decision-making in domestic cases.

The research further clarifies that legal and contextual factors enable as well as constrain the use of foreign general principles of law by highest national courts. The added value of the developed practices of the courts is nuanced by the legal factors of authority of legal sources, legal tradition and the particularities of national legal systems. Moreover, contextual factors related to individual judicial approaches and concerns of effective and efficient judicial decision-making influence the reference that is made to comparative law, including foreign general principles of law.

Keeping in mind these possibilities and constraints, general principles of law originating at the international level or in other legal systems can assist highest national courts in obtaining a better understanding as well as useful guidance concerning the interpretation of the general principles which underlie their national legal system. In this way, the use of foreign general principles of law in transnational judicial communication enables the highest national courts to work together to improve the quality of judicial decision-making in Western courts in a "global race to the top", as one of the interviewed judges put it.

Acknowledgments The research for this chapter was supported by a post-doctoral VENI grant from the Netherlands Organisation for Scientific Research (NWO). A general presentation of this research was published previously in Mak (2013).

References

Adams, Maurice. 2012. Globaliserende rechtspraak: democratisch omstreden?. *Ars Aequi* 61: 531-540.

Alpa, Guido. 1994. General Principles of Law. *Annual Survey of International and Comparative Law* 1: 1-37.

Barak, Aharon. 2006. *The Judge in a Democracy*. Princeton: Princeton University Press.

Dutheillet de Lamothe, Oliver. 2005. Constitutional Court Judges' Roundtable. *International Journal of Constitutional Law* 3: 550-556.

Dworkin, Ronald M. 1998 [1989]. *Law's Empire*. Oxford: Hart Publishing.

Errera, Roger. 2004. The Use of Comparative Law before the French Administrative Law Courts. In *Comparative Law before the Courts*, eds. Guy Canivet, Mads Andenas and Duncan Fairgrieve, 153-164. London: British Institute of International and Comparative Law.

Ferrand, Frédérique. 2012. The French Approach to the Globalisation and Harmonisation of Civil Procedure. In *Civil Litigation in a Globalising World*, eds. Xandra E. Kramer and Remco C. H. van Rhee, 335-362. The Hague: TMC Asser Press.

Glenn, Patrick H. 2007. *Legal Traditions of the World*. Oxford: Oxford University Press.

Hol, Antoine. 2012. Highest Courts and Transnational Interaction: Introductory and Concluding Remarks. *Utrecht Law Review* 8: 1-7.

Jackson, Vicki C. 2009. *Constitutional Engagement in a Transnational Era*. Oxford: Oxford University Press.

Lando, Ole et al (eds). 2000-2003. *Principles of European Contract Law*. The Hague, Boston: Kluwer Law International.

LeBel, Louis, and Andrea Gonsalves. 2006. Comments on the Integration of International Law into the Canadian Legal System (International Law and Litigation for US Judges, Federal Judicial Center, 30 October 2006). http://www.fjc.gov/public/pdf.nsf/lookup/Intl0616.pdf/$file/Intl0616.pdf.

MacCormick, Neil, and Robert S. Summers (eds). 1997. *Interpreting Precedents: A Comparative Study*. Dartmouth: Dartmouth Publishing Co Ltd.

Mak, Elaine. 2007. *De rechtspraak in balans*. Nijmegen: Wolf Legal Publishing.

Mak, Elaine. 2013. *Judicial Decision-Making in a Globalised World: A Comparative Analysis of the Changing Practices of Western Highest Courts*. Oxford: Hart Publishing.

Mattei, Ugo. 1988. *Stare Decisis: Il valore del precedente giudiziario negli Stati Uniti d'America*. Milano: Giuffrè.

Muller, Sam and Sidney Richards (eds). 2010. *Highest Courts and Globalisation*. The Hague: Hague Academic Press.

Ng, Gar Y. 2007. *Quality of Judicial Organisation and Checks and Balances*. Antwerp: Intersentia.

Piana, Daniela. 2010. *Judicial Accountabilities in New Europe: From Rule of Law to Quality of Justice*. Farnham: Ashgate.

Scalia, Antonin G. 1997. *A Matter of Interpretation: Federal Courts and the Law*, ed. Amy Gutmann, 3-47. Princeton: Princeton University Press.

Schauer, Frederick. 2008. Authority and Authorities. *Virginia Law Review* 94: 1931-1961.

Schauer, Frederick. 2012. Precedent. In *The Routledge Companion to Philosophy of Law*, ed. Andrei Marmor, 123-136. London: Routledge.

Stein, Peter S., and John Shand. 1984. *Legal Values in Western Society*. Edinburgh: Edinburgh University Press.

Steinmetz, Pierre. 2009. Contribution à la conférence mondiale sur la justice constitutionnelle (Capetown, 23–24 January 2009). http://www.venice.coe.int/WCCJ/Papers/FRA_Steinmetz_F.pdf.

Recognition of International Law: From Formal Criteria to Substantive Principles

Leonardo Marchettoni

Abstract According to traditional approaches international law and domestic law were seen either as two separate legal orders (dualism) or as two different branches within the same legal order (monism). There are reasons, however, to deem this dichotomy inadequate to capture the complexity of the contemporary legal framework. In order to overcome this trouble, it is suggested that we could resort to the Hegelian notion of recognition. The complex interrelations that tie legal orders invite focusing one's attention on the processes through which the status and rank of a legal order become acknowledged within another legal order. To achieve this task we can make use of the concept of recognition. Such a strategy presents us with a means of discarding some prevailing formalistic assumptions and opens the way to an assessment of the role that substantive principles play within international law.

1 Monism and Dualism

Until the nineteenth century international law and domestic law were seen as two separate legal orders. The founding fathers of international law, like Emmerich de Vattel, never scrutinized the impact of international law on domestic law, because they assumed that international law, regulating inter-state relationships, did not affect the content of domestic law. This assumption was well motivated, since it reflected the features of the international law they were acquainted with, a set of rules meant to govern the behaviour of States, which did not affect the positions of individuals.

L. Marchettoni (✉)
Researcher in Legal Theory, University of Parma, Parma, Italy
e-mail: leonardo.marchettoni@unipr.it

© Springer International Publishing Switzerland 2015
L. Pineschi (ed.), *General Principles of Law - The Role of the Judiciary*,
Ius Gentium: Comparative Perspectives on Law and Justice 46,
DOI 10.1007/978-3-319-19180-5_4

Things begin to change during the nineteenth century, when it becomes apparent that international law might affect the status of citizens, for example, in the case concerning agreements about international transports or communications. The awareness of this novel state of things prompted explicit theorizing about the relation between international and domestic law.[1] The issue was addressed by Heinrich Triepel in what it is now considered the first expression of the so-called dualist point of view. In his *magnum opus, Völkerrecth und Landesrecht*,[2] Triepel maintained that international law and domestic law constitute two separate spheres, dealing with different topics and governing different actors. In fact, the two legal orders might come into contact only when international rules affected individual or other groups within the State, and therefore within the realm of domestic law.[3] It followed also that an international rule might display its effects inside the domestic legal order only after being transformed in the type of rule recognized by that legal order.

In the first half of the twentieth century, dualism became the target of several critical voices, until the work of Hans Kelsen established a novel point of view regarding the relationship between international law and domestic law, namely monism.[4] While the monistic perspective, by itself, was not totally new—during the nineteenth century several voices claimed the supremacy of international law over domestic law—Kelsen did reformulate such a viewpoint, detaching it from naturalistic temptations and presenting it within the context of a positivist theory of international law. According to Kelsen and his followers, international law and domestic law are different branches of the same legal order: there is just one universal legal order, namely public international law, which overarches different suborders, the States, which complete and specify the content of international rules.

In the course of the twentieth century monism and dualism became the two poles of an endless debate. Besides the scholarly debate, the practice of national and international courts added itself as a further element of the whole picture. Under monism international law is usually regarded as immediately valid within domestic legal orders. This feature, in turn, entails that norms that can be deemed complete are self-executing, that is, capable of producing direct effects. On the contrary, dualist States consider international law and domestic law as separate spheres and require that international rules be transformed into rules recognized as valid in the domestic legal order. However, in dualist States even non-incorporated treaties may engender some effect when they are taken into account by courts interpreting domestic laws. This circumstance reinforces the suspicion that, as Jan Klabbers puts it, "the practical differences between monism and dualism may not be all that enormous".[5]

---

[1]On monism and dualism in international law see the essays contained in Nijman and Nollkaemper (2007). For a synthetic survey, see Itzcovich (2006), Chap. 2; Klabbers (2013), Chap. 16.

[2]Triepel (1899).

[3]Although, Triepel held that the concourse of law between international law and domestic law was impossible, because the two legal orders cannot regulate the same juridical relations.

[4]See Kelsen (1952).

[5]Klabbers (2013), p. 296.

Such a conclusion provides a compelling reason for downplaying the whole debate. The traditional divide between monistic and dualistic approaches is, in the best case, only narrow part of the entire problem. Moreover, there are strong reasons to think that the dichotomy between monism and dualism is nowadays scarcely useful to investigate international law and domestic law. Indeed, when one tries to apply this theoretical machinery to the analysis of recent case law, discomforting results follow. For example, when Jan Klabbers classifies both the European Court of Justice (ECJ) *Kadi* case and the United States Supreme Court *Medellín* case as two prominent instances of a new dualist trend within international jurisprudence,[6] it is difficult to assuage the feeling that something in this reconstruction has gone entirely missed out.[7] He regards the ECJ's attempt to signal the failure of the EC Regulation implementing the United Nations sanctions against terrorism to meet the human rights requirements as an illustration of dualistic attitudes, on a par with the United States Supreme Court's endeavour to restrict the same rights by negating the self-executing character of the International Court of Justice (ICJ)'s decisions. This produces the disquieting impression that the debate around monism and dualism has turned into a useless *querelle* completely detached from concrete experience.[8]

The real problem is that twenty-first century international law is quite a different thing from what it used to be when the debate between monism and dualism took off. For most of the past four hundred years, international law provided a very thin set of rules, regulating, for example, war, the conduct of diplomats, the law of the sea, or the territorial integrity of States. Since the end of World War II and particularly in the last three decades, the number of international rules has increased sharply. As a result, the international legal system is "thicker" than it has ever been before. With this scenario in sight, the classic tenets of the dualistic approach, such as those contained in some of the fundamental judgments of the discipline, like the *Lotus* case[9] or the *German Interests in Polish Upper Silesia* case[10] are no longer credible.[11]

---

[6]On the effects of the Security Council resolutions within the European legal order, see Cannizzaro (2009), pp. 39–45.

[7]Klabbers (2013), pp. 300–301.

[8]It is noteworthy that a similar impression was already expressed by several scholars in the fifties and sixties. See Itzcovich (2006), p. 35 ff.

[9]"International Law governs relations between independent States. The rules of law binding upon States therefore emanate from their own free will as expressed in conventions or by usages generally accepted as expressing principles of law and established in order to regulate the relations between these coexisting independent communities or with a view to the achievement of common aims. Restrictions upon the independence of states cannot therefore be presumed". PCIJ, Ser. A, no. 10 (1927).

[10]"From the standpoint of International law" legal rules pertaining to municipal laws "which express the will and constitute the activities of States" should be considered "as mere facts". PCIJ, Ser. A, no. 7 (1926).

[11]See also Gaja (2007).

International law is not only thicker than before; it is also more articulated. It is more sectorial, in the sense that it harvests a plurality of thematic fields that are sometimes only weakly interrelated: human rights and humanitarian law, law of the sea, trade law, environmental law, and so on. In addition, according to some scholars, there exists a hierarchy of sources within it, which includes *jus cogens*, customary law, general principles of law, treaty law. The boundaries of each subset are not sharply defined, and their status within domestic law varies with the different legal orders: while some Constitutions give the highest rank to treaty provisions, others put first different sources as customary law or *jus cogens*.[12] Moreover, beyond the traditional sources of international law, rooted in the consent—explicit or tacit—of States,[13] there is a new array of rules, regulations, standards, recommendations originating from international organizations, NGOs, multinational companies, and not easily linkable to the consent of States. This set of norms, known as "global law", is now the centre-stage of the theoretical debate,[14] because it raises formidable challenges to every attempt to define a proper criterion for distinguishing between law and non-law, and therefore for drawing a comprehensive map of valid law.

It is also worth noticing that within this landscape the role of courts, both international and domestic ones, acquires a new prominence. This fact may be viewed as a consequence of the growing complexity of international law, since such complexity precludes the formation of stable agreements and assigns to courts the creative task of reconstructing the hierarchy of normative sources. Such a predicament leads eventually to increasing the practical relevance of principles as an indispensable tool in the process of outlining the structure of valid law. In fact, while international treaties—such as European treaty law—resort widely to general principles in order to assure the dynamic character of their provisions without dismissing their universality,[15] these principles are not strictly formal like general principles of law but possess frequently substantive import.[16] Moreover, they are generally to be insulated and detailed by courts in their attempts to find the correct solution to the cases submitted to them. This state of affairs provides the reasons for searching out another interpretive key to the relationship between international law and domestic law, which does have the property of being more centred on the concrete practice of courts. It is my claim that a sounder analysis of this relationship should be based on the central notion of recognition.

---

[12]See Ginsburg et al. (2008).

[13]Actually, at least the majority of scholars, tends to see the cogency customary law as rooted more in the concrete practice of States than in their consent. However, it should be noted also that the prevailing doctrine admits that States often act voluntarily in order to influence the formation or the evolution of customary law. On this topic, see Treves (2005), p. 230 ff. For a recent critique to the role attributed to consent by international law theory, see Dworkin (2013).

[14]See, for example, Walker (2015).

[15]Maduro (2007).

[16]See Palombella (2015). The Author refers here to the idea, suggested by Anne Peters, of a "compensatory constitutionalism". See Peters (2006).

2 Recognition as a Means of Escaping the Dichotomy

As I argued above the debate between monism and dualism seems to have come to a dead end. The main problem is that this dichotomy reflects a static conception of international law, according to which international law and domestic law operate as a single—or, rather, a couple of—fixed set(s) that do(es) not undergo any substantial variation over time. On the contrary, the prevailing image of global law is one of rapid flux, where a more stable core of acts, easily identifiable as law, is surrounded by a nebula of rules, standards, etc. whose exact qualification is somewhat uncertain. Against this background an approach that centres on the processes through which new rules and regulations can gain the status of law is definitely more fruitful than one which gets lost in endless distinctions about the relationships between the international system and national legal orders.

In order to pursue this kind of inquiry it is worth building on the concept of recognition. Reference to recognition of law inevitably evokes the name of H.L.A. Hart. As it is widely known Hart thought that every legal system necessarily contains a rule setting out the criteria of legal validity, that is, a (secondary) rule which determines which rules are binding.[17] However, Hart did not think that international law could display rules of recognition comparable to those pertaining to national legal orders.[18] Be this as it may, in what follows I will try to explore a different notion of recognition that may prove useful, that is to say, the Hegelian one.

The concept of recognition is widely employed by contemporary philosophers. Yet, to avoid a long inquiry into its remote origins, it is fair to say that its probably most fertile elaboration can be found in Hegel's *Phenomenology of Spirit*.[19] Hegel introduces the concept of recognition in the fourth chapter of the *Phenomenology*, as a key element in the transition from consciousness to self-consciousness. After considering the first way in which self-conscious subjects conceive themselves, as pure will or desire that affirms itself in overcoming the world around it—which turns out to be unsatisfying, since the subject continuously needs new objects to overcome—, Hegel moves to the idea that self-conscious subjects require the recognition on the part of other self-conscious subjects: "Self-consciousness exists for and in itself when, and by the fact that, it so exists for another; that is, it exists only as something acknowledged".[20]

This cryptic statement means, by and large, that self-consciousness cannot exist in isolation but requires the presence of other self-consciousnesses in order to

---

[17]Hart (1997), p. 91 ff.

[18]Hart (1997), Chap. X. Actually the issue cannot be settled so quickly. For a recent attempt to extend Hartian positivism to the realm of international law, see Payandeh (2010). See also Kingsbury (2009).

[19]Among Hegel's predecessors it is impossible not to mention Fichte. For further details, see Siep (1979) and Redding (2008).

[20]Hegel (1977) [1807], p. 111.

gain its autonomy and identity through their acknowledgement. Indeed, this passage is of paramount importance, in that it marks a deep discontinuity with respect to the journey that the phenomenological consciousness has so far accomplished: whereas in the three preceding sections of the *Phenomenology* the consciousness sought to pick up the things in the world as objects "in themselves", the transition to the self-consciousness section is accompanied by a new awareness that the external world is, in some sense, a product of the activity of the observer and that this activity has its roots in the common space of norms and concepts disclosed as a consequence of the self-limitation that a plurality of equal self-consciousnesses effect.

At the same time, recognition is not something that can be acquired peacefully. Quite the contrary, recognition is initially marked by inequality, because each subject seeks to obtain recognition from the other without giving anything in return. Moreover, such a conflictual situation eventuates in a deep asymmetry of roles, in which the subject who prevails serves as a master and the defeated one becomes his slave.

The section of the *Phenomenology* that addresses the issue of recognition has been the subject of many influential readings, whose differences could hardly be surveyed in this context. The general ideas that I would like to extract from those pages, and which I deem to be important for my purposes, can be summarized in the following theses:

1. Valid norms cannot be separated from non-valid ones by employing a priori—formalistic—criteria of membership in some normative order. Rather, this division constitutes the outcome of the recognitive performances of the relevant subjects.[21]
2. This means also that they are not selected once and for all, but must be continuously renegotiated, as the surrounding circumstances and the identities of actors change.
3. Recognitive performances are inextricably entangled with socio-political and historical asymmetries that engender a pervasive conflict and affect the rules resulting from this process.

When we try to apply these ideas to the relationship between international law and domestic law, we can argue as follows: the key move is identifying the actors entitled to recognition with the judiciary power, not with the executive power. If we assumed that those who are legitimated to recognitive practices are governments, we would fall back in the consensual model that proved to be unable to account for the current situation. Quite the reverse, if we focus our attention on courts—more precisely, on the interplay between international and domestic courts—, the scenario becomes very different. In fact, this allows discarding completely the voluntaristic conception lurking behind the idea of State consent and replacing the

---

[21]Contra, see the attempt of Kingsbury (2009) to extend Hartian positivism to global law through the proposal of a set of formal criteria.

supposed act of will of the States with acts of recognition from the courts that, as members of an on-going practice, duck the dichotomy voluntary/necessitated.[22]

I assume that courts behave as self-consciousnesses of the legal order on the basis of which they judge.[23] So the ECJ can be portrayed as the self-consciousness of the European system, the United States Supreme Court as the self-consciousness of the United States system, and so on.[24] This function entails performing recognitive practices whenever the issue of deciding if a certain external norm constitutes law arises. So, if the ECJ must decide whether or not a certain regulation of the World Trade Organization constitutes law, it should undertake a recognitive performance. Such a performance obviously entails a conflictual dimension in which political asymmetries play a role. Without pushing the analogy with the Hegelian theses too far, we might remind that in some instances—for example, the exchange between the German Constitutional Court and the ECJ in the so called *Solange* cases—the antagonism between two legal orders expresses itself in a sequence of judgements in which each legal order—and each court—, claiming supremacy, attempts to "overcome" the other.

At this point, one could wonder on what basis the recognition is accorded or denied. Again, thinking that courts can always avail themselves of formal criteria capable of resolving the issue at stake would mean recovering the old model centred on the idea that the recognition of valid law depends on the possibility of ascertaining the existence of the consent of the relevant subject. Such a model underlies the whole debate between monism and dualism, which I addressed in the previous section. Indeed, the issue of the relationship between international law and domestic law arises only as long as the problem of identifying which norms belong to international law is already resolved, for example, because it is assumed that a consistent and neatly defined bulk of rules to which States have consented can be detected.

Once formalistic assumptions are discarded, the issue of the attitude of a given norm to become valid law may be resolved only on the basis of "substantive" criteria.[25] The move from formalistic criteria to substantive ones parallels the one from an "essentialist" view of legal orders—according to which legal orders exist

---

[22]Assigning to the courts the role of actors entitled to recognition on the international sphere does not mean assuming that they are the sole agents capable to exhibit recognitive practices in Hartian sense. The shift from States to courts is mostly important in order to highlight the obsolescence of the consensual model.

[23]Cf. also Scoditti (2004).

[24]Perhaps there may be a problem for those legal orders in which there are two or more apical courts exercising different roles. But this is a problem which I cannot tackle in this occasion.

[25]Such a move from formalism to substantive criteria reflects the shift from a formalistic interpretation of the Hartian rule of recognition, as applied to global law, to a *practical* one, according to which the rule of recognition picks up those criteria of validity that are effectively followed within a given legal system. See Palombella (2012), pp. 102–106. If the rule of recognition is understood in this second way, it really becomes closer to the notion of recognition I am attempting to develop in this chapter.

as abstract constructs with conditions of identity over time—to a "pragmatic" one—according to which legal orders exist, at most, as temporally unstable projections of the recognitive dispositions displayed by some court.[26] In practice, what most frequently happens is that the normative character of a given rule or regulation is assessed by considering whether it satisfies the requirements imposed by some theory of the necessary features of valid law—accountability of the rule-makers, requirements concerning the fairness of the procedure through which it has been emanated, publicness, compliance with customary international law and so on. In this way the basis on which the validity question is decided turns into a set of general principles concerning the properties of international law.

3 The Role of General Principles of International Law

In the previous sections of this chapter, I argued that the way in which the problem of the relationship between international law and domestic law has been discussed by international lawyers through the distinction between monistic and dualistic approaches fails to meet the challenges posed by the contemporary global landscape. I also maintained that such a scenario suggests rather an inquiry on the process whereby rules issued by external subjects become part of the domestic law and proposed to read this process through the theoretical lens provided by the Hegelian notion of recognition. In particular, I suggested that centring our attention on the recognitive practices carried out by courts entails focusing one's critical attention on the substantive principles employed to discriminate what constitutes an instance of valid law from what does not.

Article 38 of the Statute of the ICJ famously declares that the Court shall apply inter alia "the general principles of law recognized by civilized nations". According to many scholars this category comprises those generally accepted ideas and maxims—e.g., *nemo judex in causa propria, nullum crimen sine lege, ne bis in idem*—that form part of most legal systems of the world and without which it would be difficult to conceive of a legal order. They are not adopted or legislated and therefore cannot derive their validity from the consent of States.[27] However, if we get back to the preceding discussion, there are reasons to think that the category of principles of law should be enlarged so as to include also those criteria commonly employed in order to distinguish legislative rules from non-legislative ones. The main difference is that principles belonging to the latter subset do not

---

[26]Such a pragmatic character is what distinguishes the present proposal from some version of constitutional pluralism—notably that of MacCormick (1993, 2002), still centred on the idea of the existence of something like a plurality of legal orders recognizing each other. It bears more affinities to the theses expressed by Maduro (2003, 2012)—who highlights the performative character of the rules proposed by courts.

[27]See Klabbers (2013), Raimondo (2008). The leading study is still Cheng (2006) [1953].

aim at governing the behaviour of the relevant subjects but at offering some criteria that can be called upon in order to recognize valid law.

Another difference is that principles concerning the features that a given rule must possess in order to be counted as an instance of valid law cannot traced back their pedigree to an ancient tradition, as in the case of general principles *ex* Article 38 of the Statute of the ICJ. For this reason they are perhaps more indeterminate, in the sense that they require further determination by each court that formulates and employs them. They are not crystallized maxims as the general principles *ex* Article 38, but receive further content at each novel application.

This latter aspect is especially important from the point of view of our discourse, because it highlights a striking parallelism between the Hegelian concept of recognition and the recognitive practices exhibited by courts. Hegel says that the transition from consciousness to self-consciousness represents the first step within the realm of spirit. This first step is made possible because the recognition of the other as another subject exactly alike the first self-consciousness entails the opening of a supra-individual sphere, constituted through the negation of itself that each self-consciousness effects.[28] In the same way, when a given court faces the issue of determining whether a given act constitutes an instance of valid law, limiting its own legal order, it advances a criterion for the demarcation of law from non-law. Such a criterion, which stems from the recognition of the activity of another court and of the legal order which the court represents, belongs to a common patrimony of ideas that is susceptible of further employment by other courts. Other judges—or the same court that proposed it for the first time—can discuss it, accepting or refuting the rule that it proposes. But the important point is that by giving reasons for their behaviour, they contribute further content to the legal system they represent, and thus self-commit to those performances they require of other legal orders.[29]

However, it would be wrong, in my view, to conclude that the formulation of some criteria of recognition of valid law by a given court contributes to the edification of something like a universal sphere of common principles.[30] I rather think that each attempt to put down the features that a given act must possess in order to be counted as an instance of valid law may be seen as a further move within an ongoing discourse that cannot be ended by any participant.[31] In this respect, the situation is very different from that envisaged by Hegel. As I reminded some lines above, he maintained that through recognition self-consciousnesses penetrate for the first time the Realm of Spirit, that is, enter into a sphere of life distinct from

---

[28]See Redding (2008), p. 104.

[29]Cf. Palombella (2012), pp. 101–102.

[30]I think that this aspect is important because can differentiate the present proposal from ordinary pluralism. Indeed, the latter view requires that the plurality of different legal orders be situated "within a common system of international law engaged in a constructive and self-referential dialogue that consciously seeks to maintain the coherence of the overall system". See Burke-White (2004).

[31]Cf. Maduro (2012).

mere animal life and marked by the emergence of a new inter-subjectively shared substance, namely Spirit (*Geist*). I find this conclusion—for reasons that I cannot explain in this chapter—unsatisfying. I think the pluralistic structure of global law is better reflected if we think of the process of elaborating new criteria of recognition as an endless endeavour to which each court offers its contribution without any hope of saying the last word. Criteria set by a given court may be discussed by other judges but in this transit from one court to another there is no common language that actors share. On the contrary, the tragedy of global law is that each actor must operate as if it were part of a whole that cannot—and will not ever be able to—materialize.[32]

Acknowledgments The author thanks Luca Baccelli, Mariano Croce, Giulio Itzcovich, Gianluigi Palombella, Stefano Pietropaoli, Laura Pineschi, Cesare Pitea, Filippo Ruschi and Maria Zanichelli for useful comments on an earlier draft.

References

Burke-White, William W. 2004. International Legal Pluralism. *Michigan Journal of International Law* 25: 963-979.

Cannizzaro, Enzo. 2009. Security Council Resolutions and EC Fundamental Rights: Some Remarks on the ECJ Decision in the *Kadi* Case. *Yearbook of European Law* 28: 593-600.

Cheng, Bin. 2006 [1953]. *General Principles of Law as Applied by International Courts and Tribunals*. Cambridge: Cambridge University Press.

Dworkin, Ronald M. 2013. A New Philosophy of International Law. *Philosophy & Public Affairs* 41: 2-30.

Gaja, Giorgio. 2007. Dualism: A Review. In *New Perspectives on the Divide between National and International Law*, eds. Janne Nijman and André Nollkaemper, 52-62. Oxford: Oxford University Press.

Ginsburg, Tom, Svitlana Chernykh, and Zachary Elkins. 2008. Commitment and Diffusion: How and Why National Constitutions Incorporate International Law. *University of Illinois Law Review*: 201-238.

Hart, Herbert L. A. 1997. *The Concept of Law*, with a "Postscript", eds. Penelope A. Bulloch and Joseph Raz. Oxford: Oxford University Press.

Hegel, Georg W. F. 1977 [1807]. *Phenomenology of Spirit*. Trans. A.V. Miller. Oxford: Oxford University Press.

Itzcovich, Giulio. 2006. *Teorie e ideologie del diritto comunitario*. Torino: Giappichelli.

Kelsen, Hans. 1952. *Principles of International Law*. New York: Rinehart.

Kingsbury, Benedict. 2009. The Concept of "Law" in Global Administrative Law. *European Journal of International Law* 20: 23-57.

Klabbers, Jan. 2013. *International Law*, Cambridge: Cambridge University Press.

MacCormick, Neil. 1993. Beyond the Sovereign State. *Modern Law Review* 56: 1-18.

MacCormick, Neil. 2002. *Questioning Sovereignty: Law, State, and Nation in the European Commonwealth*. Oxford University Press: Oxford.

Maduro, Miguel Poiares. 2003. Contrapunctual Law: Europe's Constitutional Pluralism in Action. In *Sovereignty in Transition*, ed. Neil Walker, 501-537. Oxford: Hart.

---

[32]Cf. Palombella (2012), p. 160 ff.

Maduro, Miguel Poiares. 2007. Interpreting European Law: Judicial Adjudication in a Context of Constitutional Pluralism. *European Journal of Legal Studies* 1: 1-21.

Maduro, Miguel Poiares. 2012. Three Claims of Constitutional Pluralism. In *Constitutional Pluralism in the European Union and Beyond*, eds. Matej Avbelj and Jan Komárek, 67-84. Oxford: Hart.

Nijman, Janne, and André Nollkaemper (eds). 2007. *New Perspectives on the Divide Between National and International Law*. Oxford: Oxford University Press.

Palombella, Gianluigi. 2012. *È possibile una legalità globale? Il Rule of law e la governance del mondo*. Bologna: Il Mulino.

Palombella, Gianluigi. 2015. Principles and Disagreements in International Law (with a View from Dworkin's Legal Theory). In *General Principles of Law: The Role of the Judiciary*, ed. Laura Pineschi.

Payandeh, Mehrdad. 2010. The Concept of International Law in the Jurisprudence of H.L.A. Hart. *European Journal of International Law* 21: 967-995.

Peters, Anne. 2006. Compensatory Constitutionalism: The Function and Potential of Fundamental International Norms and Structures. *Leiden Journal of International Law* 19: 579-610.

Raimondo, Fabián. 2008. *General Principles of Law in the Decisions of International Criminal Courts and Tribunals*. Leiden: Brill.

Redding, Paul. 2008. The Independence and Dependence of Self-Consciousness: The Dialectic of Lord and Bondsman in Hegel's *Phenomenology of Spirit*. In *The Cambridge Companion to Hegel and Nineteenth-Century Philosophy*, ed. Frederick C. Beiser, 94-110. Cambridge: Cambridge University Press.

Scoditti, Enrico. 2004. Articolare le costituzioni. L'Europa come ordinamento giuridico integrato. *Materiali per una storia della cultura giuridica* 34: 198-215.

Siep, Ludwig. 1979. *Anerkennung als Prinzip der praktischen Philosophie. Untersuchungen zu Hegels Jenaer Philosophie des Geistes*. Freiburg-München: Alber.

Treves, Tullio. 2005. *Diritto internazionale. Problemi fondamentali*. Milano: Giuffrè.

Triepel, Heinrich. 1899. *Völkerrecth und Landesrecht*. Leipzig: Hirschfeld.

Walker, Neil. 2015. *Intimations of Global Law*. Cambridge: Cambridge University Press.

The "Doctrine of Principles" in Neo-Constitutional Theories and the Principle of Reasonableness in Action

Francesco De Vanna

Abstract The application of legal principles in legal argument is a fundamental claim of the neo-constitutionalist legal theory. Principles are at the top of the legal hierarchy and provide for the material unity of the judicial system, which is a pluralistic one and intertwined with various needs. Consequently, principles are to be regarded as prior and antecedent to rules, from a pre-political, fundamental point of view aiming at the judicialization of power. Considering the expansive nature of principles, in particular constitutional principles and principles proclaimed by supranational Charters of rights, it is no longer sufficient to respect the law's prescriptions about *who* and *how:* gradually, and mostly thanks to the control of constitutional legitimacy, an unavoidable question is arising about the *what* of law, the *an* of legal rulings as well as its compatibility with the standards of justice. Dworkin, in particular, affirms that principles are first of all "a requirement of justice or fairness or some other dimension of morality"; they rightly step into the world of law thanks to the adequacy and to the justification power they show. The first part of the present chapter will analyze the definitive recognition of the normative character of principles; in particular the difference of their structure and functioning from rules, and finally the different and similar aspects between principles and values. The second part of the chapter will observe more closely the functioning of principle of reasonableness, through the analysis of some passages of important judgments.

F. De Vanna (✉)
Ph.D. Candidate in Legal Theory, University of Parma, Parma, Italy
e-mail: francesco_devanna86@hotmail.it

© Springer International Publishing Switzerland 2015   79
L. Pineschi (ed.), *General Principles of Law - The Role of the Judiciary,*
Ius Gentium: Comparative Perspectives on Law and Justice 46,
DOI 10.1007/978-3-319-19180-5_5

1 Introduction

Neo-constitutionalism[1] developed in the last few decades from the theories of Ronald Dworkin: with a great variety of single expressions, it asserts the inherently pervasive power of the Constitution, emphasizes the need to specify a catalogue of fundamental rights, adopts the methodological distinction between rules and principles and highlights the norm-generative function of the latter.[2] These are assumed as parameters for the validity of the right.

Neo-constitutionalism as a theory of law, therefore, reshapes the hierarchy of sources: it subordinates ordinary law to constitutional norms, not only at a formal, logical and procedural level, but also and most importantly at a substantial, axiological level.[3] The Constitution is not only to be regarded as the founding moment of the legal system, nor only as the meta-norm concerning the production of law. On the contrary, it assumes the value of a substantial project by which the legislator must abide; it becomes a goal to attain, a "positivized world view".[4] Ultimately, then, the Constitution asserts explicitly not only the existence and validity of law, but also the conditions for its validity and the postulates of individual and collective morality.

In this respect, neo-constitutionalism sets forth arguments concerning both legitimacy and legality: it denies that legitimacy can be created only through Kelsen's nomodynamics, while it considers way more relevant the derivation of legitimacy through nomostatics. It is no longer sufficient to respect the law's prescriptions about *who* and *how*: gradually but irreversibly, and mostly thanks to the control of constitutional legitimacy, an unavoidable question is arising about the *what* of law, the *an* of legal rulings as well as its compatibility with the standards of justice acknowledged and proclaimed by all fundamental Charters and catalogues of rights.

The function of general principles, therefore, is enhanced, especially in rigid constitutional systems which include the constitutional control of laws: general principles aim not only at filling in possible legislative omissions, but also at influencing the interpretation of existing provisions.[5] In other words, while positive law

---

[1]See Dworkin (1978, 1985, 1986, 1996); Habermas (1992, ed. Ceppa 2001); Alexy (1992a, 1994); Nino (1994).

[2]For an overall view on the concept of "principle", see Dworkin (1978); Pattaro (1987), pp. 25–35; Betti (1971); Del Vecchio (1958), p. 205 ff.; Alpa (2006); Cheng (1953); Guastini (2004), pp. 199–205. See also *I principi generali del diritto, Atti del convegno*, Accademia dei Lincei, Roma, 1992 and conference proceedings of VIII World Congress of the International Association of Constitutional Law, Mexico City, 2010, available at: http://www.juridicas.unam.mx/wccl/en/i.htm.

[3]See Barberis (2011), pp. 33–41; Mazzarese (2002); Pozzolo (2001); Omaggio (2003), pp. 93–131; La Torre (2010); Bongiovanni (1999).

[4]The wording is of Mario Dogliani, quoted in Omaggio (2003), p. 108, footnote 44 (my translation).

[5]Pizzorusso (2011), p. 658; Guastini (2010), p. 328; Alpa (2006), p. 263.

codes used to consider principles as playing an essentially interstitial role, they have come to constitute a set of legal rules and standards which might potentially regulate all matters subject to law. Considering the expansive nature of principles, in particular constitutional principles and principles proclaimed by supranational Charters of rights, it has become unthinkable for any field of law to produce norms without taking into account the Constitution. Principles such as *neminem laedere* and *cuique suum tribuere,* the principle of formal and substantial equality, the inquisitorial principle in civil and criminal trials and the principles of *due process* and *favor rei*: these are only a few of the criteria and of the trial or procedural materials which constitute the soul of our systems and give them their unique "way of being".

The first part of the present chapter will analyze the definitive recognition of the normative character of principles; in particular their ontological status (juridical or moral?), the difference of their structure and functioning from rules, and finally the different and similar aspects between principles and values. The second part of the chapter will observe more closely the functioning of principles "in action", through the analysis of some passages of important judgments.

2 Principles Between Morality and Law

One of the key aspects of the neo-constitutional model is its tendency to consider law principles from a moral point of view. After admitting in his *Postscript* that he did not give principles the importance they deserve, Herbert Hart asserts that in some judicial systems (like the American one), criteria of validity may include justice principles and substantial moral values.[6] Dworkin, of course, sustains this point with even greater decision. He affirms that principles are first of all "a requirement of justice or fairness or some other dimension of morality"[7]; they rightly step into the world of law thanks to the adequacy and to the justification power they show. Dworkin bases his legal theory on an ethical objectivism according to which there are moral truths that constitute fundamental theoretical premises, capable of justifying the "truth" or "falsity" of some normative and interpretative conclusions.[8] It is thanks to the constructive work of the interpreter that moral premises, hidden in the net of the judicial system, can enter the field of law and assume the status of juridical norms. Principles, this way, fully become a part of the system and find their legitimacy in the idea of justice itself, not in a single decision by the legislator. Therefore, should a principle cease to be considered valid, tribunals would simply stop applying it, without necessarily waiting for its formal abrogation. For this reason, the interpreter is presented with the obligation

---

[6]Hart (1961) (eds. Bullock and Raz 1994).

[7]Dworkin (1978), p. 22.

[8]Dworkin (2011).

to not only represent the past, but also imagine future law, consistently with the moral and juridical history of a system. Of course, it is unthinkable that all moral principles of a community may become the basis for judicial decisions, perhaps even in contrast with precise legal dispositions, because this would destroy the functional difference set between law and morality. Before receiving a juridical form, some principles not yet included in law often show through already accepted standards. But when they assume a legal status, and gradually start to support a chain of precedents, they become "crystallized" juridical standards, and as such they determine the decisions of judges. In this respect, Dworkin suggests a precise theory, called "of the institutional support".

According to this theory, a principle, in order to receive a juridical form, must have been mentioned in previous judicial decisions or in the highest possible number of laws, not considering its appearance in their forewords, preparatory works or any other accompanying document. In conclusion, as Jürgen Habermas affirms, "principles have both a juridical and a moral nature"[9] and they are necessarily in a sort of "middle earth", halfway between the boundaries of law and morality.

3 Principles Versus Rules

In constitutional systems, principles no longer play just an "auxiliary" role, because their normative form seems particularly apt to protect primary rights, much better than classic general rules may do. Principles are at the top of the legal hierarchy and provide for the material unity of the judicial system, which is a pluralistic one and intertwined with various needs. Consequently, principles are to be regarded as prior and antecedent to rules, from a pre-political, fundamental point of view aiming at the judicialization of power.

Robert Alexy considers principles as "optimization precepts" with variable intensity (*Optimisierungsgebote*), i.e. norms prescribing something which must be realized to the furthest extent possible, but with different intensity grades and depending on legal and practical possibilities. Rules, on the contrary, are regarded as definitive precepts (*definitive Gebote*), which order, forbid, allow or authorize something in a decisive way, following an "all or nothing" logic, without anything in between.[10] The gradable and optimizable character of principles derives from the breadth of their definition and of their meaning, which affects the conditions for their application. In situations of conflict, e.g. when one principle forbids and another one authorizes, the interpreter will not disapply one in favour of the other, as he would normally do in case of colliding rules; he will rather balance the two principles and tend to give a greater or smaller relevance to each one, establishing

---

[9]Habermas (1992) (ed. Ceppa 2001), p. 17; Habermas (1996), Italian partial version (my translation).

[10]Alexy (1994, 2000).

a hierarchy between them.[11] Therefore, it is possible to assert that conflicts between principles must refer to the dimension of individual consideration (or balancing), while conflicts between rules must refer to the dimension of validity, specified through the technique of subsumption. Moreover, Alexy's balancing demands the comparison of three requirements, which derive from the need for rationality and proportionality: such requirements are "appropriateness", i.e. adequacy of the chosen means; "necessity", i.e. infringement as light as possible of the "sacrificed" principle; and finally "proportionality" in the strict sense of the word, in order to rule the application of all other possible principles in a case. This last principle follows Pareto's efficiency, which states that the poor realization of one principle must be balanced by the best possible fulfilment of the opposing principle.

One of the main points of Dworkin's theory is the distinction between *rules* and *principles*. Dworkin proved that judges do apply relevant juridical principles, through an analysis of the famous case *Riggs v. Palmer* of 1889, where the Court of Appeals of New York had to decide whether a person indicated as heir in his grandfather's will still had the right to inherit, even though he had killed his grandfather precisely for that purpose. Laws as well as judicial precedents gave the right to inherit to whoever was indicated as heir in a will, without exceptions. But the Court, basing on several other cases, elaborated the principle according to which nobody may benefit from their own crime: this justified a new interpretation of the law, thus denying the killer the right to succession. If the Court had not taken into account this principle, a literal interpretation of the law would have led to an opposite solution of the case, contrasting with reason and basic ideas of justice. This case assumed a particular relevance in jus-philosophical literature, because it is regarded as the first and most effective counter-argument against the most anachronistic statements of legal positivism.

The rule is always connected with a type of offense which can be described through Kelsen's "hypothetical imperative", i.e. through a conditional phrase establishing a connection between a conditioning cause and a conditioned consequence (*If "x"... then "y"...*). The rule, moreover, accepts only explicit exceptions; the principle is not as positive, it also accepts implicit exceptions and it needs to be put into effect by the legislator or by the judge, who will relate it to concrete types of offense and will specify its juridical consequences. The point is not to interpret the principle, as it is usually expressed with clear words; nor to create new law, as the law's field of action remains the same: the considered case is already under a field of law anyway, so the point is just to define which principles are pertinent, basing on inference and constructive reasoning.

Focusing now on the role played by norms in juridical reasoning, it is possible to distinguish between rules and principles basing on the concept of "reason to act".

---

[11]For the technique of balancing see Alexy (1992b), pp. 153–192; Alexy (2007), pp. 45–56; Dworkin (1978); Celano (2002), pp. 223–239; Pino (2009), pp. 131–158; Pino (2007); Bin (1992); Modugno (1995), pp. 643–648; Contra Waldron (1993); Ferrajoli (2013); Alexander and Kress (1995).

According to Atienza and Ruiz Manero, rules are "peremptory" reasons, while explicit principles are independent but not peremptory reasons to act, as they constitute first grade reasons whose weight needs to be evaluated by the court with respect to other reasons. Implicit principles, on the contrary, are not considered as peremptory reasons nor as independent reasons, because the courts have to analyze their qualitative content, i.e., courts have to analyze their congruence with rules and other principles mentioned in sources.[12]

Principles interact with rules; they strengthen them, they even restrict them, they justify the enunciation of new judicial rules. To use a circular image, it is possible to affirm that the principles of law receive their judicial character from their direct relation with rules, most importantly the rule of recognition, but at the same time rules receive their validity only from principles. This is almost a paradox, but, as Neil MacCormick observes:

> [W]hen we view the law in action what we see is a constant dialectic between what has been and is taken as settled, and the continuing dynamic process of trying to settle new problems satisfactorily and old problems in what now seems a more satisfactory way.[13]

This means essentially that both theory and convictions have to be gradually adjusted, until they reach a situation of satisfactory stability. With regard to this point, John Rawls theorized the "reflective balance":

> It is an equilibrium because at last our principles and judgments coincide; and it is reflective since we know to what principles our judgments conform and the premises of their derivation.[14]

The mention of "judgments" calls to mind another term for comparison of principles, that is to say, values.

4 Principles or "Tyrannical Values"?

Neo-constitutionalism often mentions how principles share some aspects with values, as the notion of value clearly explains the "fundamental" nature of principles: easy examples are equality, social dignity, democratic participation in the life of institutions. However, it is not simple to establish if, and to what extent, values affect the sphere of law, and if they are consubstantial to principles, or if, on the contrary, they belong to different normative and ideological areas.

According to MacCormick, not even positivists would ever assert that law is not based on any value; at most, they might sustain that it is not necessary to share such values in order to know that law exists and must be observed. From his point of view:

---

[12]See Atienza and Ruiz Manero (1996, 1998).

[13]MacCormick (1978), p. 245.

[14]Rawls (1971), p. 18.

> Law certainly embodies values and these values are characteristically expressed in state-ments of the principles of a given legal system. But ... values are only "embodied" in law in the sense that and to the extent that human beings approve of the laws they have because of the states of affairs they are supposed to secure, being states of affairs which are on some ground deemed just or otherwise good.[15]

Alexy's thesis, in this respect, sounds totally pertinent. It affirms that principles clearly show a "wide structural resemblance" to values; they call for the correct-ness of moral arguments and demand a rational basis for judicial discourses. It is possible to observe a set of general rules of moral argumentation which might also be regarded as rules for the justification, in a juridical sense: a certain moral order is considered right if it is based on universal premises, which are also the premises for the general practical discourse. The common demand of a juridical and moral foundation is the key to the passage from correctness to justice; law, in addition to being valid at a formal level, also becomes just at a qualitative level. Therefore, Alexy supports the correlation between principles and values on the basis of the structural characteristics of principles (which set them apart from rules); this the-ory is part of the thesis of the connection between law and morality. Judgments of values, just like judgments of principles, may be considered evaluation rules as well as evaluation criteria.

However, some German thinkers such as Hoerster and Habermas opposed this point of view, taking into consideration some critical premises of Carl Schmitt's *The Tyranny of Values*. Here it is affirmed that if the practice of law is too strictly connected to values, its rationality in scientific terms is compromised, as law becomes unclear and arbitrary; moreover, this would legitimate a constant inter-vention of the State on the freedom of citizens. For these reasons, Hoerster and Habermas strongly defend a clear logical distinction between principles and val-ues. This distinction coincides for them with the distinction between the deonto-logical status and the teleological status. Habermas asserts that principles have a deontological nature and belong to Kant's category of "right": they are universally and unconditionally valid and oblige recipients. Values, on the contrary, have a tel-eological nature and are related to Aristotle's dimension of "good life", as they express preferences about certain objects: their validity, therefore, is not universal, but historicized and local. Consequently, what is due to all (principles) should not clash with what is good only for us (values); this would destroy the famous "fire-wall"[16] which Habermas imagines inside the juridical discourse and which only a deontological concept of principles can preserve. In order to understand the core of this problem, it is necessary to refer to the concept of "complementarity", which according to Habermas constitutes the relation between law and morality. Juridical problems and moral questions arise from the same conflicts of action, but in different forms, as law is not just a symbolic system, but rather a system of action. Law and morality remain "structurally intertwined", because institutional processes require forms of argumentation which must necessarily remain open to

---

[15]MacCormick (1978), p. 234.

[16]Habermas (1996), p. 258.

moral reasons. Following post-conventional processes of foundation, law emancipated from the traditional approach, and "now morality has reached the very heart of positive law, without losing itself in the process".[17]

Distinction, not separation: this situation leads to the distinction between principles, which are potentially universal, and values, which are shared by individuals in precise, historically determined systems. It follows inevitably that "principles or higher-level norms, in the light of which other norms can be justified, have a deontological sense, whereas values are teleological".[18]

Habermas, in this respect, is closer to the point of view of American constitutionalists: they make a sharper distinction than Germans between approaches which consider fundamental rights as judicial principles and approaches which consider them as value guidelines. Alexy's perspective, on the contrary, absorbed more of the opinions issued by the German Federal Constitutional Court, which tends to consider the rights expressed in the *Grundgesetz* as an *objektive Weltordnung*, i.e. as a system of objective values capable of giving life to the whole judicial activity of the State.[19]

Also Gustavo Zagrebelsky agrees with the distinction of principles and values, and criticizes the latter with sharp arguments. In particular, he regards principles as "initial goods" which suggest to behaving in such a way that each and every action becomes an expression of the principle itself. The criterion of validity of actions will be the adequacy and predictability of the behavior with respect to the adopted principles. Values, on the other hand, are "final goods": they justify all means used between the start and the end of an action, as long as these are compatible with their *ethos*.[20] This is why values are difficult to define with rational criteria. They do not suggest, they rather order to behave in the most adequate way in order to attain a certain goal; in this case the criterion of validity of actions will not be their adequacy, but rather their mere efficiency.

5 Arguments of Principle and Arguments of Policy

A further distinction, which emerges essentially in Dworkin's theory and was partially recalled by Habermas, is the distinction between "arguments of principle" and "arguments of *policy*", in relation to the different functions conducted by the judicial and the legislative power. While the principle is a requirement of justice and equity preserving the fundamental rights of the individual, the policy is a criterion which sets a goal to achieve, a social and economic amelioration in the interest of collective purpose.

---

[17]Habermas (2001), p. 36 (my translation).

[18]Habermas (1996), p. 255.

[19]See also Amirante (1981), p. 9 ff. and Baldassarre (1991), p. 639 ff.

[20]Zagrebelsky (2002), p. 872.

Dworkin affirms that "principles are propositions that describe rights, *policies* are propositions that describe purposes":[21] they both aim at the realization of a political or moral purpose, but rights are connected to identified political purposes, while *goals* are connected to unidentified purposes. It is up to the legislator to establish general policies respectively deriving from them, but there are some cases in which the judge is asked to fill the legislator's post due to the delicacy of the matter under consideration, or due to the complexity of the arguments related to it. In these cases, the judge decides on the basis of arguments of principle as well as legislative policy, often letting the latter prevail on the former. According to Dworkin, however, the judges should always decide, even in difficult cases, on the basis of arguments of principle.

In the *Spartan Steel* case,[22] some employees of a company cut the electricity cable which provided a nearby steel plant with energy, causing the damaging of the in process casting, in addition to the loss of the three following castings due to the machineries' induced inactivity. The company was later forced to close down during the period of maintenance: for these reasons, the company asked for the reparation of all the damages, from the first to the fourth casting. Lord Denning, one of the magistrates of the judging committee, affirmed:

> It seems to me better to consider the particular relationship in hand, and see whether or not, as a matter of policy, economic loss should be recoverable, or not.

It was therefore a matter of establishing whether a duty of care subsisted at the expense of the defendant and whether the damaged company had a right to reparation for the *economic loss* derived from the interruption of the electric provision of its property. The Court upheld the request of reparation only within the first casting, but it denied it in relation to the other three, as in that case the damage was "too remote" and based only on a subjective profile of *negligence*.[23] The judge goes on:

> [I]n such a hazard as this, the risk of economic loss should be suffered by the whole community who suffer the losses—usually many but comparatively small losses—rather than on the one pair of shoulders, that is, on the contractor on whom the total of them, all added together, might be very heavy.

According to Lord Denning, if the Court had recognised the indemnification of the pure economic damage, the precedent would have been valid in every future controversy, thus increasing the risk of abuse which derives from the impossibility of positively proving the loss of income. Dworkin makes use of the case to demonstrate how different it is to consider whether the claimant has a right to reparation and to consider, instead, whether it is economically wise to distribute liability for accidents in the way the plaintiff suggested. Consequently in the first case it would

---

[21]Dworkin (1978), p. 91.

[22]*Spartan Steel & Alloys Ltd v. Martin&Co. (Contractors) Ltd.,* 3 All ER 557 (1972). See also Shiner (2005), pp. 47–48.

[23]See Gordley et al. (2006), pp. 313–314.

have been about an argument of principle, whereas, in the second one, it would have been about an argument of *policy.*

> I propose ... the thesis that judicial decisions in civil cases, even in hard cases like *Spartan Steel*, characteristically are and should be generated by principle not policy.[24]

Decisions based on arguments of policy can be sustained on an ad hoc basis, every time according to the case, while an argument of principle can justify a particular decision only if it is possible to prove it is coherent with the previous decisions and with the decisions that the magistrates would make in similar cases. As a matter of fact, in the *Spartan Steel* case, the complainant did not sustain the existence of a law establishing a right to the reparation of the suffered economic damages, but he referred to some precedents, which had allowed the reparation for other types of damages, and claimed that the principle at the bottom of those cases required a similar decision in this case too. According to Dworkin's perspective, if the plaintive makes claim of a right in relation to the defendant, in that case the latter has a correspondent duty, which, even though not traceable in any explicit legislative bill, could anyway justify a conviction against him.

Dworkin's belief that principles confer rights in opposition to goals is not shared by MacCormick, according to whom the spheres of principles and policies are inevitably related. He asserts that:

> For any goal *g*, to say that is a goal which *ought* to be secured is to enunciate a principle or a judgment dependent on some unstated but presupposed principle.[25]

Therefore, this equates with asserting that "to articulate the desiderability of some general policy-goal is to state a principle. To state a principle is to frame a possible policy-goal".[26] Nevertheless, although Dworkin does not accept the identification of principles with policies, he does not even neglect to underline how between the two normative entities there could be a logical sequence of interferences, which can result in their reciprocal inter-changeability, especially in trials of democratic deliberation.

6 Rights as "Matters of Principle"

The dynamics principles-policies are indissolubly connected to the conception of rights and to the anti-utilitarian authority they exercise in relation to functional arguments. They act both as justification of judicial decisions, and in the phases of democratic legislation as means for the limitation of the powers of the majority, wherefore, as Dworkin states, if "someone has a right to something, therefore it is

---

[24]Dworkin (1978), p. 108.

[25]MacCormick (1978), p. 263 (emphasis in the original).

[26]Ibid., p. 264.

incorrect on the part of the State to deny it, even though it would be more useful to act along these lines in the general interest". Rights are, therefore, "a matter of principle".[27]

Starting from the general principle of *equal concern and respect*, Dworkin gives rights a moral value which cannot be remitted to the contingent consideration of the majorities, if not by accepting the risk of individuals not being treated as equals. Dworkin's conviction grows out of his own experience as a jurist and of his awareness that the principles of the American constitutional history indicate the priority of moral rights of the individuals.

To some extent, the approach adopted by Habermas is analogous. He claims that the rights of individuals should be guaranteed thanks to the deontological force of the arguments of principle, and that they could be surpassed by political purposes only when the latter operate in defence of further individual rights. Considering the freedom of expression, the right to health and social dignity as juridical optimizable goods, as Alexy does, means to subdue the principles to economic rationality criteria and to an instrumental analysis of costs and benefits, which treats individual rights as collective goods.[28] Such a postulate directly founds the *rights-based* theory, according to which the principles, together with the rights and the freedoms they express, have a deontological functioning, from an anti-utilitarian point of view, beyond ethical-political preferences recognised by laws.

Although this perspective exerted a remarkable influence in Europe too, in continental theories, where the attention to social rights prevails in particular, a different awareness is proposed. Considering principles as a mere anti-utilitarian bank would deprive liberties and rights of their inner value. Hart, way before the affirmation of the neo-constitutional model, had already warned against the danger of regarding rights as opposed to collective purposes.[29] Following these views, *goal-based* and "consequentialist" conceptions of rights have been proposed: they state that there is no logical impossibility to conciliate collective purposes and the priority of fundamental rights, which, on the contrary, can even be regarded as public goals and be included in the category of principles. The best-known consequentialist theory is utilitarianism, founded on the principle of utility, according to which an action is correct if it produces the highest level of general happiness. The variations of utilitarianism can differ in the way they specify the concept of good, but they have in common the fact that they define justice according to the criterion of satisfaction and realisation of what has been previously defined as good.[30]

Amartya Sen does not accept a merely consequentialist point of view. However, he claims that rights must be granted with a certain awareness of the situation they generate, and that the promotion of a principle cannot be considered

---

[27]Dworkin (1985).

[28]See also Nino (1991a, b).

[29]Hart (1979), p. 22.

[30]See Palombella (2006), p. 147 ff.

sufficient without an evaluation of its effects on other people's freedom. Reversing Dworkin's perspective, he tries to re-dimension the "unilateral" character of rights, assuming them not as mere limits to social action, but as collective purposes and, ultimately, as goals to promote:

> If rights are fundamental, then they also have a value, and if they have a value, intrinsically and not just instrumentally, then they should appear among the purposes.[31]

In fact, rights such as education, health and assistance have an inherent value, because they grant a worthy existence; but at the same time, their effects reverberate on the community which protects them, fighting pockets of decay and poverty, just like collective purposes. This is why the question of rights does not concern only judges, but the system as a whole; not only in the form of abstention—i.e. rights as a limitation of power—but also in a positive sense, as rights become normative goals and control tests of our institutions. According to Gianluigi Palombella:

> The point is ... on the one hand, to sustain that rights are (possibly) endowed with an inherent value and, on the other hand (overcoming a centuries-old doctrinal barrier), to consider them as part of the field of public purposes, ... without depriving them of their deontological status.

It is anyway necessary to keep in mind that "every freedom requires rules and public resources in order to be granted".[32]

7 The Principle of "Reasonableness"

The *principle of reasonableness* is an essential normative parameter, not only to solve disputes in *foro domestico*, but also to allow the "communication" and mutual recognition of the argumentative standards applied by national and supranational courts. The principle of reasonableness can be referred to as a *standard* or a *canon*, because of its procedural and normative character. However, its functioning is intrinsically connected to the so called "substantial" principles and inevitably places it among the general principles of law.[33] Francesco Viola affirms that:

> In a Constitutional State of Law, reasonableness has become an internal restriction to authoritative decisions. These decisions should not only be "legal", i.e. respect the boundaries of their competence and authorization, but they should also be "legitimate" and "non

---

[31]Sen (1985), p. 12.

[32]Palombella (2002), p. 155 (my translation).

[33]See "I principi di proporzionalità e ragionevolezza nella giurisprudenza costituzionale, anche in rapporto alla giurisprudenza delle Corti europee", in "Quaderno predisposto in occasione dell'incontro trilaterale tra Corte Costituzionale italiana, Tribunale Costituzionale spagnolo e Corte Costituzionale portoghese", pp. 32–34, available at:
http://www.cortecostituzionale.it/documenti/convegni_seminari/RI_QuadernoStudi_Roma2013.pdf.
See also Atienza (1990), pp. 148–161. On "reasonableness" in general as interpretation and application technique see Perelman (1979); Aarnio (1987); Corten (1999), pp. 613–625.

arbitrary" (to use Kelsen's words), since they are confronted with positively acknowledged fundamental rights, which precede authority and do not have their origin and foundation in it.[34]

But what is the axiological foundation of the principle of reasonableness? Joergh
Luther offers a convincing answer, suggesting that:

> Reasonableness could be considered as a component of the "human identity" (*Menschenbild*)
> itself, and as a foundation of human dignity, which is acknowledged and protected by all
> modern constitutions and especially European ones.[35]

In the theories of Alexy, the conflict between two principles and the consequent
limit set to the realization of an opposing principle are solved through proportionality. This concept is one of the possible faces of the principle of reasonableness: it
is necessary to balance the adequacy and necessity of a principle with regard to its
legal and factual circumstances, in order to decide correctly. Principles considered
as "optimization precepts" are strictly connected to the concept of "proportionality". Alexy asserts that: "the principle of proportionality derives naturally from the
character of principles, and can be deduced from them".[36]

Even the Italian Constitutional Court, in its judgment no. 220 of 1995, declared
that the principle of proportionality "is a direct expression of the general standard
of reasonableness".[37]

Reasonableness, moreover, requires another element on the part of law, which
is coherence, meaning by that "congruence": this prevents the arbitrariness of
some judicial decisions and limits decisions made case by case. In this specific
function, reasonableness guarantees that identical cases will be treated in an identical way, and different cases in a different way. According to MacCormick, decisions based on the judicial reasoning must "make sense": they must be congruent
and coherent with the contents of the judicial system considered, and they must
produce acceptable consequences (*consequentialist argument*).[38]

It is clear, on the one hand, that in Alexy the principle of reasonableness acts in
the reasonable balancing of constitutionally protected interests. On the other hand,
in MacCormick's theory of law this principle is realized through the standard of
coherence. In Dworkin, coherence plays an essential role as well, so much so that
it is connected to the concept of *integrity*: as he repeatedly pointed out, integrity is
the soul of law as we know it, much more than any concern of elegance.[39]
Integrity requires judges to consider law as the product of a coherent set of
principles of justice, equity and procedural due process: these must be equally

---

[34]Viola (2000), pp. 35–71 (my translation).

[35]Luther (2007) "Ragionevolezza e dignità umana", In *La ragionevolezza nella ricerca scientifica
ed il suo ruolo specifico nel sapere giuridico*, ed. Augusto Cerri, 185-214. Roma: Aracne p. 3,
(my translation).

[36]Alexy (1994), p. 297 (my translation).

[37]Italian Constitutional Court, judgment no. 220 of 1995, *Considerato in diritto*, para. 4.

[38]MacCormick (1978), p. 132.

[39]Dworkin (1986), pp. 263–274.

applied to new cases as they show, so that the position of every individual can really be considered just, equal and based on identical criteria. Coherence, being a specification of this political value, provides for the best possible judicial decision (both by the judge and by the legislator).

In the case law of national and supranational courts, the principle of reasonableness takes essentially three different forms: (i) equality, as in reasonable equality; (ii) proportionality; (iii) reasonable balancing of interests.

8 "Reasonableness" in Action

8.1 Reasonableness as "Non-discrimination" in the Case Law of the Italian Constitutional Court

The standard of reasonableness is an expression of the principle of equality: the two are connected in an indissoluble genetic bond, so that an unreasonable norm is considered illegal precisely because it causes unreasonable discriminations. This connection appeared, for example, in the judgment no. 249 of 2010 of the Italian Constitutional Court: the aggravating circumstance of "clandestinity" (illegal status) was declared unconstitutional as it violated both principles of equality/reasonableness and offense.[40] According to judges, with regard to the protection of fundamental rights, the legal status of a foreigner cannot be considered as a legal cause for a discriminatory and detrimental treatment. It is even more so in the field of criminal law, which is strictly connected to fundamental freedoms. The Italian Constitutional Court stated that the dignity of an individual does not depend on his legal status; therefore no discrimination is possible between the position of a citizen and that of a foreigner:

> The "irregular" position … becomes a "stain" which potentially allows a discriminatory criminal treatment of the subject, … following an absolute assumption which identifies a "type of author" who will always and in any case be subject to a more severe treatment.[41]

This statement is the heart of the judgment: a person cannot be incriminated for *who he is*, but only for *what he did* (assuming that he violated something which the judicial system considers worth protecting). The first stage of the argumentation concerns the principle of equality, which is regarded as "categorical", and therefore non-negotiable: it becomes a question of justice, meaning by that what is due to all, without exception.

The core argument of the judgment by the Constitutional Court is the superior strength of the fundamental rights: the aim of the judgment is to stress their inalienable character:

---

[40]Italian Constitutional Court, judgment no. 249 of 2010.

[41]Ibid., para. 9.

> Every restriction of the fundamental rights must take into account that the value of an inviolable right cannot be restricted or limited by any established power, the only exception being an inescapable need to serve constitutionally relevant, primary public needs … It is necessary to define the constitutional ranking of the considered interests, as well as to admit that restricting fundamental rights might be unavoidable: consequently, any restricting norm must pass the test of *reasonableness* ….[42]

As previous judgments repeatedly stated:

> Article 3 of the Constitution refers indeed to citizens, but it is meant to be extended to foreigners as well, if it becomes necessary to protect the *inviolable rights of the individual* guaranteed to foreigners in accordance with international dispositions (Articles 2 and 10, paragraph 2 of the Constitution).[43]

Following this principle, another judgment by the Constitutional Court asserted:

> Foreigners are endowed with all the fundamental rights which the Constitution recognizes as human rights …; this fact obliges the legislator to respect the standards or reasonableness, considered as an expression of the principle of equality, which influences the realization of the individual's status.[44]

In Dworkin's terms, Article 3 of the Constitution is a "trump card" which prevails when compared to any other political question, in accordance with the general principle of equal concern and respect. In the ratio of the considered norm, the Court does not find any other equally relevant principle able to surpass the principle of equality or be superior to it. As a consequence, the judge ("Hercules judge", in Dworkin's words)[45] must not underestimate or lessen its deontological value, which makes it constitutively due to all.

> It is impossible to consider as *reasonable* or sufficient the purpose to combat illegal immigration, as it cannot be pursued in an indirect way, by considering the behavior of illegal immigrants more serious than an equal behavior on the part of Italian or EU citizens.[46]

The safety of citizens, on the one hand, is not as relevant as the principle of equality, which is called into question and potentially threatened by the considered norm. On the other hand, it is not even congruent with the normative instruments set out by the Italian legislator: in this situation, therefore, balancing principles is not a correct way to proceed, because the superior principle of human dignity has an "authority" which must be respected and "taken seriously" by the judicial system. In this case, two similar legal situations (two examples of criminally relevant behavior) are considered as legally distinct, without any *rational* reason, and they generate two different legal consequences (different calculations of the

---

[42]Ibid., para. 4(1).

[43]Italian Constitutional Court, judgment no. 104 of 1969 (my translation).

[44]Italian Constitutional Court, judgment no. 148 of 2008 (my translation).

[45]Dworkin (1978), p. 130.

[46]Italian Constitutional Court, judgment no. 249 of 2010, para. 5.

punishment): this constitutes the premises for a discrimination which cannot be tolerated by the system, as it implies the sacrifice of the *integrity* (the constitutive trait of all modern judicial systems).

8.2 Reasonableness as Proportionality in the Case Law of the Court of Justice of the European Union

A formal principle may guarantee substantial principles and rights. However, as Giacinto Della Cananea wrote: "... the distinction between substantial and procedural aspects is conventional, questionable, uncertain. Decisions are often determined by procedures".[47] An example may be found in the argumentation of the European Court of Justice (ECJ) in the so-called *El Dridi* case, concerning the detention of non-EU citizens in illegal stay in case of their refusal to obey a return order.[48] In this judgment, the principle of reasonableness takes the form of a test of proportionality.[49]

The Court of Appeal of Trento made a reference for a preliminary ruling to the ECJ; it asked whether the detention of a non-EU citizen in illegal stay, and the possibility to inflict a sentence of imprisonment up to four years, violated the principles of adequacy, proportionality and reasonableness of the punishment, mentioned in Articles 15 and 16 of Directive 115/2008 ("Directive").[50] This Directive determines the common norms for EU States in case of the repatriation of non-EU citizens, in respect of their fundamental rights, viewed as general principles of the EU law and also of international law.[51] The Directive does include coercive measures as well, but only as *extrema ratio*, in order to expel subjects who put up resistance; such measures, though, must not exceed a *reasonable* use of the force, and they must be applied in full respect of the dignity and physical integrity of the subject (Article 8(4)). The action must be gradual, respecting the principle of proportionality between the means deployed and the objectives pursued.

The ECJ noted that, although the Treaty on the Functioning of the European Union (TFEU; Article 79(2)(c)) admits the criminal competence of Member States on matters of illegal stay, the national legislation must abide by EU law.

---

[47]Della Cananea (2009), p. 25 (my translation).

[48]Case C-61/11 PPU *El Dridi* [2011] ECR I-3015.

[49]See Klatt and Meister (2012).

[50]Directive 2008/115/EC of the European Parliament and of the Council on common standards and procedures in Member States for returning illegally staying third-country nationals, Strasbourg (16 December 2008).

[51]Unlike illegal immigrants, who do not have valid documents, citizens in illegal stay might have entered a "guest" Country legally and later have lost the legal requirements, mostly when their residence permits expire and are not renewed.

In particular, a national norm (even though concerning criminal law) may not jeopardize or hinder the political objectives pursued by a EU Directive:

> [N]either point (3)(b) of the first paragraph of Article 63 EC, a provision which was reproduced in Article 79(2)(c) TFEU, nor Directive 2008/115, adopted inter alia on the basis of that provision of the EC Treaty, precludes the Member States from having competence in criminal matters in the area of illegal immigration and illegal stays, they must adjust their legislation in that area in order to ensure *compliance* with European Union law.[52]

The main concern of the ECJ is the coherence between the norms of the national judicial systems and EU provisions. The defense of the principle of reasonableness (and of the consequent value of human dignity) is just an indirect effect of the Court's argumentation: the point is not a conflict between two rights or two principles. If such a conflict exists, it is anyway solved by the EU disposition, which suggests (or better, orders), precisely for this reason, to proceed with proportionality and reasonableness:

> The maximum period laid down in Article 15(5) and (6) of Directive 2008/115 serves the purpose of limiting the deprivation of third-country nationals' liberty in a situation of forced removal ... Directive 2008/115 is thus intended to take account both of the case law of the European Court of Human Rights, according to which the principle of *proportionality* requires that the detention of a person against whom a deportation or extradition procedure is under way should not continue for an *unreasonable* length of time, that is, its length should not exceed that required for the purpose pursued ....[53]

As a consequence, the EU judge focuses on the protection of the direct effect of the EU Directive, which might be neutralized by the policies adopted by single Member States:

> [Member States] may not apply rules, even criminal law rules, which are liable to jeopardise the achievement of the objectives pursued by a directive and, therefore, deprive it of its effectiveness.[54]

The deontological argument, here, is not stressed, in particular since it is already implied by the ratio of the Directive, which the Court is asking to comply with. The prevailing and most persuasive argument, in this case, is the teleological one: the Court aims at safeguarding the constitutive effect of the Directive, ultimately preserving the *telos* of the European system. Human dignity is indirectly protected by the reference to the provisions of the Directive, and in particular by the principle of proportionality which constitutes the soul of the Directive itself. The judgment just considered, anyway, proves that the result is the same, no matter the approach.

---

[52]*El Dridi* cit., para. 54.

[53]Ibid., pp. 3048–3049, para. 43 (emphasis added).

[54]Ibid., p. 3052, para. 55.

8.3 Reasonableness as Balancing of Interests in the European Court of Human Rights

The previous paragraphs clearly showed the structural difference between questions of principle and policy choices, that is to say the objectives of public policy which under certain circumstances can prevail in the argumentation of the courts. On the one hand, Dworkin considers principles (as well as rights) to have a deontological nature, as they are an effective protection against the intrusion of the policies and instrumental argumentations of single governments. On the other hand, "Alexy seems to match the deontological force of the principles with their teleological function",[55] which is independent from the values and the political choices of a certain society. This may be observed in the *Belgian Linguistics* case (1968), in which the European Court of Human Rights (ECtHR) discussed the possible discriminatory character of the language policy adopted in the Belgian school system.[56]

A group of francophone citizens living in a Flemish area complained that Belgium did not provide any French-language education in local schools.[57] The Court of Strasbourg therefore analyzed the national norms dividing the Country into four language areas: each region offered education in the prevailing regional language, following a criterion of "assimilation". It should be noted that the Convention for the Protection of Human Rights and Fundamental Freddoms (ECHR) does not explicitly mention language among the forms of discrimination it forbids; the protection of languages, however, can be deduced from Article 14, which prohibits any form of discrimination based on the race or ethnic origin.[58]

The European Court explained that not all language distinctions should be forbidden. Some of these, on the contrary, may be "tolerated", if they are supported by rational reasons and pursued with proportional means:

> [T]he existence of such a justification must be assessed in relation to the aim and effects of the measure under consideration, regard being had to the principles which normally prevail in democratic societies. A difference of treatment in the exercise of a right laid down in the Convention must not only pursue a legitimate aim: Article 14 is likewise violated when it is clearly established that there is no *reasonable* relationship of *proportionality* between the means employed and the aim sought to be realised.[59]

---

[55]Zanichelli (2004), p. 46 (my translation).

[56]*Case Relating to Certain Aspects of the Laws on the Use of Languages in Education in Belgium* (App. nos. 1474/62; 1677/62; 1691/62; 1769/63; 1994/63; 2126/64), ECtHR, judgment of 23 July 1968.

[57]On this case, and on the protection of minority languages, see Torretta (2014), pp. 695–734.

[58]It is well known, though, that the "prohibition of discrimination", which is related to the principle of formal equality, does not completely cover the concept of "protection of minorities". The latter is closer to the principle of substantial equality, which requires "positive discriminations" and "affirmative actions". See Guiglia (2012), p. 8. See also D'Aloia (2002), p. 434.

[59]*Case Relating to Certain Aspects of the Laws on the Use of Languages in Education in Belgium* cit., para. 10 (emphasis added).

Consequently, balancing operations should be conducted only if they are reasonable, in respect of the guidelines and standards previously adopted by the courts of civilized nations.[60] According to Alexy, reasonableness demands an evaluation of the appropriateness, necessity and proportionality (in the strict sense) of an action with regard to its legal and factual possibilities. Proportionality concerns the legal possibilities, while the tests of necessity and appropriateness are related to the factual possibilities:

> The national authorities remain free to choose the measures which they consider appropriate in those matters which are governed by the Convention. Review by the Court concerns only the conformity of these measures with the requirements of the Convention.[61]

The prevalence of a principle, a key concept in Alexy's analysis, does not cause the invalidity or disapplication of the opposing one, but rather the coexistence of the two, in order to make space for different interests and needs in the same judicial field. In the case considered, it is surely not the right to education which is violated, but rather just one of its aspects (the linguistic one). This sacrifice appears reasonable, if compared to the needs and the resources of the State budget. In effect, the right to education:

> [B]y its very nature calls for regulation by the State, regulation which may vary in time and place according to the *needs* and *resources* of the community and of individuals. It goes without saying that such regulation must never injure the substance of the right to education nor conflict with other rights enshrined in the Convention.[62]

For this reason, this cannot be regarded as one of the cases of discrimination presented and forbidden by Article 14 of the ECHR.

The principle of proportionality, in the European Court's argumentation, constitutes a standard by which to measure the interests of the parties, the rights involved (or allegedly violated) and the general public interest. In this case, the objective pursued is considered legitimate, being based on a historical bilingual division. The normative means deployed for this purpose are considered reasonable, being characterized by proportionality. Guaranteeing a multilingual teaching in all areas would have resulted in excessive costs, which ultimately would have proven unsustainable for the community. In this situation, therefore, the access to the special measures in favor of the linguistic diversity purely depends on questions of policy, that is to say on budget needs.

---

[60]Lauterpacht observed on this matter: "[W]hen, in international disputes, rules of general jurisprudence are referred to, what is meant is that not a rule of one particular system of private law is to be applied, but only such a rule ... as has gained recognition by the general body of civilized nations. This is so for the simple reason that international law has not, in the particular sphere, developed any rules on its own. In fact, there would be no need to have recourse to general jurisprudence, if there were international rule already at hand". Lauterpacht (1975), p. 206.

[61]*Case Relating to Certain Aspects of the Laws on the Use of Languages in Education in Belgium* cit., para. 10.

[62]Ibid., para. 5 (emphasis added).

9 Conclusion

The present analysis allows to conclude that the concept of reasonableness may be considered, at the same time, as a means and as an end.[63] It is undoubtedly an "argument" when it is referred to in the course of a decisional process, but it is also a goal to attain: it is both an instrument for the realization of values and a value itself; without it, the realization of the "other" values would be jeopardized. Reasonableness, therefore, acts as a limit to the arbitrariness of the interpreter as well as to that of the legislator.

In general, the arguments based on principles are always the most convincing in the argumentations of courts at every level, in spite of several oppositions: they seem the most adequate to refer to a global, *public* dimension including tribunals as well as very diverse judicial, legal and social systems.[64] For this reason, although principles were born within the boundaries of nations, their "ordinative" function is now expressed much better by the case law which *exceeds* nations. This is evident not only in the case law of international human rights tribunals, but also in the activity of single national courts and specialized tribunals working on the new "global administrative law".[65] This way of action provides for common approaches to common problems, and opens a way to the processes of integration and harmonization. As Chester Brown noted:

> The application of customary rules and general principles of law harmonizes issues of procedure and remedies precisely because they are not derived from any specific dispute settlement regime. Rather, they are derived from rules and principles that are usually susceptible of general application. In applying such rules and principles, international courts will invariably consider the practice of other international tribunals, which leads to the adoption of common approaches to these issues.[66]

In conclusion, principles are recognized as a direct expression of justice and of the "correctness" of law.[67] With regard to this point, the theories proposed by neo-constitutionalist philosophers and jurists proved particularly convincing and were increasingly confirmed. It is not essential to know whether the status of law has been altered, that is to say, whether law is now more open to connections with morality. The point is that now, thanks to general principles, law can show its epistemic connection to justice, which will help it to adapt to the deep changes now occurring in it.

---

[63]Ruggeri (2000), pp. 567–611.

[64]On the concept of "public" in law, that is to say on a conception of law viewed as the foundation of the public dimension beyond States, see Palombella (2012), Chap. V.

[65]Kingsbury et al. (2005); Cassese (2006), pp. 663–694; D'Alterio (2010). See also the works of the "GAL" Project, available at: http://www.iilj.org/GAL/.

[66]Brown (2008).

[67]With regard to this point, judge Cançado Trindade offered a particularly pertinent observation about the International Court of Justice. He asserted: "[T]he Hague Court, also known as the World Court, is not simply the International Court of Law, it is the International Court of *Justice*, and, as such, it cannot overlook *principles*" (emphasis in the original). See *Pulp Mills on the River Uruguay (Argentina v. Uruguay)* [2010] ICJ Rep. 14. The quote is taken from Fontanelli (2012), pp. 119–136.

References

Aarnio, Aulis. 1987. *The Rational as Reasonable: A Treatise on Legal Justification*, ed. Alan Mabe. Dordrecht: Kluwer.

Alexander, Larry, and Ken Kress. 1995. Against Legal Principles. In *Law and Interpretation*, ed. Andrei Marmor, 279-327. Oxford: Clarendon.

Alexy, Robert. 1992a. *Begriff und Geltung des Rechts*. Frankfurt, New York: Campus Verlag.

Alexy, Robert. 1992b. Rights, Legal Reasoning and Rational Discourse. *Ratio Juris* 5: 143-152.

Alexy, Robert. 1994. *Theorie der Grundrechte*. Frankfurt: Suhrkamp.

Alexy, Robert. 2000. On the Structure of Legal Principles. *Ratio Juris* 13: 294-304.

Alexy, Robert. 2005. La formula per la quantificazione del peso nel bilanciamento. *Ars Interpretandi*, 10: 92-123.

Alexy, Robert. 2007. Diritti fondamentali, bilanciamento e razionalità. *Ars interpretandi* 12: 131-144.

Alpa, Guido. 2006. *I principi generali*. Milano: Giuffrè.

Amirante, Carlo. 1981. La Costituzione come "sistema di valori" e la trasformazione dei diritti fondamentali nella giurisprudenza della Corte Costituzionale tedesca. *Politica del diritto* 1: 9-70.

Atienza, Manuel, and Juan Ruiz Manero. 1990. On the Reasonable in Law. *Ratio Juris* 3,1 *bis*: 148-161.

Atienza, Manuel, and Juan Ruiz Manero. 1996. *Las piezas del derecho. Teoría de los enunciados jurídicos*. Barcelona: Ariel.

Atienza, Manuel, and Juan Ruiz Manero. 1998. *A Theory of Legal Sentences*. Dordrecht: Kluwer Academic Publishers.

Baldassarre, Antonio. 1991. Costituzione e teoria dei valori. *Politica del diritto* 4: 639-658.

Barberis, Mauro. 2011. *Manuale di filosofia del diritto*. Torino: Giappichelli.

Betti, Emilio. 1971. *Interpretazione della legge e degli atti giuridici*. Milano: Giuffrè.

Bin, Roberto. 1992. *Diritti e argomenti. Il bilanciamento degli interessi nella giurisprudenza costituzionale*. Milano: Giuffrè.

Bongiovanni, Giorgio. 1999. La teoria "costituzionalistica" del diritto di Ronald Dworkin. In *Filosofi del diritto contemporanei*, ed. Gianfrancesco Zanetti, 247-285. Milano: Raffaello Cortina Editore.

Brown, Chester. 2008. The Cross-Fertilization of Principles Relating to Procedure and Remedies in the Jurisprudence of International Courts and Tribunals. *Loyola of Los Angeles International and Comparative Law Review* 30: 219-246.

Celano, Bruno. 2002. "Defeasibility" e bilanciamento. Sulla possibilità di revisioni stabili. *Ragion Pratica* 18: 223-239.

Cassese, Sabino. 2006. Administrative Law without the State? The Challenge of Global Regulation. *New York University Journal of International Law and Politics* 37/4: 663-694.

Cheng, Bin. 1953. *General Principles of Law as Applied by International Courts and Tribunals*. London: Stevens & Sons.

Corten, Olivier. 1999. The Notion of "Reasonable" in International Law: Legal Discourse, Reason and Contradictions. *The International and Comparative Law Quarterly*. 48/3: 613-625.

D'Aloia, Antonio. 2002. *Eguaglianza sostanziale e diritto diseguale. Contributo allo studio delle azioni positive nella prospettiva costituzionale*. Padova: Cedam.

D'Alterio, Elisa. 2010. *La funzione di regolazione delle Corti nello spazio giuridico globale*. Milano: Giuffrè.

Dworkin, Ronald M. 1978. *Taking Rights Seriously*. Cambridge: Harvard University Press.

Dworkin, Ronald M. 1985. *A Matter of Principle*. Oxford: Oxford University Press.

Dworkin, Ronald M. 1986. *Law's Empire*. Cambridge: Belknap Press.

Dworkin, Ronald M. 1996. *Freedom of Law. The Moral Reading of the America Constitution*, Oxford: Oxford University Press.

Dworkin, Ronald M. 2011. *Justice for Hedgehogs*. Cambridge: Harvard University Press.

Del Vecchio, Giorgio. 1958 [1921]. *Sui principi generali del diritto*. Milano: Giuffrè.

Della Cananea, Giacinto. 2009. *Al di là dei confini statuali. Principi generali del diritto pubblico globale*. Bologna: Il Mulino.

Ferrajoli, Luigi. 2013. *La democrazia attraverso i diritti*. Roma, Bari: Laterza.

Fontanelli, Filippo. 2012. The Invocation of the Exception of Non-Performance: A Case-Study on the Role and Application of General Principles of International Law of Contractual Origin. *Cambridge Journal of International and Comparative Law* 1: 119–136.

Gordley, James, and Arthur Taylor von Meheren. 2006. *An Introduction to Comparative Study of Private Law. Readings, Cases, Materials*. Cambridge: Cambridge University Press.

Guastini, Renato. 2004. *L'interpretazione dei documenti normativi*. Milano: Giuffrè.

Guastini, Renato. 2010. *Le fonti del diritto. Fondamenti teorici*. Milano: Giuffrè.

Guiglia, Giovanni. 2012. Non discriminazione ed uguaglianza: unite nella diversità. http://www.gruppodipisa.it/wp-content/uploads/2012/05/guiglia.pdf.

Habermas, Jürgen. 1996. *Between Facts and Norms. Contributions to a Discourse Theory of Law and Democracy*. Trans. William Rehg. Cambridge: MIT Press.

Habermas, Jürgen (ed. Leonardo Ceppa). 2001 [1992]. *Diritto, morale, politica*. Torino: Einaudi.

Hart, L. A. Herbert. 1979. Tra utilità e diritti. *Sociologia del diritto* 6/1-2: 1-22.

Hart, L. A. Herbert (eds. Penelope A. Bulloch and Joseph Raz). 1994 [1961]. *The Concept of Law. With a Postscript*. Oxford: Clarendon.

Kingsbury, Benedict, Nico Krisch, and Richard B. Stewart. 2005. The Emergence of Global Administrative Law. *Law and Contemporary Problems* 68: 15-62.

Klatt, Matthias, and Moritz Meister. 2012. *The Constitutional Structure of Proportionality*. Oxford: Oxford University Press.

La Torre, Massimo. 2010. Dopo Hart: il dibattito giusfilosofico contemporaneo. In *Prospettive di filosofia del diritto del nostro tempo*, Torino: Giappichelli.

Lauterpacht, Hersch. 1975. *International Law: Being the Collected Papers of Hersch Lauterpacht*. Cambridge: Cambridge University Press.

Luther, Joerg. 2007. Ragionevolezza e dignità umana. In *La ragionevolezza nella ricerca scientifica ed il suo ruolo specifico nel sapere giuridico*, ed. Augusto Cerri, 185-214. Roma: Aracne.

Mazzarese, Tecla (ed.). 2002. *Neocostituzionalismo e tutela (sovra)nazionale dei diritti fondamentali*. Torino: Giappichelli.

MacCormick, Neil. 1978. *Legal Reasoning and Legal Theory*. Oxford: Oxford University Press.

Modugno, Franco. 1995. Chiosa a chiusa. Un modello di bilanciamento di valori. *Giurisprudenza italiana* 1: 643-648.

Nino, Carlos. 1991a. *The Ethics of Human Rights*. Oxford: Clarendon.

Nino, Carlos. 1991b. The Epistemological Moral Relevance of Democracy. *Ratio Juris* 4/1: 36-51.

Nino, Carlos. 1994. *Derecho, moral y política. Una revisión de la teoría general del derecho*. Barcelona: Ariel.

Omaggio, Vincenzo. 2003. *Teorie dell'interpretazione*. Napoli: Editoriale Scientifica.

Palombella, Gianluigi. 2002. *L'autorità dei diritti*. Roma, Bari: Laterza.

Palombella, Gianluigi. 2006. *Dopo la certezza. Il diritto in equilibrio tra giustizia e democrazia*. Bari: Dedalo.

Palombella, Gianluigi. 2012. *È possibile una legalità globale? Il Rule of Law e la governance del mondo*. Bologna: Il Mulino.

Pattaro, Enrico. 1987. Alle origini della nozione "principi generali del diritto". In *Soggetto e principi generali del diritto*, ed. Maurizio Basciu, 25-66. Milano: Giuffrè.

Perelman, Chaim. 1979. The Rational and Reasonable. In *The New Rhetoric and the Humanistics: Essays on Rhetoric and its Application,* ed. Chaim Perelman, 117-123. Dordrecht: Reidel Publishing Company.

Pino, Giorgio. 2007. Conflitto e bilanciamento tra diritti fondamentali. Una mappa dei problemi. *Ragion Pratica* 28: 219-273.

Pino, Giorgio. 2009. Principi e argomentazione giuridica. *Ars interpretandi* 14: 131-160.
Pizzorusso, Alessandro. 2011. *Delle fonti del diritto: art. 1-9*. Bologna: Zanichelli.
Pozzolo, Susanna. 2001. *Neocostituzionalismo e positivismo giuridico*. Torino: Giappichelli.
Rawls, John. 1971. *A Theory of Justice*. Cambridge: Harvard University Press.
Ruggeri, Antonio. 2000. Ragionevolezza e valori, attraverso il prisma della giustizia costituzionale. *Diritto e società* 4: 567-611.
Sen, Amartya. 1985. Rights as Goals. In *Equality and Discrimination: Essays in Freedom and Justice,* eds. Stephen Guest and Alan Milne, 11-25. Stuttgart: Franz Steiner.
Shiner, A. Roger. 2005. Legal Institutions and Sources of Law. In *A Treatise of Legal Philosophy and General Jurisprudence*, eds. Enrico Pattaro, Giovanni Sartor, Hubert Rottleuthner and Aleksander Peczenik. vol. III. Dordrecht, Berlin, Heidelberg, New York: Springer.
Torretta, Paola. 2014. I diritti delle minoranze linguistiche e il "primato" della cittadinanza europea. *Diritto pubblico comparato ed europeo* 2: 695-734.
Viola, Francesco. 2000. Costituzione e ragione pubblica: il principio di ragionevolezza tra diritto e politica. *Persona y Derecho* 46/1: 35-71.
Waldron, Jeremy. 1993. *Liberal Rights. Collected papers 1981-1991*. Cambridge: Cambridge University Press.
Zagrebelsky, Gustavo. 2002. Diritto per: valori, principi, o regole? A proposito della dottrina dei principi di Ronald Dworkin. *Quaderni fiorentini per la storia del pensiero giuridico moderno* 31: 865-897.
Zanichelli, Maria. 2004. *Il discorso sui diritti. Un atlante teorico*. Padova: Cedam.

Part II
General Principles and the Judiciary:
Legal Systems and Domestic Frameworks

Judicial Control of Juries and Just Results in the Common Law System: A Historical Perspective

Frederic N. Smalkin

Abstract The ancient common law system of England is still prevalent in many nations associated with—or previously associated with—the United Kingdom, not simply in England and Wales. Findings of fact at common law were the sole prerogative of the jury for many centuries. This chapter addresses restraints upon jurors' conduct and jury verdicts that evolved over many centuries, imposed by an increasingly active judiciary in the interest of preventing injustices stemming from jury verdicts that were unsupported by competent evidence, biased, or otherwise should not be allowed to stand in the interests of justice.

1 Introduction

It is well understood among those familiar with international law that the legal systems of England and Wales (and much of The Commonwealth) differ fundamentally from those of continental Europe. The former is generally referred to as the common law system, while the latter is generally labelled the civil law system. It is equally well understood that fundamental de jure dispute-resolution mechanisms vary significantly between the two, particularly in the common law's dependence—historically in English law, and to this day in United States law—upon a lay jury as finder of fact. What is less well understood is the evolution of the common law judges' exercise of control over the jury trial in order to achieve what is, at least in the eyes of judges, the just resolution of a case. I believe a fuller

F.N. Smalkin (✉)
LLM (Lond), MCIArb, Chief United States District Judge, District of Maryland (Ret.), Juristin-Residence, University of Baltimore School of Law, Baltimore, USA
e-mail: fsmalkin@ubalt.edu

© Springer International Publishing Switzerland 2015   105
L. Pineschi (ed.), *General Principles of Law - The Role of the Judiciary*,
Ius Gentium: Comparative Perspectives on Law and Justice 46,
DOI 10.1007/978-3-319-19180-5_6

understanding of the legal history of England in this regard will lead to an appreciation of how the general legal principle of assuring a just result has been implemented by common law judges despite the strictures of the system of law in which they have labored.

2 Overview

Legal education in the United States is focused—and quite understandably so—upon transmitting to the students both the substantive and the procedural aspects of the common law system. Much of the first year curriculum focuses upon the "black-letter" building blocks of the system. Among those are courses with clear common law roots, exemplified by the causes of action *ex delicto* and *ex contractu* which have evolved over many centuries. Anyone who has taught such courses for a long time has been asked, "Professor, what has the concept we are studying got to do with justice?" Some law professors answer sardonically, something like this: "Ours is a system of laws, not of justice".

As a general, overarching principle of law, of course, the achievement of justice as the end result of the legal process is a paramount goal. We all have an ingrained sense that a system of laws without justice is bereft of moral worth. Indeed, the fundaments of justice, it is written, issued forth directly from God to Moses:

> And the Lord spake unto Moses, saying…Ye shall do no unrighteousness in judgment; thou shalt not respect the person of the poor nor honour the person of the mighty; *but* in righteousness shalt thou judge thy neighbor.[1]

Judges are chosen and trained to achieve just results in their adjudications. In a system in which judges are not only the interpreters of law, but are also the ultimate resolvers of a case as to both facts and law, their obligation to achieve justice is fulfilled without extra-judicial influence. That is, their judgments are based solely upon their own resolutions of the legal and factual issues at play in the case. In the common law system as it stood for many centuries in England, though, the finding of fact was the sole province of a jury of local citizens, untrained in the law, not of judges. Indeed, English High Court judges lacked the power to make findings of fact in civil cases until the Common Law Procedure Act 1854; in consequence, all issues of disputed fact were necessarily decided by a lay jury from early medieval times to the middle of the nineteenth century.

When it comes to issues of fact, the common law judge's role today (where the jury trial survives as an "instructed jury") is primarily that of a gatekeeper, filtering what the jury hears and sees according to rules of evidence which allow or disallow specific sorts of evidence (e.g., hearsay) or which allow or disallow specific modes of evidence presentation (e.g., leading questions). Black-letter, focused

---

[1] King James Version (Cambridge), Lev. 19: 1, 15.

gatekeeping rules such as these are not needed in systems of law in which there is no fact-finding jury. The common law judge in all jurisdictions instructs the jury on the principles of law governing the case. Those instructions are said to be binding on the jury, but the fact that most juries return a general verdict for one party or the other, without giving reasons, makes it difficult to tell if they have, in fact, been followed. In common law jurisdictions other than the United States, the judge also customarily "sums up" the evidence to the jury before submitting the case for deliberation, reviewing and giving commentary on the evidence the jury has heard.[2]

The instructed jury of today evolved during the early modern period (roughly, the Age of Colonialism) from the common law's early, self-informing jury. The earlier jury at common law was composed of men from the vicinity of the trial, who were summoned to give witness to the royal justices as to the facts of the case stated in the plaintiff's pleadings, in civil disputes.[3] They knew, it is safe to say, the parties and the witnesses, as well as common repute as to their characters and credibility. They usually had most likely heard rumors about the underlying dispute. It is also generally thought that they knew a good bit of basic law. All Englishmen likely to be called upon for jury service were presumed to know the common law; its ubiquity is one reason why it is so named. In essence, in the days when England was very rural, the juries often were more like witnesses than like judges of the facts based on evidence. That is, they gave voice to local opinion, and the verdicts they returned were essentially adopted by the royal justices without question. Over time, though, common law judges developed tools that enabled them to see to it that a jury's verdict that judges considered unjust would not stand.

Because the history of English law is one of evolution, by and large, rather than of top-down statutory or royal direction (of course, with exceptions), it is not easy to pinpoint a time at which the polar shift in the jury system from self-instructed to instructed took place. It was a process contributed to by many factors, including the expansion of jury venires within the counties beyond the immediate locality where the dispute arose and population shifts from rural areas to manufacturing centers as the Industrial Revolution progressed, all resulting in venires unlikely to bring any foreknowledge with them to the trial. Although precise milestones in this transformative process are difficult to discern,[4] one thing that is clear is that, as the jury's role shifted over time, so did that of the judge, who took a more active role in management of the trial. Arguments of counsel were cabined by the judge; rules of evidence were applied by the judge; and in the "summing up", the jury were instructed by the judge on the law and heard his comments on the facts.

---

[2]To be sure, some summings-up may be more balanced than others, and fear of reversal for giving a slanted summing-up keeps most United States federal judges from commenting upon the evidence, even though they have the power to do so.

[3]In criminal cases, the jury were accusers (akin to the modern grand jury), with a duty to make presentment of those believed to have committed serious crimes to the royal justices. Trial by ordeal, or, later, by jury, followed and resulted in the ultimate judgment against those presented.

[4]Mitnick (1988).

The judges eventually gave themselves broad powers to nullify the result of an unjust jury verdict. It was by the exercise of their powers of jury control that the English common law judges carried out their duty to see to it that a just result was the ultimate outcome of a trial, though the journey down the road from self-instructing to instructed jury under judicial control was a long one. It might well be said that the history of the common law is one in which justice in result came to depend largely upon the judge-jury dynamic.

3 Judge and Jury in the Evolution of the Common Law

There is no easy way to shed scholarly light upon the administration of law in England before the Norman Conquest (A.D. 1066). It is generally thought that the common law, and especially the institution of judgment by one's neighbors, had its roots in Anglo-Saxon tribal custom. In fact, one of the foremost legal history texts utilized in the United States makes reference to *der Sachsenspiegel*[5] to illustrate early legal proceedings in England. The record expands after the Conquest, and a fair amount is recorded about legal developments from the thirteenth century forward.

Despite the fact that many minor disputes were resolved by lords of manors, the Crown was from early times looked to as a fount of justice, much as in Roman times the Emperor had been. The maintenance of a just and fair body of law is so important a royal duty that a substantial part of the English Coronation Oath has been traditionally devoted to it. We find this account of the Coronation Oath of Edward II in 1308[6]:

> [Bishop] Sire, will you grant and keep and by your oath confirm to the people of England the laws and customs given to them by the previous just and god-fearing kings, your ancestors, and especially the laws, customs, and liberties granted to the clergy and people by the glorious king, the sainted Edward, your predecessor?
> [Edward II] I grant and promise them.
> [B] Sire, will you in all your judgments, so far as in you lies, preserve to God and Holy Church, and to the people and clergy, entire peace and concord before God?
> [E] I will preserve them.
> [B] Sire, will you, so far as in you lies, cause justice to be rendered rightly,
> impartially, and wisely, in compassion and in truth?
> [E] I will do so.
> [B] Sire, do you grant to be held and observed the just laws and customs that the commu-
> nity of your realm shall determine, and will you, so far as in you lies,
> defend and strengthen them to the honour of God?
> [E] I grant and promise them.

---

[5]The Saxon Mirror (A Saxon chronicle). Langbein et al. (2009).

[6]See http://historyofengland.typepad.com/documents_in_english_hist/2013/02/the-coronation-oath-of-edward-ii-1308.html.

During the reign of Henry II (1154-89), the administration of justice came under increasing royal control, and the royal justices began to travel regularly on circuit, away from the *curia regis*, to major county towns to hold sessions of court, in what came to be the eyre and assize sessions. All royal itinerant justices had sworn an oath, according to Bracton, focused upon the doing of justice:

> The oath shall be this. Each will swear, one after the other, that in the counties into which they are to travel they will do right justice to the best of their ability to rich and poor alike [straight from Leviticus 19], and that they will observe the assise [sic] according to the articles set out ... and that they will execute all that is right and just in matters pertaining to the crown of the lord king. And after his oath let each of them be instructed to promote, to the best of his ability, the advantage of the lord king.

The prevailing theme of these officers' oaths was to do what is both right (presumably, being faithful to the common law) and just.[7] Although jurors also swore an oath—to return a true verdict—they did so as laymen, not as officers of the realm. The role of the jury in criminal trials held before royal justices on circuit after the Assize of Clarendon 1166 was essentially to act as an accusatory body, with ultimate resolution of the case achieved through ordeal. When the ordeal fell into disuse after the Fourth Lateran Council in 1215,[8] the English jury which had presented the accused replaced the ordeal as the ultimate finder of disputed fact, and its verdict dictated the result of the trial and the court's judgment thereon.[9] Although the historical record is sparse on the development of a separate trial jury in civil and criminal cases, by statute in the mid-fourteenth century presenting jurors were effectively precluded from acting as trial jurors, and separate juries were drawn from the local venire for presentment and trial[10] (this development was to lay one of the foundations for the later demise of the self-instructing jury, as discussed infra).

Tracing the legal history of England in the medieval period poses significant problems, albeit not so great as those involved in pre-Conquest legal historical inquiry.

---

[7]De Bracton, Henry (attrib.). Bracton: *De Legibus Et Consuetudinibus Angliæ*. Bracton Online English, Harvard Law School Library. http://bracton.law.harvard.edu/Unframed/English/v2/309.htm.

[8]Baker (2002), p. 5.

[9]Trial by combat continued in certain criminal cases (appeal of felony) in theory until 1819 (though it had become extinct in the seventeenth century). Jury trial in presented cases was not possible unless the defendant consented "to be tried by God and my Country (i.e., my fellow Englishmen)". Those who did not consent freely, however, were subjected to being pressed by heavy stones laid upon a plank on top of them while stretched out on their backs, until they consented or suffocated. This was the practice of *Peine forte et dure* (which most commentators think resulted from an unfortunate, but lost in the mists of time, miscommunication of the law French *Prison forte et dure*). Many accused felons "consented", but those with substantial property holdings often did not, for death by pressing did not work forfeiture of estate or corruption of the blood, as a jury's felony conviction would have done, thus preserving family assets for the unfortunate accused's family. See Langbein et al. (2009), pp. 61–62.

[10]Langbein et al. (2009), p. 72.

Although from the thirteenth century onwards, there exist many writs, judgment rolls, and the like, full reports of trials are sparse. There are several reasons for this.

Trials in civil matters at common law were instituted by writs. The judicial writ was a letter patent, obtained by the plaintiff from the Clerks of Chancery, in the form of a command of the King. It evolved from a simple restorative command to a wrongdoer that he right his wrong into a judicial instrument essentially directing trial of the dispute. Because the High Courts (King's Bench and Common Pleas) sat in the Palace of Westminster and because in the days of the self-instructing jury a venire of locals was needed to render a sound verdict, there evolved a clever process (*nisi prius*) to empanel a jury venire from the locality and to have that venire present at trial before the royal justices on their assize circuits throughout the kingdom. The writ directed trial on a date certain before the court at its seat at Westminster, "unless before" (*nisi prius*) the stated date, an assize were held before which the issue could be locally tried. The stated trial date at Westminster was always carefully scheduled for a date after the next scheduled assize in the locality.[11] Land ownership disputes—which were very serious matters indeed in a feudal, agrarian society—were especially suitable for adjudication by a local jury, likely to be very familiar from generation to generation with what were regarded as settled land boundaries and rights of ownership in their vicinage.

Writs also essentially acted as a grant of adjudicative and jurisdictional powers to the royal justices to try the case stated in the writ, and then to have judgment entered according to the jury's verdict. These judgments were recorded on judgment rolls at Westminster, which were preserved as permanent records. Because the writ and the judgment were the bookends of a case at common law, they were carefully recorded, along with other very formulaic pleadings which framed the legal basis for the trial and the narrowed the factual issue(s) for the jury's determination. But what of the trial itself? Relatively few complete full reports of early trials can be found. One reason for this is that the trial was likely to have been conducted in three languages: Latin was the language of the writs, pleadings and judgments; Law French (a *patois* of French, English, and Latin) was spoken amongst the lawyers and justices; and English was spoken by the witnesses and jurors. It was unlikely that, in the county towns in which assizes were held, many persons fluent enough in all three languages could be found or were interested in making any attempt at a *verbatim* record.

Lawyers and judges of the day, because pleadings and colloquies about formulaic pleadings were so foundational to the common law's perspective on achieving justice, were interested in recording (and studying as precedent) only those aspects of the case. What the jury did—evaluating the evidence and making findings of

---

[11]One of the things that makes the study of English legal history so interesting is the patchwork of clever mechanisms invented over the years to make a creaky system work efficiently, in spite of itself. Examples include, in addition to the *nisi prius* writ, the invention of "trespass on the case" (which essentially enabled the evolution of tort law), and the action of assumpsit and the Bill of Middlesex (both of which were devised to divert cases from Common Pleas to King's Bench). In many cases, there was created a "legal fiction", which is a euphemistic common-law term for a convenient falsehood that no one ever challenges.

fact—was its business. Many volumes of early reports can be found, setting forth mainly colloquies on the law between the judge and counsel. Yet, the heart of the trial itself—the testimony and documents produced by the parties before the jury—is usually missing in these reports; the evidence was not considered part of the record of the proceedings.[12] Thus, it can be difficult to tell to what extent broader principles of justice played a role in the conduct of the trial itself early on.

Nonetheless, a few interesting early case reports shedding light upon the roles of the royal justice and the jury in seeing to it that justice was done can be found. The following is the report of a latter-thirteenth century trial at gaol (jail) delivery of a man indicted for murder:

> [Justice] Sheriff, why has this man been taken?
> [Sheriff] Sir, for the death of a man who he is supposed to have killed in self defence.
> [Justice] What is your name?
> [Accused] Sir, Thomas de N.
> [J] Thomas, what was the name of the man whom you killed in premeditated attack, feloniously as a felon?
> [A] Sir, if you please, I have never been a felon and never did mischief to living man, in premeditated attack; and so I have done nothing wrong against the man whose name you ask: who, feloniously and as a felon and in premeditated attack tried to kill me on such a day, at such an hour, in such a year in my own house in such a township, for no fault on my part and solely on account of his malice.
> [J] Tell us the circumstances.
> [A] Sir, I was unwilling to hire to him a horse for the purpose of riding about his business...And because I refused him the loan of my horse he ran at me in my own house with a Welsh knife...I did not at first return his blows; but when I realized that he was set on killing me I started to defend myself: that is to say I wounded him in the right arm with a little pointed knife which I carried, making no further onslaught and acting in this way only to save my own life.
> [J] Did he die of such wound?
> [A] In truth sir, I do not know.
> [J] Thomas, you have greatly embroidered your tale and coloured your defence for you are telling us only what you think will be to your advantage, and suppressing whatever you think may damage you, and I do not believe you have told the whole truth.
> [A] Sir, I have told the whole truth, and related the affair from the beginning to the end in every detail, and of this I trust God and the country [i.e., the jury] both for good and evil.
> [J] And so let the inquest be held.
> [Reporter] And the jury said the same as Thomas had related. So the justice then says:
> [J] Thomas, these good people testify by their oaths to the truth of what you have said. So our judgment is that what you did to him, you did in self defence. But we cannot release you from this prison without the king's special grace. However we will send a report of your case to the king's court and ensure that you receive his special grace.
> [A] Sir, I thank you.[13]

The trial reported above is a crystalline example of the indeposable role of the jury as trier of fact, and that of the justice as an administrator, charged not with the determination of fact but of conducting the trial and recording the judgment.

---

[12]Baker (2002), pp. 84–85.

[13]Klerman, Daniel, *Was the jury ever self informing,* quoted in Mulholland and Pullan (2003), pp. 66–67.

Indeed, had the justice been trier of fact, Thomas would have been executed forthwith, as is quite clear from the pre-verdict colloquy between the two. But the justice, apparently without equivocation and despite his own assessment of the accused's credibility, immediately and fully embraced the verdict of the jury of assembled locals, who knew Thomas and likely knew the deceased, as well. The voice of the jury was the voice of justice, and the royal justice's immediate and unquestioning acceptance of it, including promising to see to the administrative details of the accused's release from custody, was his obedience to that voice. The jury, having heard the evidence (what evidence there was, beyond the accused's colloquy with the justice, is unreported), had done justice, prevailing over the personal predilection of the royal judge. This was the early common law at work.

4 Controlling the Jury

As time went by, English judges were faced with solving three problems inherent in the common law's reliance upon the combination of procedural formalism and a jury's verdict for a just result. The first was control over the jury during the trial; the second was jury indecision; and the third was a jury decision that the judge thought "false". Obviously, to accept and enter judgment upon a false verdict would not do justice. Approaches to resolving these questions evolved over the long history of the common law.

Control over the trial jury before its deliberations, as illustrated by the case of Thomas reported above, was not part of the early common law judge's role; the jury's determination of the facts was entirely up to them and clearly binding upon him. By the seventeenth century, though, common law judges had become much more energetic in exerting their influence upon juries during trial, as will be discussed infra.

Jury indecision had been from early times a vexation for common law judges. The following passage describes not only the evolution of judicial control over the deliberative process to bring about a unanimous verdict, but also sheds light upon the transition of the jury from a group of self-informing quasi-witnesses subject to few constraints, to a deliberative body charged with resolving disputes based upon evidence at trial, and insulated to at least some extent from outside influence:

> By the late fourteenth century, however, it was obvious that the collective, judicial character of the jury was going to prevail. The duty of the jury was not merely to answer questions, but to try sworn evidence in court. Although jurors were still allowed, even expected, to inform themselves before coming to court, by the 1380 it was clearly an irregularity to communicate with them once they were sworn other than by giving evidence in open court. If the jurors were spoken to, or treated to food or drink, by either party, their verdict could be quashed and a new trial ordered. The sequestration of the jury became a regular practice ... and it was enforced with such rigidity that its members became as prisoners to the court. After their charge [by the judge at the end of the trial], the jurors were confined "without meat, drink, fire or candle", or conversation with others, until they were agreed; and if they could not agree they were supposed to be carried round the circuit [on Assizes] in a cart until they did. The merest suspicion of misbehaviour was

punishable, and we read of Tudor jurors being fined for eating sweets. The constraints of discomfort were primarily intended to encourage unanimity....[14]

Jury indecision continues to be a problem to this day where juries still are utilized, but the harsh methods of encouraging a verdict discussed in the passage above have been replaced with gentler exhortations and, in cases of hopeless deadlock, the declaration of a mistrial, with a retrial to follow in most cases.

5 Judicial Influence upon the Jury's Verdict

Over the long history of the common law, English judges gradually developed methods for both directly and indirectly influencing the outcome of a jury trial so as to achieve a final result of the dispute that, at least to judicial sensibilities, was just. One of these methods was by direct judicial review of the verdict after trial, and another involved the instructions on law and commentary on evidence given by the judge to the jury to aid it in achieving a just result in its deliberations.

Before it was abolished, the ordeal, which followed a jury's presentment, was obviously unreviewable by any earthly power, as it represented the judgment of God.[15] Over a long period of time, judicial review of procedural and legal rulings of judges for error, at first by review by the assembled judges of the court sitting in banc, and, much later, by appellate judicial review, became entrenched.[16] But what of a jury verdict that appeared to the trial judge to be manifestly wrong? Absent accusing the trial jury of blatant misconduct, there was little that could be done early on to rectify an apparent injustice:

> The introduction of the jury [after the abolition of ordeals] nevertheless raised problems, and procedures were provided for dealing with them. Corruption and misconduct by jurors were undeniable obstacles to justice. An action called "attaint" could be brought against jurors for giving a false verdict, and if it was successful the verdict would be quashed. But attaint did not permit judicial review of decisions of fact by way of appeal, to determine their substantial correctness, nor of rulings and directions in law by the trail judge. The only question was whether jurors had perjured themselves, and the only evidence which could be considered in the attaint was that laid before the trial jury. Though not abolished until 1825, the procedure was rarely used, even in medieval times, and by Tudor times was becoming obsolete, because the punishment of perjured trial jurors was so severe that attaint juries would seldom find against them.[17]

Short of an attaint, which, as noted above, carried with it the idea that the jury had criminally misbehaved, and the very rare allied practice of fining a jury for misbehavior, there seems to have been no early mechanism by which a judge could "correct" the verdict of a jury which, in the judge's view, was flatly incorrect or

---

[14]Baker (2002), pp. 75–76.

[15]Ibid., p. 135.

[16]Ibid., p. 136.

[17]Ibid.

unjust. There arose, however, over time, processes by which a judgment could be challenged for legal error after it was rendered. Interestingly, the challenges were not addressed solely to or by the trial judge. The process involved convening all the judges of the court, sitting "in banc" at Westminster Palace and scrutinizing the record after trial. The process is well-described below:

> The procedure whereby questions could be raised after the trial, by motions "in banc" to the court at Westminster, existed in medieval times, but was limited to badly joined issues (jeofails) [defects in formal pleadings] or formal defects of the trial, such as misconduct by jurors. From the late fifteenth century, however, it was extended to enable substantive questions of law [but not of fact] to be argued after verdict. There were three basic species of motion in banc: the motion in arrest of judgment, the motion for judgment *non obstante veredicto*, and the motion for a new trial.[18]

The motion in arrest of judgment was generally a vehicle for challenging a mistake in law, but it came also in time to embrace limited review of factual determinations by a jury. This practice applied to cases in which the trial judge had required the jury to return a "special verdict", specifying the factual findings upon which it had based its general verdict:

> It later became common for the judge to put specific questions to the jury in order to ascertain the factual basis of their verdict; the answers were not part of the verdict, which was still recorded in general terms, but could be used in banc.[19]

This enabled the movant who had lost the verdict at trial to challenge its sufficiency in law based upon the facts specially found by the jury. If those facts did not support the verdict, it could be set aside in banc. Although the motion to arrest judgment has disappeared and appeals to a higher court have replaced the in banc process, individual common law trial judges still exercise the discretion in civil cases to have juries specifically state their findings of disputed facts. If the stated findings do not support the verdict, the judge can take appropriate curative measures to conform the general verdict to the specially found facts.

The motion for judgment *non obstante veredicto* ("judgment n.o.v.") is a second category of post-trial motions in banc, and it, too, is still in use today in common law jurisdictions (but today it is granted in the discretion of the trial judge alone). It had a rather narrow scope early on. It could only be made by a plaintiff against a defendant who had admitted that the plaintiff's case as pleaded had merit, but who had prevailed on an affirmative defense that was not good as a matter of law. If the error in the asserted defense was a mere matter of pleading, the defendant could correct the pleading and there would be a retrial.[20] Today, the judgment *n.o.v.* can be granted by the trial judge if the evidence presented by the prevailing party at trial is insufficient as a matter of law to support the elements of proof required to sustain the verdict. The grant of the motion acts as a final, appealable judgment, and there would be no new trial, unless ordered as the result of an appeal.

---

[18]Ibid., pp. 82–83.

[19]Ibid., p. 84.

[20]Ibid.

6 The Motion for New Trial

The third in the triad of in banc motions was the motion for a new trial. It was by far the most potent remedy for judicial review of a jury's unjust verdict.[21] Its evolution is described in the following text:

> The motion for a new trial was the last and in the end the most extensive of the methods of raising questions of law after verdict. Its medieval purpose of upsetting verdicts by reason of procedural defects on the face of the record, such as recorded misconduct by jurors, remained its principal purpose until the later seventeenth century. And it was limited by the judges' insistence could not be set aside unless the invalidity of the trial appeared on the record. But from the 1640s onwards – perhaps as a result of the abolition of the Star Chamber and the consequent loss of punitive controls over juries – the courts edged back from this principle by allowing motions in matters off the record [of pleadings], either on the trial judge's certificate the he considered the verdict contrary to his direction on the law, or contrary to the evidence, or on the basis of affidavits of misconduct. This permitted control both of the substantive finding and of the award of damages.[22]

The motion for new trial was to play a key role during the common law's next evolutionary period, with which William Murray, First Earl of Mansfield and Mansfield and Lord Chief Justice of King's Bench from 1756 to 1788, had much to do.[23]

7 Lord Mansfield, Equity, and the Instructed Jury

A great frieze wraps around the courtroom of the Supreme Court of the United States, depicting its sculptor's choice of the "great lawgivers" of recorded history, from Menes through Napoleon. A legal historian—in particular a historian of English Law—might not have made some of the same choices. The two Englishmen depicted are King John and Sir William Blackstone. King John was chosen, one assumes, for having given Royal Assent to Magna Carta 1215, but, to the extent he was a lawgiver, one might say he did not give Magna Carta so much in grace as under duress.

The second Englishman chosen was Sir William Blackstone, a Justice of Common Pleas, 1770-80. Undeniably, Blackstone's monumental work Commentaries on the Laws of England 1771 updated the great earlier compendia

---

[21]Ibid.

[22]Emphasis added. Ibid., pp. 84–85.

[23]Lord Mansfield's title is not misprinted in the text. Perhaps unique in the history of the British peerage, he was granted letters patent for two separate earldoms, both "of" the same place name—Mansfield—but located in different counties. He was childless, and the first earldom was created in 1776, with a remainder to his niece. The second was created in 1792, with a remainder to his nephew. The titles merged in one holder in 1843. The eighth and present Earl was trained as a barrister. See: http://en.wikipedia.org/wiki/Earl_of_Mansfield_and_Mansfield.

of English laws by Bracton and Fortescue, its impact being attributable to its incontrovertible, intrinsic merit both as a practice tool and an academic *magnum opus*. In gaining recognition of the common law in academia, Blackstone was truly a pioneer. He delivered what are generally acknowledged as the first lectures in common law at Oxford, the Vinerean Lectures 1753-55. Theretofore, the academic study of law had focused exclusively on civil, not common, law.

Many common law lawyers and judges might nonetheless have chosen Mansfield over Blackstone. Mansfield's singular contribution to the evolution of the common law lay not simply in cataloguing and commenting upon legal principles, but in putting them into practice, through his lucid opinions and the employment of his practical skills of judicial management.

> Mansfield presided as Chief Justice for over thirty years, and by the time he was done he had established the basic principles that continue to govern the mercantile energies of England and America down to the present day ... [A]lmost no feature of the evolving common law escaped his shaping influence.[24]

Many of Mansfield's cases are still studied in law schools (especially in England, but also in other common law jurisdictions) and are regarded in common law courts as still "good law".[25]

Born a younger son of a Scottish peer, Mansfield demonstrated a brilliant intellect from his earliest school days. Then, as now to an extent, the prevailing law of Scotland was not the common law of England, but was rooted in the civil law, which Mansfield would have studied at Oxford.[26] As will be noted infra, the civil law was to play a continuing role in his professional life.

At this point, some discussion of the two parallel systems of adjudication in England from the medieval period forward is necessary. The common law was the source of law governing ownership of land and chattels, as well as what we now categorize as torts and crimes. There were two common law superior courts, the Court of King's (or Queen's) Bench and the Court of Common Pleas. At the outset, the jurisdictions of these courts were fairly rigidly bounded. In general, matters having to do with real property were within the jurisdiction of Common Pleas, whereas Pleas of the Crown, including breaches of the King's Peace, were within the jurisdiction of King's Bench. Over the years, these courts jousted over their jurisdictional boundaries, which came to overlap considerably, in what was essentially a competition for judicial business.[27] Nonetheless, they both remained courts which exclusively based their judgments on the common law of England.

---

[24]Oldham (2004), p. 10.

[25]See, e.g., *Price v. Neal*, 3 Burrow 1354, 97 E.R. 871 (1762) (finality of payment in negotiable instruments law) and *Carter v. Boehm*, 3 Burrow 1905, 97 E.R. 1162 (1766) (duty *uberrimae fidei* in insurance law).

[26]English and Scots law slowly began a process of merger following the Acts of Union 1706 (England with Scotland) and 1707 (Scotland with England). That process of merger still continues and is still uneasy. See, e.g., Eden (2003), pp. 117–118.

[27]See Smalkin and Smalkin (2005).

From time immemorial,[28] subjects of the English monarch could petition the Crown for justice in matters of which the common law did not take cognizance. Bills for correction of injustices could also be lodged directly with parliament. As life and government grew more complex after the time of Henry II, it obviously became infeasible for the monarch personally to decide individual cases and for parliament to act corporately on bills for redress. In practice, the judicial authority of king and parliament became lodged in the Lord Chancellor, then as now considered one of the foremost English officers of State. Because such a bill of petition seeking justice was made to the Chancellor rather than a common law court, it was not governed by the precepts of common law, nor was a jury utilized. The Chancellor's court was "a court of conscience".[29] Freedom from the restrictions imposed upon common law judges by the common law's formulaic pleading and formalistic practice rules, and not least freedom from being bound by a jury's verdict on the merits of the matter, gave the Chancellor power to work justice largely unbridled in comparison to that possessed by common law judges, as will be discussed infra.

The leading English legal historian Sir John Baker gives an excellent portrayal of the evolution of equity down to Lord Mansfield's time:

> The equity of the Court of Chancery, like the [legal] fictions of the common law courts, proceeded from the premise that the course of the common law was immutable. In Chancery the just remedy was provided not by changing the law but by avoiding its effect in the special circumstances of particular cases. So long as chancellors were seen as providing ad hoc remedies in individual cases, there was no question of their jurisdiction bringing about legal change or making law. When, however, equity was regularised and reduced to known principles and rules, the overall content of English law could be said to have been thereby changed. The use and trust, the equity of redemption, the principles of relief against forfeiture, penalties, fraud and mistake, and the equitable remedies of discovery, injunction, rescission, rectification, and specific performance, were permanent additions to the law which survived the [19th century] abolition of the court.[30]

Lord Mansfield, having had roots in the civil law and—unlike many English barristers—having had an extensive equity practice, exerted a strong influence on the confluence of law and equity in his time as Lord Chief Justice:

> Equity also affected the law independent of the Chancery [Court]. It played a role in certain branches of the common law, such as action for money had and received; this was openly acknowledged under Lord Mansfield CJ, who "never liked common law so much as when it was like equity".[31]

As noted, the courts of equity did not then—and still do not—empanel juries. As a common law judge, Mansfield was bound to enter judgment on the jury's resolution of cases at law in King's Bench and could not do otherwise. Although respectful of

---

[28]By the Statute of Westminster 1275, the time prior to the reign of Richard I.

[29]Baker (2002), p. 103.

[30]Ibid., pp. 202–203.

[31]Ibid.

the traditional role of the jury in English common law, Mansfield was well aware that it had, at the same time, required the development and employment of a number of judicial restraints on the unbridled discretion of the jury; these restraints were, by Mansfield's day, so many and so complex as to lead him to oppose the introduction of jury trial into Scottish law.[32]

One of these restraints was the power of the judge to influence a jury during the course of the trial. From the following elegiac to the jury trial, written by Mansfield's contemporary Blackstone, one would think any such power did not, or at least should not, exist:

> [T]he trial by jury has ever been, and I trust ever will be, looked upon as the glory of English law.... [I]n settling and adjusting a question of fact, when entrusted to any single magistrate, partiality and injustice have an ample field to range in; either by boldly asserting that to be proved which is not so, or more artfully by suppressing some circumstances, stretching and warping others, and distinguishing away the remainder. Here therefore, a competent number of sensible and upright jurymen, chosen by lot from among those of the middle rank [of society], will be found the best investigators of truth, and the surest guardians of public justice....[33]

Despite Blackstone's commentary, the fact is that English judges by the time of Mansfield had adopted a number of practices for controlling the jury during the course of the trial, in the nature of "comments" to the jury on the law and the facts of the case. Writing in the late seventeenth century, the great commentator Sir Matthew Hale:

> [S]poke of the "Excellency" of the practice by which the trial judge is able not only to "direct" the jurors on issues of law, but "in Matters of Fact, to give them a great Light and Assistance by his weighing the Evidence before them, and observing where the Question and Knot of the Business lies, and by showing them his Opinion even in Matters of Fact, which is a great Advantage and Light to Lay Men".[34]

Mansfield's predecessor as Chief Justice, Sir Dudley Ryder, did not hesitate to exercise control of the jury during trial. His trial notebooks record many instances of commentary to the jury on the merits of the case so strong as to be a clear direction to them as to the proper outcome, in which he would sum up the evidence "for", meaning in favor of, one party or another. Even though Ryder records several instances in which the jury did not follow his direction, those were exceptional.[35] When Lord Mansfield himself was asked by the contemporary diarist and biographer James Boswell "in 1773 whether juries always took his direction, Mansfield answered, 'Yes, except in political causes where they do not at all keep themselves to right and wrong'".[36] Mansfield's background as an equity lawyer

---

[32]Oldham (2004), p. 16. In 1815, trial by jury in civil cases was extended by parliament to Scotland by statute, 55 Geo. III. c. 42, where it remains available.

[33]Blackstone, William. 1763-69. *Commentaries on the Laws of England.* Oxford, pp. 379–381. As quoted in Langbein et al. (2009), pp. 458–459.

[34]As quoted in Langbein et al. (2009), p. 431.

[35]Langbein et al. (2009), pp. 432–433.

[36]Ibid.

clearly played a role in his directions to juries; his jury instructions "not infre-
quently … encouraged the jury to take equitable considerations into account in
reaching its verdict. In addition to overt jury instructions, Mansfield could …
allow his summation to be shaped by equitable considerations".[37] A brilliant summation, based upon the judge's own painstaking notes of the evidence—as was
Mansfield's practice—became emblematic of the English common law judge.

8 Mansfield and New Trial

But what of the jury's verdict that was, in the judge's view, clearly unjust in light
of the evidence and the law, despite perhaps an attempt at judicial intervention
by instruction and summation at trial? The motion for new trial was the vehicle
for setting things right, and it had no greater advocate in the eighteenth century's
transformative period of English law than Mansfield.

   In *Bright v. Enyon*,[38] one of his landmark cases, Mansfield and the *puisne*
judges of King's Bench who joined him in their speeches on the case, firmly established and clearly articulated the modern view of the motion for new trial as the
remedy for of an injustice wrought by a jury's verdict. To be sure, incidents of
grant of a new trial in the wake of an unjust verdict are recorded as long as a century before Mansfield addressed it in *Bright v. Enyon*[39] and, indeed, as a trial judge
"Mansfield wielded or withheld the prospect of a new trial in order to achieve a
just result".[40] But, the Court of King's Bench under Mansfield's leadership gave it
the weight of authoritative, enduring precedent in English law.

   In *Bright v. Enyon,* Mansfield commented on the role of the equity court in
times before the new trial motion had been extended to review of an unjust jury
verdict. That situation was:

> [S]o intolerable, that it drove the parties into a Court of Equity, to have in effect, a new
> trial at law, of a mere legal question, because the verdict, in justice, under all the circum-
> stances, ought not to conclude [the matter]. And many bills [petitions for relief in Equity]
> have been retained upon this ground, and the question tried over again at law, under the
> direction of a Court of Equity.[41]

Clearly, and properly so, despite his respect for the equity courts, Mansfield dis-
cerned that post-trial remediation of an unjust verdict by the court in which it had
been rendered made more sense than the commencement of a de novo proceeding
in an altogether different forum.

---

[37]Oldham (2004), p. 29.

[38]1. Burrow 390, 97 E.R. 365 (1757).

[39]*Wood v. Gunston,* Sty. 462, 82 E.R. 865 (1655).

[40]Oldham (2004), p. 28

[41]As set forth in Langbein et al. (2009), p. 446.

Going on to state his views of the new trial motion as a remedy for injustice in jury verdicts at common law, Mansfield wrote in *Bright v. Enyon*:

> Trials by jury, in civil cases, could not subsist, then, without a power, somewhere, to grant new trials…
>
> [A] general verdict can only be set right by a new trial, which is no more than having the cause more deliberately considered by another jury, when there is a reasonable doubt, or perhaps a certainty, that justice has not been done. The writ of attaint is now a mere sound, in every case; in many it does not pretend to be a remedy.
>
> There are numberless cases of false verdicts, without corruption or bad intention of the jurors. They may have heard too much of the matter before trial, and imbibed prejudices, without knowing it. The cause may be intricate; the examination may be so long, as to distract their attention.
>
> Most general verdicts include legal consequences, as well as propositions of fact. In drawing these consequences, the jury may mistake, and infer directly contrary to law.
>
> The parties may be surprised, by a case falsely made at trial, which they had no reason to expect, and therefore could not come prepared to answer.
>
> If unjust verdicts, obtained under these, and a thousand like circumstances, were to be conclusive for ever, the determination of civil property, in this method of trial, would be very precarious and unsatisfactory. It is absolutely necessary to justice, that there should, upon many occasions, be opportunities of reconsidering the cause by a new trial.[42]

Of particular note above are Mansfield's repeated references to doing justice through the post-trial judicial review of the soundness of a jury's verdict.

The following passage aptly conveys the lasting and ultimately drastic influence of both Mansfield's role as judicial innovator and the liberalization of new trial motions practice:

> [Judges began] in the eighteenth century to take notes of evidence. The [trial] judge's views were generally followed as to whether a verdict was against the weight of the evidence, though the full court could refuse a new trial at its discretion. The new procedure was not confined to questions of evidence, but also enabled legal discussion in banc of facts outside the record, and this technique was perfected by Lord Mansfield CJ, particularly as a means of refining commercial law. Mansfield would state "very particularly and minutely from his own notes taken down at the trial (which he read to the audience verbatim) the exact state of the facts as they came out upon the evidence" so that the question could be agreed in banc. Mansfield's techniques were not without contemporary controversy, especially when he tried to extend them to the control of criminal juries. Like the priests who had tinkered with ordeals in which they had lost faith, the judges had begun to impose strict limits on the authority of the jury; jurors no longer had an "absolute despotic power", but their worst mistakes should be put right. The motion for a new trial went much further in this direction than the other [post-trial] procedures, by throwing the whole case before the court and not merely the formalized phrases of the record; and, since the judge's version of the facts sometimes carried more weight than the verdict, it prepared the way for the demise of the civil jury.[43]

Today, motions for new trial in United States federal practice are committed to the sound discretion of the trial judge. They may be granted essentially for the same

---

[42]1 Burrow 390, 393, 97 Eng. Rep. 365, 366.
[43]Baker (2002), p. 85; see also Civil Procedure: Power of Trial Judge to Grant New Trial Where Verdict is Against Weight of the Evidence. 1961. *Duke Law Journal*: 308–315.

wide variety of reasons for which they were traditionally granted in England at common law, including a verdict that is unjust on account of juror misconduct or is "against the clear weight of the evidence". The principle of adherence to common law criteria is set forth essentially *in haec verba* in Federal Rule of Civil Procedure 59(a)(1) and has been interpreted by seminal judicial opinions as embodying the English common law history of the curative use of the new trial remedy as discussed in this chapter.[44] To this day, though, most trial judges are hesitant to grant the motion, fearing that to do so would trespass upon the jury's franchise on making factual determinations, resulting simply in substituting the judge's resolution of the facts for that of the jury. It is safe to say that, in the absence of a rather strong showing that letting the jury's verdict stand would result in a plainly unjust outcome, the motion for new trial is likely to be denied.

Motions for new trial are also granted as part of the *remittitur* process, which offers a plaintiff the alternative of accepting a judgment reduced to an amount that the judge sees as more reasonable than the jury's award or submitting to a retrial of the case. If the plaintiff refuses the *remittitur*, a new trial is ordered. In lieu of pursuing either alternative, a plaintiff might be prompted to settle for a compromise award somewhere between the jury's verdict and the judge's *remittitur* figure.

Grant of a new trial is not immediately appealable as of right; an appeal of the grant of a new trial can only be taken in most cases after entry of the judgment at the end of the new trial. The new trial can result in a vastly different outcome to that of the first trial, of course, and it is difficult for the party losing the new trial to prevail on the ultimate appeal by arguing that the new trial was erroneously granted, as the trial judge's discretionary decision to order the new trial is given considerable deference.

9 The End Game

As the preceding discussion suggests, time was running out for the jury trial in England as it had been known from time immemorial by the end of the eighteenth century. Sir John Baker keenly summed up the rapid decline of the civil jury trial after the age of Mansfield:

> Even more drastic in its effects than the abolition of the old system of pleading has been the virtual disappearance in England of the civil jury trial. The possibility of trying facts by judge alone was introduced by the Common Law Procedure Act 1854. There were at that date already many inferior courts in which juries were not used; and in the court in banc, on motion for new trials, it was the trial judge's treatment of the facts which usually mattered. All the experience suggested that judges were more likely to understand the factual issues than laymen, and were as competent to assess evidence....The very existence of an option made the decision to ask for a jury suspicious; it suggested the hope of confusion in a weak case, or the expectation of exorbitant damages in cases involving distressing details or high feelings. When wartime conditions led to temporary prohibitions of

---

[44]See, e.g., *Aetna Casualty & Insurance Co. v. Yeatts,* 122 F.2d 350 4th Cir. (1941).

civil jury service, this was a further blow from which the civil jury never recovered. Since 1933 parties have been allowed juries only with leave of court, except in cases of libel and a few other matters, and the courts have indicated their unwillingness to give such leave.[45]

The definitive judicial death knell for civil jury trials being allowed in the discretion of the judge in ordinary tort cases in England and Wales is generally thought to have been sounded by Lord Denning, Master of the Rolls, in giving judgment in the case of *Ward v. James (No. 2)*:[46]

[T]he cases all show that, when a statute gives discretion, the courts must not fetter it by rigid rules from which a judge is never at liberty to depart. Nevertheless the courts can lay down the considerations which should be borne in mind in exercising the discretion, and point out those considerations which should be ignored. This will normally determine the way in which the discretion is exercised, and thus ensure some measure of uniformity of decision. From time to time the considerations may change as public policy changes, and so the pattern of decision may change: this is all part of the evolutionary process. We have seen it in the way that discretion is exercised in divorce cases. So also in the mode of trial. Whereas it was common to order trial by jury, now it is rare.

Relevant Considerations Today. Let it not be supposed that this court is in any way opposed to trial by jury. It has been the bulwark of our liberties too long for any of us to seek to alter it. Whenever a man is on trial for serious crime, or when in a civil case a man's honour or integrity is at stake, or when one or other party must be deliberately lying, then trial by jury has no equal. But in personal injury cases trial by jury has given place of late to trial by judge alone, the reason being simply this, that in these cases trial by a judge alone is more acceptable to the great majority of people. Rarely does a party ask in these cases for a jury. When a solicitor gives advice, it runs in this way: "If I were you, I should not ask for a jury. I should have a judge alone. You do know where you stand with a judge, and if [*296] he goes wrong, you can always go to the Court of Appeal. But as for a jury, you never know what they will do, and if they do go wrong, there is no putting them right. The Court of Appeal hardly ever interferes with the verdict of a jury." So the client decides on judge alone. That is why jury trials have declined. It is because they are not asked for. Lord Devlin shows this in his book [The Hamlyn Lectures, eighth series, Trial by Jury, ch. 6], p. 133.

This important consequence follows: the judges alone, and not juries, in the great majority of cases, decide whether there is negligence or not. They set the standard of care to be expected of the reasonable man. They also assess the damages. They see, so far as they can, that like sums are given for like injuries. They set the standard for awards. Hence there is uniformity of decision. This has its impact on decisions as to the mode of trial. If a party asks for a jury in an ordinary personal injury case, the court naturally asks: "Why do you want a jury when nearly everyone else is content with judge alone?" I am afraid it is often because he has a weak case, or desires to appeal to sympathy. If no good reason is given, then the court orders trial by judge alone. Hence we find that nowadays the discretion in the ordinary run of personal injury cases is in favour of judge alone. It is no sufficient reason for departing from it simply to provide a "guinea-pig" case.

Even in those few tort cases in which a jury trial still can be demanded as a matter of right under section 69 of the Senior Courts Act 1981 (claims of fraud, libel, slander, malicious prosecution or false imprisonment), the judge has discretion to deny the demand if "the court is of opinion that the trial requires any prolonged

---

[45]Ibid., p. 92.
[46]1 Q. B. 273 CA (1966).

examination of documents or accounts or any scientific or local investigation which cannot conveniently be made with a jury".

To sum up, the English polar shift from self-instructing jury to instructed jury was followed not very long after by another, far more consequential polar shift, i.e., from jury trials to bench trials in virtually all civil cases. The precipitating cause was the increasing control of juries by judges, resulting in the judges' eventual subsuming of the jury's role in virtually every case. If it be accepted that justice is more likely to be done in a forum in which the ultimate result is handed down by one who is trained in law, justice has prevailed.

In the United States, the right to trial by jury is enshrined for federal civil cases in the Seventh Amendment to the Constitution. The Supreme Court has interpreted this right as guaranteeing a jury trial not only in causes of action extant at common law, but also those not extant at common law if, had they been recognized in England in 1791 (the effective date of the seventh Amendment), they would have been triable by jury.[47] The Seventh Amendment is mirrored in the constitutions of the American states. It is unlikely that jury trials in the United States will be done away with in our lifetimes or at any reasonable foreseeable future date, as the forces for maintaining the status quo are tremendously powerful politically, and the right to a jury trial is seen—often with reference to Magna Carta 1215 alongside the United States Constitution—as one of the inalienable components of the American birthright. Not one in perhaps a half million Americans is likely to know that the right to a civil trial by jury is not guaranteed by the (unwritten) English Constitution or that it has essentially disappeared from its home country.

Whether the persistence of the civil jury trial in the United States is good or bad, or indeed whether it denies or assures justice to litigants, must be left to the judgment of the reader and to history as yet unwritten.

Acknowledgment The Author gratefully acknowledges the assistance of University of Baltimore Law School student Andrew Adkins, MA (East Ang), in the preparation of this chapter.

References

Baker, John H. 2002. *An Introduction to English Legal History*. IV ed. London, Dayton: Butterworths LexisNexis.
Eden, Sandra. 2003. Cautionary Tales: The Continued Development of Smith v. Bank of Scotland. *Edinburgh Law Review* 7: 107-118.

---

[47]See Wolfram (1973), p. 639. Thus, if Congress, for example, creates a right to redress (as it has) for violation of a federal statute regulating safety standards for mobile homes (which it has power to do under the Interstate Commerce Clause of the Constitution), a federal court must gaze back in time to decide whether, had there been such a thing in England as a mobile home in 1791, and had the law presented a remedy like that prescribed by Congress for safety defects in its construction, the remedy would have sounded in law or equity. Although it sounds quite absurd, this is the way in which entitlement to a jury trial in cases asserting a federal statutory right is decided, and it illustrates why a sound understanding of English legal history still is worthy of study, even in the twentieth century, and even in the United States.

Langbein, John H., Renee Lettow Lerner, and Bruce P. Smith. 2009. *History of the Common Law: The Development of Anglo-American Institutions*. Austin: Wolters-Kluwer Law & Business. New York: Aspen Publishers.

Mitnick, John M. 1988. From Neighbor-Witness to Judge of Proof: The Transformation of the English Civil Juror. *The American Journal of Legal History* 32: 201-235.

Mulholland, Maureen, and Brian Pullan. 2003. *Judicial Tribunals in England and Europe, 1200-1700, vol. 1*. Manchester: Manchester University Press.

Oldham, James. 2004. *English Common Law in the Age of Mansfield*. Chapel Hill: University of North Carolina Press.

Smalkin, Frederic N., and Frederic N. C. Smalkin. 2005. The Market for Justice, the 'Litigation Explosion', and the 'Verdict Bubble': A Closer Look at Vanishing Trials. *Federal Courts Law Review* 8: 1-23.

Wolfram, Charles W. 1973. The Constitutional History of the Seventh Amendment. *Minnesota Law Review* 57: 639-747.

General Principles of International Law: Struggling with a Slippery Concept

Elena Carpanelli

Abstract Article 38(1)(c) of the Statute of the International Court of Justice includes *general principles of law recognized by civilized nations* among the sources of international law. There has been strong debate over the meaning of this expression. One of the most disputed aspects has been whether it refers only to those principles which are recognized by the majority of the domestic legal systems or also to those principles pertaining to the international legal system per se. In support of the latter argument stands international case law that has often resorted not only to those general principles of law common to most domestic legal systems but also to those traceable back to the international legal system itself. But what this last expression means—as well as its legal nature—is anything but clear. The present chapter will look at a specific principle—the principle of humanity—as the starting point and guideline for further reflections on the meaning and legal nature of general principles of international law. This analysis will have, as an unavoidable implication, the questioning of the role of the judiciary in the process of detecting and upholding what amounts to general principles of international law.

1 Introduction

Article 38(1) of the Statute of the International Court of Justice (ICJ) (the "Statute"), which is almost identical to Article 38(I) of the Statute of its predecessor, the Permanent Court of International Justice, lists as primary sources of international law: (a) international conventions; (b) international custom; (c) general principles of law recognized by civilized nations (*principes généraux de droit reconnus par les nations civilisées*). With regard to this last category, however, there is no consensus among legal scholars on its exact nature and scope, as well as what distinguishes it

E. Carpanelli (✉)
Ph.D. Candidate in International Law, University of Milano-Bicocca, Milan, Italy
e-mail: elena.carpanelli@gmail.com

© Springer International Publishing Switzerland 2015   125
L. Pineschi (ed.), *General Principles of Law - The Role of the Judiciary*,
Ius Gentium: Comparative Perspectives on Law and Justice 46,
DOI 10.1007/978-3-319-19180-5_7

from other sources of law. As noted by Professor Bin Cheng, general principles of law have been "the most controversial of the various sources of international law enumerated in Article 38 of the Statute and thus of international law in general".[1]

A debated aspect, for instance, has been the use of the expression "civilized nations" in the context of Article 38(1)(c), which, as pointed out by Professor Gaja, might explain why international courts have so far been reluctant to refer to principles inferred from one or another municipal system.[2] With regard to this particular issue, however, a presumption exists that this expression is by now redundant and references to civilized nations should be understood to encompass all States.[3]

A more complex issue concerns the meaning of the term "general principles of law". While there is a general understanding among scholars and international courts that such an expression refers to those principles common to most domestic legal systems,[4] the methodology and evidence needed for inducing them from municipal law is controversial.

As recently noted by Professor Ellis, the positivist approach to Article 38(1)(c) of the Statute, although generating consensus, has been often disregarded by international adjudicators, who have asserted the existence of general principles of law based more on natural law assumptions than on a comparative study of domestic legal systems.[5] International judges have indeed resorted to principles found in *foro domestico* to validate their reliance on a certain principle, even without undertaking an in-depth investigation into domestic legal systems.[6]

The theoretical ground for such an approach has been well depicted by Judge Shahabuddeen, according to whom general principles of law would not amount to generalizations reached by the application of comparative law but to particularizations of a common underlying sense of what is just in the circumstances; as a consequence, an international tribunal may select an interpretation, even if it is at variance with that of some legal systems.[7] It is self-evident, however, that a similar attitude might entrust judges with excessive discretion, in breach of the drafters' intention.[8]

---

[1]Cheng (1987) [1953], xv.

[2]Gaja (2013), para. 2. So far, the International Court of Justice has never grounded a decision based on the reference to general principles of international law.

[3]Bassiouni (1990), p. 768.

[4]See, inter alia, Treves (2005), p. 248, Crawford (2012), p. 34.

[5]Ellis (2011), p. 955.

[6]Voigt (2008), p. 8.

[7]International Criminal Tribunal for the Former Yugoslavia (Appeals Chamber), *Prosecutor v. Anto Furundžija,* case no. IT-95-17/1-A, judgment of 21 July 2012, para. 264.

[8]For the *travaux préparatoires* of the Statute of the Permanent Court of International Justice (PCIJ) (whose Article 38(I)(c) has subsequently been transposed in Article 38(1)(c) of the Statute of the International Court of Justice) see PCIJ, Advisory Committee of Jurists, *Pròces-Verbaux of the Proceedings of the Committee* (16 June–24 July, 1920) with Annexes, p. 322.

Another controversial aspect is whether general principles of international legal origin (generally referred to as "general principles of international law") are encompassed within the meaning of Article 38(1)(c) of the Statute.[9]

While some commentators exclude principles of international law from the scope of the recalled provision,[10] several scholars have interpreted it to also—if not primarily—embody general principles of an international character.[11]

Whereas the *travaux préparatoires* provide no guidance on this particular issue, several arguments have been put forward in support of the inclusion of general principles of international law within the scope of application of Article 38(1)(c). Professor Lammers, for instance, has noted that, in the light of the ordinary meaning of the terms in Article 38(1)(c) of the Statute, there can be no objection to considering these principles as included in the provision.[12] The term "law" may indeed refer to both national and international law. Similarly, the expression "recognized by civilized nations" would adapt to principles found either at the domestic or international level.[13] Teleological interpretations would further support the aforesaid conclusion, given that the ratio of the debated notion was to enable the ICJ to deal with lacunae in international customs and treaties.[14]

Professor Bassiouni has also stressed that, in light of the differences between the international and domestic legal systems, principles-sources of international law might well emerge in the international legal context without having a specific parallel in national law. In his view, any attempt to exclude these principles from the meaning and scope of Article 38(1)(c) would fail to take into account what amounts to unperfected expressions of other sources of law and would therefore be incongruous with the drafters' intention.[15]

Other authors have subsumed the inclusion of general principles of international law within the meaning of Article 38(1)(c) of the Statute by upholding a unitary approach to the same concept of "general principles of law". Professor Tunkin, for instance, argued that "general principles of law" are not only those principles

---

[9]See, for instance, Shaw (2003), p. 94 (according to the Author, however, whether "general principles of law" include merely general principles derived from national legal systems or also general principles of international law is a problem easy to overcome since both these categories would fall within a unitary category).

[10]See, inter alia, Verzijl (1968), p. 62. The Author acknowledges the existence of general principles of law of such fundamental nature that, without their universal recognition, the functioning of the legal community can hardly be imagined and distinguished them from general principles accepted in municipal legal systems. However, according to the Author, these basic principles may not be rank as a separate category of sources of law, since they are necessarily already embodied in customs or treaties. See also Pellet (2012), p. 836.

[11]See, e.g., Voigt (2008), p. 8.

[12]Lammers (1980), p. 67.

[13]Ibid.

[14]Ibid.

[15]Bassiouni (1990), p. 772.

common to municipal legal systems but also peculiar to international law.[16] Therefore, for a principle to be considered as falling under Article 38(1)(c), it would be necessary to demonstrate that it also pertains to international law.[17]

As previously stated, however, this approach is not unanimous. Besides those commentators arguing that the notion of general principles of law in Article 38(1) (c) refers to general principles of both national and international law, several scholars have asserted that general principles of international law would indeed amount to either treaty or customary law and, accordingly, find their legal basis in Article 38(1)(a) or (b) of the Statute of the ICJ.[18] Other authors even proposed a broader concept of general principles of international law. According to Professor Brownlie, for instance, general principles of international law may be customary rules, general principles of law in the sense of Article 38(1)(c) of the Statute or logical propositions derived from legal reasoning that are based on existing international law and national analogies.[19]

Regardless of the above-mentioned doctrinal debate, the ICJ has somehow confirmed that Article 38(1)(c) of the Statute also includes general principles of international legal logic. Indeed, the Court has often referred to principles of international law that do not have a parallel in national legal systems.[20]

Further, Article 21 of the Statute of the International Criminal Court seems to have upheld the distinction and co-existence of the two categories of general principles by listing, among applicable law, both "general principles of law derived by the Court from national laws of legal systems of the world" and "principles of international law".[21]

The specific traits of the category of general principles of international law are, however, anything but clear. As it has been correctly observed, an exhaustive enumeration of general principles of international law amounts to a task defying

---

[16]Tunkin (1974), p. 202.

[17]Ibid.

[18]See, e.g., Raimondo (2008), p. 41. See also Waldock (1962), p. 69 (according to whom, it is necessary to keep clear the distinction between "general principles of law recognized by civilized nations", derived from domestic legal systems, and "general principles of international law", whose formal source is customary or treaty law).

[19]Brownlie (1998), p. 18. For a general overview of doctrinal opinion see also Vitányi (1982), p. 103.

[20]For a general overview see again Gaja (2013), para. 17.

[21]Statute of the International Criminal Court (Rome, 17 July 1998; entered into force on 1 July 2002). For a different interpretation of Article 21 of the Statute see Pellet (2002), p. 1070. According to the Author, the expression "the principles and rules of international law, including the established principles of the law of armed conflicts", embodied in Article 21 of the Statute, constitutes a verbal tic meant to refer exclusively to international customs. It is noteworthy, however, that in the commentary to the International Law Commission's Draft Statute, the expression principles and rules of general international law is meant to include "general principles of law, so that the Court can legitimately have recourse to the all corpus of criminal law, whether found in national forum or in international practice, whenever it needs guidance in matters not clearly regulated by treaty". See Draft Statute for an International Criminal Court, in Yearbook of the International Law Commission, vol. II, 1994, p. 51.

human capacity and, in practice, to a potentially unlimited process.[22] Professor Brownlie even asserted the inappropriateness of a rigid categorization of this source, though he noted examples of principles pertaining to it such as, inter alia, the principle of consent, reciprocity, equality of States, good faith, domestic jurisdiction and the freedom of the seas.[23]

Although relatively little attention has been paid recently to this particular aspect by legal doctrine, it is undeniable that the autonomy of the international legal system and the transnational dimension of the modern society have increasingly fostered the role of general principles of international law, especially in those areas—such as, for instance, environmental protection—where customary and treaty laws have proved to be defective. These principles have often found recognition in Declarations of principles and other soft law instruments (although a similar circumstance requires a careful distinction with those international rules articulated therein) but might also lack written transposition.

The aforementioned developments urgently call for a systematization of the category, taking into particular account their constitutive elements (practice?, States' *opinio*?) and function (as autonomous source of law, interpretative?). To this end, the present chapter will look at a specific principle—the principle of humanity—as the starting point for further analysis and reflection on the meaning and legal nature of general principles of an international legal origin. This task will be undertaken with no presumption to offer a solution or an additional value to the doctrinal debate, but with the purpose of stressing the complexity of the issue and the pre-eminent role to which the judiciary will increasingly be called to in the systematization of the category.

2 The Principle of Humanity: A Preliminary Overview of State Practice and International Jurisprudence

The principle of humanity (often referred to also as "laws of humanity" or "elementary considerations of humanity")[24] is embodied in preambles to international conventions as well as to resolutions of the United Nations General Assembly.[25]

The Preamble to the 1899 Hague Convention II containing the Regulations on the Laws and Customs of War and Land, for instance, expressly provides that:

Until a more complete code of the laws of war has been issued, the High Contracting Parties deem it expedient to declare that, in case not included in the Regulations adopted by them, the inhabitants and the belligerents remain under the protection and the rule of

---

[22]Herczegh (1969), p. 46.

[23]Brownlie (1998), p. 19.

[24]See, in general, Le Bris (2012).

[25]See, inter alia, Declaration on the prohibition of the use of nuclear and thermo-nuclear weapons, UN Doc. A/RES/1653 (XVI), 24 November 1961, Preamble.

the principles of the law of nations, as they result from the usages established among civilized people, *from the laws of humanity* and the dictates of public conscience.[26]

This provision—named "Martens clause" after its proposer—was restated, although slightly modified, in the 1907 Hague Convention IV on Laws and Customs of War on Land[27] and in the denunciations clauses to the 1949 Geneva Conventions.[28] In Article 1 ("general principles and scope of application") of the I Additional Protocol[29] and in the Preamble of the II Additional Protocol to the Geneva Conventions,[30] the expression "laws of humanity" has been substituted with the term "principles of humanity".

As observed by legal doctrine, one of the primary merits of this provision has been to approach the question of the laws of humanity for the first time under an (apparently) positivist perspective, rather than a moral one.[31] That notwithstanding, the clause remains elusive on the content and nature of the "laws of humanity" to which it refers to, as well as to the distinctive elements between the aforesaid notion and that of "usages established among civilized nations".

International tribunals and arbitrators, as well as national courts, have also often referred to the so-called principle of humanity in their case law.[32] Principles of humanity, for instance, were referred to in the High Command Trial held in Nuremberg in the wake of World War II. The Tribunal affirmed that the commanders' responsibility in occupied territories was established in the customs of war, international agreements, fundamental principles of humanity and the authority of the commander.[33] The Tribunal further observed that:

---

[26]Emphasis added. Opened for signature on 29 July 1989, entered into force on 4 September 1990.

[27]Opened for signature on 18 October 1907, entered into forced on 26 January 1910.

[28]Convention for the amelioration of the condition of the wounded and the sick in armed forces in the field, Article 63; Convention for the amelioration of the condition of wounded, sick and shipwrecked members of armed forces at seas, Article 62; Convention relative to the treatment of prisoners of war, Article 142; Convention relative to the protection of civilian persons in time of war, Article 158. All the four Conventions were opened for signature in Geneva on 12 August 1949 and entered into force on 21 October 1950. A reference to "elementary dictate of humanity" is also contained in the Preamble to the International Agreement for Collective Measures against Piratical Attacks in the Mediterranean by Submarines (Nyon Agreement), League of Nations, Treaty Series 181, 135, entered into force on 14 September 1937.

[29]Protocol Additional to the Geneva Conventions of 12 August 1949 and related to the protection of victims of international armed conflicts, opened for signature on 8 June 1977 and entered into force on 7 December 1978.

[30]Protocol Additional to the Geneva Conventions of 12 August 1949 and related to the protection of victims of non-international armed conflicts, opened for signature on 8 June 1977 and entered into force on 7 December 1978. The Preamble of the Protocol recalls that: "… in cases not covered by the law in force, the human person remains under the protection of the principle of humanity and the dictates of public conscience".

[31]Cassese (2008), p. 40.

[32]For a general overview see, inter alia, Meron (2000), pp. 78–89.

[33]United Nations War Crimes Commission, Law Reports of Trials of War Criminals, vol. XII, London, 1949, p. 75.

> From an international standpoint, criminality may arise by reason of the fact that the act is forbidden by international agreements or is inherently criminal and contrary to accepted principles of humanity as recognized and accepted by civilized nations.[34]

Thus, the Tribunal seemed to envisage generally accepted principles of humanity as autonomous source of international law, distinct from both international agreements and customs.

In 1928, the arbitral tribunal in the *Naulilaa* case applied this principle to limit the legitimacy of reprisal.[35] The Tribunal found that reprisal *"est limitée par les expériences de l'humanité et les règles de la bonne foi, applicables dans les rapports d'État à État".*[36]

In its 1949 judgment on the *Corfu Channel* case, the ICJ found that the obligations incumbent on Albanian authorities to provide notice of the existence of a minefield in its territorial waters and to warn the British ship of the danger were based not on the Hague Convention of 1907, applicable in time of war, but "on certain general and well-recognized principles, namely: elementary considerations of humanity, even more exacting in peace than in war".[37]

This passage also echoes in the separate opinion of Judge Álvarez, according to whom the characteristic of international delinquency, as a notion relevant to the damage suffered by a State in the territory of a different State owing to the negligence of the latter, "are that it is an act contrary to the sentiments of humanity".[38]

Regardless of the decision's ambiguous wording, it appears clear from the above that the Court referred to the principle of humanity as a source of legal obligations distinct from treaty law.

The International Court of Justice has further referred to the concept of "elementary consideration of humanity" in subsequent cases. In its judgment in the *Case Concerning Military and Paramilitary Activities in and against Nicaragua*, the ICJ found that, regardless of whether the United States' reservations to the Geneva Conventions constituted a bar to their application in the case, the United States might be judged according to the fundamental general principles of humanitarian law.[39] To this end, the Court recalled, in particular, that, pursuant to the same Conventions, their denunciation may in no way impair the obligations which the parties should remain bound to by virtue of the principles of the law of nations, as they result from the "usages established among civilized people, from the laws

---

[34]Ibid.

[35]*Responsabilité de l'Allemagne à raison des dommages causés dans les colonies portugaises du sud de l'Afrique (Portugal contre Allemagne)*, 31 July 1928, in *Reports of International Arbitral Awards* (vol. II), p. 1011.

[36]Ibid., p. 1026.

[37]*Corfu Channel case (United Kingdom v. Albania)* [1949] ICJ Rep. 4, p. 22.

[38]Ibid., separate opinion of Judge A. Álvarez, p. 45.

[39]*Case concerning Military and Paramilitary Activities in and against Nicaragua (Nicaragua v. United States)* [1986] ICJ Rep. 14, para. 218.

of humanity and the dictates of public conscience".[40] The Court further noted that the rules laid down in Article 3, common to all four Geneva Conventions, with regard to armed conflict of non-international character, constitute a "... minimum yardstick, in addition to the more elaborated rules which are also to apply to international conflicts ..." and "... reflect what the Court in 1949 called 'elementary considerations of humanity'".[41] By means of this reasoning, the Court again seemed to rely on "elementary consideration of humanity" as an autonomous source of international law.

The ICJ's subsequent case law, however, reveals a different approach.[42] In both its Advisory Opinions on the *Threat or Use of Nuclear Weapons* and on the *Legal Consequences of the Construction of a Wall in the Occupied Palestinian Territory*, the Court referred to "elementary considerations of humanity" not as an autonomous source of legal obligations but as an inherent character to humanitarian rules.[43]

This approach has also been upheld, although in a more nuanced manner, by the ICJ in its judgment concerning the *South West Africa* cases, where it found that:

> Humanitarian considerations may constitute the inspirational basis for rules of law ...
> Such considerations do not, however, in themselves amount to rules of law.[44]

Contrary to the ICJ, the International Criminal Tribunal for the Former Yugoslavia has firmly held that:

> Elementary considerations of humanity, emphasised by the International Court of Justice ..., should be fully used when interpreting and applying loose international rules, on the basis that they are illustrative of a general principle of international law.[45]

Thus, the Tribunal explicitly attributed to "elementary considerations of humanity" the status of general principles of international law, although it found these principles could not exert any law-making function but only serve as an interpretative means.[46]

However, the Tribunal's jurisprudence has also proved to be in some way oscillatory. In other decisions, the Tribunal seems indeed to regard at the principle of humanity as a source of law. In the *Martić* case, for instance, the Tribunal found

---

[40]Ibid.

[41]Ibid.

[42]See again Le Bris (2012), p. 130.

[43]See *Legality of the Threat or Use of Nuclear Weapons*, Advisory Opinion [1996] ICJ Rep. 240, para. 79; *Legal Consequences of the Construction of a Wall in the Occupied Palestinian Territory*, Advisory Opinion [2004] ICJ Rep. 136, para. 157.

[44]See *South West Africa (Ethiopia v. South Africa; Liberia v. South Africa)* [1966] ICJ Rep. 6, second phase, para. 50.

[45]ICTY, *Prosecutor v. Kupreskic* et al., case no. IT-95-16-T, 14 January 2000, para. 524.

[46]Ibid., para. 525.

that the prohibition against attacking civilian population and the general principle limiting the means and methods of warfare also emanate from elementary considerations of humanity, which constitute the foundation of the entire body of international humanitarian law.[47]

In addition to the abovementioned case law, it suffices here to point out that the principle of humanity has also been increasingly referred to in international legal domains different from humanitarian law and human rights law.[48] To provide an example, the International Tribunal for the Law of the Sea has expressly relied on the aforesaid principle in relation to the use of force in the arrest of ships. More specifically, the Tribunal found that:

> Although the Convention does not contain express provisions on the use of force in the arrest of ships, international law ... requires that the use of force must be avoided as far as possible and, where force is unavoidable, it must not go beyond what is reasonable and necessary in the circumstances. *Considerations of humanity must apply in the law of the sea, as they do in other areas of international law.*[49]

It follows from the Tribunal's reasoning that "considerations of humanity" would amount in and of themselves to sources of international obligations distinct from treaty law. In this respect, therefore, the Tribunal seems to have further confirmed the ICJ's *dicta* in the *Corfu Channel* and *Nicaragua* cases.

3 The Principle of Humanity: A General Principle of International Law?

Despite the fact that international arbitrators and courts have greatly relied on the principle of humanity in their case law, there is a certain amount of disagreement concerning its source, scope and function. As it has been noted in doctrinal debates, it is disputed whether this principle amounts to a separate source of obligations in international law, falling within the scope of the notion "general principles of international law", or to an aspect of public policy, *jus cogens*, morality or humanitarian law generally.[50] Accordingly, the first aspect that deserves

---

[47]ICTY, *Prosecutor v. Milan Martić*, case no. IT-95-11-R61, 8 March 1996, para. 13.

[48]The role that the principle of humanity may played also outside humanitarian and human rights law has been underlined, inter alia, by Wright, who noted that the principles embodied in the Martens clause, including the laws of humanity, constitute the animating and motivating principle of all law. See Q. Wright, Forward, in United Nations War Crimes Commission, Law Report of Trials of War Criminals, vol. XV, London, 1949, xiii. For a general overview on the concept of "humanity" in international law see also Dupuy (1991).

[49]Emphasis added. International Tribunal for the Law of the Sea, *The M/V "Saiga" (No. 2) case (Saint Vincent and the Grenadines v. Guinea)*, judgment of 1 July 1999, para. 155.

[50]Jørgensen (2000), p. 128.

preliminary reflection is whether the principle of humanity may indeed be regarded as a general principle of an international legal character.

Commentators have described the principle of humanity, as upheld in international tribunals' case law, variously, as a general principle of international law,[51] a custom,[52] a secondary source of law or a soft law principle[53] falling in none of the above mentioned categories.[54]

These differences in assessing the use made by international courts of the principle of humanity emerge if one takes into account the antithetical views expressed by Professor Waldock and Professor Fitzmaurice as regards the ICJ's statement in the *Corfu Channel* case. The former, although stressing the Court's ambiguity on the point, interpreted the Court's reference to "elementary considerations of humanity" as part of customary international law. According to him, the fact that the Court mentioned the principle of humanity alongside the principle of freedom of maritime communication and every State's obligation not to allow its territory to be used in a way contrary to the rights of other States—both belonging to customary law—was sufficient per se to conclude that the Court intended also "elementary consideration of humanity" as being part of customs.[55] That notwithstanding, it is in some ways indicative of the doubts that this reasoning may raise, especially considering the Court's express use of the word "principles", that Professor Waldock himself did not exclude that, in some instances, Article 38(1)(b) and (c) of the Statute of the International Court of Justice may be seen as a single corpus of law. In this respect, general principles of law would constitute a flexible element enabling the Court to better identify customary norms.[56]

Professor Fitzmaurice, on the contrary, regarded "elementary considerations of humanity" as a specific application of the "good neighbor principle", forming a source of obligations, which "ha[s] neither been expressly assumed nor arise from any specific rules of international law".[57]

Based on the stand taken by the ICJ in the *South West Africa* cases, other scholars have instead observed that:

> The claim that correctness as a moral principle currently provides for a sufficient condition for the legal validity of certain human rights norms, better accounts for claims made in a number of opinions issued by the International Court of Justice – such as it appeals to elementary considerations of humanity – ... than do alternative explanations drawing on custom or general principles of law.[58]

---

[51]See, e.g., Fitzmaurice (1986), p. 4.

[52]See, inter alia, Waldock (1962), p. 63.

[53]Francioni (1996), p. 173.

[54]See, for instance, Thirlway (2013), p. 236.

[55]Waldock (1962), p. 65.

[56]Ibid.

[57]Fitzmaurice (1986), p. 4.

[58]Lefkowitz (2010), pp. 189–190.

Similar statements place themselves within—and contribute to—the broad debate over the scope of "general principles of international law". While some authors have argued that this notion would encompass principles—including the prohibition of the use of force, the principle of non-intervention and elementary considerations of humanity—that are customary in nature,[59] others have firmly rejected a similar approach and support their "autonomous" nature.[60]

Legal scholars' different approaches to the nature of the principle of humanity well reflect the vagueness and inconsistency of international case law on the point. Nevertheless, there are several elements that might support the argument that this principle, as interpreted by international tribunals, may be regarded as a self-reliant "general principle of international law", distinguishable from both custom and treaty law.

First of all, the same vagueness of the statements of international courts may be seen as an inherent aspect of the category. As several commentators have stressed with regard to the ICJ, indeed, its decisions are often unclear about the process that has led it to uphold the existence of a general principle of international law.[61] Two sets of considerations—strictly related to the same nature of general principles of international law—can explain a similar ambiguity. First, in certain cases, the principle is so well accepted that the Court would be in no need to demonstrate its existence.[62] Second, the Court's reluctance in the elucidation of general principles of international law may serve their same function "by providing the necessary judicial flexibility to gap-fill where necessary".[63] It is clear that similar considerations may be easily extended to the case law of other international courts and arbitrators.

Further, regardless of the fact that international courts have apparently taken different approaches with regard to the function and content of the principle of humanity, the recurring choice of words and, in particular, the avoidance of the use of the term "custom", seems to reveal a uniform resort to the notion of "elementary considerations of humanity" or "laws of humanity" in order to refer to principles so fundamental that they are not required to crystallize in custom to be applicable.

These considerations clearly foster the idea that the principle of humanity amounts to a general principle of international law.[64] As noted by Le Bris, indeed, *"pour accéder au droit positif, 'considérations élémentaires d'humanité' se coulent dans la moule formel des principes généraux du droit international"*.[65]

In his dissenting opinion on the *Legality of the Threat or Use of Nuclear Weapons*, Judge Shahabuddeen also supported this conclusion. With reference to the principle of humanity enshrined in the Martens Clause, he observed that:

---

[59]See, e.g., Weil (1992), p. 160.

[60]For an overview of this doctrinal debate see, e.g., Meron (2006), p. 386.

[61]See Lammers (1980), p. 72.

[62]Ibid.

[63]See Zagor (2012), p. 276.

[64]See again Jørgensen (2000), p. 128.

[65]See Le Bris (2012), p. 130.

> The Martens Clause provide[s] authority for treating the principles of humanity and the
> dictates of public conscience as principles of international law, leaving the precise content
> of the standard implied by these principles of international law to be ascertained in the
> light of changing conditions, inclusive of changes in the means and methods of warfare
> and the outlook and tolerance levels of the international community.[66]

According to Judge Shahabuddeen, the reference contained in the clause to both
usages and principles excludes a priori a cumulative reading, while supporting the
view that principles of humanity do exert legal force in themselves.[67] Interesting
enough, Judge Shahabuddeen based his assertions, inter alia, on international case
law.[68]

The characterization of the principle of humanity as a general principle of international law was recently advocated also by Judge Cançado Trindade in his separate opinion to the judgment rendered by the ICJ in the *Pulp Mills* case. According
to him, general principles of international law constitute autonomous sources of
law enshrining the values that inspire the whole legal order and, at the same time,
provide for its own foundations.[69] In this respect, the principle of humanity would
represent one of the inspiring values and main foundations of several domains of
law, such as human rights law, humanitarian law and international refugee law.[70]

It is noteworthy that, regardless of whether one considers this approach persuasive or not, similar considerations seem in some ways to knit together the apparent fragmentation that has emerged in international case law. As previously noted,
even when international courts have been cautious in referring to the principle of
humanity as a free-standing principle of international law, they have nonetheless
acknowledged that they constitute inspiring values on which customary or treaties
rules are grounded on.

4 The Nature and Function of General Principles of International Law: The Principle of Humanity Between Norm-Creating and Norm-Enhancing

Even among those who identify general principles of international law as a category
distinct from both customs and treaties, there is disagreement about whether these
principles would represent merely a mean of assistance in the interpretation and

---

[66]*Legality of the Threat or Use of Nuclear Weapons* cit., dissenting opinion of Judge Shahabuddeen,
p. 406.

[67]Ibid.

[68]Ibid., p. 407.

[69]*Pulp Mills on the River Uruguay (Argentina v. Uruguay)* [2010] ICJ Rep. 14, separate opinion
of Judge Cançado Trindade, para. 208.

[70]Ibid., para. 210.

application of treaty or customary law[71] or, conversely, constitute an autonomous source of law.[72] From a theoretical perspective, the very core of the issue lies in the complex and debated distinction between principles and rules, whose analysis, however, goes far beyond the purpose of the present work.[73]

It suffices here to note that, as shown by the analysis above and as it will be further elaborated on from a functional perspective in the present section, such dichotomy has also emerged with reference to the principle of humanity. Judges and legal scholars have struggled to anchor elementary considerations of humanity to a defined international legal category and have taken different positions as to their role in the interpretation, application or creation of international norms. As previously stated, while in some cases this principle has been acknowledged as an autonomous source of international law, in other instances, authors and judges have been reluctant to entrust humanity considerations with binding legal force in lack of a clear recognition either in customary or treaty law.[74] On top of that, elementary considerations of humanity have been at times depicted as merely interpretative means enabling the judiciary to overcome doubts concerning the existence of a certain norm or, as noted by Shaw, "endowing such norms with an addition force within the system".[75]

Again, legal scholars' disagreement on this last point is a clear portrait of the ambiguity and uncertainty of jurisprudential practice. As shown above, in some instances, international courts have seemed to uphold the norm-creating nature of the principle of humanity. Professor Wright, for instance, noted that in the *Corfu Channel* case "the Court relied upon broad principles of law [elementary considerations of humanity], apparently deemed to be self-evident and stated without citation of precedent or authority".[76] In this respect, the ICJ seems to have acknowledged that fundamental principles of international law—such as the principle of humanity—may provide a norm regardless of the existence or the

---

[71]See, e.g., Tunkin (1974), p. 203.

[72]See, e.g., Lammers (1980), p. 72.

[73]See, inter alia, Dworkin (1978), pp. 22–26. On the issue, it is worth mentioning also Professor Fitzmaurice's assertion, pursuant to which "By a principle or general principle, as opposed to a rule ... of law, is meant chiefly something which is not in itself a rule, but which underlines a rule, and explains and provides the reason for it". See Fitzmaurice (1957), p. 7 (according to Fitzmaurice, the aforesaid definition of general principles would explain their importance in international law, where the practice is not uniform and there may be areas of doubt or controversy) (ibid., p. 9). See also Petersen (2007), p. 286.

[74]With reference to the principle of humanity embodied in the Martens clause and applied by national and international courts, for instance, Cassese and Meron have upheld diametrical opposite views. While the former deduced from general practice that the principle of humanity does not amount to an autonomous source of law, distinguishable from the customary process [see Cassese (2008), p. 64], according to the latter, the principle of humanity acts as a restraining factor on States from doing what is not expressly forbidden by either customs or treaty rules. See Meron (2006), p. 28.

[75]Shaw (2003), p. 102.

[76]Wright (1949), p. 494.

applicability of conventional or customary rules (and, thus, regardless of the existence of constant State practice or *opinio iuris*).

This approach, however, has not been exempted from criticism. The main objection, which is generally raised against the above-mentioned law-making argument, is that it would entrust judges with quasi-legislative powers. In this respect, however, it has been noted that the judiciary's task in no case would amount to creating "new law"; to the contrary, judges should limit themselves to evaluating standards already embodied in the existing principles.[77] Thus, with reference to the principle of humanity, judges should merely ascertain what this principle requires in a given situation.[78]

Similar conclusions also echoed in Judge Weeramantry's dissenting opinion on the *Legality of the Threat or Use of Nuclear Weapons*, where he stated that:

> Any developed system of law [including the international legal system] has, in addition to its specific commands and prohibition, an array of general principles which, from time to time, are applied to specific items of conduct or events which have not been the subject of an express ruling before. The general principle is then applied to the specific situation and out of that particular application a rule of greater specificity emerges.[79]

Pursuant to this approach, the judiciary appears as a mere "material agent", whilst a "rule of greater specificity" would emerge by itself from the application of existing principles. Judge Weeramantry's argument seems therefore to fit in between the views of those who consider general principles as sources of law in and of themselves and those who regard them as means for developing further new norms of customary and treaty law (provided that a similar distinction may effectively be upheld).[80]

Still one could argue that similar considerations fall short in identifying "what" constitutes a general principle of international law, other than the recognition made of it by the judiciary. In this respect, general principles of international law appear *"inspirés moins par la pratique des états que par l'autorité des règles en cause"*.[81] But even admitting that general principles of international law would directly derive their legal force from the inherent "authority" of the values they embody, doubts may arise as to what this expression exactly means and how it may be "detected" in practice.

Similar uncertainty surrounds those attempts to ground general principles of international law on the *status conscientiae* of the international community as a

---

[77]See again *Legality of the Threat or Use of Nuclear Weapons* cit., dissenting opinion of Judge Shahabuddeen, p. 409.

[78]Ibid.

[79]Emphasis added. See *Legality of the Threat or Use of Nuclear Weapons* cit., dissenting opinion of Judge Weeramantry, p. 493.

[80]These two different functional approaches to general principles of law have been envisaged by Bassiouni, both with reference to general principles of municipal law and general principles of international law. See Bassiouni (1990), p. 777.

[81]See Le Bris (2012), p. 132.

whole.[82] As it has been observed in legal doctrine, in the light of the difficulties in establishing the constitutive elements and the parameters on which to evaluate the *status conscientiae* of the international community, such an approach would serve as an idealistic model, rather than a practical one.[83]

On other occasions, international courts have expressly limited the function of the principle of humanity to the interpretation of existing conventional and customary law.[84] In the already mentioned *Kupreskic* case, for instance, the International Criminal Tribunal for the Former Yugoslavia expressly found that principles of humanity, as general principles of international law, play a prominent role in the interpretation and application of ambiguous customary or conventional norms, but contextually excluded that they constitute an additional source of law.[85] In these terms, general principles of international law would merely assist in the interpretation and practical application of norms of customary or treaty nature.

It is self-evident that this "interpretative approach" clashes with the view of those who consider general principles of international law as a "formal" source of international law, exerting their normative force regardless of the existence of other international rules and regardless of whether similar principles have or have not been upheld in customary or conventional provisions.[86] However, particular attention should be paid also to the argument that these apparently different approaches may well fit together, as general principles of international law might at the same time serve both as interpretative means and sources of law. As noted by Professor Bassiouni, under this perspective, general principles of international law could be regarded as a "source of law that overreaches other positive sources of international law [namely, treaties and customs], and eventually supersedes them".[87]

These last considerations bring out the additional question of whether general principles of international law might be regarded as principles so fundamental to the international legal order to even invalidate conflicting customary and conventional norms. This topic is inevitably intertwined with the more complex issues of the hierarchy among sources of international law, the notion of *jus cogens* and the emergence of a new constitutional international law; none of which constitutes the specific object of the present analysis.

---

[82]See, inter alia, *Pulp Mills on the River Uruguay* cit., separate opinion of Judge Cançado Trindade, para. 212: "In my conception, [international principles of general international law] conform to an autonomous formal "source" of international law, that no international tribunal can minimize or overlook. Their proper consideration cannot at all be limited to verifying whether they have entered the realm of international law through custom or treaties. They disclose the axiological dimension ... of the applicable law, besides being indicators of the degree of evolution of the *status conscientiae* of the international community as a whole".

[83]Pineschi (2014), p. 106.

[84]See again ICTY, *Prosecutor v. Kupreskic* et al cit., para. 524.

[85]Ibid.

[86]See, inter alia, *Pulp Mills on the River Uruguay* cit., separate opinion of Judge Cançado Trindade, para. 212.

[87]See Bassiouni (1990), p. 776.

That notwithstanding, it is worth mentioning that many commentators have relied on the principle of humanity and its application by international courts to support the argument that (some) higher general principles of international law might override treaty or customary norms.[88] Other authors, although refraining from considering the impacts of a similar categorization in relation to other sources of law, have somehow similarly listed the principle of humanity among the "normative-ideational" principles of international law, constituting the same *raison d'être* of the international legal order.[89] These principles would thus provide unity, consistency and direction to the international legal system, being the archetypal principles of the system itself. In this respect, they would differ from mere structural-operational principles—including, inter alia, the principle *pacta sunt servanda*—that would instead represent the coordinates for the organization and management of internal relations within the international legal order.[90]

These last theories much draw from Judge Tanaka's reasoning in his dissenting opinion on the *South West Africa* cases (touching upon both the notion and function of general principles of law). According to him, human rights and their protection belong to *jus cogens* (or "imperative law") and, as such, are embodied in the notion of "general principles" in Article 38(1)(c) of the Statute of the ICJ.[91] In Judge Tanaka's view, this last provision, by failing to require States' consent as a pre-condition to the recognition of general principles, extends the notion of "source of international law" beyond legal positivism.[92] As a consequence, regardless of whether States uphold or not the validity of a certain principle, they are nonetheless bound by its rule. In this way:

> From this source of law [general principles], international law could have the validity of its foundation extended beyond the will of States into the sphere of natural law and assume an aspect of its supra-national and supra-positive character.[93]

As to the *nature* of general principles of international law, however, it is clear that also this "supra-positive" approach to general principles as peremptory norms fails in overcoming the practical problem of ascertaining the existence and identifying the content of these principles in lack of clear States' consent.

---

[88]See, for instance, Christenson (1987–1988), p. 586. Although not referring explicitly to the principle of humanity, the Author implicitly encompasses it, by means of examples, among those "principles of general international law that are or ought to be so compelling that they might be recognized by the international community for the purpose of invalidating or forcing revision in ordinary norms of treaty or custom in conflict with them".

[89]Tsagourias (2007), p. 76.

[90]Ibid., p. 77.

[91] *South West Africa* cases cit., dissenting opinion of Judge Tanaka, p. 298.

[92]Ibid.

[93]Ibid.

As to their possible function, one may recall instead Professor Lauterpacht's statement, according to which:

> The difference between disregarding a rule of international law in deference to a general principle of law and interpreting it in the light of a general principle of international law may be but a play of words.[94]

5 Conclusions: General Principles of International Law and the Role of the Judiciary

The transnational nature of a growing number of human activities inevitably raises issues that neither conventional nor customary rules are apt to face. Against this vacuum, it is likely that general principles of law and, more specifically, general principles of international law may increasingly play a fundamental role in the near future. Nonetheless, as repeatedly noted, the nature, content and function of these categories are anything but clear. International case law and legal doctrine have often disagreed as to what these categories stand for.

First of all, as made evident by the analysis herein, even when taking into account a specific "principle", it is disputed whether it may be listed among "general principles of international law". International courts and scholars are reluctant to create a "catalogue" of these principles and, even when they have attempted to do so, clear discrepancies have emerged. In addition, while some authors and judges consider general principles of international law as nothing more than customary norms, others have firmly supported their "autonomous" nature. This is substantiated, inter alia, by the different approaches that international courts and legal scholars have taken with reference to the principle of humanity.

Similar considerations as to the function of general principles of international law may also be drawn. While some judges and scholars have expressly recognized the inherent normative character of such principles as an autonomous source of international law, others consider them as mere interpretative means or gap-fillers of existing customary or conventional norms.

Against this fragmented background and regardless of the functional approach that one takes—interpretative/gap-filling or law-making—the role of the judiciary appears as a pre-eminent one.

If one rejects the view that general principles of international law would merely amount to customary or treaty provisions (a view that, as noted with reference to the principle of humanity, would collide with the wording used by international courts), it appears clear that the judiciary may give an important contribution to the development and "moralization" of international law by detecting and recognizing what amounts to general principles of international law.

---

[94]Lauterpacht (1958), pp. 165–166.

This important role that the judiciary may play is, however, a delicate one, as judges are de facto called to exercise quasi-legislative powers. This is particularly true for the international legal system, in which States are unwilling to entrust judges with subjective detecting powers. It is thus no surprise that, with reference to general principles of international law, several commentators have denounced the risk of a "government of the judiciary".[95]

That notwithstanding, the exercise of quasi-legislative powers by the judiciary may allow overcoming the limits of the international legal system through ensuring the respect for fundamental rights of individuals and the interests of the whole international community anytime similar essential values are at stake.

References

Bassiouni, Cherif M. 1990. A Functional Approach to General Principles of Law. *Michigan Journal of International Law* 11: 768-818.
Brownlie, Ian. 1998. *Principles of Public International Law*. V ed. Oxford: Clarendon Press. New York: Oxford University Press.
Cassese, Antonio. 2008. *The Human Dimension of International Law. Selected Papers*. Oxford, New York: Oxford University Press.
Cheng, Bin. 1987 [1953]. *General Principles of Law as Applied by International Courts and Tribunals*. Cambridge: Grotius Publications.
Christenson, Gordon. A. 1987–1988. Jus Cogens: Guarding Interests Fundamental to International Society. Virginia Journal of International Law 28: 585-648.
Crawford, James. 2012. *Brownlie's Principles of Public International Law*. Oxford: Oxford University Press.
Dupuy. René-Jean (ed.). 1991. *Humanité et droit international*. Paris: Editions A. Pedone.
Dworkin, Ronald M. 1978. *Taking Rights Seriously*. Cambridge: Harvard University Press.
Ellis, Jaye. 2011. General Principles and Comparative Law. *European Journal of International Law* 22: 949-971.
Fitzmaurice, Gerald. 1957. The General Principles of International Law. Considerations from the Standpoint of the Rule of Law. *Recueil des Cours de l'Académie de La Haye*, vol. II. Leiden: Brill.
Fitzmaurice, Gerald. 1986. *The Law and Procedure of the International Court of Justice: General Principles and Substantive Law*. Cambridge: Grotius.
Francioni, Francesco. 1996. International 'Soft Law': A Contemporary Assessment. In *Fifty Years of the International Court of Justice. Essays in Honour of Sir Robert Jennings*, eds. Vaughan Lowe and Maurice Fitzmaurice, 167-180. Cambridge, New York: Cambridge University Press.
Gaja, Giorgio. 2013. General Principles of Law. *Max Planck Encyclopedia of Public International Law*. http://opil.ouplaw.com.
Herczegh, Geza. 1969. *General Principles of Law and the International Legal Order*. Budapest: Akadémiai Kiadó.
Jørgensen, Nina G. B. 2000. *The Responsibility of States for International Crimes*. Oxford: Oxford University Press.
Lammers, Johan G. 1980. General Principles of Law Recognized by Civilized Nations. In *Essays on the Development of the International Legal Order. In Memory of Haro F. Van Panhuys*, ed. Frits Kalshoven, 53-76. Alphen aan den Rijn: Kluwer Academic Publishers.

---

[95]This expression was used by Judge Shahabuddeen in his dissenting opinion on the *Legality of Threat or Use of Nuclear Weapons* cit. See dissenting opinion of Judge Shahabuddeen, p. 406.

Lauterpacht, Hersch. 1958. *The Development of International Law by the International Court of Justice*. London: Stevens.

Le Bris, Catherine. 2012. *L'Humanité saisie par le droit international public*. Paris: L.G.D.J.

Lefkowitz, David. 2010. Sources of International Law. In *The Philosophy of International Law*, eds. Samantha Besson and John Tasioulas, 187-203. Oxford, New York: Oxford University Press.

Meron, Theodor. 2000. The Martens Clause, Principle of Humanity, and Dictates of Public Conscience. *American Journal of International Law*. 94: 78-89

Meron, Theodor. 2006. *The Humanization of International Law*. Leiden, Boston: Martinus Nijhoff.

Pellet, Alain. 2002. Applicable Law. In *The Rome Statute of the International Criminal Court. A Commentary*, eds. Antonio Cassese, Paola Gaeta and John R.W.D. Jones, vol. II, 1051-1084. Oxford: Oxford University Press.

Pellet, Alain. 2012. Article 38. In *The Statute of the International Court of Justice. A Commentary*, eds. Andreas Zimmerman, Christian Tomuschat and Karin Oellers-Frahm, Christian Tams, 731-870. Oxford: Oxford University Press.

Petersen, Niels. 2007. Customary Law without Custom? Rules, Principles, and the Role of State Practice in International Norm Creation. *American University International Law Review* 23: 275-310.

Pineschi, Laura. 2014. I principi del diritto internazionale dell'ambiente: dal divieto di inquinamento transfrontaliero alla tutela dell'ambiente come *common concern*. In *Trattato di diritto dell'ambiente*, eds. Rosario Ferrara and Maria Alessandra Sandulli, 93-152. Milano: Giuffré.

Raimondo, Fabian O. 2008. *General Principles of Law in the Decisions of International Criminal Courts and Tribunals*. Leiden, Boston: Martinus Nijhoff.

Shaw, Malcolm N. 2003. *International Law*. Cambridge: Cambridge University Press.

Thirlway, Hugh W.A. 2013. The Law and Procedure of the International Court of Justice: Fifty Years of Jurisprudence. Vol. I. Oxford: Oxford University Press.

Treves, Tullio. 2005. *Diritto internazionale. Problemi fondamentali*. Milano: Giuffré.

Tsagourias, Nicholas. 2007. The Constitutional Role of General Principles of Law in International and European Jurisprudence. In *Transnational Constitutionalism. International and European Perspectives*, ed. Nicholas Tsagourias, 71-106. Cambridge: Cambridge University Press.

Tunkin, Grigori I. 1974. *Theory of International Law*. Cambridge: Harvard University Press.

Verzijl, Jan H.W. 1968. *International Law in Historical Perspective*. Leiden: A. W. Sijthoff.

Vitányi, Béla. 1982. Les principes généraux du droit (tendances doctrinales). *Revue générale de droit international public* 86: 48-116.

Voigt, Christina. 2008. The Role of General Principles in International Law and their Relationship to Treaty Law. *Retfaerd* 31: 3-25.

Waldock, H. 1962. General Course of Public International Law. *Recueil des Cours de l'Académie de La Haye*, vol. II. Leiden: Brill.

Weil, Prosper. 1992. Le droit international en quête de son identité. *Recueil des Cours de l'Académie de La Haye*, vol. VI. Leiden: Brill.

Wright, Quincy. 1949. The Corfu Channel Case. *American Journal of International Law* 43: 491-494.

Zagor, Matthew. 2012. Elementary Considerations of Humanity. In *The ICJ and the Evolution of International Law: The Enduring Impact of the Corfu Channel Case*, eds. Karine Bannelier, Theodore Christakis and Sarah Heathcote, 264-292. London: Routledge.

"Please, Handle with Care!"—Some Considerations on the Approach of the European Court of Justice to the Direct Effect of General Principles of European Union Law

Nicole Lazzerini

Abstract Since its inception, the European Court of Justice has conceived its mandate as encompassing the competence to identify and use in adjudication unwritten general principles of law, by drawing them, in particular, from the legal orders of the Member States or international law instruments. In order to safeguard the flexibility of this source of law, the Court has not engaged in an in-depth investigation of the very concept of "general principle of European Union law", the methodology for the identification of general principles and the reconstruction of their content, their scope of application and their effects. This chapter focuses on one specific issue that is in need of further conceptual clarification: the capacity of general principles (or at least some of them) to be relied on by individuals before national courts to have conflicting national law set aside (direct effect), in particular in disputes *vis-à-vis* other individuals (direct horizontal effect). The relevant case law of the European Court of Justice is highly ambiguous if not even obscure. For this reason, it has attracted widespread criticisms. Accordingly, the main purpose of the chapter is to understand whether that case law is more in need of argumentative clarity or of solid normative justifications.

1 Introduction

For European Union lawyers, the expression "general principles" designates an unwritten, legally-binding source of Union law whose contours have been—and continue to be—shaped by the case law of the European Court of Justice (hereafter, the "Court"). This chapter focuses on one specific issue in need of further conceptual

N. Lazzerini (✉)
Research Fellow in European Union Law, University of Parma, Parma, Italy
e-mail: nicole.lazzerini@unipr.it

© Springer International Publishing Switzerland 2015
L. Pineschi (ed.), *General Principles of Law - The Role of the Judiciary*,
Ius Gentium: Comparative Perspectives on Law and Justice 46,
DOI 10.1007/978-3-319-19180-5_8

clarification: the capacity of general principles of European Union law (hereafter, "general principles") to be invoked by individuals before national courts in order to obtain the setting aside of conflicting national law.[1] The provisions of European Union law (hereinafter, "EU law") that possess this capacity have "direct effect". This is "vertical" or "horizontal" depending on whether it is relied on by an individual against the State (or an organ of it), or against another individual.[2] In order to have direct effect, a provision must be clear, sufficiently precise, and unconditional.[3] Whilst a provision that fulfils this test may be invoked against the State, the case law of the Court suggests that this is not sufficient for horizontal effect. However, it is unclear which additional characters the provision should have. Things become even more opaque when one analyses the case law on the direct effect of general principles, as no reference can generally be found to the test of clarity, precision and unconditional character.

This lack of clarity and transparency in the reasoning of the Court is problematic from a theoretical point of view and has practical repercussions on the life of individuals. When a provision of EU law is amenable to direct effect, an individual may be able to enjoy a subjective right[4] whose exercise, or even existence, is precluded by national law. At the same time, if the provision entails direct horizontal effect, another person—the counterpart in the legal relationship—may have to take a conduct, or be the subject of consequences, different from what national law prescribes.

The topic of the direct effect of general principles therefore constitutes a privileged observatory to appreciate both the potential inherent in this source of EU law and the responsibility of the Court in handling it.[5]

---

[1]In this chapter, the expression "national law" refers to the law of the Member States of the European Union.

[2]The Court referred to direct effect since its seminal judgment in case 26/62 *van Gend & Loos* [1963] ECR 175: "the Community constitutes a new legal order of international law ... the subjects of which comprise not only Member States but also their nationals. Independently of the legislation of Member States, Community law therefore not only imposes *obligations* on individuals but is also intended to confer upon them *rights* which become part of their legal heritage".

[3]In reality, the approach of the Court to the threshold criteria for direct effect is not always consistent. As a corollary, the very meaning of "direct effect" is not uncontroversial. Based on the case law of the Court, it is possible to identify an objective notion of direct effect, which revolves around the three criteria referred to in the text, and a narrower, subjective notion, which limits the capacity to be invoked with direct effect to EU law provisions that confer rights on individuals. For further insights on this point, see Craig and De Búrca (2011), pp. 181–182. Another layer of complexity is added by the ambiguity in the case law of the Court as regards the relationship between direct effect and the principle according to which Union law has primacy over the domestic law of the Member States.

[4]This will occur when the general principle concerned confers a right on individuals. On the content of general principles see Sect. 2 below.

[5]See Mazák and Moser (2013), p. 61, who argue, at p. 63, that "the general principles of EU law ... constitute, without doubt, a powerful judicial instrument in the hands of the Court, to be handled with care and responsibility".

The attention received in recent years by two judgments where the Court has granted horizontal direct effect to a general principle, *Mangold* and *Küçükdeveci*,[6] could suggest that it is pointless to discuss the issue once again. At least two reasons support a different conclusion. First, *Mangold* and *Küçükdeveci* are complex judgments, and the granting of direct horizontal effect to a general principle is not the only issue that has attracted the criticisms of commentators.[7] By focusing solely on it, this chapter seeks to understand whether the problem lies (only) with the lack of argumentative clarity in the legal reasoning of the Court or, rather, sound legal reasons supporting the granting of direct horizontal effect to general principles are also missing. Second, the first judgment delivered by the Court on the horizontal application of the EU Charter of Fundamental Rights (hereafter, the "Charter"),[8] *Association de médiation sociale (AMS)*,[9] provides some new insight also on direct effect of general principles that is worth discussing.

As a starting point for our enquiry, it is helpful to introduce the concept and functions of general principles (Sect. 2) and to clarify in which situations their direct effect may be relevant (Sect. 3). The main challenges posed by the granting of direct horizontal effect to general principles in *Mangold* and *Küçükdeveci*, and by the legal reasoning of the Court, will then be thoroughly discussed (Sect. 4). Finally, before drawing some conclusive remarks, the relevance of *AMS* in the discourse on horizontal effect of general principles will be explored (Sect. 5).

2 General Principles as a Source of European Union Law: Concept and Functions

Against the background of the thorough discussion of these issues in other studies,[10] we can confine ourselves to observe that the Court has extrapolated general principles of law from both the EU legal order itself and from the legal orders of the Member States. The first category includes general principles drawn from specific

---

[6]Case C-144/04 *Mangold* [2005] ECR I-9981 and case C-555/07 *Küçükdeveci* [2010] ECR I-365.

[7]Two additional aspects are particularly controversial, namely: as regards *Mangold*, the way in which the Court acknowledged the existence of a general principle prohibiting discrimination on grounds of age; as regards *Küçükdeveci*, the finding that, after the expiry of the transposition period of a directive, domestic legislation concerning issues dealt with by the directive itself fall *ipso facto* within the scope of Union law. For a thorough discussion see Dougan (2011), p. 219, and de Mol (2011), p. 109.

[8]OJ 2012 C 326, 391.

[9]Case C-176/12 *AMS*, judgment of 15 January 2014, nyr.

[10]Cf., inter alia, Bernitz et al. (2013, 2008), Groussot (2006), Tridimas (2006), Adinolfi (1994), p. 521.

provisions of the EU Treaties,[11] which the Court has regarded as expression of broader rules, or from the very nature, spirit and objectives of the Union.[12] Reference can be made to the principles of solidarity,[13] of institutional equilibrium,[14] of reciprocal cooperation between the institutions and the Member States[15] and amongst the EU institution,[16] or the principle requiring Member States to compensate individuals of damages ensuing from breaches of EU law.[17] To identify the general principles of the second type, the Court has followed a comparative method, though it has never conditioned the identification of a general principle to its recognition in all the Member States. However, the dividing line between the two sets of general principles is not clear-cut. Some general principles that the Court has drawn primarily from the legal orders of the Member States find specific expression in Treaty provisions, such as, for instance, the principles of equality and non-discrimination,[18] proportionality,[19] and legal certainty.[20] At the same time, the distinction is not without any relevance: whilst the general principles with a basis in the Treaties have the status of EU primary law, the others rank in-between the Treaties and EU legislation.[21]

An important set of general principles that the Court has drawn "from outside" the EU legal order concerns the protection of fundamental rights. The founding Treaties of the European Communities[22] did not contain any express provision aimed at providing protection for individuals whose fundamental rights were adversely affected by acts adopted by the Community institutions, or by the Member States when acting within the framework of the Treaties. In its seminal judgment *Internationale Handelsgesellschaft*, the Court held that "respect for

---

[11]After the entry into force of the Lisbon Treaty on 1 December 2009, the Union is founded on two Treaties with equal legal status: the Treaty on the European Union (TEU) and the Treaty on the Functioning of the European Union (TFEU), whose last consolidated versions can be found in OJ 2012 C 326, 1.

[12]Strozzi and Mastroianni (2013), p. 220, and the Opinion of Advocate General Trstenjak in Case C-282/10 *Dominguez* (judgment of 24 January 2012, nyr.), para. 96.

[13]Joined cases 154/78, 205/78, 206/78, 226/78 to 228/78, 263/78 and 264/78 and 39/79, 31/79, 83/79 and 85/79 *Ferriera Valsabbia v. Commission* [1980] ECR 907, para. 157.

[14]Case C-138/79 *Roquette Frères* [1980] ECR 3333, para. 33.

[15]Case 230/81 *Luxembourg v. Parliament* [1983] ECR 255, para. 37.

[16]Case C-204/86 *Hellenic Republic v Council* [1988] ECR 5223, para. 16.

[17]Joined cases C-6/90 and 9/90 *Francovich* [1991] ECR I-5357, in particular paras. 31 to 35.

[18]Joined cases 117/76 and 16/77 *Ruckdeschel* [1977] ECR 1753, para. 7.

[19]Case C-174/89 *Hoche* [1990] ECR I-2681, para. 19.

[20]Case C- 169/80 *Gondrand Frères and Garancini* [1981] ECR 1931, para. 17.

[21]Gaja (1998), p. 445. In reality, this distinction does not emerge neatly in the case law of the Court. For instance, in case C-101/08 *Audiolux* [2009] ECR I-9823, para. 63, the Court affirmed that "the general principles of Community law have constitutional status". However, the case was mostly concerned with the principle of equal treatment which, as noticed, as a basis in the Treaties.

[22]Notably, the Treaty establishing the European Coal and Steel Community (1951), the Treaty establishing European Economic Community (1957), and the Treaty establishing the European Atomic Energy Community (1957).

fundamental rights forms an integral part of the general principles of law protected by the Court of Justice".[23] As sources of inspiration, it later referred to "the constitutional traditions common to the Member States", and to "international treaties for the protection of human rights on which the Member States have collaborated, or of which they are signatories".[24] Over the years, the Court has characterized as general principles several fundamental rights, very often drawing inspiration from the Convention for the Protection of Human Rights and Fundamental Freedoms (ECHR).[25] Some examples are the rights to effective judicial protection,[26] to respect for private and family life,[27] to property,[28] to human dignity,[29] the right to take collective action, including the right to strike,[30] the freedoms of expression,[31] association[32] and religion,[33] and the principle of legality of criminal offences and penalties.[34] Several fundamental rights that have been recognized as general principles are now to be found also in the Charter, which forms an integral part of EU primary law since 1 December 2009.[35]

The foregoing allows us to discard preliminary objections to the capacity of general principles to have direct effect. The "generality" of general principles does not necessarily amount to vagueness or indeterminacy. They do not correspond (or, at least, not all of them) to Dworkinian "principles".[36] Their generality rather refers to the fact that they "embody fundamental principles of the European Union and of its Member States".[37] From the point of view of their content, they "embrace rules of widely varying content and degree of completeness, ranging from interpretative maxims to fully fledged norms".[38]

The general principles of Union law perform different functions.[39] The Court has often relied on them to fill normative gaps in EU legislation, or even in the Treaties (as in the case of general principles protecting fundamental rights).

---

[23]Case 11/70 *Internationale Handelsgesellschaft* [1970] ECR 1125, para. 4.

[24]Case C-4/73 *Nold* [1974] ECR 491, para. 13.

[25]Rome, 4 November 1950.

[26]Case C-222/84 *Johnston* [1986] ECR 1651, para. 18.

[27]Case C-60/00 *Carpenter* [2002] ECR ECR I-6279, para. 41.

[28]Case 44/79 *Hauer* [1979] ECR 3727, para. 4.

[29]Case C-36/02 *Omega Spielhallen* [2004] ECR I-9609, para. 34.

[30]Case C-438/05 *International Transport Workers Federation (Viking)* [2007] ECR I-10779, para. 42.

[31]Case C-112/00 *Schmidberger* [2003] ECR I-5659, para. 80.

[32]Ibid.

[33]Case 130/75 *Prais* [1976] ECR 1589.

[34]Case C-303/05 *Advocaten voor de Wereld* [2007] ECR I-3633, para. 50.

[35]Cf. Article 6(1) TEU.

[36]Dworkin (1978).

[37]*Dominguez* (Opinion) cit., para. 95.

[38]Advocate General Mazák, case C-411/05 *Palacios de la Villa* [2007] ECR I-8531, para. 134.

[39]For a broader discussion, see Lenaerts and Gutiérrez-Fons (2010), p. 1629.

They also assist the interpretation of Union acts, and provide grounds for their review. Those based on the Treaties, having the status of EU primary law, can also affect the interpretation of other provisions with the same rank. This is the case, inter alia, of the general principles drawn from the ECHR or from the constitutional traditions common to the Member States, given that a specific Treaty provision, Article 6(3) TEU, refers to them.

General principles are binding also over the Member States whenever a situation falls "within the scope of Union law".[40] Then, national measures must be interpreted in light of the relevant general principle(s) and, in case of conflict, the national court must strive to achieve an interpretation of the domestic provision that is consistent with Union law, "taking the whole body of domestic law into consideration and applying the interpretative methods recognised by domestic law".[41] However, this duty, which is known as the duty of consistent interpretation of national law with EU law, does not allow a domestic court to rely on an interpretation of the national provision against the law (*contra legem*).[42] If the conflict between the general principle and the domestic provision cannot be overcome through consistent interpretation, the question of whether general principles can entail direct effect comes to the fore.[43]

---

[40]On the meaning of this notion, see the following Section.

[41]See the following judgments: case 14/83 *Von Colson and Kamann* [1984] ECR 1891, para. 26, case C-106/89 *Marleasing* [1990] ECR I-4135, para. 8, case C-131/97 *Carbonari and others* [1999] ECR I-1103, para. 48, joined cases C-397/01 to C-403/01 *Pfeiffer and Others* [2004] ECR I-8835, para. 113, case C-105/03 *Pupino* [2005] ECR I-5285, para. 61, and *Dominguez* cit., para. 27. Except for *Pupino*, which dealt with a Framework Decision adopted in the context of former third pillar, all the other cases mentioned concern directives. However, the duty of consistent interpretation does not exist only in relation to this source of Union law. As observed by the Court, "the requirement for national law to be interpreted in conformity with Community law is inherent in the system of the Treaty, since it permits the national court, for the matters within its jurisdiction, to ensure the full effectiveness of Community law when it determines the dispute before it" (*Pfeiffer* cit., para. 114). Thus, the duty of consistent interpretation extends to all the provisions of Union law: see Gaja and Adinolfi (2014), p. 175, *in fine*. It must also be stressed that general principles rank above Union legislation, which must itself be interpreted in conformity with the former. The application of a general principle on a national provision is usually triggered by a Union act that applies to the cases at hand (on this point, see Sect. 3). The duty to interpret national law in conformity with the general principles is then a corollary of the requirement that Union acts be themselves in conformity with those principles. Thus, in case C-275/06 *Promusicae* [2008] ECR I-271, para. 68, the Court held that: "the authorities and courts of the Member States must not only interpret their national law in a manner consistent with those directives but also make sure that they do not rely on an interpretation of them which would be in conflict with those fundamental rights or with the other general principles of Community law, such as the principle of proportionality".

[42]See *Pfeiffer* cit., para. 115, case C-268/06, *Impact* [2008] ECR I-2483, para. 100, joined cases C-378/07 to C-380/07, *Angelidaki and Others* [2009] ECR I-3071, para. 199, and *Dominguez* cit., para. 25.

[43]On the logical order between direct effect and duty of consistent interpretation, see Rosas and Armati (2010), p. 72.

3 When Is the Direct Effect of General Principles Relevant?

The notion of "scope of Union law" defines the "sphere"[44] where general principles are binding at the national level. This means, in essence, that general principles are not free-standing rules. In order to trigger their application, it is not sufficient that an individual claims that a national measure runs counter to one or more of them. One must preliminarily verify whether another binding provision of Union law, which is not a general principle itself, applies to the specific situation at issue. That "other" provision, which is sometimes referred to as "trigger rule", brings the situation within the scope of Union law, allowing the application of the general principles. It also follows from the case law of the Court that a provision of the Treaties that merely confers a power on the Union does not possess this capacity,[45] unlike the EU acts possibly adopted in the exercise of that power.

An individual can therefore seek to invoke the direct effect of a general principle only when the conflicting national provision has a connection with another rule of EU law of the kind just described. This is the case with respect to the following categories of provisions: national measures adopted in order to discharge specific duties flowing from EU primary or secondary law, such as legislation implementing EU directives,[46] or enforcing EU regulations[47]; national measures that substantially give effect to a Union obligation, though not adopted specifically on that purpose[48]; national provisions that govern or affect the enjoyment or the exercise of (ordinary) rights conferred on individuals by Union law[49]; national measures that derogate from EU primary or secondary provisions based on reasons of public interest.[50] This list, far from being exhaustive, only encompasses the situations that occur more frequently. The notion of "scope of Union law" is inherently dynamic and at present the Court is mostly elaborating it in its case law on the application of the Charter, which is similarly premised on the existence of a "trigger rule".[51]

The previous taxonomy of national measures falling within the scope of Union law also helps us to reveal a tension between the granting of direct horizontal effect to general principles and the requirement of legal certainty, which the Court has characterised as "a fundamental principle of [Union] law".[52] When a national measure

---

[44]Temple Lang (1991), p. 23.

[45]Cf., for instance, case C-427/06 *Bartsch* [2008] I-7245, para. 18.

[46]Joined cases C-64/00 and 20/00 *Booker Aquacultur* [2003] ECR I-7411, para. 126.

[47]Case 5/88 *Wachauf* [1989] ECR 2609, para. 19.

[48]Case C-442/00 *Caballero* [2002] ECR I-11915, paras. 27–30.

[49]Case C-276/01 *Steffensen* [2003] ECR I-3735, para. 71.

[50]Case C-260/89 *Elliniki Radiophonia Tileorassi (ERT)* [1991] ECR I-2925, para. 42.

[51]Cf. Case C-617/10 *Åkerberg Fransson*, judgment of 26 February 2013, nyr., paras. 17 to 22. For a discussion on the scope of application of the Charter on Member States' action, see, inter alia, Fontanelli (2014), p. 231; Rosas (2012), p. 1269, and Sarmiento (2013), p. 1267.

[52]Case C-308/06 *Intertanko* [2008] ECR I-4057.

that regulates the relationship between two individuals (for instance, a working relationship) is in conflict with a general principle, the private party who had acted in conformity with the domestic legislation could lose her case because of the direct application of the general principle. This situation is problematic from the point of view of legal certainty, which requires that rules are "clear and precise, so that individuals may ascertain unequivocally what their rights and obligations are and may take steps accordingly".[53] The concern related to legal certainty is not, however, the only one that emerges from the case law of the Court, on which we shall now turn.

4 A Troublesome Marriage: The Direct Effect of General Principles in the Recent Case Law of the Court

The Court's rulings in *Mangold* and *Kücükdeveci* arose from working disputes between private law employers and their employees, who claimed to have suffered age-discrimination. On both occasions, the Court granted horizontal effect to the general principle prohibiting discrimination on grounds of age, whose existence was established for the first time in *Mangold*. After briefly outlining the two judgments, this section reviews the main challenges stemming from the granting of direct effect to general principles, as highlighted by the two judgments. Whilst both cases concern primarily horizontal effect, some of the following criticisms and considerations are relevant also with respect to the granting of direct effect to general principles in a vertical situation.

4.1 *Mangold and Kücükdeveci*

In *Mangold*, the national court doubted the compatibility with Union law of the German legislation that, by way of derogation from the general rule, did not make the conclusion of fixed-term contracts conditional on the existence of an "objective reason" when the worker was aged 52 or over.[54] The national court submitted a preliminary reference[55] to the Court, asking it to clarify whether the applicable national

---

[53]Ibid.

[54]Reference is made to Article 14 of the *Gesetz über Teilzeitarbeit und befristete Arbeitsverträge und zur Änderung und Aufhebung arbeitsrechtlicher Bestimmungen* (Law on Part-Time Working and Fixed-Term Contracts).

[55]According to Article 267 TFEU, any court or tribunal of a Member State before whom is pending a proceeding can request the Court to give a preliminary ruling on the interpretation of provisions of the Treaties or of Union acts, or on the validity of the latter, when the Court's decision is necessary to decide the case. The national court or tribunal is, in principle, under a duty to submit a reference to the Court when under national law there is no judicial remedy against its decision. The Court has relaxed this duty in interpretation cases in case 283/81 *CILFIT* [1982] ECR 3415, whereas in case 314/85 *Foto-Frost* [1987] ECR 4199 it has established that, in certain circumstances, also national courts whose decisions can be appealed are under a duty to submit a reference to the Court concerning the validity of a Union act.

rules were in conflict with Directive 2000/78/EC, which has established a general framework for combating discrimination in the field of employment and occupation.[56] Since the previous case law of the Court showed that provisions of directives cannot entail direct horizontal effect, even when they are clear, sufficiently precise and unconditional,[57] the referring court also wondered whether the national legislation should have been set aside, had it resulted to be incompatible with EU law.

The Court found that the domestic legislation did not comply with Article 6(1) of the Directive, which allows Member States to introduce or maintain differences of treatment on grounds of age that are objectively and reasonably justified by a legitimate aim, provided that this is pursued through appropriate and necessary means. Although the promotion of vocational integration of unemployed older workers was regarded "as justifying, 'objectively and reasonably', ... a difference of treatment on grounds of age" such as that at issue, the measure failed the necessity test.[58] Therefore, the Court had to address the question of the consequences to be drawn from the incompatibility.

After reiterating its case law on the lack of direct horizontal effect of directives, the Court affirmed, crucially, that "the principle of non-discrimination on grounds of age must ... be regarded as a general principle of Community law".[59] In the Court's view, Directive 2000/78/EC has not introduced this general principle in the EU legal order; rather, it has the "sole purpose" of creating a framework aimed at strengthening the principle of equal treatment in the fields of employment and occupation.[60] As a further step, it observed that the domestic legislation fell within the scope of Union law, because it had been adopted to implement another directive,[61] notably Directive 1999/70/EC on the Framework Agreement on fixed-term work.[62] Finally, the Court instructed the national court "to provide ... the legal protection which individuals derive from the rules of Community law, and to ensure that those rules are fully effective, setting aside any provision of national law which may conflict with that law".[63] Part of the doctrine,[64] and also some

---

[56]Council Directive of 27 November 2000 establishing a general framework for equal treatment in employment and occupation, OJ 2000 *L* 303, 16.

[57]Cf. Case 152/84 *Marshall* [1986] ECR I-723, para. 48, case C-91/92 *Faccini Dori* [1994] ECR I-3325, para. 20, case C-192/94 *El Corte Inglés* [1996] ECR I-1281, para. 15, *Pfeiffer* cit., para. 108, and *Dominguez* cit., para. 37. However, the Court has introduced some exceptions or refinements to this rule: for a critical overview, see Dashwood (2006–2007), p. 81.

[58]*Mangold* cit., paras. 61 and 65.

[59]Ibid., para. 75.

[60]Ibid., para. 74.

[61]Ibid., para. 75.

[62]Council Directive 1999/70/EC of 28 June 1999 concerning the framework agreement on fixed-term work concluded by ETUC, UNICE and CEEP, OJ 1999 L 175, 43.

[63]Ibid., paras. 77 and 78.

[64]See Editorial (2006), p. 1; Schiek (2006), p. 329; Schmidt (2005), p. 505, and Dougan (2011).

Advocates General[65] within the Court, harshly criticized *Mangold*, pointing at the opaque reasoning as regards the very existence of a general principle prohibiting discrimination on grounds of age and the possibility to apply it horizontally.

In spite of this, the Court reiterated its conclusion a few years later in *Kücükdeveci*. Another German court had raised doubts on the compatibility with Union law of a national provision which, as an exception to the rule that the notice period for dismissal must be proportional to the length of the service, excluded from calculation periods prior to the completion of the employee's twenty-fifth year of age. The Court was requested to clarify whether there was a conflict with "the Community law prohibition of discrimination on grounds of age".[66] The national court also sought to establish whether the parameter to test the compatibility of the domestic provision was the general principle of non-discrimination on grounds of age, or rather Directive 2000/78/EC, whose period of transposition had expired at the time of the facts. Furthermore, since the issue arose again in the context of a dispute involving an employee and its private employer, the national judge asked whether the disapplication of the national provision was conditional on a finding of incompatibility by the Court, in order to protect the legitimate expectations of individuals.

At the outset, the Court recalled that the prohibition of discrimination on grounds of age is a general principle of Union law, and that Directive 2000/78/EC merely gives specific expression to it.[67] It then considered that the national provision at issue fell within the scope of Union law because it dealt with a matter covered by Directive 2000/78/EC.[68] For the first time, the Court held that the expiry of a directive's transposition period has "the effect of bringing within the scope of European Union law [domestic legislation] which concerns a matter governed by that directive".[69] The point raised by the national court as regards the parameter for the assessment of compatibility received a sibylline answer. Throughout the judgment, the Court referred to "the general principle of European Union law prohibiting all discrimination on grounds of age, as given expression in Directive 2000/78",[70] and assumed the coincidence between the content of the general principle and the proportionality test as established by Article 6(1) of the Directive.

Since the national provision failed the proportionality test, the Court had to address the question regarding the consequences of its incompatibility with Union law.

---

[65]Advocate General Mazák, *Palacios de la Villa* cit., paras. 134 to 138; Advocate General Geelhoed, case C-13/05, *Sonia Chacón Navas* [2006] ECR I-6467, para. 56; Advocate General Kokott, case C-321/05 *Kofoed* [2007] ECR 5795, para. 67; Advocate General Ruiz-Jarabo Colomer, joined cases C-55/07 and C-56/07 *Michaeler* [2008] ECR I- 3135, paras. 17–22.

[66]*Kücükdeveci* cit., para. 17.

[67]Ibid., paras. 20 and 21.

[68]Ibid., paras. 24 and 26.

[69]Ibid., para. 25.

[70]Ibid., paras. 32, 43, 51, 53, and 55 to 57.

It recalled that, whilst directives cannot be granted direct horizontal effect, the duty of consistent interpretation applies also in horizontal disputes.[71] Yet, the national provision at issue could not be brought in conformity with Union law without resorting to a *contra legem* interpretation.[72] Relying on *Mangold*, the Court recalled that the principle of non-discrimination on grounds of age is a general principle of Union law; if need be, national courts hearing disputes between individuals must disapply any national legislation contrary to that principle, in order to ensure the legal protection that individuals derive from EU law and its full effectiveness.[73] Finally, the Court pointed out that the disapplication of the conflicting national provision is not dependent on a finding of incompatibility by the Court itself. Unless the question arises before a last instance court, the national judge is simply entitled to make a reference for a preliminary ruling.[74]

4.2 The Reasoning of the Court on the Test Bench

In *Mangold* and *Kücükdeveci* the Court assumed that the general principles of Union law are amenable to direct effect also in horizontal disputes.[75] Two main objections can be raised in this respect, which will be referred here below as the *"technical" challenge* and the *dogmatic challenge*. A third one, the *legal certainty challenge*, cuts across the two.

4.2.1 The "Technical" Challenge

Whilst general principles are not inherently unable to have direct effect,[76] their capacity to satisfy the substantive requirements for direct effect (clarity, sufficient precision and unconditional character) is often problematic. As was seen, general principles of Union law are quite heterogeneous from the point of view of their content. The actual context in which they are invoked may also play a role. The approach of the Court in *Defrenne II*, an early case on direct horizontal effect, is worth recalling.[77]

The Court discussed whether Article 119 EEC (now, 157 TFEU) could be invoked in a horizontal dispute. This requires the Member States to ensure "the application of the principle that men and women should receive equal pay for

---

[71]Ibid., paras. 47–48.

[72]Ibid., para. 49.

[73]Ibid., paras. 50–51.

[74]Ibid., para. 55.

[75]See de Mol (2010), p. 293, and Editorial (2006), p. 4.

[76]Cf. Sect. 2 above.

[77]Case 43–75 *Defrenne II* [1976] ECR 455.

equal work". From the outset, the Court pointed out that "the principle of equal pay forms part of the foundations of the Community".[78] The whole reasoning focused more on the principle encapsulated by Article 157 TFEU than on this Treaty provision qua Treaty provision.[79] This makes the judgment pertinent to a discussion on the direct effect of general principles. The Court made a distinction between "the core and the fringe"[80] of Article 157 TFEU, arguing that this covers both discrimination, which "may be detected on the basis of a purely legal analysis of the situation", and discrimination which "can only be identified by reference to more explicit implementing provisions of a Community or national character".[81] The discrimination suffered by the applicant was ascribed to the first typology, and the national referring court was instructed to set aside contrasting provisions, including discriminatory clauses in individual contracts.[82]

The general principle prohibiting discrimination on grounds of age is itself a specific expression of the general principle of equal treatment, whose existence the Court had identified long before the adoption of Directive 2000/78/EC. Its normative core—notably, the fact that "comparable situations must not be treated differently and different situations must not be treated in the same way unless such treatment is objectively justified"—is sufficiently clear and unconditional.[83] In other words, although the Court did not emphasise this point in *Mangold* and *Kücükdeveci*, one cannot infer from them that any enquiry into the actual justiciability[84] of the general principle is not needed.[85] In fact, if that were the case, legal certainty would be seriously compromised, and so would the principle of institutional equilibrium. In the words of Advocate General Trstenjak, the latter principle requires that the Court:

> [R]espect[s] the rule-making power of the Council and of the Parliament [and] observes the necessary self-restraint in developing general principles of Community law which might possibly run counter to the legislature's aims.[86]

---

[78]Ibid., para. 12.

[79]Craig and De Búrca (2011), p. 188. In particular, the acknowledgment that Article 157 TFEU encapsulates a "foundational" principle of the Community seems to have been crucial with respect to the granting of horizontal effect to that provision: cf., paras. 39–40 and below, Sect. 4.2.2.

[80]Pescatore (1983), pp. 155, 162.

[81]*Defrenne II* cit., paras. 21 and 18.

[82]Ibid., para. 40.

[83]See the Opinion of Advocate General Tizzano in *Mangold* cit., paras. 83 and 84.

[84]According to the famous definition of Pescatore (1983), p. 176, "direct effect boils down to a question of justiciability".

[85]Note also that, in both cases, the Court regarded the general principle as mirroring Article 6(1) of Directive 2000/78/EC, which it has recognized as a directly effective provision. Investigating whether the right of workers' to paid annual leave is a general principle and satisfies the criteria for direct effect, see Advocate General Trstenjak in *Dominguez* cit., paras. 133 to 141.

[86]*Audiolux* (Opinion) cit., para. 107.

In this connection, Advocate General Jarabo Colomer has argued that the direct effect of general principles:

> [D]istorts the nature of the system of sources, converting typical [EU] acts, [the directives] into merely decorative rules which may be easily replaced by the general principles.[87]

This consideration could not be objected if the Court granted direct effect to general principles that are not justiciable as such. This, however, is more the "pathology" than the "physiology" of the direct effect of general principles.[88]

A few more lines must be devoted to the approach of the Court in *Kücükdeveci*. As already noted, the Court did not give a clear answer to the question whether the national measure should be tested against the general principle prohibiting age discrimination or against Directive 2000/78/EC. On the one hand, it checked whether the case fell within the scope of Union law, thus suggesting that the general principle was the parameter. On the other, throughout the judgment the Court referred to the general principle prohibiting age discrimination "as given expression by Directive 2000/78/EC", notably in its Article 6(1), which it regarded as fulfilling the threshold criteria for direct effect. This may create the impression that, in *Kücükdeveci*, the Court has introduced a precision to the scope of the rule that *directives* lack horizontal effect, without acknowledging the horizontal effect of the general principle concerned.[89] In other words, the provisions of a directive that meet the threshold criteria for direct effect could be invoked also in horizontal disputes when they give expression to a general principle of Union law, no matter whether directly effective by itself. This solution would maximize the effectiveness of general principles of Union law, and of a set of provisions contained in directives. It would also have the advantage to limit the differentiated treatment between public and private employees that may ensue from the rule that directives lack horizontal effect.[90] Yet, this approach is not theoretically cogent and it would significantly inhibit legal certainty. Luckily, the Court has rejected it in *AMS*.[91]

Incidentally, from the point of view of the principles of legal certainty and institutional equilibrium, the question of whether a general principle must satisfy, by itself, the threshold criteria for direct effect arises also with respect to vertical cases. This is a corollary of the broad notion of "State" endorsed by the Court, which encompasses also subjects, occasionally regulated by private law, that are not involved in the

---

[87]*Michaeler* (Opinion) cit., para. 21.

[88]Tridimas (2013), pp. 220–221. As regards the argument that the granting of direct effect to general principles is in tension with the principle of institutional equilibrium it must also be stressed that, since general principles rank higher than Union acts, the Union legislator cannot reduce their scope of application or effectiveness. On the relationship between general principles and EU legislation see: Muir (2014), pp. 219, 229–232, Lazzerini (2014), 219, 229–232, and Lenaerts and Gutiérrez-Fons (2010), pp. 1647–1649.

[89]The Opinions of Advocate General Bot in *Kücükdeveci* cit., para. 85, and of Advocate General Cruz-Villalón in *AMS* cit., paras. 76, 77 and 80.

[90]On this point, see Mastroianni (1999), p. 417.

[91]See Sect. 5 below.

process of implementing Union law.[92] Furthermore, whilst in *Kücükdeveci* the national measure breached a general principle spelt out in a provision of a directive, there may also be cases where the conflict arises with respect to a general principle not endorsed by the EU law provision that triggers its application to the case.[93]

Before moving to the dogmatic challenge, some attention must be paid to the argument that the theoretical framework underpinning *Mangold* and *Kücükdeveci* would be the principle of primacy of Union law over national law, rather than direct effect.

For the purpose of this discussion, it is sufficient to recall that the so-called "primacy model" relies on a distinction between *exclusionary* effect and *substitution* effect.[94] Exclusionary effect means that a conflict between a provision of Union law and a national provision can be solved by setting aside the latter and applying some other provisions of national law. In other words, EU law has only a foreclosing effect. By contrast, substitution effect means that, in case of a conflict, the EU law provision does not only set aside conflicting national law, but also becomes the rule that governs the (horizontal) relationship. Under the primacy model, exclusionary effect is a corollary of the primacy of Union law over national law, whereas only substitution effect amounts to direct horizontal effect. Consequently, there would be no need for a preliminary investigation of whether the general principle fulfils the "technical" requirements of clarity, precision and unconditional character. *Mangold* and *Kücükdeveci* would be about exclusionary effect only: the Court simply instructed the national court to set aside the conflicting national provisions, which in both cases were exception to general rules, and to decide the cases with the "remaining" national provisions, i.e., the general rules.

Although the Court has never upheld the distinction between substitution and exclusionary effect, some elements in *Mangold* and *Kücükdeveci*, amongst which the lack of any assessment of the justiciability of the general principle as such, may suggest that primacy, rather than direct effect, provides the theoretical underpinning of these judgments.[95] Yet, the primacy model entails a number of shortcuts. Once the conflicting national provision has been set aside, it may not be clear which other provision should apply. Furthermore, the distinction between substitution and exclusionary effect is a "false dichotomy", because in both situations "the disputes [are solved] on the basis of a rule different from the one prescribed by the national legislation".[96] Thus, in terms of legal certainty, the primacy model is no less problematic than the model, sometimes referred to as "trigger model", that

---

[92]See, also for further references, *Dominguez* (judgment) cit. paras. 38 and 39. For a critique, see Dashwood (2006–2007), pp. 87–88.

[93]Cf., Oliver (1993), p. 393.

[94]This distinction was first suggested in relation to directives: cf., Simon (1998), and the Opinion of Advocate General Saggio in joined cases from C-240/98 to C-244/98 *Océano Grupo* [2000] ECR I-4941. For a reappraisal, see Figueroa Regueiro (2002).

[95]See also the reference to cases on the principle of primacy at para. 77 of *Mangold*, among which the leading case 106/77 *Simmenthal* [1978] ECR 629, para. 21.

[96]Dashwood (2006–2007), p. 103.

rejects the distinction between exclusionary and substitution effects.[97] In fact, the primacy model also seems less theoretically cogent, if not even "arbitrary"[98]: the way in which national law is structured ultimately determines whether EU law merely forecloses, or is rather a substitute. In any event, the Court has rejected in *AMS* the possibility of relying on the principle of primacy to explain its reasoning in *Mangold* and *Kücükdeveci*, and to extend it to similar cases.

4.2.2 The Dogmatic Challenge

Assuming that *Mangold* and *Kücükdeveci* involve direct horizontal effect of general principles, the reasoning of the Court in these judgments raises a second major objection. The Court apparently assumed that, being inherent in the system established by the Treaties, general principles of Union law can be a source of rights and obligations for individuals.[99] Since the Court has resorted to the general principles of Union law as limits to the action by public authorities (of the Union and, subsequently, of the Member States, though only "within the scope of EU law"), it is not self-evident that they prevail also in horizontal relationships.[100] Moreover, direct horizontal effect is more problematic than its vertical counterpart from the point of view of legal certainty. In spite of this, the Court has evaded the issue.

In reality, such an evasive attitude is not peculiar to *Mangold* and *Kücükdeveci*: an analysis of the judgments in which the Court has acknowledged the direct horizontal effect of some Treaty provisions shows that there is no transparent, dogmatically convincing justification of that effect. At the same time, however, *Mangold* and *Kücükdeveci* fit with that case law, because both appear to be premised "on the imperative of equality as a constitutional value".[101] So far, the Court has recognized direct horizontal effect to Treaty provisions concerning the prohibitions of discrimination based on nationality (Article 18 TFEU)[102] and between male and female workers as regards "pay" (Article 157 TFEU),[103] the free movement of

---

[97]For a broader discussion on these two models, see Dougan (2007), p. 931, Lenaerts and Corthaut (2006), p. 287, de Witte (2011), p. 323, and Lenaerts and Gutiérrez-Fons (2010), p. 1640. Discussing the two judgments in light of the broader debate on the "primacy model" versus the "trigger model", see Muir (2011), p. 39.

[98]Ibid.

[99]Evidently, insofar as *horizontal* direct effect is concerned, the dogmatic challenge takes priority over the technical challenge: cf., Advocate General Kokott, case C-104/09 *Roca Álvarez* [2010] ECR I-8661, para. 55.

[100]Cf., *Dominguez* (Opinion) cit., para. 117.

[101]Tridimas (2013), p. 232.

[102]Case 36/74, *Walrave and Koch* [1974], ECR 1405, paras. 6, 16 and 17, and case C-411/98 *Ferlini* [2000] ECR I-8081, para. 50.

[103]*Defrenne II* cit., para. 39.

workers (Article 45 TFEU)[104] and services (Article 56 TFEU),[105] and the freedom of establishment (Article 49 TFEU).[106]

In particular, in *Defrenne II*, the Court based the direct horizontal effect of (now) Article 157 TFEU, which is itself an expression of the principle of equality, on the "mandatory" nature of this provision.[107] The meaning of this requirement is unclear, though it may suggest that direct horizontal effect is linked to some inherent quality (or qualities) that (only) certain EU Treaty provisions have. Indeed, the Court affirmed that the principle of equal pay "forms part of the foundations of the Community".[108]

Moreover, in the cases on fundamental freedoms, the Court has stressed their relation to Article 18 TFEU as being specific expressions of the prohibition of discrimination on nationality laid down by that provision.[109] In turn, this prohibition has been regarded as a "general rule",[110] and "a specific expression of the general principle of equality, which itself is one of the fundamental principles of Community law".[111] The Court has frequently referred also to their very nature as fundamental freedoms[112] or "fundamental objectives" of the Union,[113] to the risk that private action impairs their effectiveness,[114] and to the possibility of unequal application of working conditions amongst the Member States, due to differences in the organization of the public and private sectors.[115] However, these considerations seem to be of secondary importance with respect to that of the relation with Article 18 TFEU. The first and the second considerations could be predicated also for the free movement of goods (Article 34 TFEU), whereas in this context the

---

[104]*Walrave* cit., paras. 16 and 17, case C-94/07 *Raccanelli* [2008] ECR I-5939, para. 45, and case C-281/98 *Angonese* [2002] ECR I-4139, paras. 34 to 36.

[105]*Walrave* cit., paras. 16 and 17, and case C-415/93 *Bosman* [1995] ECR I-4921, para. 82.

[106]Case C-438/05 *Viking* [2007] ECR I-10779, paras. 57 to 59, and case C-341/05 *Laval* [2007] ECR I-11767, para. 98.

[107]*Defrenne II* cit., para. 39.

[108]Ibid., para. 12.

[109]*Walrave* cit., para. 16, *Angonese* cit., para. 31, and *Raccanelli* cit., para. 43.

[110]*Walrave* cit., para. 6.

[111]Case 810/79 *Überschär* [1980] ECR 2747, para. 16, and, more recently, case C-115/08 *ČEZ* [2009] ECR I-10265, para. 89.

[112]*Raccanelli* cit., para. 45, *Ferlini* cit., para. 50, *Angonese* cit., para. 35, and *Viking* cit., para. 58.

[113]*Walrave* cit., para. 18.

[114]Ibid., para. 18, *Bosman* cit., para. 84, *Angonese* cit., para. 32, *Viking* cit., para. 57, and *Raccanelli* cit., para. 44.

[115]*Walrave* cit., para. 19, *Defrenne II* cit., para. 9, *Bosman* cit., para. 84, and *Angonese* cit., para. 33.

case law of the Court is more convoluted.[116] Similarly, the second and third argument could support the granting of such an effect to many other Union law provisions, and possibly also of EU secondary law. By contrast, the Court has been rather cautious in this respect.

This overview could also suggest that the concept of equality from which direct horizontal effect stems from does not resemble the value of equality that can be found in domestic Constitutions. Rather, it is a concept of equality that is functional to the realization of the European *economic* constitution. Yet, *Defrenne II* breaks with this reconstruction, at least to some extent. The Court linked the foundational nature of the principle of equal pay to "its double aim, which is at once economic and social".[117] Article 157 TFEU aims at avoiding the competitive disadvantage that would otherwise suffer undertakings established in Member States that have implemented the principle of equal pay.[118] At the same time, however, it "forms part of the social objectives of the Community, which is not merely an economic Union, but is at the same time intended, by common action, to ensure social progress and seek the constant improvement of the living and working conditions of their peoples, as is emphasized by the Preamble to the Treaty".[119]

From this point of view, *Mangold* and *Kücükdeveci* seem very much similar to *Defrenne II*. The inherent value of the rule embodied by the provisions (i.e., Treaty provisions or general principles) justifies the limitation brought to the (general) principle of legal certainty by the granting of horizontal effect. However, this is a normative claim that emphasizes the need for a more transparent discourse on the dogmatic foundation(s) of horizontal direct effect. Some questions of primary importance remain on the floor: what are the (substantially) constitutional rules of the EU legal order which are also binding on individuals subject to EU law? How must these be identified by the Court? And where the boundaries of the Court's legitimacy to perform this task lie?

Whilst the Court is "an authentic interpreter of the Treaties",[120] and purposive interpretation is in line with the multifaceted and evolving nature of the EU legal order, any such interpretation should nonetheless be grounded on "principled,

---

[116]Whilst the Court acknowledged the horizontal effect of Article 34 TFEU in the early case 58/80 *Dansk Supermarked* [1981] ECR 1981, 181, para. 17, later on, in case C-159/00 *Sapod Audic* [2002] ECR I-5031, para. 74, it excluded horizontal effect. More recently, in case C-171/11 *Fra.bo*, judgment of 22 July 2012, nyr., the Court regarded as falling within the scope of Article 34 TFEU a non-profit, private-law certification body; this, however, was the only body entitled to provide the certification. In the sense that *Fra.bo* is not a case on direct horizontal effect, see Oliver (2014), p. 77. Challenging the consistency of the differentiated regime between the fundamental freedoms as regards direct horizontal effect, see Krenn (2012), p. 177.

[117]*Defrenne II* cit., para. 12.

[118]Ibid., para. 9.

[119]Ibid., para. 10. Cf. Azoulai (2010), pp. 842, 856, who argues that the granting of direct horizontal effect in *Defrenne II* shows the Court's effort to achieve "*[une] équilibre entre valeurs économiques et valeurs non économiques dans tous les régimes affectés par le droit de l'Union*".

[120]Krenn (2012), p. 184.

legal reasons".[121] In this connection, it is worth noting that, in *Defrenne II*, the Court pointed out that the question of the direct effect of Article 157 TFEU should be considered "in the light of the nature of the principle of equal pay, the aim of this provision, *and its place in the scheme of the Treaty*".[122] Similarly, it linked its reasoning on the social dimension of this provision to the Preamble to the Treaty.[123] As we shall see, the questions related to the dogmatic challenge have become even more pressing in the wake of the *AMS* judgment.

5 The *AMS* Judgment: Which Implications for the Direct Effect of General Principles?

At the end of their thoughtful "second look" on *Mangold*, Ján Mazák and Martin Moser observed:

> [T]he Court has let a genie out of the bottle; he may even grant a few wishes, but it will be as challenging as it is paramount – with a view to the legitimacy of the adjudication of the Court – to keep him within reasonable confines.[124]

In *AMS*, a case concerning the direct horizontal effect of the Charter, the Court has made some steps in the direction invoked by Mazák and Moser. By distinguishing *AMS* from *Kücükdeveci*, it offered a sort of authentic interpretation of its reasoning in the latter case (and in *Mangold*). However, whilst the "technical" challenge is to some extent addressed, the dogmatic challenge remains largely unanswered.

Before discussing *AMS* more in depth, a preliminary point requires some clarification. Since the Charter encompasses several fundamental rights that have been characterized as general principles,[125] it could be argued that the question is whether its provisions can entail direct effect, possibly also in horizontal disputes. In other words, has the same question become moot in relation to the general principles? Arguably, this is not the case. First, several general principles do not concern the protection of fundamental rights. Second, the Court may identify new general principles that aim at protecting individuals' rights (possibly, fundamental rights), which are not already reflected in the Charter.[126]

---

[121]Ibid. Emphasis in the original.

[122]Ibid., para. 7. Emphasis added.

[123]Ibid., para. 10.

[124]Mazák and Moser (2013), p. 86.

[125]For a comparison between the Charter and the fundamental rights *acquis* at the time of its proclamation in Nice, see Koukoulis-Spiliotopoulos (2002), p. 57, Lenaerts and De Smijter (2001), pp. 273, 280 and footnote 47.

[126]See De La Feria and Vogenauer (eds.) (2011), Lenaerts (2013), p. 460, and Temple Lang (2013), p. 65.

In *AMS* the Court was requested[127] to clarify whether Article 27 of the Charter (on "Workers' right to information and consultation within the undertaking")[128] could be invoked in order to set aside, in the context of a horizontal dispute, a national provision[129] whereby workers holding certain atypical contracts do not count towards the overall number of employees of the undertaking. As a first step, the Court observed that the contested national provision had implemented Article 3(1) of Directive 2002/14/EC, which lays down a general framework for informing and consulting employees in the Union.[130] Article 3(1) states that Member States can decide to apply the Directive to establishments employing at least 20 employees, or to undertakings employing at least 50 employees; it also leaves to the Member States the choice of the method for calculating the thresholds of employees employed. The Court affirmed that, irrespective of the discretion allowed to Member States, Article 3(1) lays down a precise and unconditional obligation to consider all employees, thus "fulfil[ling] all of the conditions necessary for it to have direct effect".[131] At the same time, however, it also reasserted, once again, its case law according to which directives lack direct horizontal effect.[132] Crucially, the Court then distinguished *AMS* from *Kücükdeveci*. Whilst "the principle of non-discrimination on grounds of age ... is sufficient in itself to confer on individuals an individual right which they may invoke as such", the Court stated, Article 27 of the Charter "to be fully effective ... must be given more specific expression in European Union or national law".[133] Thus, direct effect cannot be invoked in the context of a horizontal dispute in order to set aside conflicting national provisions.[134] The Court also added that:

> [S]ince [Article 27] does not suffice to confer on individuals a right which they may invoke as such, it could not be otherwise if it is considered in conjunction with [Directive 2002/14].[135]

The only remedy available to Mr Laboubi (the person appointed as workers' representative) and the trade unions supporting his claim was a liability action against France for having incorrectly transposed the directive.[136]

Thus, *AMS* has made clear that *Mangold* and *Kücükdeveci* concern direct horizontal effect of general principles of Union law. Once again, but now more clearly,

---

[127]By the *Chambre Sociale* of the French *Court de Cassation*.

[128]"Workers or their representatives must, at the appropriate levels, be guaranteed information and consultation in good time in the cases and under the conditions provided for by Community law and national laws and practices".

[129]Notably, Article L. 1111-3 of the French Labour Code.

[130]OJ 2002 L 80, 29.

[131]*AMS* cit., paras. 30 to 35.

[132]Ibid., para. 36.

[133]Ibid., paras. 45 and 47.

[134]Ibid., para. 48.

[135]Ibid., para. 49.

[136]Ibid., para. 50.

the Court has refused to uphold the distinction between exclusionary and substitution effect. Like its predecessors, *AMS* involved a situation that could be classified among those where EU law is invoked with the sole function to purge the national legal order of a provision inconsistent with the former. Yet the Court shut the door also to the—only apparently less invasive—exclusionary effect. At the same time, it rejected the alternative to create a refinement to its *mantra* that directives cannot have, *of themselves*, horizontal effect. Notably, it did not allow combining a general principle that does not satisfy the threshold criteria for direct effect with the provision of a directive expressing it in a clear, sufficiently precise and unconditional way. In stating this, the Court distancing itself from the proposal of Advocate General Cruz-Villalón, who, by contrast proposed to admit this combination—and its horizontal effect—at least with respect to the provisions of EU secondary law that "give specific substantive and direct expression to the content of the [Charter provision at issue]".[137]

General principles and fundamental rights granted by the Charter can entail direct horizontal effect only if they confer on individuals a substantive right, that is, by itself "legally perfect", or "independent", in the sense that it can be invoked without the need of further implementing legislation.

This conclusion must be welcomed. The approach endorsed by the Court is theoretically sound, and can better be reconciled with the requirements stemming from the general principle of legal certainty. Clearly, the game would become zero-sum if the narrow scope allowed to direct horizontal effect of general principles were "compensated" by the loosening of the limits to consistent interpretation of national law. Both Union courts and national courts must be scrupulous in this respect.[138]

The doubt that may emerge from *AMS* is whether the Court refers to the same test of justiciability as suggested in *Defrenne II*. As anticipated, there the Court looked for the rule behind the Treaty provision, and distinguished between its hard, autonomous normative core, and its periphery, which requires the intervention of the legislator. In *AMS*, the Court seems to closely rely on the wording of the provision of the Charter. If this were the case, there would not be perfect continuity with its previous approach, and one should reflect on the implications of the differentiated regime. It goes without saying that, when it comes to general principles, the enquiry into their justiciability cannot be based on their wording.

Most evidently, however, the clarifications provided by *AMS* concern what has been referred to as the "technical" challenge, whereas the dogmatic challenge remains in the waiting room. Better, given that the Court excluded the horizontal

---

[137]*AMS* (Opinion) cit., para. 63. The Advocate General moved from the premise that the fundamental right granted by Article 27 of the Charter is a "principle" under the (peculiar) meaning of Article 52(5) of the Charter. This provision substantially excludes (vertical and, a fortiori, horizontal) direct effect of Charter "principles". The proposal of the Advocate General aimed at enhancing the effects, and effectiveness, of Charter "principles". For more insights on his position, see Lazzerini (2014).

[138]A case in which the Court directed a quite strong exhortation to the national judge to ensure consistent interpretation in a horizontal dispute is *Dominguez* cit.. On this point, see Lazzerini (2012), p. 455.

applicability of Article 27 of the Charter on the grounds that this does not fulfil the
threshold criteria for direct effect, the underlying assumption is that the provisions of
the Charter may entail horizontal effect.[139] Should we infer from this that equality as
a foundational value of the Union is not the only additional constitutive element of
direct horizontal effect? If so, what else? And why? The question of the dogmatic
foundation of direct horizontal effect in Union law still awaits deeper discussion.

6 Conclusive Remarks

As in other international as well as domestic legal orders, the system of written
sources of European Union law is complemented by an evolving set of unwritten
legal principles, which become an integral part of that law through the activity of
European and national courts. Amongst them, the general principles of European
Union law have acquired a special importance within the case law of the European
Court of Justice. Their emergence was urged by the need to fill the gaps of the
legal order established by the founding Treaties, where the Court could not always
find the tools to address the challenges posed by the European integration process,
or to promote it.

Whilst the written rules of European Union primary law have progressively
increased in number and complexity, the general principles have not lost their
function as gap-fillers. In fact, they have acquired an important role in ensuring
not only the completeness but also the coherence of the legal order, by acting as an
aid to the interpretation of the acts of the European Union institutions and grounds
for their validity review. At the same time, the general principles of European
Union law raise problems and concerns that, irrespective of the domestic or international level of adjudication, are inherent to unwritten legal sources handled by
courts, such as the risk to trespass the boundaries of the adjudicatory function or to
harm legal certainty.

This chapter addressed the case law of the European Court of Justice on
the direct effect (in particular, direct horizontal effect) of the general principles
of European Union law. Two main challenges have been identified: the "technical" challenge (which criteria a general principle must satisfy in order for it to
have direct horizontal effect?) and the "dogmatic" challenge (which is the normative foundation of direct horizontal effect of the general principles of European
Union law?). It was argued that, as regards the technical challenge, the case law
of the Court is more in need of argumentative clarity than legal reasons. A more
recent judgment (*AMS*) sheds some light in this respect. As regards the dogmatic

---

[139]We must leave aside the question of the potential tension of this conclusion with the wording
of Article 51(1) of the Charter, which explicitly refers (only) to the Union and its Member States
as passive addressees of its provisions.

challenge, after almost thirty years, the words written by Pierre Pescatore commenting the first judgment on direct effect still go straight to the core of the issue:

> [I]t was … *a highly political idea, drawn from a perception of the constitutional system of the Community*, which is at the basis of *Van Gend & Loos*[140] and which continues to inspire the whole doctrine flowing from it.[141]

The case law on the horizontal effect of general principles fits with the narrative of the European Court of Justice as the motor of European integration. This role of the Court is a constant in the almost sixty-year life of the EU, and involves legal reasoning, judicial policy, and politics. For this same reason, the need for transparency and responsibility is all the more compelling. A clearer discourse on the rationale—or the vision of the Union—that underpins direct horizontal effect (of the general principles, but also of the provisions of the Treaties and the Charter) would be welcome. Not only as a matter important to the legitimacy of the Court, but also for the sake of the individuals that may benefit of, or be affected by, directly effective EU law provisions.

Acknowledgments I would like to thank Professors Adelina Adinolfi, Chiara Favilli, Giorgio Gaja and Laura Pineschi, and Dr Cesare Pitea for their inspiring comments and conversations on the issues covered in this chapter. Any mistakes or omissions remain of course the sole responsibility of the author.

References

Adinolfi, Adelina. 1994. I principi generali nella giurisprudenza comunitaria e la loro influenza sugli ordinamenti degli Stati membri. *Rivista Italiana di Diritto Pubblico Comunitario* 2: 521-578.

Azoulai, Loïc. 2010. Sur un sens de la distinction public/privé dans le droit de l'Union européenne. *Revue trimestrielle de droit européen* 46: 842-860.

Bernitz, Ulf, Joakim Nergelius, and Cecilia Cadner (eds.). 2008. *General Principles of EC Law in a Process of Development*. Alphen aan den Rijn: Kluwer Law International.

Bernitz, Ulf, Xavier Groussot, and Felix Schulyok (eds.). 2013. *General Principles of EU Law and Private Law*. Alphen aan den Rijn: Kluwer Law International.

Craig, Paul, and Grainne de Búrca. 2011. *EU Law: Text, Cases, and Materials*: Oxford: Oxford University Press.

Dashwood, Alan. 2006-2007. From *Van Duyn* to *Mangold* via *Marshall*: Reducing Direct Effect to Absurdity. *Cambridge Yearbook of European Legal Studies* 29: 81-109.

De La Feria, Rita, and Stefan Vogenauer (eds.). 2011. *Prohibition of Abuse of Law – A New General Principle of EU Law*. Oxford: Hart.

De Mol, Miriam. 2010. *Kücükdeveci: Mangold* Revisited - Horizontal Direct Effect of a General Principle of EU Law. *European Constitutional Law Review* 6: 293-308.

De Mol, Miriam. 2011. The Novel Approach of the CJEU on the Horizontal Direct Effect of the EU Principle of Non-Discrimination. *Maastricht Journal of European and Comparative Law* 18: 109-135.

---

[140]Cf. footnote 2 above.

[141]Pescatore (1983), p. 158. Emphasis added.

De Witte, Bruno. 2011. Direct Effect, Primacy and the Nature of the EU Legal Order. In *The Evolution of EU Law*, eds. Paul Craig and Grainne de Búrca, 323-362. Oxford: Oxford University Press.

Dougan, Michael. 2007. When Worlds Collide! Competing Visions of the Relationship between Primacy and Direct Effect. *Common Market Law Review* 44: 931-963.

Dougan, Michael 2011. In Defence of *Mangold?*. In *A Constitutional Order of States? Essays in EU Law in Honour of Alan Dashwood*, eds. Anthony Arnull, Catherine Barnard, Michael Dougan and Eleanor Spaventa, 219-244. Oxford-Portland: Hart.

Dworkin, Ronald. 1978. *Taking Rights Seriously*. Cambridge: Harvard University Press.

Editorial. 2006. Horizontal Direct Effect - A Law of Diminishing Coherence. *Common Market Law Review* 43: 1-8.

Figueroa Regueiro, Pablo. 2002. Invocability of Substitution and Invocability of Exclusion: Bringing Legal Realism to the Current Developments of the Case Law of « Horizontal » Direct Effect of Directives. *Jean Monnet Working Paper* no. 7/2002.

Fontanelli, Filippo. 2014. National Measures and the Application of the EU Charter of Fundamental Rights – Does *curia*.eu Know *iura*.eu? *Human Rights Law Review* 14: 231-265.

Gaja, Giorgio. 1998. Identifying the Status of General Principles in European Community Law. In *Scritti in onore di Giuseppe Federico Mancini – Vol. II*, 445-457. Milano: Giuffrè.

Gaja, Giorgio and Adelina Adinolfi. 2014. *Introduzione al diritto dell'Unione europea*. Bari, Roma: Laterza.

Groussot, Xavier. 2006. *General Principles of Community Law*. Groningen: Europa Law Publishing.

Koukoulis-Spiliotopoulos, Sophia. 2002. Towards a European Constitution: Does the Charter of Fundamental Rights "Maintain in Full" the *Acquis Communautaire?*. *Revue européenne de droit public* 14: 57-104.

Krenn, Cristoph. 2012. A Missing Piece in the Horizontal Effect "Jigsaw": Horizontal Direct Effect and the Free Movement of Goods. *Common Market Law Review* 49: 177-215.

Lazzerini, Nicole. 2012. Gli effetti diretti orizzontali dei diritti fondamentali in materia sociale: la sentenza *Dominguez* della Corte di giustizia e la strada del silenzio. *Rivista di diritto internazionale* 95: 455-461.

Lazzerini, Nicole. 2014. (Some of) the Fundamental Rights granted by the Charter may be the Source of Obligations for Private Parties: AMS. *Common Market Law Review* 51: 907-933.

Lenaerts, Annekatrien. 2013. The Role of the Principle *Fraus Omnia Corrumpit* in the European Union: A Possible Evolution Towards a General Principle of Law? *Yearbook of European Law* 32: 460-498.

Lenaerts, Koen, and Tim Corthaut. 2006. Of Birds and Hedges: The Role of Primacy in Invoking Norms of EU Law. *European Law Review* 31: 287-315.

Lenaerts, Koen, and Eddy De Smijter. 2001. A 'Bill of Rights' for the European Union. *Common Market Law Review* 38: 273-300.

Lenaerts, Koen and José Augustin Gutiérrez-Fons. 2010. The Constitutional Allocation of Powers and General Principles of EU Law. *Common Market Law Review* 47: 1629-1669.

Mastroianni, Roberto. 1999. On the Distinction Between Vertical and Horizontal Direct Effects of Directives in Community Law: What Role for the Principle of Equality? *European Public Law* 5: 417-435.

Mazák, Ján, and Martin Moser. 2013. Adjudication by Reference to General Principles of EU Law: A Second Look at the *Mangold* Case Law. In *Judging Europe's Judges. The Legitimacy of the Case Law of the Court of Justice*, eds. Maurice Adams, Henri de Waele, Johan Meeusen and Gert Straetmans, 61-86. London: Bloomsbury.

Muir, Elise. 2011. Of Ages in - and Edges of - EU Law. *Common Market Law Review* 48: 39-62.

Muir, Elise. 2014. The Fundamental Rights Implications of EU Legislation: Some Constitutional Challenges. *Common Market Law Review* 51: 219-245.

Oliver, Peter. 1993. General Principles of Community Law and Horizontal Effect. *Europäische Zeitschrift für Wirtschaftsrecht* 13: 393.

Oliver, Peter. 2014. L'article 34 TFUE peut-il avoir un effet direct? Réflexions sur l'ârret *Fra.bo*. *Cahiers de droit européen* 50: 77-96.

Pescatore, Pierre.1983. The Doctrine of 'Direct Effect': An Infant Disease of Community Law. *European Law Review* 8: 155-177.

Rosas, Allan. 2012. When is the EU Charter of Fundamental Rights Applicable at National Level? *Jurisprudencia/Jurisprudence* 19: 1269-1288.

Rosas, Allan, and Lorna Armati. 2010. *EU Constitutional Law. An Introduction*. Oxford, Portland: Hart.

Sarmiento, Daniel. 2013. Who's Afraid of the Charter? The ECJ, National Courts and the New Framework of Fundamental Rights Protection in Europe. *Common Market Law Review* 50: 1627-1304.

Schiek, Dagmar. 2006. The ECJ Decision in *Mangold*: A Further Twist on Effects of Directives and Constitutional Relevance of Community Equality Legislation. *Industrial Law Journal* 35: 329-341.

Schmidt, Marlene. 2005. The Principle of Non-Discrimination in Respect of Age: Dimensions of the ECJ's *Mangold* Judgment. *German Law Journal* 7: 506-524.

Simon, Denis. 1998. *Le système juridique communautaire*. Paris: Puf.

Strozzi, Girolamo, and Roberto Mastroianni. 2013. *Diritto dell'Unione europea – Parte istituzionale*. Torino: Giappichelli.

Temple Lang, John. 1991. The Sphere in which Member States are Obliged to Comply with the General Principles of Law and Community Fundamental Rights Principles. *Legal Issues of European Integration* 18: 23-35.

Temple Lang, John. 2013. Emerging European General Principles in Private Law. In *General Principles of EU Law and Private Law*, eds. Ulf Bernitz, Xavier Groussot and Felix Schulyok, 65-117. Alphen aan den Rijn: Kluwer Law International.

Tridimas, Takis. 2006. *The General Principles of EU Law*. Oxford: Oxford University Press.

Tridimas, Takis. 2013. Horizontal Effect of General Principles: Bold Rulings and Fine Distinctions. In *General Principles of EU Law and Private Law*, eds. Ulf Bernitz, Xavier Groussot and Felix Schulyok, 213-232. Alphen aan den Rijn: Kluwer Law International.

Part III
General Principles and the Judiciary
in a Comparative Perspective

Principio di determinatezza and the Void-for-Vagueness Doctrine in Constitutional Litigation: The Italian *Corte Costituzionale* and the United States Supreme Court

Michele Boggiani

Abstract This chapter offers a comparative analysis between the *principio di determinatezza* and the void-for-vagueness doctrine in the jurisprudence of the Italian *Corte Costituzionale* and the United States Supreme Court. The analysis starts by considering the theoretical underpinnings of the *principio di determinatezza*, which can be summarized in a separation-of-powers rationale, on the one hand, and a fair notice rationale, on the other. Then, the analysis moves on to an examination of the vagueness doctrine in the United States Supreme Court. The two main pillars of the principle are the necessity to assure fair notice to the common person and to prevent an arbitrary enforcement of the law by government officials. Notwithstanding some deep institutional differences, both Courts developed the two doctrines with a particular focus on the foreseeability and predictability of the law measured with the standard of the common person.

1 *Principio di determinatezza* and the Italian *Corte Costituzionale*

1.1 The Theoretical Underpinnings of the Principle

Italian criminal law is governed by many constitutional principles. Although labels such as "civil law" and "common law" legal system should not carry too much weight (since they obscure important points of contacts between the two families), it is nonetheless true that they have some residual importance. In fact, consistently with what the ordinary lawyer imagines a civil law Country to be, these constitutional principles received a conspicuous doctrinal, rather than judicial, elaboration.

M. Boggiani (✉)
Ph.D. Candidate in Criminal Law, University of Parma, Parma, Italy
e-mail: michele.boggiani@nemo.unipr.it

© Springer International Publishing Switzerland 2015
L. Pineschi (ed.), *General Principles of Law - The Role of the Judiciary*,
Ius Gentium: Comparative Perspectives on Law and Justice 46,
DOI 10.1007/978-3-319-19180-5_9

Consequently, if one wants to approach Italian criminal law, she should understand that studying what in the United States are called "secondary sources" is at least as important as studying cases.

Among these principles we find the *principio di determinatezza*, which we can roughly translate as "principle of determinacy" or "principle of precision".[1] To begin with, the principle is derived, in the first instance, from Article 25(2) of the Italian Constitution, embodying the principle of legality: "Nobody can be punished if not pursuant to a statute promulgated before the fact".[2] If we focus on the word "statute", we can understand that a vague provision would leave criminalization choices to the adjudicating court, which would in turn be free to read whatever it wants into the blurry wording. In this way, of course, *nullum crimen sine lege* would be readily circumvented.[3] At the same time, since Article 13 of the Constitution commands the utmost precision in imposing temporary incapacitating measures, it has been argued that substantive criminal law needs at least the same level of accuracy.[4]

Also, the principle is fixed at a sub-constitutional level in Article 1 of the Italian Criminal Code, where it is provided that:

> No one can be punished for a conduct unless this conduct is expressly made criminal by statute, nor can he be punished with sanctions not provided by the same statute.[5]

It is clear that, on the one hand, the principle is a defense against judicial overreaching: criminal law should be as clear as possible to bridle judicial discretion.[6] In this case, the rationale that animates the principle is guaranteeing individual liberty through the enforcement of separation of powers.[7] In fact, in the Italian constitutional design, parliament is entrusted with legislative power, while the judicial branch is in charge of adjudicating cases according to the law. Consequently, criminal laws should be clear in what they proscribe to assure that criminalization choices are effectively entrusted to the ones empowered by the people and not to unelected officials.[8]

---

[1]Cadoppi (2014), pp. 69–70. The Author provides extensive citations to the most important "classics" of Italian criminal law theory on point.

[2]Italian Constitution, Article 25(2): *"Nessuno può essere punito se non in forza di una legge che sia entrata in vigore prima del fatto commesso"*.

[3]Cadoppi (2014), p. 70.

[4]Bricola (1981), p. 256.

[5] Italian Criminal Code, Article 1: *"Nessuno può essere punito per un fatto che non sia espressamente preveduto dalla legge come reato, né con pene che non siano da essa stabilite"*.

[6]Bricola (1981), p. 257.

[7]See *Corte costituzionale*, decision no. 327 of 2008. See also, generally, Manes (2014), p. 18.

[8]In Italy, as in many other civil law Countries, judges and prosecutors are not elected nor appointed (which would guarantee at least a minimum political check). To enter the ranks of the judiciary branch, one must successfully pass a State-wide examination. One exception to the rule that is directly relevant for our inquiry, are the members of the *Corte costituzionale*, which are appointed by parliament, the President of the Republic and by the judiciary itself. Differently from American federal judges though, their appointment is time-limited and not for life.

On the other hand, though, the principle is a guarantee set up to assure informed choices of actions.[9] Consequently, its second rationale is protection of liberty through the means of clarity and predictability of the law. In fact, only a well-defined, precise statute has the capacity to inform the ordinary citizen of the consequences of her actions. This clean and neat observation has Enlightenment roots or, more precisely, it is of "Beccarian" descent: if the core of the legality principle is about preserving the citizens' right to self-determination and freedom, then we should aim for precise laws which have the capacity to guide people's actions.[10]

The *principio di determinatezza* pledges to defend the parliament's prerogative in making criminalization choices, while at the same time advocating for the citizens' freedom of choice. But whom does the principle speak to? The answer is twofold. The parliament, to be sure, is the one charged with defending its own power: if this body does not want power to slip from its own hands, it must draft precise laws. Unfortunately, sometimes parliament is counterintuitively incentivized to let its power fade in favor of judicial discretion. In fact, at times, parliament does not have the political will to thoroughly reform the criminal law and would rather leave the task to the judiciary. Then, if the reform works out well, parliament can take credit for it by saying that it wisely chose to solve the problem by allowing larger discretion, while if it does not work, parliament can always blame courts for misusing their power.

On the other hand, the principle speaks to courts, commanding them to obey the literal command of the law. The judicial branch has, in fact, all sorts of instruments to overstep the textual meaning of a provision, such as analogical reasoning, but it should refrain to use them in the field of the criminal law.[11]

Finally, it has been said that the principle speaks to legal scholars too: given the importance of scholarship in explaining the meaning of constitutional principles relevant to the criminal law, authors should concentrate their theoretical efforts toward formulating clear and comprehensible doctrines.[12]

Of course, much time has passed since the eighteenth century. Nonetheless, the fundamental insights of authors like Cesare Beccaria have been the basis on which more recent scholarship built complex theoretical conceptions. For one, Italian authors have focused on the *nexus* between *principio di determinatezza* and *principio di colpevolezza* (which can be translated as "principle of culpability"). Pursuant to the latter, in order to establish criminal liability, there should always be a psychological link between the author and the criminal conduct. This link should, at a minimum, be a "negligence" link, in the sense that either the person voluntarily acted in a certain way or at least did so negligently (by disregarding some rule of conduct that commanded him, for example, to abstain from acting).

---

[9]See *Corte costituzionale*, decision no. 327 of 2008.

[10]Cadoppi (2014), p. 70.

[11]Ibid., pp. 70–71.

[12]Bricola (1981), p. 258.

A prerequisite for establishing criminal liability is, consequently, the positive validation of this *nexus* between the person and the crime. This link, in turn, presupposes that the content of the law is reasonably clear. The concept requires some elaboration. To begin with, textual clarity is just a part of a wider idea of clarity. For the law to be "understandable" we need, to be sure, a clear text but we also need criminal provisions consonant with constitutional values and cultural norms as well as a consistent judicial interpretation of them (i.e. foreseeable and predictable).[13] Finally, we may add that overcriminalization is, in this case, an evil to be avoided too: the misuse of the criminal law to fix every societal problem renders penal provision less and less useful in governing one's conduct.[14] If the criminal law were employed to proscribe only the worst category of conduct, it could be more readily understood.[15]

At the same time though, the *Corte costituzionale*, in decision no. 96 of 1981, has added a different dimension to the principle of precision, which may not be readily apparent from the textual formulation of Article 25(2) of the Constitution and Article 1 of the Criminal Code. According to the Court, the *principio di determinatezza* imposes an additional burden on the legislator. In fact, criminal provisions must be clearly and precisely formulated, but at the same time they should also be *verifiable* in the real world. In particular, in drafting a provision, the legislator should keep in mind that the correspondence between the wording of the statute and the conduct must be empirically verifiable by the adjudicating court.[16]

In conclusion, we should keep in mind that the *principio di determinatezza* does not only mean textual clarity, but that it involves multiple additional dimensions, such as consonance with social mores, consistency of judicial interpretation, as well as a connection with the *principio di colpevolezza*.[17] These ideas have, as we mentioned noble Enlightenment origin and not surprisingly the seeds of many of them could already be seen in famous works such as *Dei delitti e delle pene*, authored by Cesare Beccaria.[18] At the same time, the principle commands that criminal provisions must have a close connection to reality: they should proscribe a "verifiable" course of conduct. Otherwise, the adjudicating court would be left in the impossibility of checking the correspondence between what is written in the statute and what happened in the real world.[19]

As we anticipated, we were able to paint the theoretical foundation of the *principio di determinatezza* in broad strokes only. A full or at least semi-comprehensive

---

[13]Manes (2014), p. 7.

[14]Bricola (1981), p. 259; Cadoppi (2014), p. 123.

[15]See Cadoppi (2014), pp. 70–85. The Author discusses and extensively cites scholarship on point. In particular, many references are made to decision no. 364 of 1988 of the Italian *Corte costituzionale*.

[16]Manes (2014), p. 21. See also immediately infra, for examples of provisions lacking such "empirical" link.

[17]Ibid., p. 7.

[18]See, for a recent edition, Beccaria (ed. Giulio Carnati) (2014).

[19]See infra, Sect. 1.2, the example of decision no. 96 of 1981.

picture would require a much bigger effort, hardly containable in the scope of the present work. To be sure, Italian legal scholarship produced a great scientific effort in illuminating the intimate nature of the "principle of precision". Nonetheless, Italian legal provisions are far from perfect or even "recognizable". If we consider that it was the *Corte costituzionale* in 1988 that finally give constitutional status to this refined conceptualization of the *principio di determinatezza*, through its connection with the *principio di colpevolezza*, we would expect to find many instances in which laws were struck down because of their vagueness. Unfortunately, we can point to only two of them and, consequently, we should analyze the reasons for this extreme paucity.

1.2 The Analysis of the Principio di determinatezza in the Decisions of the Italian Corte Costituzionale

To begin with, we should note that in the Italian system only the Constitutional Court is empowered to declare laws unconstitutional. The system is set up in a way that national courts work as a filter for the constitutional cases to be brought to the *Corte costituzionale*. A trial or appellate court that, in deciding a case, encounters a norm (directly relevant to its decision) that the court suspects to be unconstitutional should refer it to the *Corte costituzionale* through the means of a judicial motion (*ordinanza di rimessione*). In this motion, the court sets forth a theory according to which the challenged norm is unconstitutional. The *Corte costituzionale* would then evaluate the validity of the referring court's construction to decide on the constitutionality of the provision under scrutiny.

One area with which the *Corte costituzionale* was historically concerned is the use of generic expressions in legislative drafting. This writing technique usually takes different forms, such as the use of examples, "synthesizing" expressions,[20] or also of general clauses.[21] The *Corte costituzionale* has constantly upheld laws using this drafting method. Of course, this does not mean that parliament may indiscriminately legislate in this fashion, but rather that, if contained within reasonable boundaries, it might do so.[22] In fact, the law simply cannot take expressly into account every possible variation on the criminal scheme. Consequently, recapitulatory expressions may be used. More in general, this is also a distinctive feature of Italian legislative technique, which is aptly called *normazione sintetica* (synthetic drafting).[23]

---

[20]We refer to Bricola (1981), p. 265. The Author cites decisions no. 133 of 1973, no. 42 of 1972, as well as no. 88 of 1975 of the *Corte costituzionale*.

[21]Manes (2014), p. 19.

[22]In fact, the *principio di determinatezza* is to be read in connection with the *principio di ragionevolezza* (which we may imprecisely translate as "rationality principle"). To trace a quick comparison to the United States and the rational-basis review, the legislator may not act with utter irrationality. On the point, see Manes (2014), p. 24.

[23]Cadoppi (2014), p. 135.

The *Corte costituzionale* has allowed the use of such expressions by noting that general clauses or "closing" clauses are permissible as long as they do not encourage the interpreting court to overstep its legitimate interpretative boundaries. To be clearer, as long as an expression such as "other similar trades" in a provision prohibiting the performance of "wandering trades" may be expounded without resorting to impermissible means, such as analogical reasoning, it will be permitted.[24]

At the same time, it is not uncommon to see criminal provisions ending with closing provisions such as "and similar cases". In these instances, the *Corte costituzionale* has upheld the constitutionality of such "wrap-up" terms under familiar principles of statutory construction. According to the *Corte costituzionale*, this terminology is constitutionally acceptable, as in the case seen in the preceding paragraph, as long as it empowers courts to use simple interpretative powers (such as *eiusdem generis*) only, while it will not be permitted if it encourages, for example, the use of analogical reasoning (which is constitutionally forbidden).[25] In particular, the constitutional "precision" principle can to a certain extent be collapsed with the concept of analogy, in the sense that a vague provision can be defined as the one requiring the use of analogical reasoning for its application.[26]

Also the *Corte costituzionale* has consistently favored the proposition that an otherwise indeterminate provision may be clarified by reference to "common extralegal concepts" or to "ordinary or technical experience".[27] The *Corte costituzionale* has also been willing to "cure" some degree of indeterminacy in an element of a criminal provision if the offense, taken as whole, matches the parallel societal understanding of it.[28]

An example would be decision no. 191 of 1970, which upheld Articles 527, 528 and 529 of the Criminal Code. The mentioned provisions proscribe certain obscene conduct, characterized by publicity (i.e. carried out in a public place) or reproduction in printing. On the notion of "obscene", the *Corte costituzionale* stated that:

> When the criminal law protects something immaterial (such as respectability, honor, reputation, prestige, decency or others), it is inevitable to refer to notions nestled in common language and intelligence. Nobody has ever thought that this may violate the principle of legality.[29]

---

[24]See immediately infra, where *eiusdem generis* is discussed.

[25]In decision no. 27 of 1961, the *Corte costituzionale* upheld a Fascist-era restriction on "wandering trades". The defendant was working as an automobile watch-keeper. The relevant provision prohibited the practice of "wandering trades" as well as "other similar trades". On the prohibition of analogical reasoning, see Manes (2014), p. 24.

[26]Early decisions by the *Corte costituzionale* seem to adhere to this conceptualization. See decisions no. 27 of 1961 as well as decision no. 120 of 1963, cited by Palazzo (1979), pp. 6–7.

[27]See *Corte costituzionale*, decision no. 191 of 1970 and decision no. 42 of 1972. See also Manes (2014), pp. 19–20.

[28]See Palazzo (1979), p. 412.

[29]*Corte costituzionale*, decision no. 191 of 1970: *"Quando la legge penale prevede la tutela di beni immateriali (come il decoro, l'onore, la reputazione, il prestigio, la decenza ed altri) il ricorso a nozioni proprie del linguaggio e dell'intelligenza comuni, è inevitabile, né si è pensato, finora, a lamentare in proposito la violazione del principio di legalità.*

Another example would be decision no. 172 of 2014, which is the most recent example of a precedent in which the *Corte costituzionale* explicitly validated the use of "synthetic" expressions. In the case of the crime of stalking, which was introduced in 2009, the legislator chose to use this type of expression to describe the typical results of stalking acts. Article 612-*bis* of the Criminal Code describes three possible results of the criminal stalking conduct: a persistent and serious state of fear or anxiety, a well-founded concern for one's or one's relatives' safety and a change in one's life habits.[30] In the mentioned decision, the *Corte costituzionale* noted that such expressions have been constantly employed on a comparative level in other legal systems in enacting the crime of stalking. Also, the *Corte costituzionale* underscored that it is possible to assign these expressions a clear and precise meaning through an integrated, systemic and teleological approach to interpretation.[31]

In conclusion on the point, the *Corte costituzionale* is not ready to reduce itself to a narrow textual interpretation of a criminal provision. In its interpretative endeavor, the *Corte costituzionale* will read it in conjunction with other similar norms belonging to the same area of the criminal law. Also, the adjudicating court should be guided by legislative intent in promulgating the particular provision.[32]

Moreover, the *Corte costituzionale* has recognized a definite role for judicial interpretation in implementing the *principio di determinatezza*. On the one hand, a constant "clarifying interpretation" of a criminal provision can help in narrowing down its otherwise broad meaning.[33] At the same time, consistency in judicial interpretation of a certain provision can be taken as partial proof of the sufficient "clarity" of a challenged provision.[34]

It may be added though that the *Corte costituzionale*, in decision no. 327 of 2008, added two caveats to the "clarifying power" of judicial interpretation. First of all, allowing this power to sweep too broadly would unduly infringe the separation of powers, since the extreme version of such a power would allow courts to carve out a completely different meaning from the one intended by the legislator. Secondly, since the criminal law must be the guide of individual conduct, it must be able to do so from the very first moment. Individual actions cannot "wait" for the courts' intervention in clarifying an otherwise indeterminate meaning. Besides, these

---

[30]Italian Criminal Code, Article 612-bis: "*Salvo che il fatto costituisca più grave reato, è punito con la reclusione da sei mesi a quattro anni chiunque, con condotte reiterate, minaccia o molesta taluno in modo da cagionare un perdurante e grave stato di ansia o di paura ovvero da ingenerare un fondato timore per l'incolumità propria o di un prossimo congiunto o di persona al medesimo legata da relazione affettiva ovvero da costringere lo stesso ad alterare le proprie abitudini di vita*".

[31]*Corte costituzionale*, decision no. 172 of 2014.

[32]Decision no. 5 of 2004 and decision no. 327 of 2008. See also Manes (2014), p. 20.

[33]See decision no. 333 of 1991 and decision no. 133 of 1992 of the *Corte costituzionale* on the concepts of "modest amount" and "average daily dose" in the context of antidrug laws. See also Manes (2014), p. 23.

[34]See *Corte costituzionale*, decision no. 327 of 2008.

illuminating decisions may remain unknown to the ordinary citizen altogether.[35] At the same time, while the idea of an ordinary citizen actually consulting the Criminal Code to guide her actions is to a certain extent[36] fictional, it is also true that if we added the duty of relevant judicial decisions to our hypothetical citizen's burden, our image would become not only slightly fictitious but utterly unreal.

Nonetheless, the only interpretative sector of the *principio di determinatezza* under which provisions were actually struck down is the one requiring statutory provisions to have a direct, verifiable link to reality. The *Corte costituzionale* has declared the unconstitutionality of criminal laws pursuant to Article 25(2) of the Italian Constitution (in its "principle of precision" part) in only two cases.

The first decision belonging to this exclusive "club" was issued on 16 December 1980. The case[37] is interesting in a comparative perspective because it involved, like *Papachristou v. City of Jacksonville* (which we will discuss in the part dedicated to the United States Supreme Court's jurisprudence) nothing less than the Italian version of a vagrancy statute.[38] Pursuant to Article 1, no. 3 of Law no. 1423 of 1956, it was possible, for the local police commissioner, to issue a "preventive measure" against an individual that, for reason of his "behavior", gave rise to "valid motives" to conclude that he was "inclined to commit crimes". The Court concluded that the standard set forth in the statute was not judicially ascertainable. In fact, a criminal provision, to pass constitutional muster, must describe a course of conduct that is effectively verifiable by the adjudicating court.[39]

The second and last decision striking down a statute on indeterminacy grounds was laid down on 9 April 1981.[40] In this case, the *Corte Costituzionale* declared Article 603 of the Italian Criminal Code unconstitutional. Pursuant to the mentioned provision: "Anybody who exercises its power on any person, up to the point in which this person is totally subjugated, will be punished with a term of imprisonment not to be inferior to five and not to exceed fifteen years".[41]

The *Corte costituzionale* concluded, once again, that criminal provisions must have a strong link to perceivable reality. This is to mean that what is described in abstract in the law must be meaningfully comparable to the events of the real world. In other words, a court must be able to judicially verify the legal resemblance between the conduct of the defendant and the abstract provision. In this

---

[35]The point is clearly explained by Manes (2014), p. 23.

[36]We may refer to the ordinary citizen engaged in a specific occupation. It is likely that he may consult, at least cursorily, the relevant laws pertaining her sector of activity.

[37]*Corte costituzionale,* decision no. 177 of 1980.

[38]In fact, Article 1(1) of the same provision made possible the issuance of a preventive measure against "common vagabonds or idle people who, nonetheless, are able to work".

[39]Manes (2014), p. 21.

[40]*Corte costituzionale,* decision no. 96 of 1981.

[41]Italian Criminal Code, Article 603: "*Chiunque sottopone una persona al proprio potere, in modo da ridurla in totale stato di soggezione, è punito con la reclusione da cinque a quindici anni*".

case, the possible courses of conduct that may lead to the exercise of power (absent physical constraints) on the victim were absolutely unclear. Also, in preceding lower courts' decisions on Article 603 of the Criminal Code, the required "state of total subjugation" was never found nor proved. The *Corte Costituzionale* noted that this result followed from the fact that "total subjugation" is a term with no correspondence in reality. In fact, subjugation can never be "total", but it can only be partial to different degrees.[42]

1.3 Conclusion on the Principio di determinatezza in Italian Constitutional Adjudication

As we have seen, the *Corte costituzionale* has struck down only two provisions on the ground of indeterminacy. One may think that the *Corte costituzionale*, as sometimes happens in American constitutional law, is not particularly interested in breathing life into a particular constitutional clause. Nonetheless, we should conclude that this is not the case, since both the *Corte costituzionale* and legal scholarship have underscored on countless occasions how important the *principio di determinatezza* is to the legality ideal. At the same time, the *Corte costituzionale*'s self-perception of its institutional role militates against enforcing the principle more aggressively.

Apart from abstract commitments, should we conclude that the principle of precision, at least when it commands the drafting of "understandable" criminal provisions, has no bite? Not entirely, since the force of the principle is not to be measured by its judicial applications only. The *principio di determinatezza* is in fact a fundamental canon of interpretation for courts and of legislation for the parliament.[43] The *Corte costituzionale*, as we said, out of high deference and of an acute self-perception of its institutional role, is on the other side not willing to step into the "political" arena and enforce the principle vigorously.

Consequently, we should read such paucity of cases as a mirror image of the *Corte costituzionale*'s self-restraint. Also, we submit that high deference to legislative power with respect to criminalization choices can also be listed as an alternative explanation.

In conclusion, as a matter of fact, it is fair to say that the *Corte costituzionale* exercises self-restraint to a very substantial degree. It has been suggested that, according to the Court, choices concerned with "what" and "how" to criminalize cannot be disconnected from the type of judgment that the *principio di determinatezza* requires. Leaving the substantial limits on criminalization choices aside (since they concern a different even if connected constitutional principle, called the *principio di offensività*), we may at least concede that the line that separates permissible neutral review of drafting choices and impermissible overstepping into inviolable legislative discretion is a thin one.

---

[42]Manes (2014), pp. 23–24.

[43]Ibid., pp. 18–24.

This approach has sparked some critical objections.[44] Nonetheless, this course of action has been constantly followed by the *Corte costituzionale* since 1956 and it is not bound to change anytime soon.

2 The Void-for-Vagueness Doctrine in American Constitutional Law

2.1 Introduction

The vagueness doctrine is one of the three instruments employed in the United States to reach the goals of foreseeability and predictability in the interpretation of the law[45] and it also considered one of the doctrines implementing the principle of legality. Consequently, it can fairly be characterized as the most concrete means through which the rule-of-law ideal is put in practice. The doctrine requires the criminal law to be drafted as precisely as possible, to allow the common man to distinguish between what is prohibited and what is not. Also, the degree of precision reached should be enough to prevent discriminatory or arbitrary enforcement.[46]

The void-for-vagueness doctrine has not been developed in the criminal law context. In fact, it is traditionally taught and categorized within the realm of constitutional law. Nonetheless, its most relevant applications are to be found in the criminal sphere, where the government power reaches its peak.[47] The *vagueness doctrine* finds its origin in the *Due Process Clause* of the Fifth[48] and Fourteenth[49] Amendments of the United States Constitution.

The final step in establishing the Fifth and Fourteenth Amendments as the constitutional foundation of the doctrine was *Cline v. Frink Dairy Co.* (1927).[50] In *Cline*, a state antitrust statute was declared unconstitutional as impermissibly vague, citing these two constitutional provisions as the basis for the decision.[51]

---

[44]See Palazzo (1979), pp. 409–411; Bricola (1981), p. 266.

[45]Packer (1968), pp. 80–85.

[46]Jeffries (1985), p. 196.

[47]Decker (2002), p. 241.

[48]Fifth Amendment, Constitution of the United States of America: "No person shall be … deprived of life, liberty, or property, without due process of law; nor shall private property be taken for public use, without just compensation".

[49]Fourteenth Amendment, Constitution of the United States of America, para. 1: "All persons born or naturalized in the United States, and subject to the jurisdiction thereof, are citizens of the United States and of the state wherein they reside. No state shall make or enforce any law which shall abridge the privileges or immunities of citizens of the United States; nor shall any state deprive any person of life, liberty, or property, without due process of law; nor deny to any person within its jurisdiction the equal protection of the laws".

[50]*Cline v. Frink Dairy Co.*, 274 US 445 (1927).

[51]Lockwood (2010), pp. 264–266.

In the following paragraphs we will describe the main features of the doctrine (which is fundamental in implementing the legality ideal in American criminal law) with particular regard to its evolution in the jurisprudence of the United States Supreme Court. We will also keep in mind that, notwithstanding its importance, the doctrine has left many interpreters puzzled and it has many foggy corners that need to be explored.[52]

First of all, we must ascertain the intimate ratio of the void-for-vagueness doctrine. In fact, on the one hand, the doctrine has been defined "among the most important guarantees of liberty under law",[53] while on the other hand United States Supreme Courts have almost consistently failed to define its fundamental structure, except on infrequent occasions. Moreover, these rare moments of clarity have been riddled with contradictions.[54]

A problematic aspect of the doctrine is establishing the limit of judicial power in its operational sphere. In particular, it is not clear if a court could examine a provision without reference to concrete circumstances (i.e. on its face) or if, on the contrary, it should stick to an as-applied challenge (i.e. in light of the factual circumstances that surrounded the conduct). Moreover, we should establish if the boundaries of indeterminacy are the same for every norm or if, on the contrary, they are differently set for each type of provision examined. More in general, there is some uncertainty on how the court should navigate the unexplored waters of the doctrine. What should the court consider? Are there boundaries that cannot be crossed?[55]

To conclude this introduction, we should anticipate that at the heart of the doctrine lies a test that to the civil law lawyer can be represented as an equation, composed of different factors. If the result is somehow above or below a certain threshold, the scrutinized provision will or will not pass constitutional muster. So far, one would say, so good. The problem is that many factors are uncertain or indeterminate, while others are not visible to the naked eye and they need to be unearthed through the analysis of cases. As a result, the undertaking of a void-for-vagueness analysis is far from mathematical certainty and it is more akin to the art of divination.

According to courts, there are only two questions to be asked with respect in this vagueness analysis. The first one is aimed at knowing if the provision considered gives the ordinary citizen fair notice of the prohibited conduct. The second one wants to ascertain if a sufficient standard to adjudicate guilt or innocence is provided or, to the contrary, if the provision promotes discriminatory or arbitrary enforcement.[56]

---

[52]Batey (1997), p. 1.

[53]Sunstein (1996), p. 102.

[54]Amsterdam (1960), p. 71.

[55]Jeffries (1985), p. 196.

[56]Decker (2002), p. 241 and Batey (1997), p. 4.

We may summarize the tensions underlying the vagueness doctrine by noting how, on one side, while everybody agrees that a provision must give "men of common intelligence" a fair comprehension of the prohibited conduct, on the other side nobody would ever question Oliver Wendell Holmes Jr.'s statement that:

> The law is full of instances where a man's fate depends on his estimating rightly ... some matter of degree. If his judgment is wrong, not only may he incur a fine or a short imprisonment ...; he may incur the penalty of death.[57]

2.2 The Rationale Behind the Vagueness Doctrine

The most intuitive aspect of the rationale of the void-for-vagueness doctrine is the one concerned with guaranteeing fair notice to the public.

The Supreme Court has elegantly summarized the fairness element in *Connally v. General Construction Co.* (1926), which is rightly listed among the leading cases on point:

> The terms of a penal statute creating a new offense must be sufficiently explicit to inform those who are subject to it what conduct on their part will render them liable to its penalties ... and a statute which either forbids or requires the doing of an act in terms so vague that men of common intelligence must necessarily guess at its meaning ... violates the first essential of due process of law.[58]

We should ask ourselves what fair notice truly means. To be sure, it cannot be equal to "actual knowledge of the law". This is to be drawn logically from the existence of the *ignorantia legis non excusat* principle.[59] Rather, fair notice should be understood to mean "possibility of knowledge", in the sense that the individual would have known that the conduct was prohibited if he read the relevant statute.[60]

After having clarified this preliminary point, the fair notice element, intended as a means to promote informed choices of actions, has a particularly strong meaning if the prohibited conduct is not only lawful but instead constitutes the exercise of a constitutionally protected right. As an example, we may cite freedom of speech, protected by the First Amendment to the US Constitution. In this case, the lack of precision of the criminal law is, in the first place, detrimental to the uninformed individual. In the second place, though, the vague definition will impact some other potential "consumers" of free speech in a rather unique way. These hypothetical individuals, faced with a vaguely defined offense that threatens to cover some expressive conduct, would rather not exercise their right out of fear of punishment. In fact, they may not be able to determine where the line between

---

[57]*Nash v. United States*, 229 US 373 (1913), p. 377.

[58]*Connally v. General Construction Co.*, 269 US 385 (1926), pp. 221–222.

[59]Batey (1997), p. 4.

[60]Decker (2002), p. 248 e Hill (1999), p. 1304.

legality and illegality runs. In American legal thought, this perverse influence is called the "chilling effect".

Nonetheless, many scholars and courts have pointed out some shortcoming in the description of the fair notice element. This intuitive justification of the vagueness doctrine is, at first sight, clean and neat but, critics claim, behind this nice surface is nothing more than a hollow and fictional concept.[61]

To be sure, it can be fairly said that this conclusion, although truthful to some extent, is a little too extreme. Given the way in which the doctrine is currently structured, fair notice is still firmly at the core of the analysis. In fact, it embodies fundamental values such as foreseeability and predictability in the field of the criminal law. The solution to reconcile critiques with the reality of the doctrine may be to consider "fair notice" as a proxy term used to describe the necessity of clearly defining the contours of criminal liability. To put it simply, fair notice should be taken with a grain of salt.

As a partial response, in the Supreme Court's case law, attention has slowly shifted from the concept of fair notice to the idea of prevention of arbitrary or discriminatory enforcement. This different focus has the undeniable merit of shedding light on the connection between the doctrine and the protection of individual rights.[62]

The "arbitrary enforcement" rationale is usually justified under the theory that indeterminate provisions give excessive discretion to law enforcement officers, empowering them to be the final arbiters of the content of the criminal law. In leaving this decision to the law-appliers, we can see the danger of discrimination. In fact, these officials will fill in the indeterminate wording of statutes with their own personal preferences.[63] In this sense, we can see the connection with separation-of-powers values, even if focused not on courts (like in the Italian system) but rather on prosecutors and police officers.[64]

The protection of individual rights from arbitrary or discriminatory official action was finally recognized as the paramount value protected by the doctrine in *Papachristou v. City of Jacksonville* (1972).[65] The case is interesting also because of the type of statute involved, which is a vagrancy statute. The wording of the provision clearly bears the sign of legislative intention, which was punishing some individuals not for what they do but rather for what they are:

> Rogues and vagabonds, or dissolute persons who go about begging, common gamblers, persons who use juggling or unlawful games or plays, common drunkards, common night walkers, thieves, pilferers or pickpockets, traders in stolen property, lewd, wanton and lascivious persons, keepers of gambling places, common railers and brawlers, persons wandering or strolling around from place to place without any lawful purpose or object, habitual loafers, disorderly persons, persons neglecting all lawful business and habitually

---

[61]Jeffries (1985), p. 206.

[62]Amsterdam (1960), p. 88; Sun (2011), pp. 157–170.

[63]Decker (2002), p. 253.

[64]Batey (1997), p. 6.

[65]*Papachristou v. City of Jacksonville*, 405 US 156 (1972).

spending their time by frequenting houses of ill fame, gaming houses, or places where alcoholic beverages are sold or served, persons able to work but habitually living upon the earnings of their wives or minor children shall be deemed vagrants and, upon conviction in the Municipal Court shall be punished as provided for Class D offenses.[66]

To a civil lawyer, the provision is astonishing. First of all, much of the conduct proscribed does not seem to be a conduct at all, but rather a way of life. With particular reference to Italy, we may think that the mentioned ordinance would be an outright violation of the *principio di materialità*.

The Supreme Court declared the law unconstitutional. The Supreme Court's opinion also explained, in a rather exhaustive fashion, the danger brought about by vague statutes:

> Those generally implicated by the imprecise terms of the ordinance-poor people, nonconformists, dissenters, idlers - may be required to comport themselves according to the life-style deemed appropriate by the Jacksonville police and the courts. Where, as here, there are no standards governing the exercise of the discretion granted by the ordinance, the scheme permits and encourages an arbitrary and discriminatory enforcement of the law. It furnishes a convenient tool for "harsh and discriminatory enforcement by local prosecuting officials, against particular groups deemed to merit their displeasure".[67]

The test currently employed in vagueness cases is the one articulated in *Kolender v. Lawson*,[68] which, not surprisingly, involved a challenge to a *vagrancy statute*:

> The void-for-vagueness doctrine requires that a penal statute define the criminal offense with sufficient definiteness that ordinary people can understand what conduct is prohibited and in a manner that does not encourage arbitrary and discriminatory enforcement.[69]

In the process of redefining its rationale, the void-for-vagueness doctrine was transformed from a doctrine created to protect the informative function of the criminal law to one charged with the broader goal of putting a limit to discriminatory or arbitrary law enforcement.

In conclusion, this expansion in scope of the doctrine, as well as the partial demise of its "fair notice" element, was somehow anticipated. In fact, legal scholarship noted that many cases decided under the "fair notice" justification simply could not be squared with it. Many laws were struck down on that premise even if, in those same cases, the problem did not seem to be a lack of information. Also, if read with "fair notice" lenses, the fact that state laws were struck down at a much higher rate than federal ones was hardly justifiable. At the same time, scholars could not explain the continuous existence of old and extremely vague common law crimes. From these important insights came the idea that the doctrine was not only to be concerned with policing the relationship between the citizens and the

---

[66]*Jacksonville Ordinance Code* 26–57, at the time of the defendants' conduct.

[67]*Papachristou v. City of Jacksonville*, 405 US 156 (1972).

[68]*Kolender v. Lawson*, 461 US 352 (1983).

[69]Ibid., p. 357.

law, but rather with mediating between the coercive powers of the State and the constitutional guarantees.[70]

2.3 The Void-for-Vagueness Test: Explicit Factors

To the goal of ensuring a higher degree of stability to the doctrine, the Supreme Court elaborated a test to be applied in vagueness cases. Under such a construction, a challenged provision has to be examined in distinct phases, each of which is constituted of a formula that will guide the court in its decision. Since the formula is in itself composed of words, it will be inevitably imprecise to a certain degree, leaving a (healthy) space to the interpreter.

The current test was set forth in *Kolender v. Lawson*[71] and it is two-pronged. First of all, the law must define the proscribed conduct in a way that "ordinary people can understand what conduct is prohibited". Secondly, the provision must be drafted in a way that "does not encourage arbitrary and discriminatory enforcement". If the analysis will lead to the conclusion that either of the two parts of the test is not satisfied, the statute will be struck down:[72]

> The void-for-vagueness doctrine requires that a penal statute define the criminal offense with sufficient definiteness that ordinary people can understand what conduct is prohibited and in a manner that does not encourage arbitrary and discriminatory enforcement.[73]

Notwithstanding the fact that a large part of legal scholarship is concerned with the excessive power bestowed on courts by the current formulation of the vagueness doctrine, the adjudicating officials employ self-restraint to a substantial extent. This is exemplified by the fact that laws are presumed constitutional and by the fact that additional factors are considered in addition to the goal of "saving a statute", such as narrowing judicial interpretation.[74]

In reality, it is fair to say that the vagueness analysis implies a balancing between opposite needs. On one side, allowing judicial interpretation to save a provision in every instance would lead to even bigger fair notice problems. On the other side, it is to a certain extent natural that interpretation will eventually lead to a specification, or even to an integration of the meaning of the law.[75]

This theory of adjudication of void-for-vagueness cases may seem reasonable at first but, if we take the fair notice rationale at its face value, it seems

---

[70]Amsterdam (1960), pp. 80–85, had this intuition in 1960. See also Jeffries (1985), pp. 217–218.

[71]*Kolender v. Lawson* cit.

[72]Decker (2002), p. 246.

[73]*Kolender v. Lawson* cit., p. 357.

[74]Decker (2002), p. 247 and Goldsmith (2003), pp. 295–296. See also *Hamling v. United States*, 418 US 87 (1974), *United States Civil Serv. Comm'n v. National Ass'n of Letter Carriers*, 413 US 548 (1973) and *Screws v. United States*, 325 US 91 (1945).

[75]Goldsmith (2003), p. 296.

unwarranted: in fact, if the vagueness doctrine is bound to defend the "ordinary person's" freedom of choice, how much sense does it make to include the judicial gloss of a provision in the analysis? In fact, an average citizen is not likely to consult case books or reports.[76]

On the same tone, the judicial scrutiny performed under the vagueness doctrine is taken a step further by considering, in a clarifying fashion, legislative history as a means to determine the legislator's intent.[77] Notwithstanding the fact that part of legal scholarship would favor the use of such an instrument,[78] we may nonetheless look suspiciously at the practice, for it would be unrealistic to charge an ordinary person, or maybe even a professional, with the task of ascertaining legislative history.

In addition to this, the Supreme Court has also considered the "timing factor" of interpretation. In fact, the reasoning goes, if a statute went unchallenged for a long time, this may signify that, probably, its meaning is relatively clear.[79]

At the same time, the Supreme Court has also considered the type of provision challenged. First of all, the vagueness doctrine has a stronger bite in the criminal rather than in the civil arena. Secondly, if the challenged provision proscribes individual conduct as opposed to collective conduct, such as that happening in a professional or business setting, the level of information provided must be higher. This conclusion is reached by considering that it is at least plausible that a collective entity would have consulted the relevant applicable law before acting. Also, it may well be that such an entity would have resorted to professional legal advice, if in doubt.[80]

Moreover, if the provision is targeted to a limited group of people (e.g. butchers, bakers, venture capitalists), it could be possible that an otherwise unclear term would acquire a specific meaning in the specific sector considered.[81]

Finally, if the criminal provision borders with the constitutionally protected area of individual liberties (such as freedom of speech), the level of precision should rise to the highest level.[82] This is due to the fact that a vague provision discourages every activity situated on its fuzzy border. Moreover, if many of these activities are also constitutionally protected activities, there is the additional problem that this conduct is not only permissible but desirable. Examples may be brought regarding freedom of expression,[83] as well as freedom of movement[84] or also the right to abortion.[85]

---

[76]Amsterdam (1960), pp. 73–74.

[77]*United States Civil Serv. Comm'n v. National Ass'n of Letter Carriers* cit., and *United States v. Bramblett*, 384 US 503 (1955).

[78]Goldsmith (2003), p. 298.

[79]*United States v. Ragen*, 314 US 513 (1942), *Screws v. United States* cit.

[80]Robinson (2005), p. 358.

[81]See, e.g., *McGowan v. Maryland*, 366 US 420 (1961).

[82]Decker (2002), p. 249.

[83]Batey (1997), pp. 16–18.

[84]*Kolender v. Lawson* cit., p. 358.

[85]*Colautti v. Franklin*, 439 US 379 (1979), p. 394.

Another element that is usually considered in this delicate balancing is the presence of a *scienter* element in the definition of the crime. In fact, if the conduct is punished only if done intentionally, this element may partially excuse imprecision.[86] On the point, unfortunately, there seems to be some confusion between intention in carrying out the single elements of the *actus reus* (which, unfortunately, is where judicial interpretation focuses) and knowledge of the criminality of the conduct (which should be the correct focus of the analysis).

2.4 The Void-for-Vagueness Test: Implicit Factors

So far, the "factors" we have considered in the vagueness "equation" belong somehow to the physiology of judicial interpretation. However, there are additional factors that can be observed at a closer scrutiny of case law. These other elements are, to a large extent, of political-discretional nature and they are not made explicit by interpreting courts.

First of all, the courts are willing to evaluate the availability of less indeterminate alternatives to reach the legislative goal. Also, directly connected to this first idea, there is a second element which is the importance of the legislative objective. Consequently, the level of tolerance of imprecision is given also by the combination between the necessity of using indeterminate wording and the importance of the provision in the general criminal law framework. To conclude on the point, a vague but fundamental provision will pass constitutional scrutiny with relative ease.[87]

Also constitutional rights are, to a certain extent, put on the scale of vagueness. Freedom of speech usually seems to come first and weigh the most, while other rights[88] are assigned lesser weight.[89]

We may cite, once again, *Kolender v. Lawson*:[90] in the opinion authored by J. O'Connor, the Court justified facial analysis[91] on the ground that *Kolender* involved the right to not be discriminated against in law enforcement while previous cases disavowing such analysis (*Flipside*[92] and *Levy*[93]) were simply concerned with regulating economic activity and military life (to be kept distinct from civilian life) respectively.

---

[86]Decker (2002), p. 249.

[87]Batey (1997), pp. 10–12.

[88]Third Amendment to the United States Constitution: "No Soldier shall, in time of peace be quartered in any house, without the consent of the Owner, nor in time of war, but in a manner to be prescribed by law".

[89]Batey (1997), pp. 17–20.

[90]*Kolender v. Lawson* cit., pp. 358–359, footnote 8.

[91]See infra on the concept of facial challenge.

[92]*Hoffman Estates v. The Flipside, Hoffman Estates*, 455 US 489 (1982).

[93]*Parker v. Levy*, 417 US 733 (1974).

In conclusion, there seem to be a strong political component to the vagueness doctrine. To recall a scheme of analysis set forth in legal scholarship, if the challenged provision is not among the core crimes (which were already known at common law) whose "importance" is proved per se, the court may go on to evaluate the significance of the legislative goal sought. If this goal is deemed significant, a higher degree of vagueness will be tolerated. If on the other side, the goal is not considered paramount, the provision would be struck down more easily.[94] Finally, after this first implicit evaluation is carried out, the court may weigh the necessity of using vague terms: in this evaluation, the adjudicator might consider the feasibility of a more precise drafting as well as the impact on constitutional rights.[95]

2.5 Facial Challenge Versus As-Applied Challenge

In applying the vagueness doctrine, American courts usually distinguish between facial challenges and as-applied challenges. In the first type of cases, the provision is examined "on its face", which is to say that the provision is examined directly, without considering the actual circumstances of the case. This type of analysis is generally employed when constitutional rights are involved.

We can already see how circumstances matter to help the common citizen understand the significance of her conduct. In fact, the degree of precision of a criminal statute may vary "in action" according to the concrete situation in which the defendant acted.

Coming back to our analysis, we may take child pornography as an example. This type of pornography is clearly not covered by the right to free speech. Nonetheless, if a law prohibiting child pornography has the potential to impinge, in some hypothetical case, on freedom of expression, courts would allow the child pornographer to argue "on behalf" of the hypothetical individuals whose "speech" may be chilled by challenged provision.[96] This proxy challenge on behalf of others is a facial challenge.

On the other hand, in as-applied challenges, we should consider that concrete circumstances help clarifying the otherwise abstract meaning of the provision. Consequently, courts will carefully consider them. To understand the point, we should take an example: *Davis v. State*, decided by the Indiana Court of Appeals.[97]

In the case, an Indiana criminal provision provided, in relevant part, that:

> (a) A person having the care of a dependent ... who knowingly or intentionally: (1) places the dependent in a situation that endangers the dependent's life or health; ... commits neglect of a dependent, a Class D felony.[98]

---

[94]Batey (1997), pp. 4–39.

[95]Ibid.

[96]Please refer, for citations, supra, Sect. 2.2, where "chilling effect" is discussed.

[97]*Davis v. State*, 476 N.E.2d 127, Ind. Ct. App. (1985).

[98]*Indiana Code*, 35-46-1-4, *Neglect of a dependent; child selling*.

In the case, the defendants abandoned their few-hour-old son on the side of a gravel road in the Indiana countryside. After being indicted, they argued that the expression "endangers the dependent's life or health" was excessively vague. They further submitted that the conduct of a parent allowing his child to play, for example, football, may well fall within the provision.

The Indiana Court of Appeals rejected the argument. Since, in vagueness cases, we have to ask if a person of ordinary intelligence would reasonably understand that his conduct is criminal, it must be concluded that, if we took into account the actual circumstances, it was absolutely crystal clear that abandoning a newly-born baby to the side of a gravel road was within the core meaning of "endangers the dependent's life or health".[99]

3 A Comparative Analysis of the *Principio di determinatezza* and the Vagueness Doctrine as Applied in Constitutional Adjudication

In analyzing the two doctrines one may, first of all, notice the "oceanic" distance that separates the two Courts considered. A cursory analysis of the institutional and systemic differences between the two could take a whole book. Let us indulge then, for a moment, on only one particularly striking difference. The *Corte costituzionale* is as self-restrained as a Constitutional Court can ever be. In fact, it has avoided political controversy with utmost care and it has contained its decisions, which nonetheless carry great weight, within the boundaries of technical adjudication.

On the other hand, the United States Supreme Court is at the very center of the American political life. During history, many fundamental social questions have been solved in the austere marble palace of Washington, D.C.. Among them, we may refer to racial segregation in schools, slavery, and the right to abortion as well as same-sex marriage.

On the topic of vagueness, though, the institutional and physical distance between the two Courts is greatly reduced. In fact, the vagueness doctrine as well as the *principio di determinatezza* have an inescapable technical component which allows us to compare the decisions of the two constitutional adjudicators.

We may notice, as a first point of contact, that both Courts are willing to refer to the effects of judicial interpretation on the degree of precision of criminal provisions. On the one hand, the *Corte costituzionale* referred to judicial interpretation first as a way to additionally clarify the meaning of a provision. Also, the *Corte costituzionale* has stated that the absence of contrasting judicial interpretations may be taken as a sign of the clarity of the language. On the other hand, the Supreme Court has pointed to a similar theory when it has allowed clarifying glosses on an otherwise indeterminate language. In concluding on this point, it may be said that both Courts recognized that the meaning of a provision is

---

[99]*Davis v. State* cit., pp. 130–131.

not to be ascertained from the text only, but from its judicial interpretation too. Nonetheless, neither of them is willing to allow extreme interpretations just to the goal of saving a provision, even though it has been noticed that both the Italian and the United States Supreme Court have done, from time to time, precisely that.

A difference between the two Courts may be seen in their approach to the separation of powers issue. Starting from the United States, the Supreme Court has over time discarded the separation-of-powers rationale of the vagueness doctrine, in favor of an enhanced attention to the fair notice and discriminatory enforcement rationales. Notwithstanding the fact that it has been abandoned, this part of the vagueness analysis keeps on living, although implicitly, in the other two prongs of the doctrine. In fact, the separation of powers ensures at a more general level against both unfair surprise (by prohibiting judicial legislation) as well as against abuses of discretion.

Coming to the *Corte costituzionale*, the separation-of-powers *leitmotif* is, to these days, an essential part of the application of the "principle of precision". In fact the *Corte costituzionale*, supported by legal scholarship in its entirety, customarily repeats that the principle guards against the appropriation of legislative power by courts, in the sense that vague laws would allow them to specify the meaning of a statute in whichever way it may suit their liking.

Another point worth noting about the Italian system is that the *principio di determinatezza* showed some actual bite when the *Corte costituzionale* found that what the legislator described in the statute had no way of being judicially ascertained. For example, when the law asked the police commissioner to decide who may be "inclined to commit crimes", the *Corte costituzionale* struck down the provision on the ground that no official, belonging to the judicial or executive branch alike, may possibly link such a description to an "observable phenomenon".

We noted that the provision challenged in the mentioned case was the exact equivalent of an American vagrancy statute, such as the one seen in *Papachristou*. These statutes were targeted at socially undesirables and they armed police forces with a legal tool to take them out of public view.

The United States Supreme Court, instead of focusing on the link between abstract description and perceptible reality, chose to concentrate on the great amount of discretion that such a provision grants police officers. Nonetheless, both Courts were troubled by these street-cleaning statutes and both reacted in the same way, even if under slightly different theories.

One striking difference in the application of the two doctrines is the sheer volume of cases decided under each of them. In the United States Supreme Court, there are numerous cases on the books in which laws have been struck down as unconstitutionally vague. On the other hand, the Italian *Corte costituzionale* issued such rulings only twice since 1956. This is probably to be attributed to the different institutional architecture in which the two Courts are posited. The United States Supreme Court has over the course of history commanded more and more deference and this accumulated gravitas has allowed it to descend, from time to time, into the political arena, even if formally maintaining neutrality. In this respect, we may point to the arch-famous *Bush v. Gore*,[100] in

---

[100]*Bush v. Gore*, 531 US 98 (2000).

the context of which an argument can be made that there was not much "law" to the decision. In particular, conservative justices, which usually take an aggressive stance in policing federalism, had no problem in telling the Florida Supreme Court how to interpret its own state law. On the other side, liberal justices instantaneously became defenders of States' prerogatives.

On the other side, the Italian *Corte costituzionale* practices self-restraint to a high degree. If we look at the two decisions striking down statutes on the ground of indeterminacy, we may think that the *Corte costituzionale* had no other way to go. These two provisions were, first of all, textually indeterminate. Secondly, there was no corresponding "ordinary-man" or technical meaning for expressions such as "to subject an individual to one's power into total subjugation" or to "inclined to commit crimes". Finally, there was absolutely no link with perceivable reality and, as a consequence, the citizen and the interpreter were left completely in the dark.

Finally, we may notice that both Courts focus on the individual ordinary citizen. In both the Italian and American version of the principle of precision in the criminal law, it is recognized that the law, on one side, should guide individuals' conduct while, at the same time, should be drafted narrowly to assure that the contours of the criminal sphere are drawn by elected, rather than unelected, officials.

References

Amsterdam, Anthony G. 1960. The Void-for-Vagueness Doctrine in the Supreme Court – A Means to an End. *University of Pennsylvania Law Review* 109: 67-116.
Batey, Robert. 1997. Vagueness and the Construction of Criminal Statutes – Balancing Acts. *Virginia Journal of Social Policy & the Law* 5: 1-96.
Beccaria, Cesare (ed. Giulio Carnazzi). 2014. Dei delitti e delle pene. Milano: BUR.
Bricola, Franco. 1981. Art. 25, 2° e 3° comma. In *Commentario della Costituzione*, ed. Giuseppe Branca, 227-316. Bologna: Zanichelli; Roma: Società editrice del foro italiano.
Cadoppi, Alberto. 2014. *Il valore del precedente nel diritto penale. Uno studio sulla dimensione in action della legalità.* II ed. Torino: Giappichelli.
A.E. Goldsmith. 2003. The Void-for-Vagueness Doctrine in the Supreme Court, Revisited, *American Journal of Criminal Law* 30: 279-314.
Decker, John F. 2002. Addressing Vagueness, Ambiguity, and Other Uncertainty in American Criminal Laws. *Denver University Law Review* 80: 241-344.
Hill, Alfred. 1999. Vagueness and Police Discretion: The Supreme Court in a Bog. *Rutgers Law Review* 51: 1289-1318
Jeffries, John C. 1985. Legality, Vagueness, and the Construction of Penal Statutes. *Virginia Law Review* 71: 189-245.
Lockwood, Cristina D. 2010. Defining Indefiniteness: Suggested Revisions for the Void-for-Vagueness Doctrine. *Cardozo Public Law, Policy & Ethics Journal* 8: 255-340.
Manes, Vittorio. 2014. Principi costituzionali in materia penale (diritto penale sostanziale). http://www.cortecostituzionale.it/documenti/convegni_seminari/Principi_costituzion ali_in_materia_penale_ottobre_2014.pdf.
Packer, Herbert L. 1968. *The Limits of the Criminal Sanction.* Stanford: Stanford University Press.
Palazzo, Francesco C. 1979. *Il principio di determinatezza nel diritto penale. La fattispecie.* Padova: Cedam.

Robinson, Paul H. 2005. Fair Notice and Fair Adjudication: Two Kinds of Legality. *University of Pennsylvania Law Review* 154: 335-398.

Sun, Tammy W. 2011. Equality by Other Means: The Substantive Foundations of the Vagueness Doctrine. *Harvard Civil Rights-Civil Liberties Law Review* 46: 149-194.

Sunstein, Cass R. 1996. *Legal Reasoning and Political Conflict*. New York: Oxford University Press.

Anti-discrimination Law and Limits of the Power of Dismissal: A Comparative Analysis of the Legislation and Case Law in the United States and Italy

Fabio Pantano

Principia communia legis naturae non eodem modo applicari possunt omnibus, propter multam varietatem rerum humanarum: et ex hoc provenit diversitas legis positivae apud diversos.

Tommaso D'Aquino, *Summa theologiae*, 1a 2ae, Quaest. 95, Article 2

Abstract The prohibition of discrimination in employment relationships is core to the fundamental principle of human dignity that underlies the law of the most developed Countries. Nonetheless, under a comparative approach, anti-discrimination law assumes different roles and functions according to the historical development of each legal system. In the United States the implementation of anti-discrimination provisions has been one of the main instruments for US legislative institutions to promote the emancipation of the most disadvantaged groups of workers. On the other hand, United States courts have narrowly interpreted anti-discrimination statutory laws emphasizing the necessity of protecting employers' prerogatives under the common law doctrine of "at will employment". Within the European and Italian experiences, political concerns for the emancipation of the working class have informed the evolution of labor law since the nineteenth century. Case law and statutes provide for general limits to the powers of employers, in order to counterbalance the economic submission of workers to the supremacy of companies. This chapter focuses on discriminatory dismissals and is founded on the idea that the relationship between anti-discrimination law and the power of employers to dismiss acquires different roles and functions according to the peculiar features of the different legal systems, and in relation to their historical development. On the basis of these arguments a narrow interpretation of the most recent provisions of Italian legislations on discriminatory dismissals is to be preferred under a comparative approach.

F. Pantano (✉)
Researcher in Labor Law, University of Parma, Parma, Italy
e-mail: fabio.pantano@unipr.it

© Springer International Publishing Switzerland 2015
L. Pineschi (ed.), *General Principles of Law - The Role of the Judiciary*,
Ius Gentium: Comparative Perspectives on Law and Justice 46,
DOI 10.1007/978-3-319-19180-5_10

1 Introduction

The prohibition of discrimination in employment relationships is core to the fundamental principle of human dignity that underlies the law of the most developed Countries. Nonetheless, under a comparative approach, anti-discrimination law assumes different roles and functions according to the historical development of each legal system.

In the United States, social class conflict has never been central to the political agenda. Non-class ties, in particular ethnicity, have been the dominant way for political parties to create attachments with immigrant and American-born workers. Thus, the implementation of anti-discrimination provisions has been one of the main instruments for US legislative institutions to promote the emancipation of the most disadvantaged groups of workers. On the other hand, US courts have narrowly interpreted anti-discrimination statutory laws, emphasizing the necessity of protecting employers' prerogatives under the common law doctrine of "at will employment".[1]

Within the European experience, political concerns for the emancipation of the working class have informed the evolution of labor law since the nineteenth century. Case law and statutes provide for general limits to the powers of employers, in order to counterbalance the economic submission of workers to the supremacy of companies.

Within American law, the dialectic between the common law "employment at will" doctrine and statutory anti-discrimination provisions constitutes the core of American jurisprudence on the limits to the employers' power to terminate the employment relationship. Within Italian system employers can dismiss employees only on the basis of justified reasons, while the existence of a discriminatory motive affects only the kind of remedy enforced by courts in order to redress an unjustified dismissal. Thus, anti-discrimination principles play a residual role in this field.

Recently, Italian parliament has enacted a very remarkable reform on the consequences of the unlawful dismissal. Statute no. 92/2012[2] has modified Article 18 of the statute no. 300/1970.[3] Currently the "discriminatory dismissal" and the "dismissal due to an illicit motive" are the only circumstances that imply the strongest remedy against unlawful discharge (reinstatement + back pay + front pay). This new regime has increased the debate on the role of the non-discrimination principle. The two main approaches shared by Italian scholarship, in this regard, are highly conflicting.

On the one hand, a strict interpretation has been held, that minimizes the systemic importance of the non-discrimination principle and, consequently, the scope

---

[1]According to American common law all employers "may dismiss their employees at will, be they many or few, for good cause, for no cause, or even for morally wrong cause, without being thereby guilty of legal wrong". Among others: *Payne v. Western & A. R.R. Co.*, 81 Tenn. 507 (1884).

[2]Law no. 92 of 28 June 2012.

[3]Law no. 300 of 20 May 1970.

of the application of the strongest remedy against unlawful dismissal. On the other hand, the idea of an extensive interpretation of the statutory provision on discriminatory dismissal has been affirmed. According to this approach, the more intense remedy should apply every time that there is no legitimate reason for the termination of the employment relationship, on the basis of the assumption that each unlawful dismissal should be considered as "discriminatory".

The idea of this chapter is that a comparative approach might produce the insights necessary to clarify the interpretative doubts of Italian scholarship and jurisprudence. I will try to demonstrate that the relationship between anti-discrimination law and the power of employers to dismiss acquires different roles and functions according to the peculiar features of the different legal systems, and in relation to their historical development.

Italian law pursues the aim of rebalancing the socio-economic and contractual disparities, within the employment relationship, by establishing a set of specific limits to every legal power of the employer; thus statute no. 604/1966 provides for a specific set of rules that limits the power of dismissal. The employer can terminate the employment relationship only for justified reasons, due to the economic organization of the business or to unlawful behavior of employees. The discrimination principle plays a very limited role. The discriminatory nature of the discharge does not affect the validity of the decision but only the kind of remedy that the court will enforce.

By contrast, in the United States the non-discrimination principle constitutes (at least within federal law) the most relevant limit to the "employment at will" doctrine. Nonetheless, American courts have always applied a strict interpretative approach, in order to protect employers' prerogatives. Even with a more permissive approach, if compared to Italian case law (for instance as regards some decisions on the necessity of demonstrating the discriminatory intent), American courts have not opened the door to a massive application of the non-discrimination principle and to its extensive interpretation, notwithstanding the most remarkable systematic role that this principle plays within US employment law.

On the basis of these observations, a comparative approach corroborates the idea that a broad interpretation of the recent Italian provision on the legal remedies against discriminatory dismissals is not to be shared.

2 The Non-discrimination Principle: Some Preliminary Remarks

The general analysis of the principle of non-discrimination and of its systematic meaning outside the scope of labor and employment is not among the main aims of this chapter. Nonetheless, some preliminary remarks are necessary. On the basis of the traditional analysis of the general principles of law,[4] some doubts about the existence of such a principle itself could be raised, at least as regards Italian law.

---

[4]Bobbio (1966), p. 888 ff.; Bartole (1986); Del Vecchio (1921).

Nevertheless, even omitting the discussion on its very existence, this principle has ambiguous content that can be easily confused with the principle of equal treatment. Such a misunderstanding seems to be very frequent.

Equal treatment means treating similar situations in the same way, and distinguishing the different ones. Within European and American law, such a rule is not applied to the private relationships, but is commonly recognized as regards the relationships between public authorities and private subjects. Modern liberal law systems, founded on the rule of law, establish that the State and public administrations have to treat private individuals fairly and reasonably and that the legislator will enact statutory provisions that will not favor anyone in an unreasonable way. But such a principle is not granted within the relationships between the enterprise and workers.

On the contrary, a remarkable protection is recognized to the right of the employer to run his/her business[5] and to take any decision that he/she finds convenient in order to manage his/her economic activity, unless it is in contrast with a specific rule provided for by statutes or case law.

Taking decisions implies differentiating between, and providing in different ways for, customers, enterprises, contractors and subcontractors. The employer is responsible for the results of his/her economic activity, for the destiny of his/her enterprise and the interests of his/her shareholders and stakeholders. In order to grant the freedom of enterprise of the employer, her/his judgment on economic choices cannot be subject to any external revision, unless the decision taken is contrary to a precise statutory provision or case law rule.

Things do not change when the treatment of workers and employees is at stake. Italian case law is decidedly clear on this point. There is no binding principle for employers to treat similar situations in the same way, in the absence of an explicit contrary provision. Exemptions are provided in order to protect only those specific interests of workers that are deemed to deserve protection equal or superior to that of the freedom of enterprise.[6] American law does not seem to differ greatly, in this regard.

It might seem paradoxical but, while doubts about the existence of a general non-discrimination principle within Italian employment law could be raised, it is sure that, in any case, the general principle of law that grants the employer's right to differentiate—I would say, in a provocative manner, to "discriminate"—prevails on it, unless the differentiation/discrimination is specifically prohibited.

Many provisions prohibit specific discriminatory behaviors within Italian law. Most of them derive from European law; others from the implementation of rules of international law; some were already contained in domestic provisions, even before the implementation of the European directives on discrimination, of first and

---

[5]Within Italian law this principle receives a constitutional recognition by Article 41 of the Constitution.

[6]See Sect. 3 below.

second generation.[7] In fact, the number of provisions is such that the existence of a general principle of non-discrimination could hardly be contested. Nonetheless, it is quite clear that, even if such a general principle exists, it is not an inference of the equal treatment rule provided for by Article 3 of the Italian Constitution.

In my point of view, the content of this principle is that the prohibition of discrimination among private subjects directly derives from the protection of human dignity, and thus relates to Article 2 of Italian Constitution.[8] Since the right to differentiate (therefore to "discriminate") is highly protected by the Italian Constitution, it would be surprising if the fundamental right not to be discriminated against were recognized in such a general and wide manner to all workers and employees within the same constitutional legal system. Provisions on discrimination do not protect the right to equal treatment, but the dignity of human beings, involved within the economic activities of the enterprise.

This assumption has many remarkable consequences. If such a principle exists, its normative effect is not intended to provide for a general limitation of employers' power. On the contrary it is directly focused on the aspect of human dignity that would be under attack.

Italian and international scholars debate on the question of whether or not the express prohibitions of discrimination provided for within national and international law systems constitute a closed or open list. According to the approach proposed herein, even where the second idea is accepted,[9] a deep analysis of the nature of the protected specific aspect of human dignity is necessary, since this specific interest is to be balanced with the freedom of enterprise.

3 United States: The Historical Development of Inequalities Founded on Ethnicity and Gender

Given these general remarks on the content of the non-discrimination principle, it is necessary to define the role that prohibitions of discriminatory forms of treatment play within the two different law systems under investigation, since I believe that it significantly affects the way in which relevant provisions are to be interpreted.

The main idea of this chapter is that the function of the non-discrimination provisions differs according to the historical development of the legal systems these provisions belong to. This is particularly apparent when one compares the US and the Italian systems.

---

[7]Lassandari (2010), p. 7 ff.

[8]"The Republic recognizes and grants the inviolable rights of the human being, as an individual or within the social groups where he expresses his personality, and demands the fulfillment of the mandatory duties of political, economic and social solidarity".

[9]See Barbera (2013), p. 148.

Sociologists and historians consider the United States as a "categorically unequal" society,[10] where the "exploitation" of one group of individuals, and "opportunity hoarding" by another, dominant, category regulates the functioning of socio-economic dynamics. It has been maintained that "the motor of American history has been the continual reconfiguration of racial inequality in the Nation's social, political, and economic institutions".[11]

One could observe that European societies (and, in particular, the Italian one) are not very different in this regard. Nonetheless, sociologic studies[12] demonstrate that Europe has developed a less dramatic difference between the wealthiest and the most disadvantaged strata of society. The development of more effective systems, for the redistribution of wealth, has protected Europe from the more evident phenomena of economic social exclusion present within the American society. Nevertheless, the problem of poverty is still notable, even in Europe, and has seen a very conspicuous increase in consequence of the recent economic crisis.

The most evident difference between the two social systems is not the quantity of disadvantaged individuals, or the level of differentiation regarding access to economic resources or opportunities. The cornerstone of the problem is that in the United States the differentiation between social groups has operated on the basis of essentialist definitions of individuals, especially in terms of ethnicity and gender.[13] Within American society the economic situation of individuals has historically been highly affected by essentialist definitions of identity. The situation of social exclusion primarily operates in terms of essentialist distinctions (for instance being black, Latino or female) and poverty or economic disadvantages are invariably their consequence.

Since its origin, American society has supported the development of this form of "inequality" through the endorsement of slavery and its wide use within the productive system.[14] The racial segregation of Afro-Americans from Whites continued even after the civil war, through the Jim Crow system, and "racial segregation was enforced not only formally, in public settings, but also informally, in private practice, through a racial etiquette negotiated, daily, by black and white Southerners".[15] The New Deal political compromise "legitimated racial discrimination in employment", maintaining the formal disparity between the status of Afro-Americans and Whites within US institutions, up until the sixties.[16] Before the Civil Rights Act (CRA), African Americans were subject to a strong form of segregation and the employment was one of the most relevant fields in which their

---

[10]Massey (2007), p. 28 ff.

[11]Quadagno (1995), pp. 14–15, 188.

[12]Massey (2007), p. 258 ff.

[13]Ibid., p. 51 ff.; Katznelson (2006), p. 25; Quadagno (1995), p. 4 ff.

[14]Quadagno (1995), p. 187 ff.

[15]Massey (2007), p. 7.

[16]Quadagno (1995), pp. 10, 22.

exclusion from the best opportunities took place.[17] In the South, most of the work requiring "unskilled labor" was performed by black people and the situation was not very different in the North, even if the segregation there was less overt.[18]

The consequences of this form of alienation were destined to extend for many generations of Afro-Americans, because the inherited economic disempowerment of families prevented the possibility of access to the highest levels of education, and, thereby, to the highest "skilled labor" wages and more satisfactory forms of employment.[19]

For these reasons, there is still a significant lack of employment equity within the American labor market.[20] Black people still form the majority of those holding unskilled labor positions and of those unemployed.[21] This distribution of employment also affects the demography of the major cities, thus further entrenching the segregation based on ethnic classification.

The situation is similar for other minorities, such as Chinese people and Latinos. In the case of Latinos the social segregation has different and more recent origins, but similar issues and, in some cases, more serious consequences for the conditions of the people concerned. In most cases, individuals with South or Central American origins, living permanently within United States territory, do not possess a regular authorization. The percentage of undocumented Latinos is continuously increasing. They constitute a "better underclass",[22] since not only are they exploited and forced to accept the most menial and badly paid jobs, but they are themselves "outside the law", without the possibility of claiming any right, and under the continuous menace of being incarcerated for the felonious crime of being on US soil without permission.

However, "race", or "ethnicity", is not the only basis for the construction of "categorical inequalities" within American society. One of the most deeply embedded reasons for social segregation is gender or sex. Sociological studies demonstrate that women have significantly less access to the highest levels of education, and hold far less high status positions than men.[23]

From a general perspective, it is clear that "race and gender ... continue to function in powerful ways, to generate categorical inequalities"[24] and to operate as

---

[17]Ibid., pp. 17 ff., 188 ff.

[18]Massey (2007), p. 55 ff; Quadagno (1995), p. 56 ff.

[19]Massey (2007), p. 250 ff; Quadagno (1995), p. 53.

[20]Pitts (2008), p. 39 ff.

[21]Ibid., p. 41 ff.

[22]Massey (2007), p. 157 ff.

[23]Moreover, in the last decades, the economic crisis has distributed the burden of inequality proportionally to the increase of the polarization of economic wealth. While women more easily reach a fair distribution of roles within the family and more remunerated working positions among the richest classes, their situation is worsening among the lower layers of society. See Massey (2007), p. 157 ff.

[24]Ibid.

a "categorical mechanism of stratification" in the United States.[25] Therefore, the weight acquired by non-discrimination provisions in US employment law is strictly related to the development of American society.[26]

4 Social Inequalities and Employment Law in the United States and Italy

Social class conflict has never been central to the political agenda in the United States. Non-class ties, in particular ethnicity, have been the dominant way for political parties to create attachments with immigrants and American-born workers. Thus, the implementation of anti-discrimination provisions has been one of the most relevant instruments for US legislative institutions in the promotion of the emancipation of the most disadvantaged categories of workers.[27]

Moreover, while labor movement and unions' activism have been the motors for the emancipation of most disadvantaged classes in Europe, in the United States trade unions have always fought in order to exclude Afro-Americans from the most remunerated and qualified professional positions, preserving the privileges of their white members. Thus anti-discrimination law has been also used as an instrument for political institutions to undermine trade unions power to control the labor market in favor of white, more skilled workers.[28]

In the industrial and post-industrial era, labor law has represented the most important legal instrument for the emancipation of disadvantaged categories. Since American social stratification is fundamentally grounded on gender and ethnicity (or "race"), it is not surprising that the economic disparity between positions within the employment relationship and the labor market have been prevalently tackled by measures aimed to eliminate discrimination.

For these reasons anti-discrimination law constitutes the major part of American employment law and the most relevant body of limits to the powers of the employer.[29] This is quite clear from the words of Mr. Justice Powell, in the seminal opinion delivered by the US Supreme Court on discrimination. In *McDonnell Douglas Co. v. Green*, the Court held that:

> The language of Title VII makes plain the purpose of Congress to assure equality of employment opportunities and to eliminate those discriminatory practices and devices which have fostered racially stratified job environments to the disadvantage of minority citizens.[30]

---

[25]Ibid.

[26]Quadagno (1995), p. 4.

[27]Forbath (1991), p. 29 ff.

[28]Quadagno (1995), pp. 58, 61 ff., 188, 192 ff.

[29]Kittner and Kohler (2000), p. 276 ff.

[30]*McDonnell Douglas Corp. v. Green*, 411 US 792 (1973).

From this point of view, the US case is remarkably different from the European one. In Europe political concerns related to the emancipation of the working class have determined the evolution of labor law since the nineteenth century. The economic disadvantages of certain groups of individuals were not related to other factors concerning their personal conditions. More schematically, in Europe you are poor because you are poor; while in America you are poor because you are African-American, Latino or Chinese.

The case of gender discrimination necessitates a different reasoning, since it has always been spread both within American and European society, and it is not by chance that the prohibitions of gender discrimination are key to European anti-discrimination law. Nonetheless, in Europe anti-discrimination provisions have developed in a general framework where case law and statutes had already provided for general limits to the powers of employers, in order to counterbalance the economic submission of workers to the supremacy of companies.

On the contrary, in US employment law, anti-discrimination provisions provide for the strongest and more extended body of limits to the legal prerogatives of employers.[31] The Congress has adopted them in order to counteract an original and unlimited power of the enterprise to decide the destiny of the employment relationship, based on the common law "at will employment doctrine", on whose basis "all may dismiss their employees at will, be they many or few, for good cause, for no cause, or even for morally wrong cause, without being thereby guilty of legal wrong".[32]

It is clear that anti-discrimination law performs an extremely different role within US employment law and the employment laws of European Countries. Instances for challenging economic and social exclusion have issued in two different normative techniques within the two different contexts. American employment law provides for a structured body of anti-discrimination provisions in order to limit the discretionary power of the employer to dismiss the worker. European legal systems originated a more general and systemic technique for regulating the employer's power, based on the reasonableness principle.

It is not by accident that, within the European context, anti-discrimination law has seen a massive development at the European level and not at the level of the single Member States. In fact, unlike domestic laws, the European legal system does not have a highly developed social legislation and already consolidated techniques for counterbalancing the social primacy of employers over workers and employees.

---

[31]As a matter of fact, anti-discrimination law is not the only body of rules aimed to limit entrepreneurial powers. More specifically, as regards the power of dismissal, the legitimate discharge of employees is to fulfill other requirements provided by the common law, both within federal case law and the one contained within States' courts decisions; statutory provisions of the States, in some case establishing the "just cause" principle; limits provided for by collective agreements. See Kittner and Kohler (2000), p. 276 ff.

[32]Among others: *Payne v. Western & A. R.R. Co.* cit.

Moreover, the possibility that the increase of anti-discriminatory measures could respond to the general improvement of the conditions and treatments of workers has recently been challenged. It has been argued that this legislative trend has a causal relation with the dismantling of the traditional welfare state system. Thus, the anti-discrimination principle would have nothing to do with a project of emancipation of disadvantaged classes. On the contrary, it would represent the "appealing" face of "a process whereby the protection of the interests of employees becomes secondary to securing their interest in employment and employability, for the sake of economic stabilization"[33] and "disguise the unions' lack of ability to address social concerns".[34]

Within Italian law the Civil Code and the statutory provisions determine an organic body of rules, imposing a reasonable exercise of enterprise's prerogatives.[35] Anti-discrimination law is relegated to a residual role, aimed at counteracting only specific behaviors[36] that undermine the personal dignity of workers, with more effective actions.

In Italy the economic conflict between social classes has always played a more significant role than the fight for the emancipation of groups discriminated against on the basis of ethnicity, gender and other essentialist features, as demonstrated by the origin itself of anti-discrimination law within the Italian legal system. Indeed the first relevant Italian case law is related to cases of discrimination for political reasons or for affiliation to trade unions.[37]

But what are the main consequences of these general and systematic remarks? Do the different historical developments of anti-discrimination laws and the related different functions encompassed by this field of law, within the US and the Italian legal systems, result in a specific and effective interpretation of the inherent provisions?

I would assert that an analysis of the inherent statutory and case law clearly demonstrates that this question deserves a positive answer. In the United States, especially if one looks to the laws that regulate the termination of the employment relationship, it is clear that anti-discrimination law constitutes the main limit to the power of the employer to discharge workers, at least at a federal level. By contrast, within Italian law the same power is determined by the existence of justified reasons (or "motives"), and anti-discrimination provisions have a residual role, related to the type of remedy the court can enforce.

---

[33]Somek (2011), pp. 10–11.

[34]Ibid., p. 9.

[35]Gragnoli (2011), p. 511 ff.

[36]More specifically, according to the Directives 2000/43/EC and 2000/78/EC, implemented within Italian law by *Decreto legislativo* no. 215 of 9 July 2003 and *Decreto legislativo* no. 216 of 9 July 2003, the illicit behaviors are the ones motivated by race ethnic origin, religion or belief, disability, age or sexual orientation.

[37]Lassandari (2010), p. 188.

5 Anti-discrimination Provisions in US Employment Law

The main principles regulating the termination of the employment relationship, in US law, are due to the "at will employment doctrine". Therefore, there is no specific regulation governing the discharge of workers, at least at federal level.[38] In general, the power of dismissing workers is subject to the same general limits provided for all the employer's prerogatives. Therefore, anti-discrimination limits apply to dismissals in the same way that they do for all the other cases of discriminatory behavior.

In US employment law, the body of statutory provisions against discrimination is highly developed and the CRA represented a sort of breakthrough of Congress' policy in this field. It recognized the equality of citizens, despite their ethnicity, even within private relationship, ending the "Jim Crow" regime and, furthermore, permanently changing the equilibrium of the US political scenario.[39]

The US Constitution already contained an explicit provision on equal treatment. The Equal Protection Clause, at the end of Section 1 of the Fourteenth Amendment, establishes that "no State shall ... deny to any person within its jurisdiction the equal protection of the laws". The US constitutional provision has the same normative structure as Article 3 of the Italian Constitution. It cannot be considered the basis for a general principle of law on non-discrimination.

The CRA remains the fundamental provision of US law, as regards anti-discrimination law. It was modified in 1991, seeing the addition of new forms of remedies against unlawful employers' behavior.

Title VII of the CRA provides that:

It shall be an unlawful employment practice for an employer -
(1) to fail or refuse to hire or to discharge any individual, or otherwise to discriminate against any individual with respect to his compensation, terms, conditions, or privileges of employment, because of such individual's race, color, religion, sex, or national origin; or
(2) to limit, segregate, or classify his employees or applicants for employment in any way which would deprive or tend to deprive any individual of employment opportunities or otherwise adversely affect his status as an employee, because of such individual's race, color, religion, sex, or national origin.

Beside the CRA, the Congress has enacted other statutory provisions, aimed to prevent discriminatory treatments related to specific personal conditions of workers.[40]

The Age Discrimination in the Employment Act of 1964 (ADEA) prohibits any discrimination based on age. It has not simply added a new instance of unlawful discriminations to the list of Title VII, but enacted a new body of rules explicitly dedicated to discrimination on the basis of age. Nonetheless, the normative structure of ADEA and Title VII are similar, and most of the theories on discrimination and proof developed under one statute have been transposed into the other.

---

[38]See Kittner and Kohler (2000), p. 263 ff.

[39]Massey (2007), p. 74 ff.

[40]See Kittner and Kohler (2000), p. 268 ff.

The Equal Pay Act (EPA) of 1963 requires the payment of equal wages to male and female employees within the same establishment, performing "equal work on jobs, the performance of which requires equal skill, effort, and responsibility, and which are performed under similar working conditions".

More recently, Congress (1990) has enacted the American with Disabilities Act (ADA). Unlike the other main anti-discrimination statutory provisions (Title VII, EPA, ADEA), ADA only protects a "qualified individual with disability" and the question of whether or not the plaintiff falls within this category is the primary—if not the only—issue in a large percentage of litigated cases.

5.1 Controversial Aspects of US Case Law on Discriminations: The Burden of Proof

US employment law (at least at federal level) does not establish any general statutory provision on the justification of dismissal. The unilateral termination of the employment relationship by the employer is only subject to the general body of principles and doctrines created by courts. Among them, anti-discrimination provisions acquired a fundamental role. This is not the case for Italian law, where the termination of workers has a specific statutory regulation, which has to be coordinated with anti-discrimination law.

Even if anti-discrimination rules constitute the only instrument for reviewing the choices of the enterprise, US courts have often interpreted the relevant statutory provisions strictly, emphasizing the necessity of protecting employers' prerogatives under the common law doctrine of "at will employment".[41]

Within American case law, the necessity to assess the *discriminatory intent* and the way in which the *distribution of the burden of proof* is to be articulated in the trial are among the most contested issues. In its seminal opinion on the application of Title VII, the Supreme Court provided for precise rules on these subjects.[42]

In *McDonnell Douglas*, the Court elaborated the following scheme for the distribution of the burden of proof:

1. *Prima facie* case;
2. Demonstration of a legitimate non discriminatory reason;
3. Pretext.

The burden of a *prima facie* case is on the worker who claims to have been discriminated. He has to demonstrate that:

> [H]e belongs to a racial minority; (ii) that he applied and was qualified for a job for which the employer was seeking applicants; (iii) that, despite his qualifications, he was rejected;

---

[41]Somek (2011), p. 6.

[42]*McDonnell Douglas Corp. v. Green* cit.

and (iv) that, after his rejection, the position remained open and the employer continued to seek applicants from persons of complainant's qualifications.[43]

If the worker is able to prove a *prima facie* case, then the burden shifts to the employer, who is required to articulate some legitimate, non-discriminatory reason for the employee's rejection.

At this point the worker "must be given a full and fair opportunity to demonstrate by competent evidence that the presumptively valid reasons for his rejection were in fact a cover-up for a racially discriminatory decision".[44]

Such a distribution of the burden of proof clearly demonstrates that a certain level of review on the behavior of the employer is possible through the anti-discrimination provisions. The enterprise has to articulate the reasons for the dismissal and the court will assess whether they are able to rebut the *prima facie* case.

Nonetheless, in *McDonnell Douglas Corp.*, the Court has made clear that this possibility has to be applied in a very rigorous manner. In the relevant case, the Court of Appeals held that employers' justifications were based only on subjective—and not objective criteria—"which carried little weight in rebutting charges of discrimination".

The Supreme Court rejected the argumentations of the Court below, stating that "nothing in Title VII compels an employer to absolve and rehire one who has engaged in ... deliberate, unlawful activity against it".[45]

The meaning of the Supreme Court's statements appears clear. On the basis of Title VII, the court's evaluation has to be focused on the existence of a non-discriminatory reason for the choice of the employer. Judges are not to review the enterprise's decision, since there is no rule that requires that decision to be "justified".

The Supreme Court has confirmed this approach in a series of opinions. They made it clear that there is no violation of anti-discrimination law when the factor that motivates the employer is any other reason than the one prohibited, even if this justification is "implausible", "silly" or "fantastic".[46] According to the Supreme Court the "presumption raised by the *prima facie* case is rebutted, and the factual inquiry proceeds to a new level of specificity" when the employer presents the non-discriminatory reason "with a sufficient clarity so that the plaintiff will have a full and fair opportunity to demonstrate pretext".[47]

The absence of any obligation to justify the discharge affects the nature of the review of the decision of the employer carried out by the court. He/she is only required "to articulate" the reason, whatever it is.

---

[43]Ibid.

[44]Ibid.

[45]Ibid.

[46]*Hazen Paper Co. v. Biggins*, 507 US 604 (1993).

[47]*Texas Dept. of Commun. Affairs v. Burdine*, 450 US 248 (1981).

According to what the Court affirmed, one could say that judges would not be allowed even to evaluate whether the reason presented by the employer exists. But this approach does not seem feasible. The most acceptable construction is that courts have to assess whether the reason articulated by the employer is real and "feasible" or not; but cannot establish whether it is a "good" or a "bad" one.

5.2 The Discriminatory Intent

The necessity of demonstrating the "discriminatory intent" is one of the most contested questions as regards the implementation of anti-discrimination provisions. The problem is debated both in Italy and in the United States. The most relevant question is whether the worker is required to demonstrate that discrimination was the real reason for the employer's behavior.

Within the Italian system, scholars and courts are radically divided on this issue. Courts systematically require the worker to demonstrate the discriminatory intent;[48] on the contrary, for the most part, scholars support the view that, once the discriminatory impact of the employer's decision is proved, the plaintiff acquires the right to obtain the judicial remedy provided for by law.[49]

US case law is ambiguous on this point. In its seminal case on the "disparate impact doctrine", referring to Title VII, the Supreme Court held that "Congress directed the thrust of the Act to the consequences of employment practices, not simply the motivation".[50] In particular, "the Act proscribes not only overt discrimination but also practices that are fair in form, but discriminatory in the operation".[51] In this case, the worker would be required only to demonstrate the "disparate impact" of the employment practice on a minority of workers and not—for what appears from this opinion—the "discriminatory intent". At this point the burden of proof shifts to the employer, who has to demonstrate the existence of a "business necessity", meaning that the employment practice under consideration is "related to job performance".[52]

Nevertheless, in most recent cases the same Supreme Court seemed to depart from this course, stressing the idea that the demonstration of the discriminatory intent is, however, required. In *Hicks* the Court held that, even where a persecutory behavior of the enterprise is demonstrated, the worker is explicitly required to proving that that behavior is due to his personal condition that would constitute the reason of discrimination.[53]

---

[48]Corazza (1998), p. 403 ff.

[49]Lassandari (2010), p. 44 ff.; contra Bellocchi (2013), p. 803 ff.

[50]*Griggs v. Duke Power Co.*, 401 US 424 (1971).

[51]Ibid.

[52]Ibid.

[53]*St. Mary's Honor Ctr. v. Hicks*, 509 US 502 (1993).

These uncertainties give a clear indication on how the anti-discrimination principle works within American employment law. Despite the fundamental role played by anti-discrimination law for Congress' policy of combatting social exclusion and promoting emancipation of more disadvantaged groups of individuals, US courts did not provide for a very broad interpretation of anti-discrimination provisions. The Supreme Court is especially cautious; attempting to maintain a fair balance between the protection of weaker members of the society and the preservation of enterprise's economic freedoms.

6 The Discriminatory Discharge Within Italian Law

Italian anti-discrimination law is, for the most part, comprised of principles and rules stemming from European directives.[54] Other principles, relating to discriminatory practices, derive from international sources. Furthermore, the domestic legislator has enacted statutory provisions of primary importance. A general prohibition of employers' discriminatory behavior is contained in Article 15 of the statute no. 300/1970 (*Statuto dei lavoratori*).

As regards the discharge, Italian anti-discrimination law has to be coordinated with the general limits to the employer's power to terminate the employment relationship. Statute no. 604/1966 regulates the power of the employer to dismiss workers. It provides that the discharge of the employee has to be grounded on a justified motive. In particular, Article 3 clarifies that the discharge can be justified by "a remarkable breach of contractual obligations of the employee, or by reasons related to the productive activity, to the organization of work and its regular functioning".

Article 4 of the same statute establishes that "the discharge due to political beliefs, religious faith, being member of a trade union or taking part in trade unions activities is null, notwithstanding the justification deduced". Therefore, the legislator has provided for two different bodies of limits to the power of dismissing employees, within the same normative contest.

One of the most contentious questions in the current scientific debate is how these two different provisions have to be coordinated and, in particular, what are the respective scopes of implementation.

The discussion has become more controversial because of a recent modification[55] of Article 18 of statute no. 300/1970, which defines the remedies for unlawful discharge. In its previous version, Article 18 provided for the reinstatement and the payment of back pays and front pays (R.BP.FP+) each time the discharge was unjustified (according to Article 3 of statue no. 604/1966), only within all the

---

[54]Lassandari (2010), p. 8 ff.; Borelli (2007), p. 94 ff.
[55]Statute no. 92/2012.

enterprises or the establishments with more than fifteen employees. While, in case of discriminatory discharges, the same remedy has to be granted to each employee unlawfully terminated, notwithstanding the dimension of the enterprise.

According to the current language of Article 18, this remedy is applied only for discriminatory discharges or when the termination of the employment relationship is due to an illicit motive.[56] However, when the dismissal is only unjustified,[57] but not discriminatory, two different and weaker kinds of remedies will be applied. Depending on some complicated criteria more explicitly defined by the same provision,[58] the employer will be condemned either to the restatement plus a reparatory compensation quantified by the court, with a maximum amount of 12 monthly salaries (R.BP.FP−); or to only a reparatory compensation quantified between a minimum of 12 and a maximum of 24 monthly salaries (RC).

7 The Application of Anti-discrimination Law to the Discharge of Employees in Italian Law

Two different reconstructions of this new normative asset have been proposed by Italian scholarship. The first one holds that the strongest remedy (R.BP.FP+) will apply only in case of discriminatory discharge. In all the other cases R.BP.FP− will apply.[59] Of course this interpretation implies a decrease of the level of protection for workers unlawfully dismissed.

On the other side, it has been affirmed that, because of the fundamental importance of the constitutional principle of non-discrimination, anti-discrimination provisions have to be applied in an extensive manner. Therefore, each time the employer terminates the employment relationship without any legitimate reason the dismissal is to be considered discriminatory.[60] This approach would extend dramatically the cases the enforcement of R.BP.FP+;[61] in fact, this remedy would be enforced for all unjustified dismissals.

Can a comparative approach provide for some hints in order to solve up this controversy?

In Italy and the US anti-discrimination provisions acquire a different role on the basis of the historical evolution of the two different legal systems. In US (at least

[56]Meaning for "illicit motive" any motive in contrast with an imperative provision, and that has been the only determining reason for the discharge.

[57]Meaning that the employment relationship has been terminated without any justified reason, as defined by Article 3, or that the court has found that the employer has not demonstrated the existence of the reason he had articulated.

[58]And whose more specific explanation is not useful for the aim of this investigation.

[59]Bellocchi (2013), p. 830 ff; Carinci (2013), p. 461 ff.; Cester (2012), p. 816 ff.; Marazza (2012), p. 612 ff.; Maresca (2012), p. 415 ff.

[60]Carinci (2012).

[61]Cf. Barbieri (2013), p. 28.

federal) law, they perform a more systematic function, since they constitute the basic body of limits to the discretional power of employers and the main instrument, within employment relationship, to implement Congress' policies for the emancipation of disadvantaged social categories.

On the contrary, within Italian system, anti-discrimination law performs the only function of contrasting some specific employer's behaviors challenging the most fundamental constitutional principles, related to the personal dignity of workers. This mere observation should induce a stricter implementation of anti-discrimination provisions in Italian employment law.

Moreover, even within the US system, courts have delivered a very cautious interpretation of anti-discrimination statutory measures. Notwithstanding the more pronounced importance of anti-discrimination law within American system, case law has constantly pursued a fair balance with the protection of economic freedoms, so as not to impose excessive interferences with the prerogative of the enterprises.

Notwithstanding the more preeminent role performed by the non-discrimination principle in that legal system, US courts have always been very careful in applying anti-discrimination provisions outside the specific list of discriminatory reasons defined by statutory law.[62]

As has already been noted above (Sect. 1), the constitutional origin of the anti-discrimination principle in Italian law is the protection of human dignity, and not a general principle of equal treatment, deriving from Article 3 of the Constitution. This reasoning is much more feasible within US constitutional law, where, in the field of employment law, the Equal Protection Clause refers even more expressly to the relationships between States and the federal government—as employers—and public workers.

These observations demonstrate that the implementation of new anti-discrimination prohibitions have to be considered carefully also in Italian law, both with respect to the personal condition upon which the disparate treatment is based, and to its balance with the necessary protection of entrepreneurial prerogatives. Therefore, even if the statutory list of the personal conditions related to discrimination is not considered as closed, each time the list is extended by judicial interpretation, the interest concerned has to be strictly connected with the constitutional notion of "human dignity".

The necessity of a particular caution in the extension of the scope of discriminatory discharge provisions is also due to the peculiarities of the Italian system, emphasized by the comparative approach.

Because of Article 3 of statute no. 604/1966, the unjustified discharge has a peculiar regulation within Italian law, which is not related to anti-discrimination provisions. This is not the case in the US system, where anti-discrimination law constitutes the only significant limit to the decisions of the enterprise. It would be anomalous if, in Italian law, anti-discrimination provisions were to be interpreted in such an extensive way as to create an alternative set of limits for the unlawful

---

[62]See *Dawson v. Bumble & Bumble*, 398 F.3d 211 (2005).

dismissal, since the two different bodies of laws have to be coordinated but cannot overlap.[63] In any case, in the presence of a possible overlapping, it cannot be maintained that anti-discrimination principles prevail on the general rule of the necessary justification; for the very reason that the former creates a specific limit and have to be applied only in cases in which workers' human dignity is at stake, while the latter is general, so endowed with a broader applicability.[64]

In US law, the attempts of some courts[65] to allow an extensive interpretation of anti-discrimination provisions have been justified by the necessity of limiting the effects of the "at will employment" theory, in order to implement the project of social emancipation pursued by the Congress. This is not the case with the Italian system, where the aim of providing for a general judicial review on the powers of employers is achieved by autonomous provisions, not concerning discrimination. Besides, even within the American scenario, the Supreme Court has always "moderated" the most extensive interpretations delivered by the courts below.

The remarkable differences in the way anti-discrimination provisions work within the two legal systems is made clear by the distribution of the burden of proof. In US law, the related scheme is common to all the cases of discriminatory choices adopted by the enterprise, since a specific set of limits for the unjustified discharge does not exist. The trial for assessing discriminatory behavior is introduced by the *prima face* case. Only as a second measure, is the employer required to articulate a reason alternative to discrimination. It is by this procedural requirement that anti-discrimination provisions introduce the broadest room for a judicial review on the decisions of enterprise, even if the justified reason is not required to be "reasonable" or "justified", but only to be feasible.

Within Italian law, the separate nature of the provisions regarding the justification of the dismissal makes discrimination a very specific case within the wider category of the unlawful termination of the employment. The proof scheme of discrimination is separated from the one of the justified motive of the dismissal, since they imply the implementation of two separate bodies of provisions.

According to Article 5 of the statute no. 604/1966, the burden of proving that the termination of the employment relationship was justified is on the employer. The uncertainty of the authenticity of the justified motive implies the invalidity of the dismissal. In this case the employee will obtain only the R.BP.FP− regime.

If the employer does not convince the court that the reason for the discharge is feasible and just, the worker's claim will be successful. In this case, it would be completely unreasonable to apply the remedy for the case of discriminatory discharge, since the worker has articulated no proof of discrimination. On the contrary, it is clear that one thing is the proof of the justified motive, another is the one of the discrimination, because, in the case of dismissal, they imply the application

---

[63]Most recently, Bellocchi (2013).

[64]See Chieco (2013), p. 287 ff.

[65]Among the others, *Hicks v. St. Mary's Honor Ctr., Div. of Adult Insts. of Dep't of Corrections & Human Resources*, 970 F.2d 487 (1992).

of two different bodies of rules. In order to get the R.BP.FP+ the employee has to demonstrate the discriminatory nature of the discharge.[66]

For these reasons, Italian courts are unanimous in requiring the worker to give proof of the discriminatory intent; while, for the most part, Italian scholarship does not agree on this point.

US jurisprudence is far less unanimous in this regard. The disparate impact doctrine concentrates the trial only on the discriminatory effects of employer's decisions, but the Supreme Court seems not to have found a definite position.[67]

It is very significant that even the US Supreme Court, which usually adopts a strict interpretation of anti-discrimination provisions, is ambiguous on this point. But this approach is due to the different function of the anti-discrimination law within the American system, which naturally drives the interpretation toward a more extensive approach.

Within the Italian system, the trend should be the opposite. The unlawful discharge is regulated by the "justified reason" principle. The implementation of the provisions on discriminatory discharge is not necessary in order to review the decision of the enterprise. From this perspective, it is clear that the discriminatory intent has to be proved, since it is the specific element that distinguishes the discriminatory from the unjustified discharge and, thus, the criterion that leads to the implementation of one remedy instead of the other.

The idea that the non-discrimination principle induces focus on the discriminatory effects of the employer's decisions,[68] and not on the "intent", is not feasible for the discharge.[69] This perspective can be applied only to behavior that has no other specific limits and whose presumed discriminatory nature is the only possible reason for invalidity.

8 Conclusions

Through a comparative approach, it appears that anti-discrimination law has acquired different roles and functions according to the historical development of each legal system.

In the United States, the implementation of anti-discrimination provisions has been one of the main instruments to promote the emancipation of the most disadvantaged categories of workers. The dialectic relationship between the common law "employment at will doctrine" and statutory anti-discrimination provisions constitutes the core of American jurisprudence on the limits to the employers'

---

[66]It has recently be argued that unjustified and discriminatory discharge do not function according to a "binary logical reasoning". See Barbera (2013), p. 150.

[67]See Sect. 5.2 above.

[68]Lassandari (2010), p. 331 ff.

[69]Bellocchi (2013), p. 830 ff.

power of dismissal. Nonetheless, US courts have often narrowly interpreted anti-discrimination statutory laws, emphasizing the necessity of protecting employers' prerogatives.

Italian law pursues the aim of rebalancing the socio-economic and contractual disparities within the employment relationship by establishing a set of limits to the exercise of every legal power attributed to the employer grounded, in the final analysis, on the evaluation of its reasonableness. Within Italian labor law, employers can dismiss employees solely on the basis of justified reasons. The existence of a discriminatory motive affects only the sanctions provided against unfair dismissals. Thus, anti-discrimination principles play a residual role in this field.

In constitutional law (both Italian and American), the prohibition of discrimination among private subjects does not derive from a general principle of "equal treatment". Provisions on discrimination protect the dignity of human beings, involved within the economic activities of the enterprise.

This assumption has many remarkable consequences. One is that each time the list of the personal conditions that imply discrimination is extended by judicial interpretation, the interest concerned has to be strictly connected to the constitutional notion of "human dignity", and balanced with the economic freedoms of the employer.

On the basis of these systematic observations, the anti-discrimination principle plays a very limited role in the Italian regulation of dismissals. The demonstration of a discriminatory intent for the discharge of the employee does not affect the validity of the decision, but only the kind of remedy that the court will apply.

The approach of the courts gives fundamental hints in order to understand the implementation of non-discrimination principle in both legal systems and its effect. Notwithstanding the more preeminent role performed by the non-discrimination principle within US legal system, the courts of this Country have always been very cautious in applying anti-discrimination provisions outside the specific list of discriminatory reasons defined by statutory law. Also Italian courts have been quite strict on this regard and in requiring the evidence of a discriminatory intent. However, Italian scholarship has promoted a very extensive interpretation of anti-discrimination provisions.

The comparative approach provides for rigorous arguments against this idea, especially as regard the first paragraph of Article 18 of the statute no. 300/1970 and the theory holding that each unjustified dismissal has to be considered as discriminatory in order to extend the scope of the application of the more severe remedy enabled in that case.

References

Barbera, Marzia. 2013. Il licenziamento alla luce del diritto antidiscriminatorio. *Rivista giuridica del lavoro e della previdenza sociale* 64: 139-168.

Barbieri, Marco. 2013. La nuova disciplina del licenziamento individuale: profili sostanziali e questioni controverse. In *Il licenziamento individuale nell'interpretazione della legge Fornero*, eds. Marco Barbieri and Domenico Dalfino, 9-56. Bari: Cacucci Editore.

Bartole, Sergio. 1986. Principi generali del diritto. In *Enciclopedia del diritto*, XXXV: 494-533. Milano: Giuffrè.

Bellocchi, Paola. 2013. Il licenziamento discriminatorio. *Argomenti di diritto del lavoro* 18: 830-858.

Bobbio, Norberto. 1966. Principi generali di diritto. In *Novissimo digesto italiano*, 887-896. Torino: Utet.

Borelli, Silvia. 2007. *Principi di non discriminazione e frammentazione del lavoro.* Torino: Giappichelli.

Carinci, Franco. 2013. Ripensando il "nuovo" art. 18 dello Statuto dei lavoratori. *Argomenti di diritto del lavoro* 18: 461-505.

Carinci, Maria Teresa. 2012. Il rapporto di lavoro al tempo della crisi: modelli europei e "flexicurity" "all'italiana" a confronto - The Employment Relationship in a Time of Crisis: A Comparison between European Models and "Flexicurity" "Italian style". *Giornale di diritto del lavoro e delle relazioni industriali* 34: 527-572.

Cester, Carlo. 2012. La disciplina dei licenziamenti dopo la riforma Fornero: metamorfosi della tutela reale. *Il lavoro nella giurisprudenza* 20: 861-868.

Chieco, Pasquale. 2013. Il licenziamento nullo. In *Flessibilità e tutele nel lavoro. Commentario della legge 28 giugno 2012 n. 92*, ed. Pasquale Chieco, 277-304. Bari: Cacucci Editore.

Corazza, Luisa. 1998. Il licenziamento discriminatorio. In *Diritto del lavoro*, ed. Franco Carinci, 349-354. Torino: Utet.

Del Vecchio, Giorgio. 1921. Sui principi generali del diritto. *Archivo giuridico* LXXXV: 33-90.

Forbath, William E. 1991. *Law and the Shaping of the American Labor Movement*. Cambridge: Harvard University Press.

Gragnoli, Enrico. 2011. Considerazioni preliminari sui poteri del datore di lavoro e sul loro fondamento. *Rivista giuridica del lavoro e della previdenza sociale* 62: 511-541.

Katznelson, Ira. 2006. *When Affirmative Action Was White: An Untold History of Racial Inequality in Twentieth-Century America*. New York: W. W. Norton & Company.

Kittner, Michael, and Thomas C. Kohler. 2000. Conditioning Expectations: The Protection of the Employment Bond in German and American Law. *Comparative Labor Law and Policy Journal* 21: 263-330.

Lassandari, Andrea. 2010. *Le discriminazioni nel lavoro: nozioni, interessi, tutele*. Padova: Cedam.

Marazza, Marco. 2012. L'art. 18, nuovo testo, dello Statuto dei lavoratori. *Argomenti di diritto del lavoro* 17: 612-635.

Maresca, Arturo. 2012. Il nuovo regime sanzionatorio del licenziamento illegittimo: le modifiche dell'art. 18 Statuto dei lavoratori. *Rivista italiana di diritto del lavoro* 31: 415-459.

Massey, Douglas S. 2007. *Categorically Unequal: The American Stratification System*. New York: Russel Sage Foundation.

Pitts, Steven. 2008. Bad Jobs. The Overlooked Crisis in the Black Community. *New Labor Forum* 16: 39-47.

Quadagno, Jill. 1995. *The Color of Welfare: How Racism Undermined the War on Poverty*. New York: Oxford University Press.

Somek, Alexander. 2011. *Engineering Equality: An Essay on European anti-discrimination Law*. Oxford: Oxford University Press.

Principle of Non-discrimination on the Grounds of Sexual Orientation and Same-Sex Marriage. A Comparison Between United States and European Case Law

Veronica Valenti

Abstract By way of a comparison between European and United States case law regarding same-sex marriages, this chapter aims at stressing the important role of judicial activity in implementing the full meaning of equality in exercising the fundamental right to marry. From an analysis of different judgments concerning the same-sex marriage, it is possible to observe a gradual global prevailing of the "paradigm of heterosexual marriage", as a result of the non-discrimination principle on the grounds of sexual orientation, which is consolidated by the occidental juridical culture. The study of this case law also points out the relationship between social consent, judicial activity and legislative power. The European supranational courts as well as the US Supreme Court seem to check in a more stringent manner the discretion of the domestic/State legislators, in accordance with the growing social consent in favor of same-sex marriages. The "new approach" of the European supranational courts and the US Supreme Court has the merit to trigger a virtuous dialog among lower courts, State legislators and civil society in order to gradually give fullness to the meaning of the non-discrimination principle on the grounds of sexual orientation. Hence, it is possible to say that the current question is not if the same-sex marriage is constitutional but who decides about it. Judicial action, in the absence of legislative answers, risks guaranteeing only a fragmentary (and often contradictory) protection of fundamental rights. It should be desirable that the legislator will choose suggestions coming from the "living law" and that the "dichotomy" between the two powers will be reduced to unity, according to the rules of a democratic system, based on the separation of and loyal cooperation between the same powers.

V. Valenti (✉)
Researcher in Constitutional Law, University of Parma, Parma, Italy
e-mail: veronica.valenti@unipr.it

© Springer International Publishing Switzerland 2015
L. Pineschi (ed.), *General Principles of Law - The Role of the Judiciary*,
Ius Gentium: Comparative Perspectives on Law and Justice 46,
DOI 10.1007/978-3-319-19180-5_11

1 United States and European Case Law: The History of "Parallel Routes"

Despite many differences between the United States and the European legal system,[1] we can find some "assonances" when we compare the United States (federal and State level) case law and the European (supranational and national level) case law about the non-discrimination principle on the grounds of sexual orientation and, particularly, with regard to the *same-sex marriage*.

Initially both in the Unites States and in Europe, the principle of non-discrimination based on sexual orientation rooted thanks to the "judicial activism".

Indeed, without any specific normative framework to refer to, the European courts—in particular, the European Court of Human Rights (ECtHR)—and the US Supreme Court declared the principle of non-discrimination on the grounds of sexual orientation, emphasizing its potential application in various fields, including the familiar one. In addition, the judicial approach concerning non-discrimination principle on the grounds of sexual orientation created the pre-conditions for the implementation of a "gradual protection" of gay rights.

As noticed by some authors,[2] the "step by step approach" of judges has enabled conquests that perhaps would not have been possible to obtain through legislative action, if we consider historical times or if we consider the dominant public opinion toward sexual freedom.

This is demonstrated by the fact that, almost globally, the jurisprudential excurses concerning gay rights developed through four phases:

(1) important decisions of the US Supreme Court and the ECtHR have led to the decriminalization of sodomy in States where this was a crime and/or an aggravating circumstance of the crime. Three leading cases can be mentioned: the *Dudgeon* case (ECtHR, 1981)[3]; the *Romer*[4] and the *Lawrence*[5] cases (US Supreme Court, 1996, 2003);

(2) a second phase began in the late nineties, in particular in the European Union, thanks to important judgements of the European Court of Justice (ECJ) relating to the non-discrimination principle on the grounds of sexual orientation in

---

[1]Clear differences, if we only compare the US government system—US Federalism—with the EU governing system (a Union of States) and if we consider the role played by European courts—the European Court of Human Right and the European Court of Justice—at the European supranational and at national level.

[2]See Sperti (2013).

[3]*Dudgeon v. United Kingdom* (App. no 7525/76), ECtHR, judgment of 22 October 1981.

[4]*Romer v. Evans*, 517 US 620 (1996).

[5]*Lawrence v. Texas*, 539 US 558 (2003).

the workplace (*Grant* case,[6] 1998; *D. and Kingdom of Sweden* case,[7] 2001). This judicial trend was then followed by European Union institutions that:

- established the general principle of non-discrimination (Article 13 European Community Treaty—Amsterdam 1997, today Article 19 Treaty on the Functioning of the European Union—Lisbon 2007);
- adopted the Directive 2000/78/EC, establishing a general framework for equal treatment in employment and occupation or the Directive 2004/38 on the rights of European Union citizens and their family members to move and reside freely within the territory of Member States, with which the EU opened the notion of family member to the same-sex spouses and to same-sex partners;
- included the non-discrimination principle between the fundamental EU values (Article 2 Treaty on European Union—Lisbon, 2007);
- and, finally, mentioned the principle of non-discrimination on the grounds of sexual orientation in the EU Charter of Fundamental Rights (Article 21), a document legally binding all Member States;

(3) the Courts passed the purely "individualistic" approach of previous decisions in order to assert a "pluralistic view" of human dignity and the freedom to live in their own familiar dynamic, respecting sexual orientation, as a "new declination" of the self-determination of the individual within his/her private sphere.

From this point of view, it is clear the influence that the decisions of the courts have exercised on the legislative evolution, with regard to same-sex marriages and/or civil unions.[8]

As a result of this "global" judicial trend, many States and national legislators intervened to recognize same-sex couples in a more or less deep manner, also in accordance with national social consensus.

---

[6]Case C-249/96 *Grant,* [1998] ECR I-00621.

[7]Joined cases C-122/99 and C-125/99 *D. and Kingdom of Sweden* [2001] ECR I-04319.

[8]E.g. *Baehr v. Lewin,* 74 Haw. 852 P.2d 44 (1993); *Goodridge v. Department Public Health,* 440 Mass. 309 (2003); *Lewis v. Harris,* 188 N.J. 415, 908 A 2d 196 (2006). In Europe: the decisions of the German *Bundesverfassungsgericht,* 1 BvF 1/01, 1 BvF 2/01 of 2002 and 1/11 and 1 BvR 3247/09 of 2013; the judgments of the Portuguese *Tribunal Constitucional,* no. 359 of 2009 and no. 192 of 2010; the decisions of the Italian Constitutional Court, no. 138 of 2010 and no. 170 of 2014; the ruling of the French *Conseil Constitutionnel* no. 663 of 2013 and the decision of the Spanish *Tribunal Constitucional* no. 198 of 2012. We can also mention the case law of the ECtHR (in particular: *Schalk and Kopf v. Austria,* App. no. 30141/04, ECtHR, judgment of 24 June 2010, and *Vallianatos v. Greece,* App. nos. 29381/09 and 32684/09, ECtHR [GC], judgment of 7 November 2013) and of the US Supreme Court (*United States v. Windsor,* 133 S. Ct. 2675, 2013, and *Hollingsworth v. Perry,* 133 S. Ct. 2652, 2013).

Looking to these results, it is possible to draw a "mapping" of different laws that came into force in the United States but also in many European Countries. Indeed, we can distinguish:

(1) States that follow the "separate but equal" approach have introduced a civil institution that is, now, for the same-sex couples, like marriage is for heterosexual couples. This implies that the progressive and gradual extension of the rights linked to marital status, to the same-sex couples is, from time to time, "filtered" by the legislator and controlled by the Constitutional Court. The German *Lebenspartnerschaft* could be an example. As a result of important decisions of the *Bundesverfassunggericht*, it was possible to extend to homosexual partners the same social security rights (i.e. the same survivor's pension that is recognized for heterosexual married couples[9] or some parental rights, like the right to adopt a biological child or an adopted child of the respective partner)[10];

(2) States that have opened the institution of marriage to the same-sex couples, (e.g. Belgium, Finland, France, Portugal, Spain, The Netherlands and the United Kingdom. In the United States it is thought that as a result of the *Windsor* case, and also the recent decisions of the other federal judges, thirty-six States now recognize the same sex marriage);

(3) States, such as Italy, in which same-sex couples can not marry; or where there is not any specific institution (like the German one) for the same-sex couples or where any institution does not exist, like the French *pact civil de solidarieté (Pacs)*, that could protect homosexuals as heterosexual couples, that do not wish to marry. In Italy same-sex couples could only benefit from judicial protection, with regard to these specific situations.

With regard to this mapping, we can note that, at least, since 2010 to the present, a further "season" for the protection of same-sex couples has started.

In this new phase, "the challenge" (legal, political and ethical) is represented by the overcoming of the "paradigm of heterosexual marriage" and by the overcoming of the "separate but equal" approach, that has inspired many State laws. From this point of view, judicial protection for some specific situations (i.e. the Italian model) can not satisfy the need of equality, as imposed by the constitutional principle of non-discrimination on the grounds of the sexual orientation.

This consideration leads us to point out the *fourth assonance* between the US context and the European one. Indeed, at State level, some inhomogeneity in the protection of the homosexual family can record.

This situation depends on the discretion that both the US Supreme Court and the European courts recognize the State/national legislator.

---

[9]BVerfG, 1 BvR 1164/07 of 2009; BVerfG, 1 BvR 611/07 of 2010.

[10]BVerfG, BvR 1/11, BvR 3247/09 of 2013.

Neither the American Federation nor the European Union have the formal power, the "formal authority" to impose to all Member States a unique notion of marriage.[11]

This has been said, as in the US Supreme Court in *Windsor* case of 2013 in which the Supreme Court declared the unconstitutionality of section 3 of the Defense of Marriages Act, because it infringes the Fifth Amendment of the Federal Constitution.[12] As a result of that decision, the Supreme Court asserted (but also going further beyond this) that the imposition at the federal level of the "heterosexual paradigm" of marriage is an invasion of the legislative competence of the State.

Similarly, this "opening" to the discretion of the national legislators, emerges also in the ECtHR or ECJ case law. It could be mentioned, for example, the *Schalk and Kopf v. Austria* case, where, for the first time, the ECtHR has been required to assess whether the refusal by State authorities to the same-sex marriage could be a violation of the Convention for the Protection of Human Rights and Fundamental Freedoms (ECHR) (especially, Articles 12, 8 and 14).[13]

In its judgment, the European Court asserted that, because of the social evolution of the family concept, as recorded in some States, "it [would be] artificial to maintain the view that, in contrast to a heterosexual couples, a same-sex couple [could not] enjoy 'family life' for the purposes of art. 8".[14]

Similarly the US Supreme Court and the ECtHR abandoned "the paradigm of heterosexual marriages", in order to adopt "a more neutral" concept of marriage, with respect to the peoples' sexual orientation. However, at the same time, the same judges asserted that:

[A]s matters stand, the question of whether or not to allow same-sex marriages is left to regulation by the national law of the Contracting State.[15]

One could question as to why. The answer seems to be the same in the United States as in Europe:

Marriage has deep-rooted social and cultural connotations which may differ largely from one society to another. The Court reiterates that it must not hurry to substitute its own judgment in place of that of the national authorities, who are best placed to assess and respond to the needs of society.[16]

The same "opening" to the discretion of the national legislators also emerges from the ECJ case law (i.e. *D. and Kingdom of Sweden* case), as well as from later cases (i.e. *Maruko* case[17] and *Römer* case[18]).

---

[11]See Perelli (2013), p. 3.

[12]See, for an Italian issue about this decision, D'Aloia (2014a, b).

[13]*Schalk and Kopf v. Austria* cit.. See for the analysis of this decision Crivelli (2011).

[14]See *Schalk and Kopf v. Austria* cit., para. 94.

[15]Ibid., para. 61.

[16]Ibid., para. 62.

[17]Case C-267/06 *Maruko* [2008] ECR I-1757.

[18]Case C-147/08 *Römer* [2011] ECR I-3591.

I would like to anticipate that in the latest European case law, the European judges seem to pay more attention to the social trends. It appears as well that European judges are prepared to check in a more stringent manner the discretion of domestic legislators, in accordance to a growing social consent in favor of same-sex marriage.

From this point of view, it is important to stress the relationship between "the social consent" and the judicial activity: without a clear position of the legislator on same-sex marriage, the casuistic approach of the judges could test and, at the same time, influence the social consent on this matter. In addition, through particular argumentative techniques, the judges are able, crosswise, to create conditions to encourage a homogeneous legislative framework in favor of same-sex marriages.

The use of comparison by judges, for example, shows that the "others have done so" may represent an important resource in order to decide difficult cases, to overrule a decision, to better support similar arguments, to "soften" the reactions of the public opinion, with regard to "social consequences" of the decision.

Both in United States and European case law, there are frequent references to foreign leading cases relating to non-discrimination based on sexual orientation. There is also a circulation track of different models,[19] and, as many authors have noted, this has become a real "dialogue between Courts".[20]

This dialog describes, in a symptomatic manner, the stronger interaction between courts, as result of the globalization process, of the creation of "global standards" in the protection of fundamental rights and of the "new universalism of rights protection, built on a cooperative constitutionalism, projected beyond the boundaries of the State".[21]

Emblematic is a decision of the Spanish Constitutional Court (judgment no. 198 of 2012). In order to justify the evolutionary interpretation of marriage, as protected by Article 32 of the Spanish Constitution, the Court referred many times to international and foreign experiences, especially when the same remembered:

---

[19]See, for example, *Dudgeon v. United Kingdom* cit., a real "leading case" in the history of the gay rights, that continues to be mentioned in many decisions of the national Constitutional Courts of different Countries. See the decision of the Italian Constitutional Court no. 138 of 2010 but also the *Lawrence* case, ruled by the US Supreme Court, which is the first case in which the Supreme Court referred to a foreign European case (*Lawrence v. Texas* cit.).

[20]On this issue see Sperti (2006, 2013); De Vergottini (2010); Ruggeri (2013, 2014b). About the notion of "community of judges", are also interesting the considerations outlined in the Seminar "Implementation of the judgments of the European Court of Human Rights: a shared judicial responsibility?" (Strasbourg, 31 January 2014), available at http://www.echr.coe.int/Documents/Dialogue_2014_ENG.pdf.

[21]For the problematic relationship between national judges, Constitutional Courts, supranational and international courts see D'Aloia (2014a). See also Ruggeri (2013), Tega (2012).

> The equality between same sex marriages and opposite sex marriages has been consolidated by the occidental juridical culture.[22]

It is interesting to point out the definition of "occidental juridical culture": for the Spanish Court, it includes, not only the doctrine, international law, the judgments of the international and European courts but also comparative law and the foreign experiences that have the same social and cultural conditions.[23] Consequently, as correctly noted by some Italian authors,[24] we can say that the referral to foreign experiences is used, most of the time, to demonstrate the existence of some common (both European and American) values and to promote the evolutionary interpretation of marriage.

In principle, it could be said that, if the concept of "occidental juridical culture" is linked to the idea of the legal system as social phenomenon bound to reality, then the judge is the *trait d'union* between law and society and, in a dynamic way, an important entrance door for the social change.

2 The Judicial "Development" of the Principle of Non-discrimination of Same-Sex Couples and the Growing Conditioning by Supranational Judges on the Discretion of State/National Legislators

2.1 European Supranational Level: The ECHR System

As previously mentioned, the principle of non-discrimination on the grounds of sexual orientation has emerged, both in the American case law and in the European case law, primarily on the basis of an evolutionary interpretation of the

---

[22]*Tribunal Constitutional de España*, decision no. 198/2012, 6 November 2012, available at http://www.tribunalconstitucional.es/es/jurisprudencia/Paginas/Sentencia.aspx?cod=20674. The Court wrote: "*Si se acude al Derecho comparado, en la balanza de la integración del matrimonio entre personas del mismo sexo en la imagen actual del matrimonio pesa el hecho de que la equiparación del matrimonio entre personas de distinto sexo y entre personas del mismo sexo se ha consolidado, en los últimos años, en el seno de varios ordenamientos jurídicos integrados en la cultura jurídica occidental*".

[23]In the same decision, the Court wrote: "*Pues bien, la cultura jurídica no se construye sólo desde la interpretación literal, sistemática u originalista de los textos jurídicos, sino que también contribuyen a su configuración la observación de la realidad social jurídicamente relevante, sin que esto signifique otorgar fuerza normativa directa a lo fáctico, las opiniones de la doctrina jurídica y de los órganos consultivos previstos en el propio ordenamiento, el Derecho comparado que se da en un entorno socio-cultural próximo y, en materia de la construcción de la cultura jurídica de los derechos, la actividad internacional de los Estados manifestada en los tratados internacionales, en la jurisprudencia de los órganos internacionales que los interpretan, y en las opiniones y dictámenes elaboradas por los órganos competentes del sistema de Naciones Unidas, así como por otros organismos internacionales de reconocida posición*". See for a comment Ibrido (2012, 2013).

[24]See Sperti (2013).

concept of privacy and self-determination of individuals (as guaranteed by Article 8 of the ECHR and by the Fourteenth Amendment of the US Constitution).

Starting at the end of the nineties, the ECtHR has inaugurated a combined interpretation of Articles 8 and 14 (prohibition of discrimination on many grounds—but not expressly on the grounds of sexual orientation—in the exercise of freedoms protected by the European Convention), never more be abandoned.[25]

To say that there has been a discrimination in the exercise of rights protected by the ECHR on the grounds of sexual orientation implies to subject, under *strict scrutiny*, the arguments used by the State to support the legitimacy of the national measures that restricted the same rights.

This is clear in *Karner v. Austria*,[26] about the succession of the surviving same-sex partner in a tenancy. In this case, the ECtHR stated that the protection of the "traditional family" is an important and legitimate reason to justify different treatment based on sexual orientation. However, at the same time, the same Court stated that the Austrian government did not adequately prove the national *ingérence* (the denial of the right of the surviving same-sex partner) with respect to the purpose (the protection of a traditional family).

For many years, the European Court has abandoned the "individualistic" approach in interpreting Articles 8 and 14 and begun to consider homosexual unions as "family life". Doing so, the Court has begun to use the ECHR as a "living instrument"; paying more attention to the evolution of the contemporary society; and to the raising an European consensus in favor of a more broad concept of family life.

We can see this approach, in particular in the *Schalk and Kopf* case,[27] in which the European Court greatly enriched the arguments presented to that date. This is a very important decision: first, the parameter used is not only the result of a combined reading of Articles 8 and 14 or because, as said, the ECtHR arrived to a notion of marriage (Article 12), which opens to the discretion of legislator; second, at the supranational level, "marriage" no longer appears as a traditional notion of marriage.

As we have already seen, the European Court links the same-sex relationship to the notion of private-family life (Article 8) and, taking into account the social evolution of the concept of family registered in many States, it states that:

> It [would be] artificial to maintain the view that, in contrast to a different-sex couples, a same-sex couples [could not] enjoy the "family life" for the purposes of art. 8.[28]

Recently, the ECtHR has returned to rule on the issue of the legal recognition of same-sex couples, in the case *Vallianatos v. Greece*.[29] The Court ruled on an

---

[25]In particular, see *Salgueiro da Silva Mouta v. Portugal* (App. no. 33290/96), ECtHR, judgment of 21 December 1999.

[26]*Karner v. Austria* (App. no. 40016/98), ECtHR, judgment of 24 July 2003.

[27]*Schalk and Kopf v. Austria* cit..

[28]See cit., footnote 12.

[29]*Vallianatos v. Greece* cit.. See for a comment Rudan (2014), p. 1; Valenti (2013).

application submitted by a number of Greek same-sex couples, alleging infringement of Articles 8 and 14, because they were excluded—and therefore discriminated against compared to the heterosexual couples—by the Greek law on civil unions, entered into force in 2008.

On its merits, the decision of the ECtHR does not appear innovative. The Court confirms the well-established case law based on the evolutionary interpretation of Article 8 of the European Convention, as asserted in the *Schalk and Kopf* case. Other aspects, however, can lead us to reflect how interesting are the procedural aspects of this decision. In particular, the attention is to be focused on:

(a) the fact that the couples of Greek citizens decided to refer the matter directly to the ECtHR, asserting that Greek law does not offer an effective domestic remedy;

(b) the assignation of the case directly to the Grand Chamber of the European Court.

With regard to the first aspect, considering the "substantial" meaning that has been the rule of the prior exhaustion of domestic remedies in the European case law, the ECtHR asserts that, in the Greek system, there are no effective remedies available to assert the right protected by Articles 8 and 14 of the European Convention. According to the Court, also Article 105 of the Introductory Law to the Civil Code (that states that "the State shall be under a duty to make good any damage caused by the unlawful acts or omissions of its organs in the exercise of public authority") cannot be considered as an effective remedy. Likewise, in the opinion of the ECtHR, the Greek constitutional control is not sufficient, because it is not a concrete control.

The European Court does not consider positively the fact that, in the Greek system, as in the Italian one, the ECHR is a source of law superior to the ordinary legislation (Article 28 of the Greek Constitution), as it results from some decisions of the national supreme courts which declared unconstitutional several domestic laws that infringed the European Convention (and so Article 28 of the Constitution that expressly states that international law shall prevail over any contrary provision of the law).

These statements appear slightly "forced"; it seems that, in this case, there has been almost an "invasion of the field", an overlap of the ECtHR in respect to national judges and, in particular, with respect to constitutional judges.[30]

With regard to the second aspect—the referral of the case directly to the Grand Chamber—it is known that, according to Article 30 of the European Convention and to Article 72 of its Rules of Procedure, a Chamber may divest its own jurisdiction in favor of the Grand Chamber, where the case raises deep problems of interpretation of the ECHR or is at odds with a previous judgment of the European Court.

The present case, however, does not seem to present both of the hypothesis mentioned above; the decision seems rather to confirm, on its merits, the well-established case law by the ECtHR. Therefore, it appears that, with the referral to

---

[30]On the relationships between different courts, see Gallo (2012), Ruggeri (2013).

the Grand Chamber, the European Court wanted to confer "authoritativeness" to this new way of interpreting the rule of prior exhaustion of domestic remedies.

Within the European system of "multilevel protection of rights", it conveys that the ECtHR shows the tendency to "centralize", as much as possible, the judgment of "conventionality" of national laws, exercising therefore, in relation to the recognition of same-sex couples, a tighter control on the discretion of the domestic legislator.

There is also another aspect of this judgment that seems very significant. I refer to the attitude of the judges of Strasbourg in assessing the European growing social consent concerning the recognition of same-sex couples: they materially count the European Countries that introduced a legal protection to same-sex couples.[31]

According to the European Court, even if it cannot be said that there is homogeneity among European Countries, this growing trend has an impact on the domestic legislation, because it imposes on the State "in a isolated position" the obligation to justify, in a more stringent manner, the choice to not recognize same-sex couples. This means that the ECtHR has to use *strict scrutiny* on the arguments of the State; therefore, in the absence of "convincing and weighty" arguments, the Court can declare the infringement of the Convention.[32]

In this judgment, it would seem there is a will to "close the circle" on Article 8 of the ECHR, in order to repair almost the "minimum level" of legal protection for same-sex couples, that, on the basis of a growing European social consensus, could influence the discretion of national legislators. From this point of view, it seems clear, at least, that a national legislator, which intends to introduce a law in order to protect unmarried couples, cannot exclude, from such protection, same-sex couples.

In my opinion, what the ECtHR has decided in the *Vallianatos* case, does not seem to be entirely contradicted by what the same Court decided in the most recent *Hämäläinen* case, in July 2014.[33]

There are different factual requirements between the two cases. In the *Hämäläinen* case, the European Court assessed the compliance with Article 8 (autonomously and also in conjunction with Article 14) and with Article 12 of the

---

[31]We can read in that decision: "the trend emerging in the legal systems of the Council of Europe member States is clear: of the nineteen States which authorize some form of registered partnership other than marriage, Lithuania and Greece are the only ones to reserve it exclusively to different-sex couples ... In other words, with two exceptions, Council of Europe member States, when they opt to enact legislation introducing a new system of registered partnership as an alternative to marriage for unmarried couples, include same-sex couples in its scope. Moreover, this trend is reflected in the relevant Council of Europe materials ..." (para. 91).

[32]The judges of Strasbourg write: "The fact that, at the end of a gradual evolution, a country finds itself in an isolated position as regards one aspect of its legislation does not necessarily imply that aspect conflicts with the Convention ... Nevertheless, in view of the foregoing, the Court considers that the government have not offered convincing and weighty reasons capable of justifying the exclusion of same-sex couples from the scope of Law no. 3719/2008" (para. 92).

[33]*Hämäläinen v. Finland* (App. no. 37359/09), ECtHR [GC], judgment of 16 July 2014.

ECHR, of the Finnish legislation concerning sex change of one of the spouses and the protection of the previous family relationship.

In the absence of a law on same-sex marriages in Finland, the sex change of a spouse implied also the change of the same qualification of the family relationship. In order to give recognition to the new sexual identity of the spouse, the Finnish legislator established the automatic conversion of the previous marriage in a registered civil union (i.e. an institution reserved only to same-sex couples that guaranteed, more or less, the same rights that the marriage offered to the heterosexual couples).

The applicants claimed the possibility to maintain, as same-sex couples, the effects of the marriages previously contracted.

Compared to the *Vallianatos* case, in the *Hämäläinen* case, the judgment does not concern the illegal exclusion of same-sex couples from the legal protection offered by some institutes like the civil union, but the legal recognition of the right of the same-sex couples to marry. Unlike the position of the applicants in the *Vallianatos* case, in this case, the applicants, according to the Finnish legislation at the time, could still have a guarantee of their rights, at least through the registered civil unions.[34]

In my opinion, also for this reason, in the *Hämäläinen* case, the ECtHR has excluded the violation by the Finnish legislator of the provisions of the European Convention mentioned above, stating that "the current Finnish system as a whole has not been shown to be disproportionate in its effects on the applicant"[35] and that there is "a fair balance between the competing interests in the present case"[36] (i.e. between the individual's right to obtain a new sexual identity and the discretion of the legislator to define who can get married).

However, this recent judgment is significant, because once again, the ECtHR recognizes a broad discretion to the domestic legislator, relating to the same-sex marriages.[37] This is, as stated by the Court, because there is not a European social consensus on this issue.

From this point of view, the judgment raises some doubts with regard to the "European social consensus approach".

In the *Vallianatos* case, the European social consensus theory seems to play an "additional" role, compared to the arguments used by the ECtHR in order to justify the violation by the Greek legislator of Article 8 in conjunction with Article 14

---

[34]The Court writes: "Same-sex marriages are not, for the time being, permitted in Finland although that possibility is currently being examined by Parliament. On the other hand, the rights of same-sex couples are currently protected by the possibility of contracting a registered partnership" (para. 69).

[35]*Hämäläinen v. Finland* cit., para. 88.

[36]Ibid.

[37]Ibid., para. 71: "The Court reiterates its case law according to which Article 8 of the Convention cannot be interpreted as imposing an obligation on Contracting States to grant same-sex couples access to marriages".

of the European Convention (and then, in order to state the discrimination that the same-sex couples suffered on the grounds of their sexual orientation).

Furthermore, this approach doesn't exempt the European Court from examining, through *strict scrutiny*, the Greek government's arguments.

In the *Vallianatos* case, then, the social consensus approach would seem to be symptomatic of the evolutionary interpretation of the ECHR. Adversely, in the *Hämäläinen* case, the lack of the European social consensus concerning same-sex marriages is a central argument for the ECtHR, in order to exclude the violation of the European Convention. The consensus approach, here, is used as "an autonomous hermeneutic criterion",[38] that is difficult to define, and that it seems to be applied, by the European Court, without limits.[39]

Referring to this issue, it is also to be mentioned that the judgment of the ECtHR has been overcome by the Finnish parliament that, on 28 November 2014, passed a civil initiative to introduce same-sex marriage.

Nevertheless, if we consider the overall activity of the ECtHR regarding the rights of the same-sex couples, we have to give credit to some recent studies that point out how the European Court has become increasingly progressive on this issue and its rulings have increased the likelihood of national policy reforms; even the likelihood of policy reforms of Countries whose laws and policies the Court have not explicitly been found to violate the ECHR.[40]

2.2 European Supranational Level: The EU Case Law

We can reach a similar conclusion, if we analyze the latest decisions of the ECJ, after the entry into force of Directive 78/2000—which introduced the prohibition of direct and indirect discrimination in the workplace—as well as after the entry into force of the Treaty of Lisbon and also of the Charter of Nice/Strasbourg that

---

[38]See Pustorino (2014).

[39]As noticed by judges Sajó, Keller e Lemmens in their dissenting opinion: "In this context, we note that proof of the existence of a consensus, when adduced, must not depend on the existence of a common approach in a super-majority of States: the Court has some discretion regarding its acknowledgment of trends (compare *Vallianatos and Others v. Greece* [GC], nos. 29381/09 and 32684/09, para. 91, ECHR 2013)".

[40]See Helfer and Voeten (2014), p. 105: "In the context of ECtHR judgments on LGBT rights, we find evidence that even where international judges take social trends into consideration, they nonetheless retain considerable discretion and can encourage policy change by noncompliant Countries under the right domestic political and institutional conditions. In particular, ECtHR judgments increase the likelihood that all European nations—even Countries whose laws and policies the court has not explicitly found to violate the European Convention—will adopt pro-LGBT reforms. The effect is strongest in Countries where public support for homosexuals is lowest".

now has binding character. I refer specifically to three cases: *Maruko*,[41] *Römer*[42] and *Hay*.[43]

In the *Maruko* and *Römer* cases, the judges of Luxembourg asserted that the German legislator had infringed the Directive 78/2000, because German law denied the right to a survivor's pension to the surviving same-sex partner (a right guaranteed, however, to heterosexual married couples). For that reason, the German legislator had discriminated on the grounds of sexual orientation for same-sex couples.

In the *Hay* case, the judges of Luxembourg stated that the French legislator had discriminated against same-sex couples (that have contracted a *Pacs*), denying them some benefits guaranteed to same-sex married couples, like special leave and award salary in the case of marriage (benefits that, only after 2008, were extended also to the same-sex couples that contracted a *Pacs*).

In all three cases, in order to verify the existence of any discrimination, the ECJ made a comparison between the situations that, at national level, are comparable.

In the *Hay* case, in order to assess the discriminatory nature of the national legislation (according to Article 2 of Directive 7/2000), the judges of Luxembourg pointed out that it "is required not that the situations be identical, but only that they be comparable" and that "the assessment of that comparability must be carried out not in a global and abstract manner, but in a specific and concrete manner in the light of the benefit concerned"[44] and, regardless of the fact that "national law generally and comprehensively treats registered life partnership as legally equivalent to marriage".[45]

However, from the comparison of the three decisions, the judgment in the *Hay* case appears to be more inclusive and incisive.

Indeed, in the *Maruko* and *Römer* cases, a comparison was made between opposite-sex married couples and same-sex couples, that have contracted a *Lebenspartnerschaft* (the German institution that is, for the same-sex couples, what marriage is for the opposite-sex couples).

In the *Hay* case, the parameter for comparison is broader, because a comparison is made between married couples and homosexual couples joined in a *Pacs*. On the one hand, this offers legal protection to the *more uxorio* cohabiting couples, homosexual or heterosexual couples and it doesn't produce the same effects of marriages; on the other hand, it is no longer the only "comparable situation" for heterosexual marriages, because the French legislator has "opened" the marriage also to the same-sex couples. As a consequence, the "comparable situation" to the

---

[41]*Maruko* cit..

[42]*Römer* cit..

[43]Case C-267/12 *Frédéric Hay* [2013] nyr.

[44]Ibid., para. 33.

[45]Ibid., para. 34.

status of worker/spouse ends up covering situations—both legal and factual—that do not depend on peoples' marital status.

Doing so, the judges of Luxembourg find a discrimination pursuant to Article 2 (2)(a) of Directive 78/2000. More specifically, they asserted that there is a direct discrimination based on sexual orientation, if:

> [T]he national rules of the Member State concerned do not allow persons of the same sex to marry, in so far as, in the light of the objective of and the conditions relating to the grant of those benefits, that employee is in a comparable situation to an employee who marries.[46]

In light of the situation, the potential and the "revolutionary" charge of this decision truly emerges, considering the effects of the decision in Countries where the legislator guarantees the protection of same-sex couples through legal arrangements other than marriage or when, a fortiori, same-sex couples do not have any legal protection, as in the Italian legal system.

Precisely, with regard to these legal systems, the decision of the judges of Luxembourg sounds like a warning: expanding so the concept of "comparable situation", as has been said, the ECJ seems to "sanction" and remedy, time to time, the omissions of national legislators who discriminate a single worker on the grounds of sexual orientation.[47] This is the core of the decision, the "most delicate" and strongest point.

Accordingly, the judges of Luxembourg indirectly extended the judgment of reasonableness on areas "reserved" to the discretion of the domestic legislator and to the national courts.

Under this aspect, two things can be said.

First, the *Whereas* no. 22 of Directive 78/2000 provides that the Directive is "without prejudice to national laws on marital status and the benefits dependent thereon". The ECJ appears not to dwell on the actual legal implications of this *Whereas*. If this is so, the judges of Luxembourg actually seem to want to embark on a path of "indirect communitarization of the national family laws".[48]

Focusing on mutual and natural interconnections between labor policies and family policies and "expanding" the meaning of the principle of non-discrimination based on sexual orientation of individual workers, the judges of Luxembourg recognize that this principle is a general principle of the EU legal system and, at the same time, they recognize "a kind of *ultra* efficacy", "compared to other values".[49]

If someone talks about a (even if only indirectly) "communitarization" of the national family law may seem like a gamble, it is not unreasonable to argue that, with that decision, the ECJ aims to restrict the discretion of national legislators on

---

[46]Ibid., para. 47.

[47]Cf. Valenti (2014).

[48]Cf. De Pasquale et al. (2012).

[49]See Winkler (2011), p. 10. See also Rijpma and Koffeman (2014), Orzan (2014).

the family policies in order to ensure an effective implementation of the principle of non-discrimination based on sexual orientation.

In other words, the discretion of Member States relating to the marital status can no longer be an alibi to continue to discriminate against homosexual workers, excluding them from individual economic or security-welfare performances, if these workers live a (legal or de facto) familiar relationship, that could be comparable to that of heterosexual married workers. This leads, inevitably, to EU judges exerting an "external" and "indirect" control on how that discretion is exercised by national legislators.

Secondly, the *Hay* case not only marks a turning point in the European path in (indirectly) "communitarization" of national family law, but also emphasizes the important role, in this context, that EU judges have assumed.

According to this point of view, it can certainly be argued that, in the *Hay* case, the judges of Luxembourg have been much more incisive than in the past; the decisional space that has previously been left to the "dialog" with the national courts has been regained.

Indeed the *Whereas* no. 15 of Directive 78/2000 provides that:

> The appreciation of the facts from which it may be inferred that there has been direct or indirect discrimination is a matter for national judicial or other competent bodies, in accordance with rules of national law or practice.

In compliance with this Directive, in the *Maruko* and *Römer* cases, the EU judges stressed that "the assessment of comparability is within the jurisdiction of the national Courts".[50] It is not so in the *Hay* case, where, in any part of the decision, the ECJ seems to replace the national courts, causing itself the same "assessment of comparability" that the national court should have done.

As the ECtHR seems to have done in enforcing the ECHR, at the same manner, the ECJ seems to operate a tighter control on the discretion of the Member States in order to ensure, in a more rigorous way, the uniform application and interpretation of EU law, especially in contexts where there is not a strong social consent about the level of protection of same-sex couples.

2.3 United States: The Judicial Activism After the Windsor Case. Waiting for Another Decision by the US Supreme Court

In my opinion, the American context is not "so far" from the European one.

As known, referring to the two decisions of 2013 (*United States v. Windsor* and *Hollingsworth v. Perry*),[51] the US Supreme Court has actually written an important page in the battle for same-sex couples rights.

---

[50]*Maruko* cit., paras. 67–69; *Römer* cit., para. 4.

[51]US Supreme Court, *United States v. Windsor* cit., and *Hollingsworth v. Perry* cit..

In particular, in the *Windsor* case[52] the US Supreme Court declared the unconstitutionality of section 3 of the Defense of Marriages Act (DOMA), according to which, at the federal level, the accepted concept of marriage was the opposite-sex marriage. This implied that Congress could adopt acts to recognize certain benefits for heterosexual spouses, excluding same-sex couples.

For the Supreme Court, the imposition, at the federal level, of such traditional concept of marriage is an arbitrary invasion in the legislative competence of each State.

In addition, the Supreme Court evaluates the constitutionality of section 3 of DOMA in light of the due process clause, established by the Fifth Amendment. After having asserted that section 3 of DOMA violated the federal balance, the US Supreme Court emphasizes the social, "pluralistic" dimension of the concept of dignity.

The Supreme Court qualified the choice of a State to guarantee to a group of citizens the right to marry, as an important moment "to give further protection and dignity to that bond".[53] In particular:

This status is a far-reaching legal acknowledgment of the intimate relationship between two people, a relationship deemed by the State worthy of dignity in the community equal with all other marriages. It reflects both the community's considered perspective on the historical roots of the institution of marriage and its evolving understanding of the meaning of equality.[54]

For that reason, the Supreme Court assessed whether section 3 of DOMA had or had not a legitimate aim, starting from the parliamentary works of DOMA, that show a "discriminatory animus" as based on "both moral disapproval of homosexuality and a moral conviction that heterosexuality better comports with traditional (especially Judeo-Christian) morality".[55]

As a consequence, the US Supreme judges recognized that "DOMA writes inequality into the entire United States Code".[56]

From these words it is clear that, as some authors have noted,[57] this case is only an apparent "case" about the distribution of legislative powers.

The argument appears to have been used by the Supreme Court to maintain a self-restraint that, as well as in Europe, has triggered a virtuous mechanism among lower courts, State legislators and civil society, with different effects.

First, this self-restraint creates, gradually, the conditions to justify the social evolution of certain legal institutions and it favors the "climate" for its acceptance by local communities. Second, the dialog with the legislators/lower courts

---

[52]For some Italian comments on this decision see: D'Aloia (2014a, b), Massa Pinto (2013), Schillaci (2013).

[53]US Supreme Court, *United States v. Windsor* cit., opinion of the Court, III.

[54]Ibid.

[55]Ibid.

[56]Ibid.

[57]Sperti (2013).

becomes spontaneously tighter; this fosters the consolidation of a more homogeneous social consent, and gradually gives fullness to the meaning of non-discrimination principle on the grounds of sexual orientation.

Not without a certain circularity, therefore, on the grounds of a growing social consent in favor of the same-sex marriage, we can note that the judges could endorse the same-sex marriage, as "inevitable conclusion" of the non-discrimination principle. On the grounds of the same consent, the control on the legislator in "an isolated position" will become inevitably stricter (as *Vallianatos* case shows).

If we read the American ruling after the *Windsor* case concerning same-sex marriages, we gain the perception of what has been said above, i.e. the growing tendency of federal judges to maintain a tighter control on the discretion of the individual States.

Example of what said above is the decision of the Supreme Court of New Mexico, adopted on 19 December 2013,[58] which moves away from a context that is very similar to the Italian one. Same-sex marriage was not expressly banned in New Mexico, but the ban could be deduced from various legal provisions that expressly refer to the sex diversity of the spouses.

The Court declared that the traditional concept of marriage "violates the Equal Protection Clause under Article II, section 18 of the New Mexico Constitution"[59] because it discriminates against same-sex couples on the basis of either their sex or their sexual orientation.

In order to prove this, the Supreme Court made a comparison between homosexual couples and heterosexual couples. Initially, the Court examines whether the argument of the "potential procreative capacity"—used also by other national Constitutional Courts (such as the Italian one)—may justify a different treatment between same-sex and heterosexual couples. Focusing on the validity of marriages contracted with the desire not to have children, the Court states that "procreation is not the overriding purpose of the New Mexico marriage laws" because:

> The purpose of the New Mexico marriage laws is to bring stability and order to the legal relationships of committed couples by defining their rights and responsibilities as to one another, their property, and their children, if they choose to have children.[60]

The Court adds that with respect to children, the general marriage laws provide that "[a] child born to parents who are not married to each other has the same rights pursuant to the law as a child born to parents who are married to each other", and so the same say "same-gender and opposite-gender couples who want to marry are similarly situated".[61]

---

[58]*Griego v. Oliver,* 316 P.3d 865 (2013).

[59]Ibid.

[60]Ibid., para. 33.

[61]Ibid.

Once the conditions for comparability are fixed, the New Mexico Supreme Court examines the constitutional validity of the State law, through the intermediate scrutiny:

[B]ecause the LGBT community is a discrete group that has been subjected to a history of purposeful discrimination, and it has not had sufficient political strength to protect itself from such discrimination.[62]

Through such scrutiny, the Court considers that the arguments used to deny marriage to the same-sex couples (for example, the public interest to promote a responsible procreation, responsible education of children, not to have deinstitutionalization of the marriage, as well as the moral disapprobation of homosexual activity and the "traditions") are not able to justify the prohibition and discrimination currently existing. Hence it declares the unconstitutionality of the same-sex marriage State ban.

The decision of the Supreme Court of New Mexico is only an example. Indeed, a growing acceptance to same-sex marriage by other States is quickly emerging.

Currently, there are thirty-six States in which same-sex marriages is legal. In twenty-five States,[63] this was possible thanks to the activism of the judges (State courts, district courts and courts of appeal), that overturned the same-sex marriage bans, declaring them unconstitutional.[64] Some States (Indiana, Oklahoma, Virginia, Utah, and Wisconsin) submitted petitions for the *writ of certiorari* to the US Supreme Court in order to obtain renewal of the decisions of the same Court of Appeals that struck down the same-sex marriage ban.

With the order issued on 6 October 2014, the US Supreme Court denied the petitions for the *writ of certiorari*, perhaps because of the almost unanimous view expressed by the different courts about the constitutionality of same-sex marriages. Hence the Circuit Court of Appeals' ruling went into effect in these five States.

---

[62]Ibid., para. 53.

[63]Alaska, Arizona, California, Colorado, Connecticut, Florida, Idaho, Indiana, Iowa, Kansas, Massachusetts, Montana, Nevada, New Jersey, New Mexico, North Carolina, Oklahoma, Oregon, Pennsylvania, South Carolina, Utah, Virginia, West Virginia, Wisconsin, Wyoming. See: National Center for Lesbian Rights. 2015. *Marriages, Domestic Partnerships and Civil Unions: Same-sex Couples within the United States*, available at http://www.nclrights.org. See also for an Italian comment Sperti (2014).

[64]See for example: *Latta v. Otter*, no. CV-00482-CW (2014); *Kitchen v. Herbert*, 755 F.3d 1193 (2014); *Baskin v. Bogan*, 766 F.3d 648 (2014); *Wolf v. Walker*, 986 F. Supp.2d 982 (2014); *Whitewood v. Wolf*, 992 F. Supp.2d 410 (2014); *Geiger v. Kitzhaber*, 994 F. Supp.2d 1128 (2014); *Wright v. Arkansas*, no. CV-14-414 (2014); *Garden State Equality* et al. *v. Dow*, 82 A.3d 336 (2013). See also the pending cases: US Court of Appeals for the Sixth Circuit, *DeBoer v. Snyder*, *Bourke v. Beshear*, *Tanco v. Haslam*, *Obergefell v. Hodges*; and US Court of Appeals for the Fifth Circuit, *De Leon v. Perry*.

Likewise, other six States (Colorado, Kansas, North Carolina, South Carolina, Virginia and Wyoming), that are under the same Circuit jurisdiction, were affected by the same ruling.

The order issued last October has not been the "final word" of the Supreme Court. For the first time, after the *Windsor* case and in contrast with the recent rulings of other courts and in contrast with this recent order of the US Supreme Court, the Court of Appeals for the sixth Circuit has overturned lower-court rulings in Michigan, Ohio, Tennessee and Kentucky, upholding the State bans.[65]

In order to justify the argument that the choice of introducing same-sex marriages should be only as result of democratic decision-making and therefore it should be left to the law-maker (not to the judges), the Court of Cincinnati recalled European experiences and in particular the decision of the ECtHR in the *Schallk and Kopf* case and in the *Hämäläinen* case.

As recollected by the judges, both European decisions recognize the existence of the margin of appreciation for States in the matter of marriages:

> Yet foreign practice only reinforces the impropriety of tinkering with the democratic process in this setting ... Even more telling, the European Court of Human Rights ruled only a few years ago that European human rights laws do not guarantee a right to same sex marriage. *Schalk and Kopf v. Austria*, 2010. "The area in question", it explained in words that work just as well on this side of the Atlantic remains "one of evolving rights with no established consensus", which means that States must enjoy [discretion] in the timing of the introduction of legislative changes. It reiterated this conclusion as recently as this July, declaring that "the margin of appreciation to be afforded" to States must still be a wide one. *Hämäläinen v. Finland*.[66]

On 18 November 2014, the plaintiffs filed a petition for a *writ of certiorari* with the Supreme Court. At the moment of writing, the case is pending before the Supreme Court; however, it is reasonable to think that it could "force" the US Supreme Court to intervene again, in order to definitively settle the "debate" about same-sex marriages.

What it is happening in the United States and in Europe confirms that:

> The recognition of rights is not something that develops at an even pace. It is rather a history of struggles in which Courts act as watchdogs of the legislative branch and sometimes succeed in developing a "civilization" of fundamental rights ... Thus it is not surprising that same sex marriages are legalized following fluctuating vicissitudes.[67]

In this perspective, the question "who should decide concerning same sex marriages?" seems incorrect, as incorrect is to believe that only the law-maker could decide about this issue, because only the law is the result of a democratic decision-making.

---

[65]*DeBoer v. Snyder, Bourke v. Beshear, Tanco v. Haslam, Obergefell v. Hodges* cit..

[66]Ibid., para. II.G.

[67]See Romeo (2014).

If we agree, we deny the important democratic role of the judiciary power, which is to ensure that the constitutional rights, liberties, and duties do not become hostage by popular whims and by majority decisions.[68]

3 The Same-Sex Couples at a National Level: The Italian Case

3.1 The Decisions of the Italian Constitutional Court (no. 138 of 2010, no. 170 of 2014) and the … "Italian Avoiding Ability" Concerning Same-Sex Marriages

As stated above, a growing European trend is developing in favor of the same-sex marriage: Countries like Belgium, Denmark, Finland, France, Netherlands, Norway, Portugal, Sweden, Spain and the United Kingdom have already introduced it in their legal systems.

But there are also Countries, such as Germany, that, on the grounds of the special constitutional protection of the marriage institution (*die Ehe*), have followed the "separate but equal" approach, and introduced a similar institution (*Lebenspartnerschaft*), now fully equipped as heterosexual marriages.

In this scenario, the Italian situation is particular if not "isolated". The Italian parliament has never enacted a law on same-sex marriages; currently, it is only being discussed as a bill for the introduction of a legislative framework for civil unions.

In Italy, the Civil Code does not expressly refer to the diversity of sex as a requirement for marriage. Nevertheless, considering that heterosexuality is deeply rooted within Italian society, the diversity of sex has been considered as an essential pre-requisite.

---

[68]In this regard, the words of Martha Craig Daughtrey, in her dissenting opinion to the decision of the Court of Appeals for the Sixth Circuit (*DeBoer v. Snyder* case), seems to me very significant: "Today, my colleagues seem to have fallen prey to the misguided notion that the intent of the framers of the United States Constitution can be effectuated only by cleaving to the legislative will and ignoring and demonizing an independent judiciary. Of course, the framers presciently recognized that two of the three co-equal branches of government were representative in nature and necessarily would be guided by self-interest and the pull of popular opinion. To restrain those natural, human impulses, the framers crafted Article III to ensure that rights, liberties, and duties need not be held hostage by popular whims. More than 20 years ago, when I took my oath of office to serve as a judge on the United States Court of Appeals for the Sixth Circuit, I solemnly swore to 'administer justice without respect to persons', to 'do equal right to the poor and to the rich', and to 'faithfully and impartially discharge and perform all the duties incumbent upon me … under the Constitution and laws of the United States'. … If we in the judiciary do not have the authority, and indeed the responsibility, to right fundamental wrongs left excused by a majority of the electorate, our whole intricate, constitutional system of checks and balances, as well as the oaths to which we swore, prove to be nothing but shams".

So much so that, in the past, marriages contracted between persons of the same sex were judged not only as an invalid act, but even as a non-existent act, because it was contrary to public order.

In 2010 (before *Schalk and Kopft* case), for the first time, the Italian Constitutional Court dealt with a question concerning the constitutionality of some Articles of the Civil Code, with reference to Articles 2 (pluralism principle), 3 (equality principle), 29 (right to marry), 117(1) (constitutional, international, European limits to the legislative power) of the Constitution "insofar as, interpreted systematically, they do not allow homosexual individuals to celebrate marriages with persons of the same sex".[69]

Article 117 of the Constitution states that:

> Legislative powers shall be vested in the State and in the Regions in compliance with the Constitution and with the constraints deriving from EU legislations and international obligations.

Relating to the alleged violation of this Article, the Constitutional Court ruled inadmissibly on the question: international and European laws—says the Court—do not impose upon the national legislator a duty to introduce the same-sex marriages.

We have already seen that Article 12 of the ECHR and Article 9 of the EU Charter of Fundamental Rights expressly refer to the national legislative discretion for the definition of marriage.

With regard to Article 2 of the Italian Constitution ("The Republic recognizes and guarantees the inviolable rights of the person, both as an individual and in the social group where human person is expressed" as it requires compliance with the mandatory duties of political, economic and social solidarity), the Constitutional Court maintains that this Article promotes a constitutional pluralist model: "social groups" must be deemed inclusive of all communities forms in which a person can freely develop his or her own personality; as a result, it encompasses every stable "familiar" relationship of people, including same-sex unions.

However, the Italian Constitutional Court finds that this Article does not impose upon the legislator the duty to recognize the same-sex marriages; the legislator has the discretion to choose to introduce other institutions to protect same-sex couples.

Owing to a comparative approach, the Constitutional Court notices that the experience of other Countries is inhomogeneous; indeed, not all foreign legislators have introduced same-sex marriages.

The Italian Court also rules that the question referred to Article 2 of the Constitution is inadmissible, because an Italian legislator can exercise his discretion and choose many legal instruments to guarantee to the rights of same-sex couples, not necessarily the marriage itself.

At the same time, the Court says that judges, with their decisions, may protect specific situations concerning same-sex couples, as they already do so for the opposite-sex cohabiters.

---

[69]Italian Constitutional Court, decision no. 134 of 2010.

The Constitutional Court then moves to consider Article 29 of the Constitution, according to which "The Republic recognizes the rights of the family as a natural society founded on marriages", without explicitly stating that spouses have to belong to opposite sexes. Using the words "natural society", the Constituent Assembly intended to recognize the "pre-existence" (and the autonomy from the State) of the first social group (family) that the State has only to recognize.

On account of this, the Italian Court moves to reconstruct the meaning of "family" and "marriage"; yet, in a different way from other Constitutional Courts, the Italian ones use an original argument:

1. the concept of family and marriage cannot have been crystallized with reference to the time when the Constitution entered into force, because they were endowed with the flexibility that is inherent within constitutional principles;
2. the concept of family and marriage has also to be interpreted taking account not only the transformations within the legal system, but also the evolution of society and its customs;
3. however, such an interpretation "cannot go so far as to impinge the core of this constitutional provision [Article 29], modifying it in such a way as to embrace situations and problems that were not considered at all when it was enacted".[70]

In the opinion of the Court, proof of this could be found in the Constituent Assembly debate with regard to Article 29 of the Constitution: the Assembly did not address the question of homosexual unions, even though homosexuality was not unknown.

For this reason, the Court considers that the meaning of the constitutional provision under discussion cannot be set aside through interpretation, because this would not involve a simple re-reading of the system or the abandonment of a mere interpretative practice, rather a creative interpretation of Article 29.

Constitutional judges, on the other hand, going over, and, dealing with the alleged violation of Article 3 of the Constitution (principle of non discrimination) justify the different treatment of heterosexual couples on the basis of their "(potential) ability to procreate".[71]

The Constitutional Court reiterated its position in judgment no. 170 of 2014,[72] where more clearly it excluded that the legislator could introduce, by ordinary law, same-sex marriages.[73] The legislator could protect same-sex couples as every social formation, in light of the principle of social pluralism (Article 2 Constitution), but not as married couples: under Article 29 of the Constitution, only heterosexual couples can get married.

---

[70]Ibid.

[71]In my opinion, the core of the decision is represented precisely by the word "potential".

[72]With this judgment, the Court states the constitutional illegitimacy of the norm that provides the automatic nullity of the marriage in case of change of sex of one of the spouses. At the same time, the Court doesn't consider the couple (become same-sex couples) as married or joined in a civil union.

[73]As suggested by some authors: see, for example, Cartabia (2012), Pinto and Tripodina (2010).

This decision is clearly dissonant with respect to the general European trend[74] and to the decisions of other Constitutional Courts that, in another way, found their rulings on an evolutionary interpretation of the constitutional concepts of marriage and family.[75]

The Italian Constitutional Court does not seem to take into account the supranational normative and the European case law that is gradually imposing, as mentioned before, the full meaning of the equality, recognizing the same fundamental right to marry, for both homosexual and heterosexual couples.[76]

3.2 The Approach of Italian Judges to the Same-Sex Marriage

Despite the judgments of the Constitutional Court, or better taking advantage of the "glimmers" of these decisions, Italian judges have begun to offer a guarantee for same-sex couples in specific situations. We can mention the decision no. 4184 of 2012 of the Italian Court of Cassation,[77] where it ruled on whether two same-sex Italian citizens, married abroad, were entitled to record their marriage certificates at an Italian Civil Registry Office.

For the first time, the Court of Cassation asserted that same-sex marriages could not be considered as inexistent; it is only an act that cannot produce effects in Italy. In other words, the Court did not consider this type of marriage as contrary to the public order.

The Supreme judges, indeed, said that, as with the *Schalk and Kopf* case, the ECtHR recognized the existence, at the European level, of a "neutral concept" of marriage that the national parliament, in its full discretion, has to define. So it could be said that same-sex marriage is still an act that does not exist.

Moreover, the Supreme Court "invited" national judges to intervene to protect specific legal situations of same-sex couples. In doing so, the Supreme Court confirmed the role of the judiciary in implementing the conditions of the integrated protection of fundamental rights and the importance of the "dialog" between national judges with the ECtHR.

---

[74]See Ferrando (2014), at 2.

[75]See, for examples, the decisions nos. 359 of 2009 and 210 of 2010 of the Portuguese Constitutional Court; the decision no. 198 of 2012 of the Spanish Constitutional Court or the ruling no. 669 of 2013 of the French Constitutional Court.

[76]See Pezzini (2014), at 2; Brunelli (2014), at 2.

[77]This decision is available at http://www.giurcost.org/casi_scelti/Cassazione/Cass.sent.4184-2012.htm.

Indeed, as determined by the rulings of the Constitutional Court (nos. 348 and 349 of 2007), in the domestic hierarchy of sources law, the ECHR is placed above statutes and laws yet is below the Constitution, with the result that:

(1) the judges are required to interpret the rules in a consistent manner with the European Convention (therefore, they shall apply the civil rules concerning marriage registration according to Article 12 of the same Convention as interpreted by the European Court in the *Schalk and Kopf* case);
(2) if this is not possible, they should raise a question of constitutionality to the Constitutional Court, for infringement of Article 117(1) of the Constitution.

Through the duty of consistent interpretation to the European Convention, judges have become "the first" interlocutors of the ECtHR:

> [T]he protection of a particular situation is the result of a virtuous combination between the obligation of the national Legislator to adapt to the European Convention and the obligation of the judge to interpret the rules in a consistent manner with the Convention and the obligation of the Constitutional Court not to allow that a rule, of which it has been found the deficit with respect to a fundamental right, continues to have effect.[78]

Several judges show a lot of courage in developing the "potentiality" of the judgment of the Court of Cassation of 2012. For example, the trial court of Reggio Emilia (judgment of 13 February 2012) that judged a case about the free movement of same-sex couples.[79]

A Uruguayan citizen who got married to an Italian citizen in Palma Majorca requested the residence card on the grounds of family reunification that was refused by the *Questura* (police headquarters). The judge of Reggio Emilia upheld the application on the basis of EU Directive 38/2004 on the right of citizens of the Union and their family members to move and reside freely within the territory of the Member States, transposed by the Italian legislator in 2007.

According to the judge, the subject of assessment is only the applicant's right to obtain a permit to stay in Italy, with respect to the EU Directive mentioned above and not the legitimacy of the same-sex marriage, contracted in Spain. Asserting this, the judge recalled the fundamental right of each person to live freely in a relationship, without discrimination based on sexual orientation as recognized by the ECtHR.

It can then be addressed the decisions concerning temporary custody of children to homosexual couples (Family Proceedings Court of Bologna, Decree, 31 October 2013; Trial Court of Parma—Tutelary Judge—Decree, 3 July 2013; Family Proceedings Court of Palermo, 4 December 2013) or the decision of the Court of Grosseto of 9 April 2014.[80] The latter ordered the transcript of a same-sex marriage, celebrated in New York City, asserting that, after the ruling of the

---

[78]See Italian Constitutional Court, decision no. 317 of 2009.

[79]Decision available at http://www.articolo29.it.

[80]Decision available at http://www.articolo29.it.

ECtHR on the *Schalk and Kopf* case, a same-sex contract abroad is no longer contrary to the public order.[81]

4 Conclusion

The analysis of US and European case law allows us to draw some brief concluding remarks.

The supranational courts seem to prefer the spontaneous emergence of a homogeneous European social consensus; they also appear to recognize the wider discretion of the domestic legislator on whether to introduce same-sex marriages or not. With the effect, that the control over its margin of appreciation, in the face of such social change, will become more strict.

At the same time, however, both in Europe and in the United States, the supranational/federal courts are monitoring the national normative changes in the light of a new trend, with the effect, that the control over the margin of appreciation of a single legislator, in the face of such social change, will become stricter. This is clear in the US case law: in the *Windsor* case, for example, the US Supreme Court qualified the choice of a State to guarantee the right to marry to the same-sex couples as an important moment "to give further protection and dignity to that bond".[82] This is also clear if we consider ECtHR case law: the Court counts the Countries that protect same-sex couples and emphasizes that the isolated position of the State, that does not protect such couples, will be subject to stricter scrutiny.

Similar conclusion may be drawn if we analyze the ECJ case law: exploiting the natural interconnections between EU work/social security policies and national family policies, the Court could exercise an indirect control on the discretion of the national legislator in the matter of marital status.

At the national/State level, judges are exercising "from below" the same "pressure" on the legislator and their decisions may foster the emergence of a homogeneous social consensus in favor of same-sex marriages. From this point of view, the Italian experience is emblematic. As we have seen, through the duty of interpretation in conformity to the ECHR, Italian judges represent "the first port of entry" for European and international law.

The analysis of same-sex marriage case law underlines another important aspect: the close link between legal system and society. The *sollen sein* of each institution is influenced by the consequential dynamism that reflects, in its *sollen sein* and in its *sollen werden,* the historical and social perception of the community, at any given time.

---

[81]To the contrary, see, Tribunal of Pesaro, Decree, 14 October 2014; Tribunal of Milan, Decree, 17 July 2014, available at http://www.articolo29.it.

[82]See cit., footnote 52.

If we consider—as the Spanish Constitutional Court states—"*El Derecho come un fenómeno social vinculado a la realidad en que se desarrolla*"[83] it seems clear that judges represents the essential *trait d'union* between social reality and legal reality. In other words, the judge is the privileged subject to intercept change, to implement it.

With regard to same-sex marriages and the role of the judiciary, many scholars highlight the dichotomy between the "Legislative State" and the "Jurisdictional State",[84] often condemning the overexposure of the judiciary, in the silencing of the legislator. In this perspective, we can say that now the question is not if same-sex marriage is constitutional but who decides it. Judicial action alone, in the absence of any legislative action, risks guaranteeing only a fragmentary (and often contradictory) protection of fundamental rights.

Hence it is correct to hope that the legislator will choose suggestions coming from the "living law" and that the dichotomy between the two powers will be united, according to the rules of a democratic system, based on the separation/loyal cooperation between the powers.[85]

References

Brunelli, Giuditta. 2014. Dimensione antidiscriminatoria del principio di eguaglianza e diritto fondamentale di contrarre matrimonio. *GenIus: Rivista di studi giuridici sull'orientamento sessuale e l'identità di genere* 2: 6-11.

Cartabia, Marta. 2012. Avventure giuridiche della differenza sessuale. *Iustitia* 6: 43-64.

Crivelli, Elisabetta, 2011. Il caso *Shalk e Kopf* c. *Austria* in tema di unioni omosessuali. In *Dieci casi sui diritti in Europa*, ed. Marta Cartabia, 59-69. Bologna: Il Mulino.

D'Aloia, Antonio. 2014a. Europa e diritti. Luci e ombre dello schema di protezione *"multilevel"*. *Diritto dell'Unione Europea* 1: 1-45.

D'Aloia, Antonio. 2014b. From Gay Rights to Same-sex Marriages: A Brief History through the Jurisprudence of US Federal Courts. In *Same-sex Couples before National, Supranational and International Jurisdictions*, eds. Daniele Gallo, Luca Paladini and Pietro Pustorino, 33-71. Berlin: Springer.

De Pasquale, Tiziana, Agata A. Genna, and Laura Lorello. 2012. Diritto pubblico delle relazioni familiari e processo di europeizzazione dei diritti. *Rivista Italiana di Diritto Pubblico Comparato* 5: 787-817.

De Vergottini, Giuseppe. 2010. *Oltre il dialogo tra Corti. Giudici, diritto straniero, comparazione*. Bologna: Il Mulino.

Ferrando, Gilda. 2014. Le coppie dello stesso sesso in Italia: matrimonio o partnership? *GenIus: Rivista di studi giuridici sull'orientamento sessuale e l'identità di genere* 2: 26-34.

Gallo, Franco. 2012. Rapporti fra Corte costituzionale e Corte EDU, Bruxelles, 24 maggio 2012. http://www.cortecostituzionale.it.

---

[83]See Spanish Constitutional Court, decision no. 198 of 2012. See also supra, footnotes 21 and 22.

[84]See about this matter Ruggeri (2014a).

[85]For the same conclusions see again Ruggeri (2014a).

Ibrido, Renato. 2013. Ritorno alla comparazione. Note a margine della sentenza del *Tribunal Constitucional* spagnolo sul matrimonio omosessuale. http://www.nomos-leattualitaneldiritto.it.

Ibrido, Renato. 2012. Spagna. Il *Tribunal Constitucional* spagnolo riconosce la legittimità costituzionale della legge sul matrimonio omosessuale. http://www.dpce.it.

Helfer, R. Laurence, and Erik Voeten. 2014. International Courts as Agents of Legal Change: Evidence from LGBT Rights in Europe. *International Organization* 68: 77-110.

Massa Pinto, Ilenia. 2013. Il potere di definire la sostanza veicolata dalla parola 'matrimonio' tra politica e giurisdizione: note in margine alle recenti sentenze della Corte Suprema degli Stati Uniti. http://www.costituzionalismo.it.

Massa Pinto, Ilenia, and Chiara Tripodina. 2010. Su come per la Corte le unioni omosessuali non possono essere ritenute omogenee al matrimonio, ovvero tecniche argomentative impiegate per motivare la sentenza n. 138/2010. http://www.dircost.unito.it.

Orzan, Massimo F. 2014. Employment Benefits for Same-sex Couples: The Case Law of the ECJ. In *Same-sex Couples before National, Supranational and International Jurisdictions*, eds. Daniele Gallo, Luca Paladini and Pietro Pustorino, 493-510. Berlin: Springer.

Perelli, Andrea. 2013. Il matrimonio omosessuale dinanzi alla Corte suprema degli USA: brevi considerazioni in ottica comparata. http://www.dpce.it.

Pezzini, Barbara. 2014. Riconoscere, negare o giustificare la discriminazione matrimoniale delle persone omosessuali? A proposito dell'interpretazione sistematico-originalista del matrimonio nell'art. 29 Cost. *GenIus: Rivista di studi giuridici sull'orientamento sessuale e l'identità di genere* 2: 12-25.

Pustorino, Pietro. 2014. La Corte europea dei diritti dell'uomo e cambiamento di sesso: il caso *Hämäläinen* c. *Finland*. http://www.articolo29.it.

Rijpma, Jorrit, and Nelleke, Koffeman. 2014. Free Movement Rights for Same-sex Couples Under EU Law: What Role to Play for the ECJ? In *Same-sex Couples before National, Supranational and International Jurisdictions*, eds. Daniele Gallo, Luca Paladini and Pietro Pustorino, 455-492. Berlin: Springer.

Romeo, Graziella. 2014. The Recognition of Same–sex Couples Rights in the US between Counter-Majoritarian Principle and Ideological Approaches: A State Level Perspective. In *Same-sex Couples before National, Supranational and International Jurisdictions*, eds. Daniele Gallo, Luca Paladini and Pietro Pustorino, 15-32. Berlin: Springer.

Rudan, Delia. 2014. Unioni civili registrate e discriminazione fondata sull'orientamento sessuale: il caso Vallianatos. *Diritti umani e Diritto internazionale* 8: 232-236.

Ruggeri, Antonio. 2013. Diritto euro unitario e diritto interno: alla ricerca del sistema dei sistemi. http://www.diritticomparati.it.

Ruggeri, Antonio. 2014a. Dal legislatore al giudice, sovranazionale e nazionale: la scrittura delle norme in progress, al servizio dei diritti fondamentali. http://www.forumcostituzionale.it.

Ruggeri, Antonio. 2014b. Famiglie, genitori e figli, attraverso il "dialogo" tra Corti europee e Corte costituzionale. Quali insegnamenti per la teoria della Costituzione e delle relazioni interordinamentali? http://www.giurcost.it.

Schillaci, Angelo. 2013. "This case is not routine". La Corte Suprema USA e il *same-sex marriage*, tra tutela dei diritti e limiti della giurisdizione. http://www.rivistaaic.it.

Sperti, Angioletta. 2006. Il dialogo tra le corti e il ricorso alla comparazione giuridica nell'esperienza più recente. http://www.associaizionedeicostituzionalisti.it.

Sperti, Angioletta. 2013. *Omosessualità e diritti. I percorsi giurisprudenziali ed il dialogo globale delle Corti Costituzionali*. Pisa: Pisa University Press.

Sperti, Angioletta. 2014. Il matrimonio *same-sex* negli Stati Uniti a un anno dalla sentenza Windsor. Una riflessione sugli sviluppi giurisprudenziali a livello statale e federale. *GenIus: Rivista di studi giuridici sull'orientamento sessuale e l'identità di genere* 2: 143-157

Tega, Diletta. 2012. *I diritti in crisi. Tra corti nazionali e Corte Europea di Strasburgo*. Milano: Giuffrè.

Valenti, Veronica. 2013. Dalla CEDU una tutela per direttissima delle coppie omosessuali. http://www.confronticostituzionali.it.

Valenti, Veronica. 2014. Verso l'europeizzazione del diritto nazionale di famiglia? Brevi osservazioni a margine del caso Hay. http://www.forumcostituzionale.it.

Winkler, Matteo. 2011. I trattamenti pensionistici delle coppie dello stesso sesso nell'Unione europea. Il caso Romer. *Responsabilità civile e previdenza* 10: 1979-1996.

Healthcare Right and Principle of "Minimum Standards": The Interpretation of the Judiciary in a Comparative Perspective

Monica Cappelletti

Abstract This chapter explores how general principle of minimum standards regarding medical treatment is applied and interpreted by the judiciary in Italian and European case law. Firstly, the attention will be focused on the interpretation of the Italian Constitutional Court, that has defined and applied this principle since 1978, even before its introduction in the Constitution (Article 117(2)(m)), after its revision in 2001. Secondly, the chapter will examine the application of healthcare standards right by the Court of Justice of the European Union defining patients' rights in cross-border healthcare between European Member States. Finally, the chapter will highlight the legal implications regarding the definition of patients' rights and, in a more general perspective, social rights within an everchanging welfare system due to the economic crisis.

1 Preliminary Remarks: Healthcare Right in the Interpretation of the Judiciary

Within the framework of social rights[1] recognized by the Constitutions of the second postwar period, healthcare right is particularly important, since it represents a

---

[1]Social rights, as it is known, configure such rights to benefits and imply a positive intervention by States authorities. Although this concept is a typical reconstruction of European continental constitutionalism, derived from the Weimar Constitution of 1919, even in the Anglo-Saxon constitutionalism these rights have found direct success in Beveridge Report of 1942 (United Kingdom) and in the New Deal Plan of United States President Roosevelt. In this regard, scholars have pointed out that the United States State of Union Address of 1944 is a kind of US Second Bill of Rights, which included "the right to earn enough to provide adequate food and clothing and recreation, the right to adequate medical care, a decent home and a good education, the right to adequate protection from economic fears of old age, sickness, accident and unemployment". See Jackson and Tushnet (1999), pp. 1436–1437. See also Carrozza et al. (2009), p. 1068; Romeo (2013), p. 505.

M. Cappelletti (✉)
Research Fellow in Comparative Public Law, University of Parma, Parma, Italy
e-mail: monica.cappelletti@unipr.it

© Springer International Publishing Switzerland 2015   243
L. Pineschi (ed.), *General Principles of Law - The Role of the Judiciary*,
Ius Gentium: Comparative Perspectives on Law and Justice 46,
DOI 10.1007/978-3-319-19180-5_12

preliminary right for the concrete realization of substantial equality principles and for the exercise of other fundamental rights. In fact, scholars have highlighted, in particular with regard to the Italian constitutional context, that:

> Social rights substantiate the priority dimension, although not the only one, of the substantial equality principle. It is actually a circular dimension, a two-way dimension: the identification of the "full development of person" and "the participation in the political, economic and social development of the Italian Republic" are the real finalistic values of Article 3, second paragraph of the Italian Constitution, that project social rights beyond a mere containment of social and economic inequality, as well as solidarity.[2]

As with other social rights, healthcare right needs legislative implementation, as the recognition in a fundamental Charter of a legal system is not in itself sufficient to ensure the effective fulfillment of the rights themselves. At the same time, the effectiveness of these rights does not only depend on the enforcement of the legal provisions, but also on the interpretation of judges, and in particular the constitutional ones, as they are requested to find a balance between different interests.[3]

This chapter aims at examining the interpretative activity of judges with respect to the protection of healthcare right, studying the evolution of case law within two different legal systems, Italy and the European Union. The choice of these two legal systems is not random, but is justified by the peculiarities of their legislative provisions and their judicial interpretation of healthcare right. The Italian Constitution was one of the first to recognize the health right and the Italian Constitutional Court has undertaken a complex interpretative approach to the definition of the minimum standards within healthcare throughout the Country since the seventies. The European Union recognizes the healthcare right in the EU Charter of Fundamental Rights, but it has no legislative competence in healthcare matters. However, this did not prevent the European Court of Justice (ECJ) to rule on a particular form of exercise of the healthcare right (i.e. patients' cross-border healthcare rights)[4] and to outline a set of parameters to exercise it at European level.

Although these two cases may seem very different, these two interpretive judicial settings have two points of contact: one derived from the fact that decisions of the EU judge may well have an effect on the Italian legislation and on any future cases settled by the national judges; another being the common need for interpretation of judges to protect the healthcare right in the economic crisis context and for the redefinition of the welfare State.

---

[2]My translation. See D'Aloia (2002), p. 10.

[3]D'Atena (2006), pp. 10–11.

[4]In this chapter we use different terminology to describe the phenomenon of healthcare mobility, in other words moving from their own Country to another one to receive medical treatment. The terms of cross-border healthcare, patients' mobility, or medical tourism must be considered synonyms for the purposes of this chapter.

2 The Role of the Italian Constitutional Court in the Definition of Minimum Standards Regarding Medical Treatment

Healthcare right, as set out in Article 32 of the Italian Constitution,[5] represents a rare constitutional provision, since in contemporary Constitutions it is not common to find explicit rules for health protection.[6] This provision recognizes healthcare as a fundamental right of the individual.[7] At the same time, it provides a number of implicit rights, connected with healthcare protection: the right of mental and physical integrity, the right to live in a healthy environment, the right to receive healthcare assistance or medical treatment, the right not to be treated or to refuse medical treatment.[8]

For the purposes of this chapter, the attention will be focused on one of these aspects, namely the right to receive healthcare assistance or medical treatment (Article 32(1)) and its interpretation by the Italian Constitutional Court. In this perspective, the right to receive healthcare requires positive actions by public institutions or, in general, by the State.

Within the Italian legal system, the parliament first implemented the constitutional provisions relating to healthcare with law no. 833 of 23 December 1978, which established the National Health Service. This legislative measure was aimed at defining uniform standards of performance across the whole Country, which was guaranteed for all citizens, regardless of their region of residence.[9]

In reality, long before this law was adopted, the Italian Constitutional Court had declared the need for the State to ensure "equal standards" for healthcare throughout the Country, since "hospital care services and healthcare right, which are connected, cannot be changed from region to region".[10]

Based on this setting and interpreting law no. 833/1978, the Italian Constitutional Court has developed a jurisprudence that has helped to better define the concept of "uniformity" of healthcare services. In particular, it is possible to identify three different periods of judicial interpretation: a first phase in the seventies and eighties; a second in the nineties; and a third one, after the constitutional revision of the Italian Constitution.

---

[5]Article 32(1) of the Italian Constitution: "*La Repubblica tutela la salute come fondamentale diritto dell'individuo e interesse della collettività, e garantisce cure gratuite agli indigenti*" (The Republic safeguards health as a fundamental right of the individual and as a collective interest, and guarantees free medical care to the indigent).

[6]Luciani (1992), p. 1; D'Arrigo (2001), p. 1009; Ferrari (2011), p. 268.

[7]Italian Constitutional Court decisions nos. 103 of 1977; 88 of 1979; 184 of 1986; 559 of 1987; 992 of 1988; 1011 of 1988; 298 of 1990; 455 of 1990; 356 of 1991; 107 of 2012.

[8]Ferrara (2010), p. 3; Tripodina (2008), p. 321; Simoncini and Longo (2006), p. 655; Ferrara, (1997), p. 513; Montuschi and Vincenzi Amato (1976), p. 146; Minni and Morrone (2013).

[9]France (2001).

[10]My translation. See Italian Constitutional Court decision no. 116 of 1967, *Considerato in diritto* no. 2. See Anzon (1967), p. 1549.

At first, immediately following the approval of the law on the National Health Service, the Constitutional Court interpreted the concept of essential levels (or uniform standards) regarding healthcare services, that should have been provided uniformly across the whole Country without differences between regions.[11] For example, in decision no. 245 of 1984, regarding different mechanisms for allocation of healthcare costs between Italian regions, the Italian Constitutional Court held that healthcare funds:

> [H]ave been established to ensure minimum standards of medical treatment uniformly for the National territory …. On the contrary, it is precisely the equality of citizens *vis-à-vis* healthcare services that risked being compromised if it had continued to apply a differentiated mechanism of allocation of health funds, which might favor the inhabitants of the Trentino-Alto Adige region, to the detriment of all other parts of the Country.[12]

In other words, medical treatment had to be available equally and uniformly, i.e. according to uniform standards, in all Italian regions.

Differently, the nineties marked both a legislative[13] and a judicial transition. The definition of healthcare standards, due to the necessary financial planning and cost restraints in the healthcare system, began to be balanced with other constitutional interests, such as financial ones. It was during this period that the Constitutional Court set out the concept of healthcare right as a "conditioned constitutional right". In particular the Italian judge highlighted that:

> The right to receive medical treatment, being based on a programmatic constitutional provisions that impose a specific goal to be achieved, it is guaranteed to every personas a conditioned constitutional right by the implementation of Parliament through the balance of the constitutionally protected interests, taking into account the objective limits that it may be in the implementation of organizational and financial resources at its disposal.[14]

In this perspective, healthcare right is not absolute, but may encounter restrictions in its implementation. In particular, the parliament and the government may

---

[11]Italian Constitutional Court decisions nos. 245 of 1984; 177 of 1986; 294 of 1986; 64 of 1987; 1011 of 1988.

[12]My translation. See Italian Constitutional Court decision no. 245 of 1984, *Considerato in diritto* no. 9: "*È stato istituito per garantire livelli minimi di prestazioni, in modo uniforme su tutto il territorio nazionale …. Al contrario, è proprio 'l'eguaglianza dei cittadini nei confronti del servizio' che rischiava di venire compromessa, qualora si fosse continuato ad applicare un differenziato meccanismo di riparto del fondo medesimo, suscettibile di privilegiare gli abitanti del Trentino-Alto Adige, a detrimento di tutte le altre componenti del Paese*".

[13]During the nineties the Italian government adopted a series of legislative measures to amend the National Health System, as legislative decree no. 502 of 1992, legislative decree no. 112 of 1998 and legislative decree no. 229 of 1999.

[14]My translation. See Italian Constitutional Court decision no. 455 of 1990, *Considerato in diritto* no. 3: "*Il diritto a ottenere trattamenti sanitari, essendo basato su norme costituzionali di carattere programmatico impositivo di un determinato fine da raggiungere, è garantito a ogni persona come un diritto costituzionale condizionato dall'attuazione che il legislatore ordinario ne dà attraverso il bilanciamento dell'interesse tutelato da quel diritto con gli altri interessi costituzionalmente protetti, tenuto conto dei limiti oggettivi che lo stesso legislatore incontra nella sua opera di attuazione in relazione alle risorse organizzative e finanziarie di cui dispone al momento*".

balance healthcare right with objective limits, such as those relating to organizational and financial resources at its disposal in an enclosed period.[15]

Furthermore, the Italian Constitutional Court settled the concept of "human dignity" as insurmountable to the restriction of healthcare right, a parameter which the parliament has always to take into account.[16] Standards of medical treatment do not have to be only uniformed, but the concept of essentiality of these standards has begun to better take shape. In other words standards have to ensure at least a minimal protection (minimum standards).[17] In this sense, in the decision no. 509 of 2000, for example, the Constitutional Court reiterated that the balance between the healthcare right and the economic and financial interests should not affect:

> [T]he core healthcare right, protected by the Italian Constitution as an inviolable sphere of human dignity, which prevents the creation of situations without protection, that can indeed affect the implementation of that rights.[18]

In other words, even though there may be actual economic needs of containment of public health costs, the parliament has to provide for a minimum healthcare protection.[19]

In 2001, the constitutional revision of Title V, Part II of the Italian Constitution constitutionalized the minimum standards principle of performance for civil and social rights, which has to be guaranteed for the whole Country (Article 117(2) (m)). This provision attributes the exclusively legislative competence to the State in the determination of these levels.[20]

The Italian Constitutional Court has been called, immediately after the approval of the constitutional amendment, to interpret this new constitutional provision primarily with reference to the distribution of legislative competence between State and regions. In this regard, the constitutional judge asserted the cross-cutting and flexible nature of the minimum standards of performance, because:

> It is not a "issue" in the strict sense, but it is a competence of the Parliament to invest in all matters, with respect to which it has to establish necessary rules to ensure everyone,

---

[15]Italian Constitutional Court decisions nos. 40 of 1991; 247 of 1992; 356 of 1992; 218 of 1994; 304 of 1994; 416 of 1995; 226 of 2000. See Cocconi (1998); Colapietro (1996).

[16]Italian Constitutional Court decisions nos. 304 of 1994; 309 of 1999; 509 of 2000; 252 of 2001; 432 of 2005; 354 of 2008; 269 of 2010; 299 of 2010; 61 of 2011.

[17]D'Aloia (2003), p. 1070; Balduzzi (2005), p. 49; Messineo (2012).

[18]My translation. See Italian Constitutional Court decision no. 509 of 2000: "*Il nucleo irriducibile del diritto alla salute protetto dalla Costituzione come ambito inviolabile della dignità umana, il quale impone di impedire la costituzione di situazioni prive di tutela, che possano appunto pregiudicare l'attuazione del diritto*".

[19]Italian Constitutional Court decisions nos. 304 of 1994; 267 of 1998; 185 of 1998; 309 of 1999; 252 of 2001; 111 of 2005; 432 of 2005.

[20]Giorgis (2003).

throughout the Nation, the enjoyment of a guaranteed performance, such as the essential content of these rights, without regional restrictions or conditions.[21]

With reference to the balance between the healthcare right and the economic-financial interests, the Italian Constitutional Court, in line with its previous case law, has further stressed human dignity as an insurmountable parameter against organizational healthcare service needs, even if healthcare right remains a "financially conditioned right". This approach has proven to be constant in relation to the need of users sharing National Health Service costs and, therefore, it is not incompatible with the constitutional provisions;[22] moreover it has been legitimated with reference to the healthcare planning principles, as a means to contain public spending within this sector.[23]

In conclusion, the Italian Constitutional Court has contributed to the definition and specification of the inherently ambiguous concept of healthcare minimum standards. Healthcare right is not absolute, but can be declined in relation to economic and financial needs. Minimum and essential levels of medical treatment have to be ensured, referring to human dignity expressly protected by the Italian Constitution.

3 The Role of the Court of Justice of the European Union in the Definition of Patients' Rights in Cross-Border Healthcare

Within the European legal order, the ECJ has always played a key role in the implementation of Community law as well as in the juridical integration between Member States. Hence, this Court has been identified as the real engine of European integration.[24] In fact, many decisions have marked the evolution of the European legal system with a greater convergence and harmonization between the different national legal systems.[25]

The central role of the Court may also be found in matters related to healthcare right of European citizens. As already mentioned before, healthcare matter is not a

---

[21]My translation. See Italian Constitutional Court decision no. 282 of 2002, *Considerato in diritto* no. 3: "*Non si tratta di una 'materia' in senso stretto, ma di una competenza del legislatore statale idonea ad investire tutte le materie, rispetto alle quali il legislatore stesso deve poter porre le norme necessarie per assicurare a tutti, sull'intero territorio nazionale, il godimento di prestazioni garantite, come contenuto essenziale di tali diritti, senza che la legislazione regionale possa limitarle o condizionarle*". See also decisions nos. 88 of 2003 and 134 of 2006. See Bin (2002), p. 1445; Morana (2002), p. 2030; Violini (2002), p. 1450.

[22]Italian Constitutional Court decisions nos. 203 of 2008 and 187 of 2012.

[23]Italian Constitutional Court, decisions nos. 111 of 2005; 200 of 2005; 94 o 2009; 248 of 2011; 193 of 2007; 52 of 2010; 163 of 2011; 91 of 2012; 79 of 2013; 104 of 2013; 180 of 2013; 256 of 2014.

[24]Weiler (1987), p. 555; Starr-Deelen and Deelen (1996), p. 81; Martinico (2009); De Waele (2010), p. 3; Martinico and Pollicino (2012) Schiek (2012) p. 113.

[25]Case C-6/54 *Costa* [1964] ECR 585; case C-70/77 *Simmenthal* [1978] ECR 1453 and cases C-286/82 and 26/83, *Luisi and Carbone* [1984] ECR 377.

competence of the European Union, being a strictly national legislative competence.[26] Indeed, Article 168 of the Treaty on the Functioning of the European Union (TFEU) (formerly Article 152 of the European Community Treaty) specifies that the European Union has to ensure a high level of human health protection in the definition and implementation of all Union policies and activities; as a result, Member States have to regulate, in particular, the management of health services and medical care and the allocation of the resources assigned to them. The European Union may only coordinate policy actions between Member States (Article 6 TFEU). These provisions have been confirmed in Article 35 of the EU Charter of Fundamental Rights, which protects the rights of every person to have access to preventive healthcare and to receive medical treatment, under the conditions established by national laws.

Nevertheless, as early as the seventies, in the implementation of the free movement of person principle between Member States and in particular with regard to workers, the European Community has initiated a process of recognition of some rights for citizens of a Member State who are temporarily or permanently in another Member State. Regulations 1408/71 and 574/72[27] have specifically tried to coordinate different Member States' social security systems, providing a range of social security rights for this particular category of citizens (employees, self-employees and their families).[28] Among these rights, there is also the opportunity for an employee to request medical treatment in another Member State (under Article 22), first obtaining advance authorization of the State of residence. The original framework established that the State of residence could refuse this authorization if the demand for medical treatments were not legislatively provided by the national legislation of the State of residence, and if this treatment could be practiced in the State of residence within a reasonable amount of time.

Since the nineties, thanks to the interpretation of the judiciary of the European Treaties and the provisions of Regulations 1408/71 and 574/72, the ECJ has begun to outline a different and additional possibility to access healthcare in another Member State and, above all, the right to receive reimbursement for medical treatment abroad. This judiciary term has seen the Court as the main player in the definition of the right for reimbursement of cross-border healthcare and later (in 2011) a specific legislative provision in this matter has been adopted.[29]

During this period the Court has also defined what could be identified as "parameters" or minimum elements to access cross-border healthcare for European citizens ("movement of patients"), not just limited to the workers, in the European competence of free movement of persons, goods and services.

---

[26]Carboni (2012), Obermaier (2009).

[27]Now see Regulation 883/2004/EC of the European Parliament and of the Council of 29 April 2004 on the coordination of social security systems.

[28]Van der Mei (2003), p. 222.

[29]See further below.

The first two leading cases[30] concerned two residents in Luxembourg, who, after having obtained healthcare in another Member State, had demanded reimbursement. In the first case, Mr. Kohll requested an authorization for orthodontic treatment for his younger daughter in Germany. His request was denied due to the medical treatment not being necessary and urgent and the fact it could have been obtained directly in Luxembourg. The ECJ, while assessing the Member States competence in determining their social security systems, considered the national legislation, under which reimbursement of healthcare treatment costs provided by an orthodontist established in another Member State is subject to prior authorization by the national institution, was in contrast to the free movement principle of services and consequently the European Treaty (Articles 59 and 60 of the European Community Treaty, now Articles 56 and 57 TFEU):

> It must be recalled that aims of a purely economic nature cannot justify a barrier to the fundamental principle of freedom to provide services ... However, it cannot be excluded that the risk of seriously undermining the financial balance of the social security system may constitute an overriding reason in the general interest capable of justifying a barrier of that kind. But, contrary to the submissions of UCM and the Luxembourg Government, it is clear that reimbursement of the costs of dental treatment provided in other Member States in accordance with the tariff of the State of insurance has no significant effect on the financing of the social security system.[31]

In the second case, Mr. Decker had purchased spectacles in Belgium and his reimbursement was denied for lack of prior authorization. Even in this case, the EU judge said the contrast of the national legislation concerning prior authorization to have right to reimbursement for medical treatment with European Treaty and, specifically, in contrast to the free movement principle of goods (Article 30 of the European Community Treaty, now Article 34 TFEU).[32]

Both the *Kohll* and *Decker* cases led to the affirmation of a new parameter within healthcare treatment and reimbursement of healthcare costs incurred in a State other than that of residence. In particular, the ECJ determined that it is not necessary a prior authorization for non-hospital treatment for European citizens applying directly the free movement principles of services and goods.

These first two cases have opened, as mentioned, a judicial season that has led the ECJ to further specify the right for reimbursement of cross-border healthcare for European citizens. Among several key decisions, in the *Geraets-Smits and Peerbooms* case[33] the Court not only specifies the characteristics of the reimbursement, but also applies the free movement principle of services even those provided by a hospital.

Firstly, the ECJ asserts the neutrality of social security system adopted in a Member State to obtain reimbursement of medical treatment abroad, in the sense

---

[30]Case C-158/96 *Kohll* [1998] ECR I-1931 and case C-120/95 *Decker* [1998] ECR I-1831. See Van der Mei (2003), p. 222; Bonomo (1998) p. 2391.

[31]*Kohll* cit., paras. 41–42.

[32]*Decker* cit., paras. 39, 40 and 42.

[33]Case C-157/99 *Geraets-Smits and Peerbooms* [2001] ECR I-5473.

that it is not important whether it is a system which the patient has selected and paid directly to the health operator and then subsequently is reimbursed by health insurance institution, as in this case, or if it is a system that allows free care to patients at affiliated health operators. In both social security systems, reimbursement of cross-border healthcare cannot be denied. In fact, the Court points out that:

> With regard more particularly to the argument that hospital services provided in the context of a sickness insurance scheme providing benefits in kind, such as that governed by the ZFW, should not be classified as services within the meaning of Article 60 of the Treaty, it should be noted that, far from falling under such a scheme, the medical treatment at issue in the main proceedings, which was provided in Member States other than those in which the persons concerned were insured, did lead to the establishments providing the treatment being paid directly by the patients. It must be accepted that a medical service provided in one Member State and paid for by the patient should not cease to fall within the scope of the freedom to provide services guaranteed by the Treaty merely because reimbursement of the costs of the treatment involved is applied for under another Member State's sickness insurance legislation which is essentially of the type which provides for benefits in kind.[34]

The *Geraets-Smits and Peerbooms* case marks then a further step in the affirmation of the cross-border healthcare right, when the ECJ recognizes and admits the possibility of reimbursement for hospital treatment:

> [T]he fact that hospital medical treatment is financed directly by the sickness insurance fund on the basis of agreements and pre-set fees scales is not in any way to remove such treatment from the sphere of services.[35]

While, on the one hand, the ECJ verifies that, in the implementation of the principle of free movement of services, there is no distinction between the two different types of healthcare treatments (hospital or non-hospital treatment), on the other, the EU judge introduces parameters for the reimbursement of cross-border healthcare. In order to safeguard the financial balance of national healthcare systems, the Court recognizes the need for prior authorization to access to hospital treatment in a State other than that of residence. However, in this case the refusal of the authorization should be based on objective, non-discriminatory criteria which should be identified in advance.[36]

The interpretative activity of the ECJ did not stop there. Later, until the first legislative codification,[37] the Court has intervened both to determine the criteria for the amount of reimbursement for patient who decides to seek medical treatment abroad, and to further specify parameters for the national authorization for cross-border hospital treatment.

Regarding the first aspect (the amount of reimbursement for cross-border healthcare treatment), in an extensive case law the ECJ has noted, first, that the legislation, under which medical costs must be calculated, must be that of the

---

[34]Ibid., para. 55. See Cancilla (2009) p. 228.

[35]Ibid., para. 56. See also case C-385/99 *Müller-Fauré* [2003] ECR I-4509.

[36]*Geraets-Smits and Peerbooms* cit., para. 90. See Van der Mei (2004), p. 67.

[37]See further below.

State where patient receives the healthcare treatment, since it would be illogical to quantify the costs based on the regulations of the State of residence. In fact, the EU judge emphasizes that:

> The insured person must in principle be entitled to the benefits in kind provided on behalf of the competent institution by the institution of the place where the insured person is staying, in accordance with the provisions of the legislation of the State in which the benefits are provided, as if the covered person were insured in that State. ... By guaranteeing that insured persons covered by the legislation of one Member State and granted authorisation have access to treatment in the other Member States on conditions as favourable as those enjoyed by persons covered by the legislation of those other States, that provision helps to facilitate the free movement of persons covered by social insurance.[38]

Nevertheless, this solution highlights two problematic aspects: on the one hand, the issue of reimbursement when there is a different cost between the medical treatment incurred abroad and that the patient would have paid if the same healthcare service had been provided in the State of residence; on the other hand, the issue of optional costs, such as travel expenses. In several judgments the ECJ has reiterated that any partial reimbursement of cross-border healthcare costs could be an obstacle to the free movement of services:

> There is no doubt that the fact that a person has a lower level of cover when he receives hospital treatment in another Member State than when he undergoes the same treatment in the Member State in which he is insured may deter, or even prevent, that person from applying to providers of medical services established in other Member States and constitutes, both for insured persons and for service providers, a barrier to freedom to provide services.[39]

Therefore, it follows, that States have to fully reimburse the cost for cross-border healthcare. For the optional costs, the Court admits the possibility for Member States to define a maximum amount reimbursable, instead:

> The obligation imposed on the competent institution by Article 22 ... relates exclusively to the expenditure connected with the healthcare received by the insured person in the host Member State, namely, such as that at issue in the case in the main proceedings, in the case of hospital treatment, the cost of medical services strictly defined and the inextricably linked costs relating to the stay and meals in the hospital.[40]

Turning then to the parameters of the authorization (or contrary to the criteria for defining a refusal to authorize), the ECJ has dealt with these aspects in the *Mrs. Watts* case.[41] In this regard, it is useful to highlight that Regulation 1408/71 provides that authorization to receive medical treatment abroad may not be refused where the treatment cannot be provided for the person concerned within the territory of the Member State in which he resides (Article 22(2)). In the

---

[38]Case C-368/98 *Vanbraekel* [2001] ECR I-5363, para. 32.

[39]Ibid., para. 45. See also case C-372/04 *Watts* [2006] ECR I-4325, para. 130.

[40]Case C-466/04 *Herrera* [2006], ECR I-5341, para. 28. See also case C-444/05 *Stamatelaki* [2007], ECR I-3185, para. 35; case C-8/02 *Leichtle* [2004], ECR I-2641, para. 48.

[41]*Watts* cit.. See Cousin (2007), p. 183.

Watts case, the Court has defined the concept of "reasonable time" to receive medical treatment, precisely in order to safeguard the patients' healthcare.[42] This concept is undoubtedly important especially with regard to those healthcare systems based on the mechanism of waiting lists. In defining the meaning of "reasonable time", the ECJ has substantially offset the States interest in the economic integrity of the hospital system, the needs of healthcare planning and the patient's rights to healthcare protection. In the opinion of the EU judge, the mechanism of waiting lists should not hinder the particular situation of the patient. In fact in each individual case the medical circumstances and the clinical needs of the person must be evaluated:

> The interpretation of the time ... is not liable to undermine the national competent authorities' power to manage the available hospital capacity in their territory by the use of waiting lists, provided that the existence of such lists does not prevent the taking account in each individual case of the medical circumstances and the clinical needs of the person concerned when he requests authorisation to receive hospital treatment in another Member State at the expense of the system with which he is registered. ... In order to be entitled to refuse to grant the authorisation referred to in Article 22(1)(c)(i) of that regulation on the ground that there is a waiting time for hospital treatment, the competent institution is required to establish that that time does not exceed the period which is acceptable on the basis of an objective medical assessment of the clinical needs of the person concerned in the light of all of the factors characterising his medical condition at the time when the request for authorisation is made or renewed, as the case may be.[43]

Therefore, if it is not possible in the State of residence to receive the healthcare service within a period compatible with the disease and the clinical situation of the patient, the national institution cannot refuse to allow cross-border healthcare.[44]

4 From the Codification of European Case Law to Recent *Petru* Case

Since 1998, the ECJ has defined the right to cross-border healthcare for European citizens, legitimizing two ways to access medical treatment abroad. Firstly, for hospital services, it is necessary the prior authorization by the State of residence, while for non-hospital services patients could directly request a reimbursement after the treatment. Then, the Court, as described above, helped to better define the quantum of reimbursement and the conditions under which patients may request authorization to cross-border healthcare, balancing Member States' interests with that of the economic and financial performances of national healthcare systems and the need to have medical treatment in a reasonable time for patients.

---

[42]Differently see case C-56/01 *Inizan* [2003] ECR I-12403. See Antoniazzi (2004), p. 593; Cisotta (2007), p. 168; Longo (2007), p. 662.

[43]Case C-372/04 *Watts* cit., paras.75 and 79.

[44]See also case C-173/09 *Elchinov* [2010] ECR I-8889.

Thus, the ECJ has contributed to recognizing primarily workers cross-border healthcare rights and, in general, the definition of healthcare mobility right for all European citizens who require medical treatment.

This interpretative activity of the Court has fuelled an uncertain legal framework, especially with regard to European legislation on the coordination of social security systems for workers, pushing the European Commission to adopt a specific directive.[45] After a lengthy approval procedure,[46] the Directive 2011/24/EU of the European Parliament and of the Council of 9 March 2011 on the application of patients' rights in cross-border healthcare is approved. It aims at codifying the principles established by the ECJ with regard to cross-border healthcare right.[47]

This legislative measure has been better defined as an "act of minimum harmonization".[48] The European Commission, unable to fully determine the discipline in this area, for the reasons mentioned above regarding the division of legislative competences between Union and Member States, tried to ensure greater legal certainty for cross-border healthcare, as well as to reconcile different particularities of the national health systems, and their economic and financial needs. Consequently, the entire regulatory framework of the Directive leaves wider discretion for Member States in determining cross-border healthcare right.[49]

In fact, this Directive[50] establishes precisely cases where this is not applied (services in the field of long-term care, organ transplants and public vaccinations)[51] in addition to the two kinds of healthcare treatments (hospital and non-hospital)

---

[45]In this matter there was a preliminary proposal of codification on occasion of the approval of Directive Services, that should have also provided on healthcare services; see European Commission, Proposal for a Directive of the European Parliament and the Council on Services in the Internal Market, COM(2004) 2, 5 March 2004. See also Barnard (2008), p. 323.

[46]There was a first proposal of the European Commission in June 2006, that contributed to the approval of the Conclusions of the Council on common values and principles in European Union Health Systems. During the approval procedure the original draft text of the Directive had been modified and amended by Member States and the European Parliament. Finally, the Directive was adopted on 28 February 2011. See Meyer (2013), p. 95.

[47]"This Directive aims to establish rules for facilitating access to safe and high-quality cross-border healthcare in the Union and to ensure patient mobility in accordance with the principles established by the ECJ and to promote cooperation on healthcare between Member States, whilst fully respecting the responsibilities of the Member States for the definition of social security benefits relating to health and for the organisation and delivery of healthcare and medical care and social security benefits, in particular for sickness", Directive 2011/24/EU, *Whereas* no. 10. See also *Whereas* nos. 11 and 12.

[48]Meyer (2013), p. 87.

[49]Member States had to bring into force the laws, regulations and administrative provisions necessary to comply with this Directive by 25 October 2013. See Prudil (2014), p. 15; Kattelus (2014), p. 23; Requejo (2014), p. 79; Bongers and Townend (2014), p. 65; Schwebag (2014), p. 56; Olsena (2014), p. 46; Vidalis and Kyriakaki (2014), p. 33; Santuari (2014), p. 77.

[50]Inglese (2012), p. 109; Di Federico (2012), p. 683; Meyer (2013), p. 95; Nys (2014), p. 5; Peeters (2012), p. 32; Uccello Barretta (2014), p. 19; Di Federico (2014), p. 177; Santuari (2014), p. 69.

[51]See Directive 2011/24/EU, Article 1(3).

where it depends on the procedures required for prior authorization or for reimbursement. Member States have to determine the cases of limitation to cross-border healthcare right,[52] the authorization procedure[53] and the method of calculation for reimbursement,[54] as well as, give accomplished determination to different generic terms, that have not been declined previously by the European Directive. For example, although one of the cardinal principles of the Directive is the non-discrimination with regard to nationality,[55] it is presented that Member States could limit (temporally) access to the national healthcare system for "overriding reasons of general interest" to other Member States' patients.[56]

This Directive will undoubtedly be an opportunity for Member States to better define the content of the cross-border healthcare right. Nevertheless, it is not possible to exclude that in the future other cases could be examined by national judges and the ECJ, when the national rules will not guarantee effective access to cross-border healthcare equally to all European citizens, or if national rules will pose excessive restrictions to this right.

Recently, the ECJ[57] has again affected patients' mobility. This decision does not mention the Directive 2011/24/EU; there is no doubt, however, that this judgment will have an effect on its future implementation.

This recent case, very similar to the *Watts* one, concerns the interpretation of the concept of "reasonable time" within which a particular medical treatment should be received, given the different clinical and pathological circumstances of the patient in his or her State of residence or the authorization to healthcare mobility. A Romanian woman, Mrs. Petru, suffering from severe cardiovascular disease, having to undergo open heart surgery, had requested authorization to cross-border healthcare treatment before travelling to Germany. Considering the lack of material conditions of the Romanian hospital (lack of medicines, medical supplies and basic necessities, insufficiency of beds available) where Mrs. Petru should have had to undergo surgery, she requested the authorization for cross-border healthcare, while she was abroad to receive the medical treatment. The Romanian administration refused the authorization, as the medical treatment required could be completed within a reasonable time in Romania. Mrs. Petru had subsequently then filed for reimbursement of costs incurred during the medical operation abroad.[58]

This judgment of the Court is extremely innovative as it adds an additional parameter to the interpretation of the *Watts* case; however, it imposes an additional "burden assessment" for national judges.

---

[52]Ibid., Article 4(3).

[53]Ibid., Articles 8 and 9.

[54]Ibid., Article 7.

[55]Ibid., Article 4(3).

[56]Ibid., Articles 4(3) and 7(9).

[57]Case C-268/13 *Petru* [2014] nyr.

[58]Ibid., paras. 9–12.

The ECJ proposes healthcare swiftness according to two different sets of circumstances: those linked closely to the organization of healthcare services (such as waiting lists, as analyzed in the *Watts* case), and those relating to structural deficiencies of the healthcare service itself (such as shortage of medicines as in the *Petru* case). It is precisely in the light of these two circumstances (organizational and structural reasons) that the Court assesses the "reasonable time" aspect of a healthcare service, and consequently the ability to allow or deny cross-border healthcare mobility. The ECJ highlights that:

> One of the circumstances that the competent institution is required to take into account may, in a specific case, be the lack of medication and basic medical supplies and infrastructure, such as that alleged in the main proceedings. As the Advocate General observes … the second subparagraph of Article 2(2) of Regulation no. 1408/71 does not distinguish between the different reasons for which a particular treatment cannot be provided in good time. Clearly, however, such a lack of medication and of medical supplies and infrastructure can, in the same way as the lack of specific equipment or particular expertise, make it impossible for the same or equally effective treatment to be provided in good time in the Member State of residence.[59]

This interpretation is certainly innovative, since it opens up a series of symptomatic circumstances relating to structural deficiency of a healthcare system, not merely linked to the managerial or organizational situation. These deficiencies justify even potential hospital tourism, especially for people resident in those Member States that are facing major economic difficulties within their healthcare systems.[60]

The ECJ adds, however, some parameters to verify if these structural deficiencies determine whether there is an inability to have the healthcare service within a reasonable time. In fact the Court imposes a double evaluation, both with reference to the entire healthcare system of the Member State, as well as its timelines. In other words, it has to be verified if the medical treatment requested could be received in any other structure of the national healthcare system as a whole and if this treatment could be obtained within a reasonable time, because of the patient's clinical and pathological circumstances.[61]

As a result, the ECJ seems to have clamped down on the possibility of European patients to decide where to receive healthcare treatments, which should primarily be received in their State of residence. Obviously this evaluation, especially with reference to the fact that there may be other hospitals in the Country where the patients live, it is not an omen of exclusivity. The *Petru* case marks

---

[59]Ibid., para. 33.

[60]Consider, for example, the Italian regions subjected to the procedure of recovery plans (*piani di rientro*) of healthcare systems. These plans imposed in some cases the closure of hospitals or the redefinition of the health service.

[61]*Petru* cit., para. 34.

in any case a step forward in the interpretation of cross-border healthcare right. Nevertheless, there is also no doubt that, even with the implementation of the Directive on patients' mobility, the process of recognition of this right has yet to come to thorough legal solution.

5 Healthcare Right, Courts and Economic Crisis

Analyzing the jurisprudence of the Italian Constitutional Court and the ECJ on the healthcare right, as the right to receive healthcare, in recent years these judges seem to have aimed mainly at defining not so much healthcare minimum standards, as to establish the core of the healthcare right beyond where no restrictions are permissible. The Italian Constitutional Court, as the previous section has demonstrated, relied on the concept of human dignity; the ECJ referred to the waiting times to receive healthcare treatment in the interpretation of the term "reasonable time".

In the light of these two different interpretive paths, it is possible to draw two focal considerations. The first relates to the relationship and possible influences between national and supranational judges in the European legal order; the second regards the need for minimum standards definition relating to medical treatment in face of the containment of public spending.

With reference to the relationship between the two Courts and in particular their mutual influences, as mentioned above, the new Directive on patients' mobility may surely lead to both national and EU judges dealing with the European vague rules and with national transposition measures. Any refusal to allow cross-border healthcare mobility or the non-reimbursement of healthcare treatment obtained abroad may be brought first to national courts (and perhaps Constitutional Courts) to examine individual and specific citizen cases and, secondly, to the ECJ to examine the compatibility of these national laws with European Directive. It is not excluded, as it has been since 1998, that the ECJ will be specifically called upon to define and interpret European law case by case.

It has been acknowledged that the ECJ might go beyond the interpretation of the principles of free movement of persons, services and goods, principles already in use for the solution of previous cases referring to issues of cross-border healthcare right. As it has been argued, the Court might directly apply the EU Charter of Fundamental Rights (in particular Article 35 on healthcare) to expand the European citizens' rights.[62] This would certainly constitute a fundamental step not only towards the recognition of social rights at an European level, but also towards the strengthening of the European Union integration, not only in an economic

---

[62]Di Federico (2013), p. 681.

sense.[63] In the recent *Petru* case, the ECJ had the occasion to give effective protection to the cross-border healthcare right, admitting in cases of a national healthcare system structural deficiency to obtain medical treatment abroad directly. The Court seems to have chosen to stop halfway: it is acceptable to go abroad to receive medical treatment, only if the same treatment is not available in another healthcare structure of the State of residence. In this way, the ECJ has reiterated the responsibility of Member States in this matter.

The judiciary activity in the definition of healthcare standards also allows more general consideration with regard to the protection of social rights and the balance of public finances.[64] In fact, the definition of healthcare minimum standards, reconciled with the primary need to protect, may ensure sustainable healthcare systems, especially with reference to those who are either totally or partially public financed, as in the case of European States.

The economic crisis, as well as the requirements for the definition of uniform standards, could further aggravate those healthcare systems already overly affected by structural and systemic deficiencies (lack of medicines, lack of staff, etc ...). In these cases, healthcare tourism could become not only a way of delivering healthcare services, but also (perhaps) the only way in order to receive them. According to this perspective, the European case may be an example, as the ECJ has ruled a fundamental parameter to frame the phenomenon of patients' mobility, i.e. a reasonable time frame within which to receive medical treatment.

The jurisprudence on healthcare right is therefore definitely crucial, especially to give effective and concrete protection to different legal situations. In the end, healthcare right is guaranteed by judges, but it needs, perhaps even more in a period of economic crisis, to have effective legal recognition and concrete legislative implementation.[65]

References

Annas, George. 2013. Health and Human Rights in the Continuing Global Economic Crisis. *American Journal of Public Health* 103: 967-967.

Antoniazzi, Sandra. 2004. Sistema sanitario nazionale e principio comunitario di libera prestazione dei servizi: la scelta dell'utente per prestazioni mediche erogate in un diverso Paese membro, subordinata alla necessaria autorizzazione amministrativa dello Stato membro di appartenenza per il rimborso delle spese sostenute. *Rivista italiana di diritto pubblico comunitario* 2: 603-631.

Anzon, Adele. 1967. Esigenze unitarie e competenze regionali. *Giurisprudenza costituzionale* 3: 1549-1556.

---

[63]D'Aloia (2014), pp. 44–45.

[64]Ciolli (2012); Grasso (2012); D'Aloia (2012); Tega (2012); Trucco (2012); Luciani (2013); Gabriele (2013); Salazar (2013); Morana (2013); Benatar et al. (2011), p. 646; Annas (2013), p. 967; Aoife (2014).

[65]D'Aloia (2012), p. 13.

Aoife, Nolan. 2014. *Economic and Social Rights after the Global Financial Crisis*. Cambridge: Cambridge University Press.

Balduzzi, Renato. 2005. Livelli essenziali di assistenza *versus* livelli minimi. In *La politica economica tra mercati e regole*, eds. Guido Barberis, Italo Lavanda, Giorgio Rampa, Bruno Soro, 49-67. Soveria Mannelli: Rubbettino.

Barnard, Catherine. 2008. Unraveling the Services Directive. *Common Market Law Review* 45: 323-394.

Benatar, Solomon, Stephen Gill, and Isabella Bakker. 2011. Global Health and the Global Economic Crisis. *American Journal of Public Health* 101: 646-653.

Bin, Roberto. 2002. Il nuovo riparto di competenze legislative: un primo, importante chiarimento. *Le Regioni* 6: 1445-1450.

Bongers, Lisette, and David Townend. 2014. The Implementation of the Directive on the Application of Patients' Rights in Cross–border Healthcare in the Netherlands. *European Journal of Health Law* 1: 65-78.

Bonomo, Annamaria. 1998. La libera circolazione dei malati. *Giustizia Civile* 10: 2391-2401.

Cancilla, Francesco A. 2009. *Servizi di welfare e diritti sociali nella prospettiva dell'integrazione europea*. Milano: Giuffrè.

Carboni, Giuliana G. (ed.). 2012. *La salute negli Stati composti. Tutela del diritto e livelli di governo*. Torino: Giappichelli.

Carrozza, Paolo, Alfonso Di Giovine, and Giuseppe F. Ferrari (eds). 2009. *Diritto costituzionale comparato*. Roma-Bari: Laterza.

Ciolli, Ines. 2012. I diritti sociali. In *Il diritto costituzionale alla prova della crisi economica*. eds. Francesca Angelini and Marco Benvenuti, 83-114. Napoli: Jovene.

Cisotta, Roberto. 2007. Principi giurisprudenziali e nuove iniziative della Commissione in materia di *patient mobility* nell'Unione europea: un piccolo (o grande?) terremoto in atto. *Studi sull'integrazione europea* 1: 161-182.

Cocconi, Monica. 1998. *Il diritto alla tutela della salute*. Padova: Cedam.

Colapietro, Carlo. 1996. *La giurisprudenza costituzionale nella crisi dello Stato sociale*. Padova: Cedam.

Cousin, Mel. 2007. Patient Mobility and National Health System. *Legal issues of economic integration* 2: 183-193.

D'Aloia, Antonio. 2002. *Eguaglianza sostanziale e diritto diseguale*. Padova: Cedam.

D'Aloia, Antonio. 2003. Diritti e Stato autonomistico. Il modello dei livelli essenziali delle prestazioni. *Le Regioni* 6: 1063-1140.

D'Aloia, Antonio. 2012. I diritti sociali nell'attuale momento costituzionale. http://www.gruppodipisa.it.

D'Aloia, Antonio. 2014. Europa e diritti: luci e ombre dello schema di protezione *multilevel*. *Diritto dell'Unione europea* 1: 1-45.

D'Arrigo, Cosimo. 2001. Salute (diritto alla). In *Enciclopedia del Diritto*. Milano: Giuffrè.

D'Atena, Antonio. 2006. Costituzionalismo e tutela dei diritti fondamentali. In *Lezioni di diritto costituzionale*, ed. Antonio D'Atena, 1-13. Torino: Giappichelli.

De Waele, Henri. 2010. The Role of the European Court of Justice in the Integration Process: A Contemporary and Normative Assessment. *Hanse Law Review* 1: 3-26.

Di Federico, Giacomo. 2012. La direttiva 2011/24/UE e l'accesso alle prestazioni mediche nell'Unione europea. *Rivista di diritto della sicurezza sociale* 3: 683-703.

Di Federico, Giacomo. 2013. L'accesso alle cure mediche nell'Unione europea tra diritti fondamentali e sovranità nazionali. *Quaderni costituzionali* 3: 679-687.

Di Federico, Giacomo. 2014. Access to Healthcare in the Post-Lisbon Era and the Genuine Enjoyment of EU Citizens' Rights. In *The EU after Lisbon*, eds. Lucia Serena Rossi and Federico Casolari, 177-212. New York: Springer.

Ferrara, Rosario. 1997. Salute (Diritto alla). In *Digesto delle Discipline Pubblicistiche*, 513–538.

Ferrara, Rosario. 2010. Il diritto alla salute: i principi costituzionali. In *Salute e sanità*, ed. Rosario Ferrara, 3-64. Milano: Giuffrè.

Ferrari, Giuseppe F. 2011. *Le libertà: profili comparatistici*. Torino: Giappichelli.

France, George. 2001. *Federalismo, regionalismo e standard sanitari nazionali*. Milano: Giuffrè.

Gabriele, Francesco. 2013. Diritti sociali, unità nazionali e risorse (in)disponibili: sulla permanente violazione-inattuazione della Parte prima (quella "intoccabile"!) della Costituzione. *Rivista Associazione italiana costituzionalisti* 3: 1-29.

Giorgis, Andrea. 2003. Le garanzie giurisdizionali dei diritti costituzionali all'uguaglianza distributiva. In *Diritti e Costituzione. Profili evolutivi e dimensioni inedite*, ed. Antonio D'Aloia, 111-140. Milano: Giuffrè.

Grasso, Giorgio. 2012. *Il costituzionalismo della crisi. Uno studio sui limiti del potere e sulla sua legittimazione al tempo della globalizzazione*. Napoli: ESI.

Inglese, Marco. 2012. Le prestazioni sanitarie transfrontaliere e la tutela della salute. *Diritto comunitario e degli scambi internazionali* 1: 109-138.

Jackson, Vicki, and Mark Tushnet. 1999. *Comparative Constitutional Law*. New York: Foundation Press.

Kattelus, Mervi. 2014. Implementation of the Directive on the Application on Patient's Rights in Cross-border Healthcare (2011/24/EU) in Finland. *European Journal of Health Law* 1: 23- 32.

Longo, Erik. 2007. Il diritto ai migliori trattamenti sanitari nella giurisprudenza di Lussemburgo. *Quaderni costituzionali* 3: 662-666.

Luciani, Massimo. 1992. Diritto alla salute. In *Enciclopedia Giuridica Treccani*, vol. XXXII, 1-14.

Luciani, Massimo. 2013. Costituzione, bilancio, diritti e doveri dei cittadini. *Astrid Rassegna* 3: 1-47.

Martinico, Giuseppe. 2009. *L'integrazione "silente". La funzione interpretativa della Corte di giustizia e il diritto costituzionale europeo*. Napoli: Jovene.

Martinico, Giuseppe, and Oreste Pollicino. 2012. *The Interaction Between Europe's Legal Systems. Judicial Dialogue and the Creation of Supranational Laws*. Cheltenham: Edward Elgar Publishing.

Messineo, Donato. 2012. *La garanzia del "contenuto essenziale" dei diritti fondamentali. Dalla tutela della dignità umana ai livelli essenziali delle prestazioni*. Torino: Giappichelli.

Meyer, Hilko. 2013. Current Legislation on Cross-border Healthcare in the European Union. In *The Globalization of Health Care*, ed. Glenn Cohen, 83–110. Oxford: Oxford University Press.

Minni, Francesca, and Andrea Morrone. 2013. Il diritto alla salute nella giurisprudenza costituzionale della Corte Costituzionale italiana. *Rivista Associazione italiana dei costituzionalisti* 3: 1-12.

Montuschi, Luigi, and Diana Vincenzi Amato. 1976. Articolo 32. In *Commentario della Costituzione. Rapporti etico-sociali*, ed. Giuseppe Branca, 146-209. Bologna: Zanichelli.

Morana, Donatella. 2002. La tutela della salute, fra libertà e prestazioni, dopo la Riforma del Titolo V. A proposito della sentenza n. 282 del 2002 della Corte Costituzionale. *Giurisprudenza Costituzionale* 3: 2034-2042.

Morana, Donatella. 2013. I diritti a prestazione in tempo di crisi: istruzione e salute al vaglio dell'effettività. *Rivista Associazione italiana dei costituzionalisti* 4: 1-13.

Nys, Herman. 2014. The Transposition of the Directive on Patients' Rights in Cross-Care Healthcare in National Law by the Member States: Still a Lot of Effort to Be Made and Questions to Be Answered. *European Journal of Public Health* 1: 1-14.

Obermaier, Andreas. 2009. *The End of Territoriality? The Impact of ECJ Ruling on the British, German and French Social Policy*. Farnham: Ashgate.

Olsena, Solvita. 2014. Implementation of the Patients' Rights in Cross-border Healthcare Directive in Latvia. *European Journal of Health Law* 1: 46-55.

Peeters, Miek. 2012. Free Movement of Patients: Directive 2011/24 on the Application of Patients' Rights in Cross-border Healthcare. *European Journal of Public Health* 1: 29-60.

Prudil, Lucas. 2014. Implementation of the Directive 2011/24/EU in the Czech Republic. *European Journal of Health Law* 1: 15-22.

Requejo, Teresa. 2014. Cross-border Healthcare in Spain and the Implementation of the Directive 2011/24/EU on the Application of Patient's Rights in Cross-border Healthcare. *European Journal of Health Law* 1: 79-96.

Romeo, Graziella. 2013. I diritti sociali. In *Diritti e doveri*, ed. Luca Mezzetti, 505-529. Torino: Giappichelli.

Salazar, Carmela. 2013. Crisi economica e diritti fondamentali, Relazione al XVIII Convegno dell'Associazione italiana dei costituzionalisti. *Rivista Associazione italiana costituzionalisti*, 4: 1-39.

Santuari, Alceste. 2014. Profili giuridici di tutela del paziente e diritto alla mobilità sanitaria. Opportunità e vincoli finanziari. http://www.giustamm.it.

Schiek, Dagmar. 2012. *Economic and Social Integration. The Challenge for EU Constitutional Law*. Cheltenham: Edward Elgar Publishing.

Schwebag, Mike. 2014. Implementation of the Cross-border Care Directive in EU Member States: Luxembourg. *European Journal of Health Law* 1: 56-64.

Simoncini, Andrea, and Erik Longo. 2006. Articolo 32. In *Commentario alla Costituzione*, eds. Raffaele Bifulco, Alfonso Celotto and Marco Olivetti, 655-674. Torino: Utet.

Starr-Deelen, Donna, and Bart Deelen. 1996. The European Court of Justice as a Federator. *Publius: The Journal of Federalism* 26: 81-97.

Tega, Diletta. 2012. I diritti sociali nella dimensione multilivello tra tutele giuridiche e crisi economica. http://www.gruppodipisa.it.

Tripodina, Chiara. 2008. Articolo 32. In *Commentario breve alla Costituzione*, eds. Sergio Bartole and Roberto Bin, 321-332. Padova: Cedam.

Trucco, Lara. 2012. Livelli essenziali delle prestazioni e sostenibilità finanziaria dei diritti sociali. http://www.gruppodipisa.it.

Uccello Barretta, Laura. 2014. Il diritto alla salute nello spazio europeo: la mobilità sanitaria alla luce della direttiva 2011/24/UE. http://www.federalismi.it.

Van der Mei, Anne P. 2003. *Free Movement of Persons within the European Community*. Portland: Hart Publishing.

Van der Mei, Anne P. 2004. Cross-Border Access to Medical Care: Non Hospital Care and Waiting Lists. *Legal Issues of Economic Integration* 1: 57-67.

Vidalis, Takis, and Irini Kyriakaki. 2014. Cross-border Healthcare: Directive 2011/24 and the Greek Law. *European Journal of Health Law* 1: 33-45.

Violini, Lorenza. 2002. La tutela della salute e i limiti al potere di legiferare: sull'incostituzionalità di una legge regionale che vieta specifici interventi terapeutici senza adeguata istruttoria tecnico scientifica. *Le Regioni* 6: 1450-1461.

Weiler, Joseph H. H. 1987. The Court of Justice on Trial; A Review of Hjalte Rasmussen: On Law and Policy in the European Court of Justice. *Common Market Law Review* 24: 555-589.

Part IV
The Role of the Judge and General Principles in Selected Issues and Case Studies

The (Mis)-Use of General Principles of Law: *Lex Specialis* and the Relationship Between International Human Rights Law and the Laws of Armed Conflict

Silvia Borelli

Abstract The maxim *lex specialis derogat legi generali* is widely accepted as constituting a general principle of law. It entails that, when two norms apply to the same subject matter, the rule which is more specific should prevail and be given priority over that which is more general. In the international legal system, the concept is frequently resorted to by courts and tribunals as a tool of legal reasoning in order to resolve real or perceived antinomies between norms. One area in which the notion of *lex specialis* is frequently invoked is in the articulation of the relationship between international human rights law and international humanitarian law in situations of armed conflict. This has particularly been the case following the use of the term by the International Court of Justice in the *Nuclear Weapons* and *The Wall* Advisory Opinions. On closer analysis, it appears that those seminal decisions of the International Court of Justice, in using the language of *lex specialis,* did not intend that international humanitarian law should prevail over international human rights law. Rather, when it comes to the relationship between these two branches of law, what is commonly referred to as an application of the *lex specialis* principle is in reality no more than an application of the principle that treaties should be interpreted in the light of any relevant rules of international law binding on the parties. The chapter suggests that, due to the implications that international humanitarian law prevails over international human rights law, the language of *lex specialis* should be abandoned when discussing the relationship between the two bodies of law.

S. Borelli (✉)
Principal Lecturer in International Law and Director of Research, School of Law,
University of Bedfordshire, Bedfordshire, UK
Visiting Professor, University of Parma, Parma, Italy
e-mail: silvia.borelli@beds.ac.uk

© Springer International Publishing Switzerland 2015   265
L. Pineschi (ed.), *General Principles of Law - The Role of the Judiciary,*
Ius Gentium: Comparative Perspectives on Law and Justice 46,
DOI 10.1007/978-3-319-19180-5_13

1 Introduction

The principle commonly expressed in the maxim *lex specialis derogat legi generali* is a general principle of legal reasoning which has roots dating back—at least—to Roman law,[1] and is accepted in the majority of legal systems. The purpose of the principle may be seen as being to provide a basis for choice to resolve the normative antinomy resulting from two conflicting rules which apply to and regulate the same subject matter. In order to solve such conflicts, the principle *lex specialis derogat legi generali* entails that, when two rules regulating the same subject-matter conflict, priority is to be given to that which is more specific.[2]

The present chapter analyzes the way in which the principle *lex specialis derogat legi generali* has been utilized in international legal discourse, and in particular by international courts and tribunals, in order to articulate the relationship between the norms of two branches of international law, namely international humanitarian law and international human rights law, which are concurrently applicable to situations of armed conflict. Although much discussion in that regard has turned on the application of the *lex specialis* principle, it is suggested that the principle is not in fact an appropriate mechanism to resolve those situations in which international humanitarian law and international human rights law provide for diverging standards.

2 The Principle *Lex Specialis Derogat Legi Generali* in International Law

Within the international legal system, Article 38(1) of the Statute of the International Court of Justice (ICJ) is widely accepted as an enumeration of the sources of international law.[3] Article 38(1)(c) includes among those sources "the general principles of law recognized by civilized nations". Such "general principles" were similarly previously included in the equivalent provision contained in Article 38 of the Statute of the Permanent Court of International

---

[1]For discussion of the origins of the maxim, see, e.g., Lindroos (2005), p. 35.

[2]The precise operation of the principle is of course far more sophisticated and nuanced than this basic description implies and there exists a wealth of literature which attempts to identify the exact contours of the principle, including, e.g., when two rules should be regarded as regulating the same subject-matter. For an overview of the principle and discussion of many of these issues from the perspective of international law, see Koskeniemi (2004); International Law Commission Study Group on Fragmentation (2006a), pp. 30–114; see also Prud'homme (2007). For a jurisprudential discussion, see, e.g., Zorzetto (2013).

[3]Statute of the International Court of Justice (San Francisco, 24 October 1945), 25 UNTS 993. The provision in question formally constitutes merely a definition of the law which the ICJ is to apply in fulfilling its function of deciding "in accordance with international law such disputes as are submitted to it" [ibid., Article 38(1)].

Justice (PCIJ), on which Article 38 of the Statute of the present Court is substantially based.[4]

The PCIJ never referred expressly to Article 38(1)(c) of its Statute, whilst the ICJ, for its part, has only rarely made express reference to the category of general principles referred to in Article 38(1)(c),[5] and has refrained from outlining the contours of the notion, or expressly confirming that specific principles fall within it.[6] As a result of the reticence of the PCIJ and ICJ in expressly relying on Article 38(1)(c), "international lawyers have never reached agreement on the definition of the general principles mentioned in Art. 38".[7] Nevertheless, it is relatively clear that their essential characteristics are that they should be "unwritten legal norms of a wide-ranging character", which are "recognized in the municipal laws of States", and which must be capable of transposition at the international level.[8]

There is little doubt that the principle *lex specialis derogat legi generali*, together with its sister principles *lex posterior derogat priori* and *lex superior derogat inferior*, fit the definition of "general principles of law" as contained in Article 38(1)(c) of the ICJ Statute, insofar as they are (a) norms of general legal reasoning, which (b) are recognized in the majority (if not all) domestic legal systems, and (c) can be transposed to and applied at the international level.[9]

The resolution of conflicts between norms through application of the maxim *lex specialis derogat legi generali* has frequently been resorted to in the international legal system. In contrast to the principles of *lex posterior* and *lex superior*, the

---

[4]Statute of the Permanent Court of International Justice (Geneva, 16 December 1920), League of Nations, Treaty Series 6, 390. The drafting history of the provision reveals that the intention of the Advisory Committee of Jurists in including general principles amongst the sources of law which the PCIJ could apply was in large part to avoid any possibility of a *non liquet* resulting from the silence of the positive rules of conventional or customary international law: see the discussion of the debate in the Advisory Committee in Pellet (2012), pp. 739–742 (paras. 21–33) and 832 (para. 250).

[5]See Wolfrum (2011), para. 36; Pellet (2012), pp. 833–834 (para. 253). In a number of cases, the Court referred to the concept in summarizing the arguments of the parties, but then avoided taking any firm position as to whether the particular principle invoked qualified as a general principle within Article 38(1)(c) on other grounds: see, e.g., *Right of Passage over Indian Territory, Merits* [1960] ICJ Rep. 6, p. 43; *North Sea Continental Shelf (Federal Republic of Germany/Denmark; Federal Republic of Germany/Netherlands)* [1969] ICJ Rep. 3, p. 21 (para. 17). Notwithstanding the lack of express reference to Article 38(1)(c), the Court (and individual judges) have frequently invoked "general principles": for discussion, see Pellet (2012), pp. 838–839 (para. 265).

[6]In *South West Africa (Ethiopia v. South Africa; Liberia v. South Africa)* [1966] ICJ Rep. 6, p. 47 (para. 88), the Court denied that the "*actio popularis*", or right resident in any member of a community to take legal action in vindication of a public interest was at that time recognized as a matter of public international law, and held that it could not be "imported" into international law as constituting a general principle within the meaning of Article 38(1)(c).

[7]Pellet (2012), p. 834 (para. 254).

[8]Ibid., p. 834.

[9]The principle *lex specialis generalibus derogat* was indeed one of the examples given during the drafting of the provision which become Article 38(1)(c) of the Statute of the PCIJ; see Cheng (1953), p. 26, citing PCIJ, Advisory Committee of Jurists, *Procès-Verbaux of the Proceedings of the Committee, June 16th–July 24th, 1920, with Annexes*, 1920, p. 337. Cf. however Matz-Lück (2010), para. 14.

principle *lex specialis* does not figure among the rules of coordination included in the Vienna Convention on the Law of Treaties (VCLT),[10] nor has it been codified elsewhere as a rule of general application in international law. Nevertheless, it is frequently given effect in specific circumstances.

By way of example, Article 55 of the Articles on Responsibility of States for Internationally Wrongful Acts adopted by the International Law Commission (ILC) in 2001, entitled *"lex specialis"*, provides that the norms embodied in the remainder of the Articles do not apply "where and to the extent that the conditions for the existence of an internationally wrongful act or the content or implementation of the international responsibility of a State are governed by special rules of international law".[11]

In addition, the *lex specialis* principle has been recognized and applied by international courts and tribunals in a variety of contexts.

A first manner in which the *lex specialis* principle has been used is in order to explain the point that, in general—and to the extent that the relevant customary rule does not constitute *jus cogens*—States are free by entering into a treaty to modify the obligations which would otherwise be applicable between them under customary international law.[12] In other words, as a general matter, a treaty obligation, being more specific, will prevail over customary international law, as the more general.[13]

---

[10]Vienna Convention on the Law of Treaties (23 May 1969), 1155 UNTS 331. The principle of *lex posterior* as a principle of coordination is given effect in Article 30(3) of the VCLT as regards the relationship between subsequent treaties dealing with the same subject matter; see also Article 59 of the VCLT (Termination or suspension of the operation of a treaty implied by the conclusion of a later treaty). The *lex superior* principle finds expression in the provisions relating to the concept of *jus cogens* in Articles 53 and 64 of the VCLT; see also Article 103, Charter of the United Nations (San Francisco, 26 June 1945), 1 UNTS 16.

[11]International Law Commission, *Articles on Responsibility of States for Internationally Wrongful Acts* (2001), in *Report of the International Law Commission, 53rd Session, ILC Yearbook 2001*, vol. II, part two, pp. 26–143. See similarly, Article 64 of the ILC's Articles on Responsibility of International Organizations (2011), in *Report of the International Law Commission, 63rd Session*, UN Doc. A/66/10 (2011), chapter V. Cf. Article 17 of the ILC's 2006 Articles on Diplomatic Protection, in *Report of the International Law Commission, 58th Session, ILC Yearbook 2006*, vol II, part two, p. 24.

[12]See, e.g., *Continental Shelf (Tunisia/Libyan Arab Jamahiriya)* [1982] ICJ Rep. 18, p. 38 (para. 24).

[13]The point was implicitly recognized by the ICJ in *Military and Paramilitary Activities in and against Nicaragua (Merits)* [1986] ICJ Rep. 14. In the specific circumstances of that case, the Court ruled solely on the basis of the relevant obligations of the United States under customary international law, which were the only obligations over which it had jurisdiction. Nevertheless, it emphasized that, where parallel rules exist as a matter of both custom and conventional obligation, "in general, treaty rules being *lex specialis*, it would not be appropriate that a State should bring a claim based on a customary-law rule if it has by treaty already provided means for settlement of such a claim" [ibid, p. 137 (para. 274)]. For a particularly clear statement of the point (although without express reference to *lex specialis*), see *Dispute regarding Navigational and Related Rights (Costa Rica v. Nicaragua)*, [2009] ICJ Rep. 213, p. 233 (para. 35). For an application of the *lex specialis* principle in the context of investment treaty arbitration, see, e.g., *García Armas and García Gruber v. Venezuela*, Decision on Jurisdiction, 15 December 2014, paras. 158 and 167–175.

The application of the principle in this manner is qualified, in the sense that a treaty will only apply as *lex specialis* if and to the extent that the relevant treaty obligations between the parties make special provision for the specific question in issue, and the parties may thus be taken, to that extent, to have agreed to exclude the otherwise applicable rules of customary international law.[14]

The second manner in which the *lex specialis* principle may be used is as a means for articulating the relationship between norms contained in the same treaty, or in connected instruments, which are potentially applicable to the same subject-matter.[15] The principle of *lex specialis* has been extensively used in this way by the European Court of Human Rights (ECtHR) to explain the articulation between provisions within the Convention for the Protection of Human Rights and Fundamental Freedoms (ECHR)[16] which deal with the same subject matter. For example, the European Court has emphasized that the right pursuant to Article 5(4) of the ECHR of anyone deprived of their liberty to have the legality of their detention determined by a competent judicial body (*habeas corpus*) constitutes *lex specialis* as regards the more general right under Article 13 of anyone whose rights under the Convention have been violated to an effective remedy at the domestic level.[17] Similarly, it has held that the right to a fair trial under Article 6(1) of

---

[14]As put by the Tribunal in the *OSPAR Convention* arbitration, "our first duty is to apply the OSPAR Convention. An international Tribunal will also apply customary international law and general principles unless and to the extent that the parties have created a *lex specialis*" (*Dispute Concerning Access to Information under Article 9 of the OSPAR Convention*, Final Award, 2 July 2003, RIAA, vol. XXIII, 59, p. 87 (para. 84). The Tribunal added, ibid, that "even then, it must defer to a relevant *jus cogens* with which the Parties' *lex specialis* may be inconsistent". See also *Amoco International Finance Corporation v. Iran*, Iran-US C.T.R, vol. 15, 1987-II, p. 222 (para. 112).

[15]For instance, in the *Beagle Channel* arbitration, the Court of Arbitration had recourse to the principle as a subsidiary ground for rejecting the existence of a supposed conflict between the terms of Articles II and III of the Boundary Treaty of 23 July 1881 between Chile and Argentina insofar as those provisions attributed particular territory to one or other of the Parties. In that regard, the Court of Arbitration observed that: "all conflicts or anomalies can be disposed of by applying the rule *generalia specialibus non derogant*, on which basis Article II (*generalia*) would give way to Article III (*specialia*), the latter prevailing"; *Beagle Channel Arbitration (Argentina/ Chile)*, Award of 18 February 1977, RIAA, vol. XXI, 53, p. 100 (para. 39).

[16]Convention for the Protection of Human Rights and Fundamental Freedoms as amended by Protocols no. 11 and no. 14 (Rome, 4 November 1950).

[17]See, e.g., *Nikolova v. Bulgaria*, judgment of 25 March 1999, ECtHR, Rep. 1999-II, p. 25, para. 69. For a recent restatement of the relationship between the remedy enshrined in Article 5(4) and the more general right to an effective remedy under Article 13, see *A. v. United Kingdom* (App. no. 3455/05), ECtHR [GC], judgment of 19 February 2009, para. 202; see also ibid., para. 225, where the Court held that, in light of the findings as to Art. 5(4), it was not necessary separately to examine applicants' complaint under Article 13. Cf., however, *Georgia v. Russia (I)* (App. no. 13255/07), ECtHR [GC], judgment of 3 July 2014, paras. 210–16.

the ECHR constitutes *lex specialis vis-à-vis* the right to an effective remedy under Article 13.[18]

As regards articulation of rules relating to the same subject matter contained in different treaties, an example is given by the ILC Study Group on Fragmentation, which notes that, whilst the Ottawa Convention on Anti-Personnel Landmines[19] may be regarded as laying down the general law as to landmines, from another perspective it regulates "a 'special' aspect of the general rules of humanitarian law".[20] As a consequence, to the extent that the general rules of international humanitarian law (both treaty-based and customary) permitted the use of land-mines by belligerents in an armed conflict, for the parties to the Ottawa Convention, their right to do so is now limited.

Nevertheless, the application of rule *lex specialis* in such circumstances is not automatic. In the *Southern Bluefin Tuna* arbitration, the UNCLOS Annex VII arbi-tral tribunal recognized that there was some support in international law for the proposition that, where there was a framework treaty and an implementing treaty, the latter might operate as "*lex specialis* that governs general provisions of an antecedent treaty".[21] However, it went on to emphasize that:

> [I]t is a commonplace of international law and State practice for more than one treaty to bear upon a particular dispute. There is no reason why a given act of a State may not vio-late its obligations under more than one treaty. There is frequently a parallelism of trea-ties, both in their substantive content and in their provisions for settlement of disputes arising thereunder. The current range of international legal obligations benefits from a process of accretion and cumulation; in the practice of States, the conclusion of an imple-menting convention does not necessarily vacate the obligations imposed by the framework convention upon the parties to the implementing convention.[22]

---

[18]See, e.g., *Yankov v. Bulgaria* (App. no. 390847/97), ECtHR, judgment of 11 December 2003. By contrast, the Court has rejected the argument that Article 5(5) of the ECHR, which provides that everyone who has been the victim of an arrest or detention in contravention of Article 5, "shall have an enforceable right to compensation", constitutes *lex specialis* vis-à-vis the general power of the Court, contained in what is now Article 41 of the ECHR, to grant just satisfaction; see, e.g., *Neumeister v. Austria (Article 50)* (App. no. 1936/63), Series A, no. 17 (1974), paras. 29 and 30. The ECtHR has also invoked the *lex specialis* principle in order to justify examining complaints relating to an interference with freedom of assembly only under Article 11, despite the fact that Article 10 was, at least potentially, also implicated; see, e.g., *Ezelin v. France*, judg-ment of 26 April 1991, *Series A*, no. 202 (1991), para. 35; *Djavit An v. Turkey*, judgment of 20 February 2003, ECtHR, Rep. 2003-III, p. 251, para. 39.

[19]Convention on the prohibition of the use, production, stockpiling, and transfer of anti-personal mines and on their destruction (Ottawa, 18 September 1997), 2056 UNTS 241.

[20]ILC Study Group on Fragmentation (2006a), para. 111.

[21]UNCLOS Annex VII Arbitral Tribunal, *Southern Bluefin Tuna (Australia-Japan; New Zealand-Japan)*, Award on Jurisdiction and Admissibility, 4 August 2000, RIAA, vol. XXIII, 1, p. 40 (para. 52).

[22]Ibid.

The operation of the *lex specialis* principle in the international legal system has been the subject of in-depth (if not always clear) discussion in the context of the work of the ILC on Fragmentation of International Law. In its "Conclusions" adopted in 2006, the ILC's Study Group on Fragmentation described the maxim *lex specialis derogat legi generali* as "a generally accepted technique of interpretation and conflict resolution in international law",[23] and noted that it "suggests that whenever two or more norms deal with the same subject matter, priority should be given to the norm that is more specific".[24]

In the more detailed study underlying those final conclusions, the Study Group postulated that "the *lex specialis* principle" might operate in two ways, "[a] particular rule may be considered an *application* of a general standard in a given circumstance. The special relates to the general as does administrative regulation to law in domestic legal order. Or it may be considered as a *modification, overruling* or a *setting aside* of the latter".[25] However, in that regard, the ILC also noted that "whether a rule is seen as an 'application', 'modification' or 'exception' to another rule depends on how we view those rules in the environment in which they are applied, including what we see as their object and purpose".[26]

3 *Lex Specialis* as the Coordinating Principle Between International Humanitarian Law and International Human Rights Law?

In light of the preceding overview of the application of the *lex specialis* principle generally in public international law, the focus turns to the manner in which it has been used (and arguably abused) in articulating the relationship between international humanitarian law and international human rights law.[27] The present section will examine first the approach of the ICJ to the relationship between the two branches of law, before briefly surveying the way in which selected international human rights monitoring bodies and courts have dealt with the issue.[28]

---

[23]ILC Study Group on Fragmentation (2006b), para. 5.

[24]Ibid. see also ILC Study Group on Fragmentation (2006a), pp. 34–64, para. 55 ff.

[25]ILC Study Group on Fragmentation (2006a), para. 88 (footnotes omitted).

[26]Ibid. para. 97.

[27]For overviews, see e.g. Doswald-Beck and Vité (1993) and Arnold and Quénivet (2008). See also Sassòli and Olson (2008).

[28]The discussion in Sect. 3.2 below is limited to some of the most significant examples. For a detailed survey of the practice of UN human rights bodies and regional systems, see van den Herik and Duffy (2014).

3.1 The Approach of the International Court of Justice

The classic statement that *lex specialis* in some way constitutes the principle governing the interrelationship of international humanitarian law and international human rights law as applied in situations of armed conflict is the ICJ's *Nuclear Weapons* Advisory Opinion. There the Court, in discussing the applicability of the International Covenant on Civil and Political Rights (ICCPR)[29] in situations of hostilities, observed that:

> [T]he protection of the [ICCPR] does not cease in times of war, except by operation of Article 4 of the Covenant whereby certain provisions may be derogated from in a time of national emergency. Respect for the right to life is not, however, such a provision. In principle, the right not arbitrarily to be deprived of one's life applies also in hostilities. The test of what is an arbitrary deprivation of life, however, then falls to be determined by the applicable *lex specialis*, namely, the law applicable in armed conflict which is designed to regulate the conduct of hostilities. Thus whether a particular loss of life, through the use of a certain weapon in warfare, is to be considered an arbitrary deprivation of life contrary to Article 6 of the Covenant, can only be decided by reference to the law applicable in armed conflict and not deduced from the terms of the Covenant itself.[30]

The notion that international humanitarian law constitutes "*lex specialis*" in relation to the rules of international human rights law was subsequently reiterated and expanded upon by the ICJ in 2004 in *The Wall* Advisory Opinion.[31] The Court, having cited the relevant passage from the *Nuclear Weapons* Opinion, reiterated that, subject to the possibility of derogation recognized by human rights treaties, international human rights law continued to apply in case of armed conflict.[32] It then went on to explain that:

> As regards the relationship between international humanitarian law and human rights law, there are thus three possible situations: some rights may be exclusively matters of international humanitarian law; others may be exclusively matters of human rights law; yet others may be matters of both these branches of international law.[33]

Although the ICJ did not in that context suggest any general coordinating criterion for the third situation (i.e. those in which the rights in question were "matters of both … branches of international law"), the language of *lex specialis* again made an appearance in the following lines. The Court went on to note that, in order to answer the question facing it, i.e. whether the actions of Israel were inconsistent with its international obligations, and, if so, what were the consequences, it had to "take into

---

[29]International Covenant on Civil and Political Rights (New York, 16 December 1966), 999 UNTS 171.

[30]*Legality of the Threat or Use of Nuclear Weapons*, Advisory Opinion [1996] ICJ Rep. 240 (hereinafter "*Nuclear Weapons*"), para. 25.

[31]*Legal Consequences of the Construction of a Wall in the Occupied Palestinian Territory*, Advisory Opinion [2004] ICJ Rep. 136 (hereinafter "*The Wall*").

[32]Ibid., para. 106.

[33]Ibid.

consideration both these branches of international law, namely human rights law and, as *lex specialis*, international humanitarian law".[34]

The Court's recourse to the term *lex specialis* in its two Advisory Opinions to denote the role of international humanitarian law is problematic, and raises as many questions as it answers.

As Marko Milanovic has convincingly shown in his recent study on the "lost origins" of the *lex specialis* principle as the mechanism for articulating the relationship between international humanitarian law and international human rights law,[35] it appears that the principle was not generally invoked in the academic literature as regulating the relationship between the two bodies of law prior to the *Nuclear Weapons* Opinion.[36] Further, the "*lex specialis*" principle was not widely relied upon by the States which made submissions in *Nuclear Weapons*; it would appear to be traceable back to a single (ambiguous) passage in the written submission of the United Kingdom before the Court, which itself did not make reference to the Latin maxim in extenso.[37]

In the two Advisory Opinions, the ICJ itself did not invoke the full form of the maxim *lex specialis derogat legi generali*, nor did it as such refer to the "*lex specialis* principle*"; rather, it used the abbreviated tag *lex specialis* to characterize international humanitarian law. Indeed, the manner in which the Court used the tag does not appear to correspond to the principle as contained in the Latin maxim as such. That maxim, in its strict sense, and as is clear from the word "derogat", implies the (partial or total) disapplication or displacement of the general law in favor of the special law. However, in both *Nuclear Weapons* and *The Wall* the starting point of the Court's analysis was precisely that—subject to any relevant derogation permitted in accordance with the terms of the relevant instrument—international human rights law was *not* disapplied or displaced by the existence of an armed conflict, and instead continued to apply *in parallel* with international humanitarian law.

In any case, the use of the words *lex specialis* in *Nuclear Weapons* occurred in the specific context of the Court's discussion of the narrow question of the operation in situations of armed conflict of the right to life under Article 6 of the ICCPR, which prohibits the "arbitrary" deprivation of life. In that regard, what the Court appeared to have envisaged by its reference to *lex specialis* is that, whilst both international humanitarian law and international human rights law apply to situations of armed conflict, the relevant rules of international humanitarian law can be taken into account in determining when a deprivation of life is to be considered "arbitrary" for the purposes of Article 6. Far from being an application of

---

[34]Ibid.

[35]See Milanovic (2014b).

[36]In his review of the literature predating the *Nuclear Weapons* Advisory Opinion (Ibid.), however, Milanovic omits to mention the use of *lex specialis* in this sense in Bothe et al. (1982), p. 619.

[37]See Milanovic (2014b).

the *lex specialis* principle, such an approach is, in fact, far closer to the principle of systemic interpretation. That principle, which is embodied in Article 31(3)(c) of the VCLT, and forms part of the generally applicable rules of treaty interpretation, requires that, in interpreting a treaty provision, the interpreter should take into account "any relevant rules of international law applicable in the relations between the parties".

Understood in this sense, the reference to the *lex specialis* nature of international humanitarian law has nothing to do with international humanitarian law *prevailing over* or *displacing* international human rights law, but rather would appear to be used as shorthand for the proposition that, where human rights obligations fall to be applied in a situation of armed conflict, due effect should be given to the requirement to interpret the relevant obligations in light of, and consistently with, the equally applicable rules of international humanitarian law.

In order to elucidate what the ICJ may have intended by referring to *lex specialis*, it is instructive to examine the manner in which the Court went on to apply the relevant standards of international humanitarian law and international human rights law in *The Wall*.

The ICJ identified a variety of applicable obligations, under both international humanitarian law and international human rights law, which were potentially implicated by Israel's construction of the security barrier and the associated regime,[38] before proceeding to examine whether the conduct of Israel was in principle inconsistent with those obligations. In considering the potential violation of the relevant international human rights law instruments, the Court did not use international humanitarian law to inform its reading of the scope of Israel's obligations under the ICCPR, the International Covenant on Economic, Social and Cultural Rights (ICESCR)[39] and the Convention on the Rights of the Child.[40] The Court discussed both the possibility of derogation under some of the instruments, and the "qualifying clauses" contained therein, solely in terms of international human rights law[41] and held that neither affected the conclusion that Israel's

---

[38]*The Wall*, paras. 132–134.

[39]International Covenant on Economic, Social and Cultural Rights (New York, 16 December 1966), 993 UNTS 3.

[40]United Nations Convention on the Rights of the Child (New York, 20 November 1989), 1577 UNTS 3. Prior to considering the relevant obligations under international human rights law, the Court discussed the consistency of Israel's conduct with the various relevant rules of international humanitarian law. Whilst acknowledging that some rules of international humanitarian law enabled account to be taken of "military exigencies in certain circumstances", the Court held that either the relevant norms did not permit such considerations to be taken into account, or (to the extent that they did) that it had not been established that the relevant conduct had been "absolutely necessary" (*The Wall*, para. 135).

[41]Ibid., para. 136.

conduct was inconsistent with its obligations under international human rights law.[42] As observed by Bethlehem, the Court "did not undertake any further analysis of the relationship between the applicable international humanitarian law rules and those of the ICCPR that it held to apply, simply commingling in its analysis various provisions from both strands".[43]

It thus appears that the ICJ, in characterizing international humanitarian law as *lex specialis* in its two Advisory Opinions, did so in a very particular sense. It is relatively clear that it did not intend to refer to the maxim *lex specialis derogat legi generali*, or, at least, that it did not intend the consequence to be the disapplication of international human rights law in favor of international humanitarian law. Rather, the recourse to Latin appears to have been used merely to indicate that the rules of international humanitarian law were to be given effect, as far as possible, where relevant in the assessment of whether there had been compliance with obligations under international human rights law.

The ILC, in its 2006 Study on Fragmentation, appears to have perceived the difficulty in characterizing the ICJ's approach in *Nuclear Weapons* as one involving application of the maxim *lex specialis derogat legi generali* in its strongest form. On the one hand, it recognized that the Court had expressly affirmed that international human rights law continued to apply, noting that "the two fields of law applied concurrently, or within each other".[44] Nevertheless, in an apparent attempt to square the Court's use of the term with the fact that the maxim *lex specialis* implies the disapplication of the general norm in favor of the special, it went on to suggest that:

> [F]rom another perspective ... the law of armed conflict – and in particular its more relaxed standard of killing – set aside whatever standard might have been provided under the practice of the Covenant.[45]

The suggestion by the ILC that international humanitarian law had "set aside" the standard otherwise applicable under the "practice" of the ICCPR in respect of the right to life is misleading. Notwithstanding the Court's reference to *lex specialis*, the applicable standard under Article 6 of the ICCPR remained at all times that of arbitrariness; what the Court suggested was rather that what was to

---

[42]As regards the ICESCR, the Court found that the *regime* created by Israel infringed several of its obligations thereunder, and noted merely that this was the case since the restrictions on the relevant rights "fail to meet a condition laid down by Article 4 [ICESCR], that is to say that their implementation must be 'solely for the purpose of promoting the general welfare in a democratic society'" (Ibid.). Similarly, in verifying whether the interference with the right to freedom of movement under Article 12 of the ICCPR constituted a permissible limitation, the ICJ adopted wholesale, and without further elaboration, the relevant standards as articulated by the Human Rights Committee, and made no reference to any qualification in that regard resulting from the rules of international humanitarian law (Ibid.).

[43]Bethlehem (2013), p. 185.

[44]ILC Study Group on Fragmentation (2006b).

[45]Ibid., 53, para. 96 (emphasis added).

be considered as "arbitrary" had to be interpreted taking account of the circumstances, including the fact that the situation in question was an armed conflict to which the laws of armed conflict applied.

It is notable that, since *The Wall*, the ICJ appears to have deliberately avoided making use of the language of *lex specialis* in articulating the relationship between international humanitarian law and international human rights law. In its 2005 judgment in *Armed Activities on the Territory of the Congo*, one of the questions facing the Court was whether the conduct of members of the Uganda People's Defence Force (UPDF), which the Court had found to be attributable to Uganda, constituted a breach of the latter State's obligations under international humanitarian law and international human rights law. Having cited the passage from *The Wall* as to the three possible situations as regards the applicability of international humanitarian law and international human rights law,[46] it summarized its finding in that case as having been that "both branches of international law, namely international human rights law and international humanitarian law, would have to be taken into consideration".[47] Notably, it omitted the specification that, in doing so, international humanitarian law was to be treated as *lex specialis*.

Thereafter, in assessing whether Uganda had breached its various obligations under international human rights law,[48] the Court did not discuss how the relevant standards were to be interpreted in light of the existence of an armed conflict and the concurrent applicability of international humanitarian law rules. Admittedly, the absence of any reference to the fact that international humanitarian law was to be taken into consideration as *lex specialis* might be explained on the basis that the conduct at issue was blatant and egregious, and was prohibited equally under both international humanitarian law and international human rights law. Nevertheless, it is striking that the Court carved out the citation from *The Wall* in such a way as to avoid any reference to the notion of *lex specialis*.

Most recently, in *Application of the Convention on the Prevention and Punishment of the Crime of Genocide (Croatia v. Serbia)*, the parties had debated the issue of whether acts which were lawful as a matter of international

---

[46]*Armed Activities on the Territory of the Congo (Democratic Republic of the Congo v. Uganda)*, [2005] ICJ Rep. 168 (hereinafter "*Armed Activities*"), para. 216.

[47]Ibid., para. 216.

[48]Ibid., para. 117. The ICJ listed a variety of international humanitarian law and international human rights law instruments without making distinction as between *lex generalis* and *lex specialis*, namely the 1907 Hague Regulations (which the Court deemed to be applicable to both Uganda and the Democratic Republic of Congo due to its customary status); the Fourth Geneva Convention; the ICCPR; Additional Protocol I to the Geneva Conventions; the African Charter on Human and Peoples' Rights (ACHPR) (Banjul, 27 June 1981); the Convention on the Rights of the Child, and its Optional Protocol on the Involvement of Children in Armed Conflict (New York, 25 May 2000), 2133 UNTS 161.

humanitarian law could constitute the *actus reus* of genocide. In that regard, the Court emphasized that the Genocide Convention and international humanitarian law:

> [A]re two distinct bodies of rules, pursuing different aims. The Convention seeks to prevent and punish genocide as a crime under international law (Preamble), "whether committed in time of peace or in time of war" (Article I), whereas international humanitarian law governs the conduct of hostilities in an armed conflict and pursues the aim of protecting diverse categories of persons and objects.[49]

Although it took the position that, in light of the limited scope of its jurisdiction, it was not required to "rule, in general or in abstract terms, on the relationship between the Genocide Convention and international humanitarian law",[50] the Court nevertheless added that:

> [I]n so far as both of these bodies of rules may be applicable in the context of a particular armed conflict, the rules of international humanitarian law might be relevant in order to decide whether the acts alleged by the Parties constitute genocide within the meaning of Article II of the Convention.[51]

Further, later in its judgment, in the context of its examination of Serbia's counter-claim, the Court observed that:

> [T]here can be no doubt that, as a general rule, a particular act may be perfectly lawful under one body of legal rules and unlawful under another. Thus it cannot be excluded in principle that an act carried out during an armed conflict and lawful under international humanitarian law can at the same time constitute a violation by the State in question of some other international obligation incumbent upon it.[52]

The Genocide Convention, to the extent it may properly be characterized as a human rights instrument, is obviously of a very different type from the ICCPR or ICESCR; it is concerned with the prohibition, prevention and criminalization of the crime of genocide at the international level, rather than with the conferring of specific rights on individuals with corresponding obligations to respect those rights imposed upon States. Nevertheless, the Court's observations resonate with the overarching question of the articulation of the relationship between different standards in different areas of law. They appear to mark both a further step in the careful retreat from use of the term *lex specialis*, and recognition that the question of the interaction of norms deriving from different areas of law is substantially more complex, and cannot be resolved solely through an application of the *lex specialis* principle.

---

[49]*Application of the Convention on the Prevention and Punishment of the Crime of Genocide* (*Croatia v. Serbia*), *Merits*, Judgment of 3 February 2015 (hereinafter "*Croatian Genocide*"), para. 153.

[50]Ibid., para. 154.

[51]Ibid. See also ibid., para. 85.

[52]Ibid., para. 474.

3.2 The Relationship Between International Humanitarian Law and International Human Rights Law in the Practice of Human Rights Bodies

Despite the somewhat different perception by some academic commentators, the majority of human rights bodies appear not to have subscribed to the suggestion by the ICJ that the relationship between international humanitarian law and international human rights law is one of *lex specialis/lex generalis*.

The terminology of *lex specialis* is notably absent from the practice of the Human Rights Committee. The Committee's General Comment no. 31 was adopted on 29 March 2004, several years after the *Nuclear Weapons* Advisory Opinion and only a few months before the ICJ handed down its decision in *The Wall*.[53] In dealing with the question of the continued applicability of the ICCPR in times of armed conflict, the Committee noted that:

> [T]he Covenant applies also in situations of armed conflict to which the rules of international humanitarian law are applicable. While, in respect of certain Covenant rights, more specific rules of international humanitarian law may be specially relevant for the purposes of the interpretation of Covenant rights, both spheres of law are complementary, not mutually exclusive.[54]

This approach, whilst corresponding in broad terms to the approach of the ICJ to the applicability of the ICCPR to armed conflict, is far more subtly and carefully phrased. On the one hand, whilst not specifying which, the Committee limits the potential relevance of international humanitarian law to the interpretation of only certain rights under the ICCPR. On the other, although recognizing that the rules of international humanitarian law "may be specially relevant" for the *interpretation* of the Covenant, it eschews the use of the language of *lex specialis*, and the corresponding ambiguity as to whether the relationship is one in which international humanitarian law prevails over the ICCPR.

Other monitoring bodies have adopted the notion of *lex specialis* in part, although without giving priority to international humanitarian law. For instance, in *Coard v. United States*, in discussing the continued applicability of the American Declaration on Human Rights[55] in situations of armed conflict and occupation, and rejecting the argument by the United States that "the situation denounced was governed wholly by international humanitarian law",[56] the Inter-American Commission on Human Rights observed that:

> [I]n a situation of armed conflict, the test for assessing the observance of a particular right, such as the right to liberty, may, under given circumstances, be distinct from that

---

[53]Human Rights Committee, "General Comment No. 31. Nature of the General Legal Obligation Imposed on States Parties to the Covenant", 29 March 2004, UN Doc. CCPR/C/21/Rev.1/Add.13.

[54]Ibid., para. 11.

[55]American Declaration on the Rights and Duties of Man, OAS Res. XXX, adopted on 2 May 1948, reprinted in *American Journal of International Law Supplement* 43, 133.

[56]*Coard v. United States* (Case 10.951), I/ACommHR, Rep. no. 109/99, 29 September 1999, para. 38.

applicable in a time of peace. For that reason, the standard to be applied must be deduced by reference to the applicable *lex specialis*.[57]

The Commission went on to emphasize, however, that:

[A]s a general matter, while the Commission may find it necessary to look to the applicable rules of international humanitarian law when interpreting and applying the norms of the inter-American human rights system, where those bodies of law provide levels of protection which are distinct, the Commission is bound by its Charter-based mandate to give effect to the normative standard which best safeguards the rights of the individual.[58]

The Commission has adopted a similar approach under the American Convention on Human Rights (ACHR),[59] Article 29(b) of which provides that no provision of the Convention "shall be interpreted as ... restricting the enjoyment or exercise of any right or freedom recognized by virtue of the laws of any State Party or by virtue of another convention to which one of the said states is a party". For instance, in *Abella* the Commission noted that that the provisions of the American Convention and humanitarian law instruments may apply concurrently, and observed that Article 29(b) of the ACHR required it "to take due notice of and, where appropriate, give legal effect to applicable humanitarian law rules".[60] However, at the same time, it observed that:

[W]here there are differences between legal standards governing the same or comparable rights in the American Convention and a humanitarian law instrument, the Commission is duty bound to give legal effort to the provision(s) of that treaty with the higher standard(s) applicable to the right(s) or freedom(s) in question. If that higher standard is a rule of humanitarian law, the Commission should apply it.[61]

By contrast, the Inter-American Court of Human Rights (IACtHR) has taken a different approach. It has implicitly rejected any application of the *lex specialis* principle, and has adopted a far more radical line, according to which, for parties to the ACHR, their obligations thereunder prevail, and the conduct of a State falls to be assessed solely in accordance with the obligations under the American Convention, whether or not that conduct is permitted under any other body of law.

In *Las Palmeras (Preliminary Objections)*, the IACtHR held that it was competent "to determine whether any norm of domestic or international law applied by a State, in times of peace or armed conflict, is compatible or not with the American Convention".[62] At the same time, it emphasized that it was con-

---

[57]Ibid., para. 42 (footnote omitted; the relevant footnote referred to the *Nuclear Weapons Opinion*).

[58]*Coard v. United States*, para. 42.

[59]American Convention on Human Rights (San José, 22 November 1969), 1144 UNTS 123.

[60]*Abella v. Argentina* (Case 11.137), I/ACommHR, Rep. no. 55/97, 18 November 1997, para. 164.

[61]Ibid., paras. 164–165; for further discussion, see Zegveld (1998).

[62]*Las Palmeras* Case (*Preliminary Objections*), I/ACtHR, Series C no. 67 (2000).

cerned only with the compatibility with the American Convention of the conduct of States in purported application of international law, and that it had no jurisdiction as such to assess compliance with instruments of international humanitarian law:

> [I]n order to carry out this examination, the Court interprets the norm in question and analyzes it in the light of the provisions of the Convention. The result of this operation will always be an opinion in which the Court will say whether or not that norm or that fact is compatible with the American Convention. The latter has only given the Court competence to determine whether the acts or the norms of the States are compatible with the Convention itself, and not with the 1949 Geneva Conventions.[63]

On the other hand, although applying solely the American Convention (and/or other relevant instruments over which it has jurisdiction), the Inter-American Court has asserted the possibility of having recourse to considerations deriving from international humanitarian law in interpreting the provisions of the American Convention in situations of armed conflict.[64] In addition, although not going so far as to assert its competence to declare a State internationally responsible for violations of international humanitarian law, it has stated that it is able to "observe" whether the conduct of the respondent State was also contrary to international humanitarian law.[65]

By contrast, at least until very recently, the ECtHR has refrained from making any reference to the possibility of inconsistency between the ECHR and international humanitarian law. Further, it has not sought to apply (nor has it until comparatively recently even mentioned) the notion of *lex specialis* in this context. Even when faced with cases involving alleged violations of provisions of the European Convention which had occurred in situations of occupation or armed conflict, the Court made no mention of the relevant observations of the ICJ in the *Nuclear Weapons* and *The Wall* Advisory Opinions in its reasoning, and did not even refer to the relevant passages.[66]

Most notably, in a number of cases arising out of the internal armed conflict in Chechnya, the Court was faced with questions relating to the conduct of the

---

[63]Ibid., paras. 32–34.

[64]See, e.g., *Bámaca Velásquez v. Guatemala*, IACtHR, Series C no. 70 (2002), where the Inter-American Court, having noted that the capture and disappearance of a former guerilla commander had occurred in a situation which was properly characterized as an internal conflict (paras. 121(b) and 207), found that "the relevant provisions of the Geneva Conventions may be taken into consideration as elements for the interpretation of the American Convention" (para. 209). Nevertheless, as noted by van den Herik and Duffy (2014), p. 15, a more careful look at the Court's approach in applying the relevant norms "brings into question to what extent it really used international humanitarian law as a tool of interpretation of the relevant Convention provisions"; see further Moir (2003).

[65]*Bámaca Velásquez v. Guatemala* cit., para. 208.

[66]The first instance in which the Court made reference to the relevant passages from the case law of the ICJ in the "Relevant International Law Materials" section of its judgment (which does not form part of its reasoning on the merits) was *Al-Skeini v. United Kingdom* (App. no. 55721/07), ECtHR [GC], judgment of 7 July 2011, where the Court set out the relevant passage from *The Wall* (para. 90), as well as referring to *Armed Activities* (para. 91). See previously the joint dissenting opinion of judges Fura-Sandström, Björgvinsson and Ziemele attached to the Chamber judgment in *Kononov v. Latvia* (App. no. 36376/04), ECtHR, judgment of 24 July 2008 (para. 5); the notion does not make an appearance in the subsequent Grand Chamber judgment of 17 May 2010.

Russian armed forces resulting in the killings of civilians.[67] In those cases, which raised issues of violations of Article 2 of the ECHR in both its substantive and procedural aspects, the Court, whilst recognizing the fact that the conduct at issue had taken place in the context of the State response to an armed insurgency, made no express mention of the relevant standards under international humanitarian law. Rather, it simply sought to apply, in a way which took into account the fact that the conduct at issue had taken place in the context of military operations, the standards on the use of force which it had elaborated in its case law under Article 2 of the ECHR in cases involving law enforcement operations.[68]

More recently, an express mention of international humanitarian law appeared in the decision of the Grand Chamber in *Varnava v. Turkey*, handed down in 2009. In that case, which concerned disappearances in Cyprus during the Turkish invasion and subsequent occupation of the northern part of the island in 1974, the Court limited itself to holding that Article 2 of the ECHR had to "be interpreted in so far as possible in light of the general principles of international law, including the rules of international humanitarian law which play an indispensable and universally accepted role in mitigating the savagery and inhumanity of armed conflict".[69] However, the Court did not make any mention of international humanitarian law as constituting *lex specialis*, but squarely based its recourse to relevant rules of international humanitarian law on the principle of systemic interpretation.

4 Recent Developments: Testing the *Lex Specialis* Approach

The vast majority of the cases in which the *lex specialis* approach has been applied in practice, as well as most theoretical musings on the principle, deal with the "textbook" example of protection of life in armed conflict. Two recent cases, however, have thrown into stark relief the complex and difficult issues resulting from the parallel application and inter-relationship of international humanitarian law and international human rights law in relation to other rights, notably the right to liberty.

---

[67]*Isayeva v. Russia* (App. no. 57950/00), ECtHR, judgment of 24 February 2005; *Khashiyev and Akayeva v. Russia* (App. nos. 57942/00 and 57945/00), ECtHR, judgment of 24 February 2005; *Isayeva, Yusupova, and Bazayeva v. Russia* (App. nos. 57947/00, 57948/00, and 57949/00), ECtHR, judgment of 24 February 2005. For commentary, see Abresch (2005), Orakelashvili (2008), Bowring (2009).

[68]See, e.g., *Isayeva v. Russia* cit., para. 175.

[69]*Varnava and others v. Turkey* (Apps. nos. 16064-6/90 and 16068-73/90), ECtHR [GC], judgment of 18 September 2009, para. 185; see also, although less explicitly, the Chamber judgment of 10 January 2008, para. 130.

The cases in question are the decision of the Grand Chamber of the European Court in *Hassan v. United Kingdom*[70] and that of the High Court of England and Wales in *Serdar Mohammed v. Ministry of Defence*.[71] Both cases arose under the ECHR, and approach the question of the interaction between the European Convention and international humanitarian law on the assumption that the Convention is in principle applicable extraterritorially, including in situations of armed conflict.[72] In both cases, the ECtHR was confronted with the question of the compatibility of detention in armed conflict with Article 5 of the ECHR, a provision which, both in its terms and in the way in which it has been interpreted by the European Court, is extremely specific both as to the limited nature of the catalogue of permissible grounds for deprivation of liberty, and as to what is required in terms of procedural guarantees for those detained.[73]

4.1 Hassan v. United Kingdom: Disapplication by Interpretation?

The decision of the Grand Chamber of the ECtHR in *Hassan v. United Kingdom*, handed down in September 2014, concerned the alleged violation of Convention rights arising out of the arrest, detention, and interrogation of an Iraqi civilian in the period immediately preceding the declaration of the "end of active hostilities" in the 2003 invasion of Iraq.[74] The application to the Court complained of violations of, inter alia, Article 5 of the ECHR, on the ground that the detention of Mr. Hassan

---

[70]*Hassan v. United Kingdom* (App. no. 29750/09), ECtHR [GC], judgment of 16 September 2014 (hereinafter "*Hassan*").

[71]*Serdar Mohammed v. Ministry of Defence* [2014] EWHC 1369 (QB) (2 May 2014) (herein after "*Serdar Mohammed*").

[72]See, e.g., *Al-Skeini v. United Kingdom* cit.; *Al-Jedda v. United Kingdom* (App. no. 27021/08), ECtHR [GC], judgment of 7 July 2011.

[73]The Court has consistently emphasised (including as regards cases of domestic preventive detention) that the grounds for detention set out in Article 5(1) are an exhaustive list: see, e.g., *Ireland v. United Kingdom* (App. no. 5310/71), ECtHR, judgment of 18 January 1978, para. 194; *Saadi v. United Kingdom* (App. no. 13229/03), ECtHR [GC], judgment of 21 January 2008, para. 43; *A and others v. United Kingdom* (App. no. 3455/05), ECtHR [GC], judgment of 19 February 2009, paras. 162–163; *Al-Jedda v. United Kingdom* cit., paras. 99–100.

[74]The applicant was the brother of Tarek Hassan who had been arrested by UK troops on 23 April 2003, a few days before the declaration by the Coalition that "major hostilities" had ended (1 May 2003) and the commencement of the occupation the Coalition. Following his arrest, Tarek Hassan was detained in the US-run military facility at Camp Bucca and interrogated by UK intelligence agents. Having been cleared for release, he was released on 2 May in an unspecified location in Basra province. His body was discovered several months later in a location some 700 km from Basra. In addition to the alleged violation of Article 5, the application before the Court alleged violations of Articles 2 and 3 of the ECHR.

had not been in compliance with Article 5(1), and that he had been denied the procedural guarantees enshrined in Article 5(2) to (4).

The *lex specialis* rule played a central role in the arguments of the UK government before the European Court. The point was first raised in relation to the question of whether the victim had been within the "jurisdiction" of the UK for the purposes of Article 1 of the ECHR. In that regard, the United Kingdom argued, inter alia, that the jurisdictional link of "State agent authority"—according to which an exercise of jurisdiction for the purposes of Article 1 might be found to exist "where the Contracting State's agents operating outside its territory exercised 'total and exclusive control' or 'full and exclusive control' over an individual"[75]— did not find application during the active phase of an international armed conflict. It did so on the basis that in such a situation "the conduct of the Contracting State would, instead, be subject to all the requirements of international humanitarian law".[76] The European Court rejected that argument, noting that "to accept the government's argument on this point would be inconsistent with the case law of the International Court of Justice, which has held that international human rights law and international humanitarian law may apply concurrently".[77]

The language of *lex specialis* then appeared again in the primary argument of the UK government in resisting the merits of the claim as to violation of Article 5. In this regard, the United Kingdom argued that, where the ECHR fell to be applied in an international armed conflict, "the application had to take account of international humanitarian law, which applied as the *lex specialis*, and might operate to modify or even displace a given provision of the Convention".[78] In the alternative, it argued that, if the Convention were not as such modified or displaced, nevertheless, Article 5 had to be interpreted consistent with other rules of international law, and that, in particular, the list of permissible grounds for detention under Article 5(1) "had to be interpreted in such a way that it took account of and was compatible with the applicable *lex specialis*, namely international humanitarian law".[79]

Finally, as regards the possibility of derogation from Article 5 under Article 15 of the ECHR, the United Kingdom argued that "consistently with the practice of all other Contracting Parties which had been involved in such operations" it had not derogated. In a somewhat circular, question-begging manner, it suggested that:

> [T]here had been no need to do so, since the Convention could and did accommodate detention in such cases, having regard to the *lex specialis*, international humanitarian law.[80]

---

[75]*Hassan*, para. 71.

[76]Ibid.

[77]Ibid., para. 77. The Grand Chamber also noted that in *Al-Skeini v. United Kingdom* cit., which was also concerned with a period when international humanitarian law was applicable, it had found that the United Kingdom exercised jurisdiction under Article 1 of the ECHR (ibid.).

[78]Ibid., para. 88.

[79]Ibid., para. 89.

[80]Ibid., para. 90.

Having noted that detention under the Third and Fourth Geneva Conventions could not be regarded as "congruent" with any of the grounds set out in Article 5(1)(a) to (f),[81] the Court went on to note the possibility of derogation under Article 15, and that the United Kingdom had not availed itself of that possibility in respect of its operations in Iraq.[82]

The Court then noted that the case was the first in which a Contracting State had requested the Court to "disapply its obligations under Article 5 or in some other way to interpret them in the light of powers of detention available to it under international humanitarian law".[83]

The Court concluded that there had been no violation of Article 5(1), on the basis that, in an international armed conflict, Article 5 was to be interpreted in the light of international humanitarian law, and as permitting detention in compliance with the Third and Fourth Geneva Conventions.[84]

In reaching that conclusion, although referring to the case law of the ICJ on the relationship between international humanitarian law and international human rights law, the Court did not invoke any version of the *lex specialis* principle. Rather, it justified its conclusion on the basis of the rules of interpretation contained in the VCLT and, in particular, the principle of systemic interpretation contained in Article 31(3)(c).[85]

In that regard, having referred to and quoted, inter alia, the views expressed by the ICJ in *The Wall* as quoted in *Armed Activities*, the Court stated that it was required "to interpret and apply the Convention in a manner which is consistent with the framework under international law delineated by the International Court of Justice".[86]

On that basis, it accepted that the absence of derogation under Article 15 did not prevent taking international humanitarian law into account in interpreting Article 5[87] and held that:

> [I]n situations of international armed conflict, the safeguards under the Convention continue to apply, albeit interpreted against the background of the provisions of international humanitarian law.[88]

---

[81] Ibid., para. 97.

[82] Ibid., para. 99.

[83] Ibid. The issue had previously arisen in *Cyprus v. Turkey* (Apps. nos. 6780/74 and 6950/75), Report of the Commission of 10 July 1976, in which the Commission had refused to examine allegations of breach of Article 5 relating to detention of prisoners of war (para. 313). Somewhat pointedly, the Grand Chamber in *Hassan* noted that in *Al-Jedda v. United Kingdom* cit., which had likewise concerned detention by the UK military in an international armed conflict, the UK had not sought to argue that Article 5 had been modified or displaced by reason of the powers of detention contained in the Third and Fourth Geneva Conventions (*Hassan*, para. 99).

[84] Ibid., para. 102.

[85] Ibid., paras. 100 and 102.

[86] Ibid., para. 102.

[87] Ibid., para. 103. That conclusion was reached on the basis that there existed a subsequent practice among the States parties not to derogate from Article 5 in respect of military operations abroad.

[88] Ibid., para. 104.

As a consequence, it accepted that:

> [B]y reason of the co-existence of the safeguards provided by international humanitarian law and by the Convention in time of armed conflict, the grounds of permitted deprivation of liberty set out in subparagraphs (a) to (f) of that provision should be accommodated, as far as possible, with the taking of prisoners of war and the detention of civilians who pose a risk to security under the Third and Fourth Geneva Conventions.[89]

The Court accordingly concluded that:

> [I]n cases of international armed conflict, where the taking of prisoners of war and the detention of civilians who pose a threat to security are accepted features of international humanitarian law, ... Article 5 could be interpreted as permitting the exercise of such broad powers.[90]

The Court emphasized that any detention nevertheless had to be "lawful" under international humanitarian law, and had to be in keeping with the fundamental purpose of Article 5(1) of protecting individuals from arbitrariness,[91] but then in practice proceeded to read down the remaining provisions of Article 5 relating to procedural safeguards in light of international humanitarian law. In particular, it held that, as concerns detention in an international armed conflict, the safeguards contained in Article 5(2) and (4) (information as to the reasons for detention, and the right to judicial review of the legality of detention) were to be interpreted "in a manner which takes into account the context and the applicable rules of interna tional humanitarian law".[92] As regards the requirement under Article 5(3) (i.e. that persons detained pursuant to Article 5(1)(c) must be brought promptly before a judge, and are entitled to trial within a reasonable time, or release pending trial), it somewhat disingenuously held that the safeguard was not applicable on the basis that, in the case of security detention or internment under international humanitarian law, individuals were not detained pursuant to Article 5(1)(c).[93]

The decision of the Court in *Hassan* is indicative of the dangers of conceptualizing or describing the relationship between international humanitarian law and international humanitarian law as one of *lex specialis/lex generalis*, with the implied assumption that, in case of conflict, international humanitarian law should necessarily prevail.

Whilst the Court avoided any express reliance on the principle of *lex specialis* to justify its decision, the effect of the decision is that international humanitarian

---

[89]Ibid.

[90]Ibid.

[91]Ibid., para. 105.

[92]Ibid., para. 106. In that regard, the Court accepted that the "competent body" for periodic review of detention as foreseen by Articles 43 and 78 of the Fourth Geneva Convention need not necessarily be a "court" as required by Article 5(4). Nevertheless it was careful to add that the competent body "should provide sufficient guarantees of impartiality and fair procedure to protect against arbitrariness", and that the first review should take place shortly after the start of detention, with subsequent reviews taking place at frequent intervals thereafter (ibid.).

[93]Ibid.

law displaces the relevant rules of the ECHR just as effectively as if the Court had simply treated international humanitarian law as *lex specialis*, and applied the principle *lex specialis* in its strongest form.

As noted above, the constant jurisprudence of the ECtHR treats the grounds for detention set out in Article 5(1) as constituting an exhaustive list.[94] Yet in *Hassan*, basing itself on the principle of systemic interpretation, the Court effectively implied into Article 5(1) an entirely new additional basis for detention (i.e. detention consistent with international humanitarian law), albeit limited only to situations of international armed conflict. This interpretation finds no foothold in the text of the provision, nor in the previously consistent jurisprudence of the Court interpreting it.

Insofar as the Court's approach in *Hassan* is incompatible with the express terms of that provision, it involves resort to a *contra legem* interpretation which is, in itself, clearly inconsistent with the fundamental principles of textual and teleological interpretation set out in Article 31(1) of the VCLT, i.e. that a treaty is to be interpreted "in good faith in accordance with the ordinary meaning to be given to the terms of the treaty in their context and in the light of its object and purpose".[95]

The Court's approach to the other provisions of Article 5 is likewise symptomatic of the same approach. Insofar as it was held that the stringent procedural safeguards applicable under Article 5 either had to be effectively equated to the less demanding requirements under international humanitarian law, or were held to be inapplicable, they were effectively gutted of any content. Although the Court attempted to soften the effect of its ruling by purporting to require that the competent body should be offered sufficient guarantees of impartiality and due process so as to protect against arbitrariness, those requirements add little to the (very basic) protections which are commonly understood to exist under international humanitarian law itself. The net result is, again, in substance, precisely the same as if the Court had concluded that Article 5 of the European Convention had been fully displaced by the applicable provisions of international humanitarian law as *lex specialis*.

4.2 *Serdar Mohammed v. Ministry of Defence: A "Modest" Role for the Lex Specialis Principle*

In contrast to *Hassan*, the decision of the High Court in *Serdar Mohammed* contains a detailed and insightful discussion of the relationship between the ECHR and international humanitarian law in terms of *lex specialis*.

---

[94]See cit., footnote 71.

[95]Cf. *Serdar Mohammed*, para. 291, where Leggatt J. expressed the view that, "given the specificity of Article 5, there is little scope for *lex specialis* to operate as a principle of interpretation".

The complaint concerned the prolonged detention of an Afghani citizen, suspected of being a high-ranking member of the Taliban forces, by UK troops operating as part of the United Nations International Security Assistance Force (ISAF).[96] The applicant claimed that his detention had no legal basis, and constituted a violation of Article 5 of the European Convention.

The decision grappled with a number of complex, controversial and inter-linked issues relating to the interpretation and application of the ECHR. Those issues included the relationship between the Convention and the applicable rules of international humanitarian law, which, in light of the circumstances of the case, it was common ground were the rules applicable in non-international armed conflict.[97]

In that context, one of the principal arguments advanced by the UK government in denying any breach of Article 5 of the ECHR, as summarized by Leggatt J., was that:

> [A]rmed conflict is an exception to the normality of peace. Human rights law is designed to apply in peace time or, even if also applicable during an armed conflict, is not specifically designed for such a situation. By contrast, international humanitarian law is specifically designed to apply in situations of armed conflict. In such circumstances, rules of international humanitarian law as *lex specialis* qualify or displace applicable provisions of a human rights treaty, such as Article 5 of the Convention.[98]

In order to address that argument, Leggatt J. engaged in a detailed discussion of the issue of the relationship between the Convention and international humanitarian law, in the process carrying out an analysis of the meaning and effect of what he termed the "*lex specialis* principle".[99]

Having observed that, "although easy enough to state in general terms, the exact meaning and effect of the *lex specialis* principle is more elusive ...",[100] the judge distinguished three ways in which the *lex specialis* principle could be said to operate.[101] The three potential variants identified by the judge were:

(a) the "total displacement" version of the principle, according to which "in a situation of armed conflict, international humanitarian law as the *lex specialis* displaces Convention rights altogether";[102]

(b) a "weaker version" of the principle, which, whilst accepting that the ECHR continued to apply generally in a situation of armed conflict, required that, in case of a conflict between international humanitarian law and the ECHR,

---

[96]Serdar Mohammed was captured by UK soldiers in 2010 in the course of a military operation in northern Helmand. He was detained by the UK in military bases for 110 days, before eventually being handed over to the Afghan authorities.

[97]*Serdar Mohammed*, paras. 231 and 232.

[98]Ibid., para. 271.

[99]Ibid., para. 272. Although the judge made reference to the maxim *lex specialis derogat legi generali* (ibid.), it is clear that, as used in the judgment, the term "*lex specialis* principle" was intended to have a far wider scope.

[100]Ibid., para. 273.

[101]Ibid.

[102]Ibid., para. 274.

international humanitarian law should prevail "as the body of law more specifically tailored to the situation";[103] and

(c) a "more modest" version of the principle which operates merely as a principle of interpretation.[104]

The judge dismissed the total displacement proposition as "impossible to maintain",[105] including in light of the relevant case law of the ICJ.

As for the second version of the principle, the judge observed that even the "weaker" form of *lex specialis*, which would require disapplication of specific ECHR provisions insofar as they actually conflicted with international humanitarian law, was not apt to regulate the relationship between the European Convention and international humanitarian law, since the Convention included a provision (Article 15) which was expressly designed to allow States to derogate from certain obligations in states of emergency, including war.[106]

Finally, as regards the third possible version of the *lex specialis* principle, which treated it not "as a principle for resolving conflicts between different bodies of law but as a principle of interpretation",[107] the judge observed that he could "see no difficulty with this, most modest version of the argument that international humanitarian law operates as *lex specialis*",[108] and its requirement that "in conditions of armed conflict, Article 5 (and other relevant articles) of the Convention should be interpreted so far as possible in a manner which is consistent with applicable rules of international humanitarian law".[109]

The High Court thus, in effect, rejected any application of the maxim *lex specialis derogat legi generali*, in its strict sense of displacement, as a suitable principle of coordination between the ECHR and international humanitarian law. To the extent that it accepted the "modest" version of the *lex specialis* principle as a means of interpretation, the approach adopted is not, in reality, an application of the *lex specialis* in its proper sense at all. Rather, its effects are so close as to be virtually indistinguishable from the principle of systemic interpretation contained in Article 31(1)(c) of the VCLT, as applied by the Grand Chamber in *Hassan*.

5 Conclusion

At base, the general principle *lex specialis derogat legi generali* is a rule to resolve antinomies between norms which concurrently regulate, in different manners, the same subject-matter. It does so by applying the special norm in preference to the

---

[103]Ibid., para. 282.

[104]Ibid., paras. 288 and 289.

[105]Ibid., para. 275.

[106]Ibid., para. 284.

[107]Ibid., para. 288.

[108]Ibid., para. 289.

[109]Ibid., para. 288.

general norm, which is thereby displaced, in whole or in part. As discussed in Sect. 2 above, the principle has the credentials to be regarded as a "general principle of law recognized by civilized nations" under Article 38(1)(c) of the ICJ Statute. Further, it is frequently relied upon by international courts and tribunals in order to resolve potential normative conflicts between general international law and treaties and to coordinate the interaction of potentially conflicting or redundant rules contained within a single treaty or in interrelated instruments.

When utilized in this fashion, the *lex specialis* principle is undoubtedly a useful tool in the arsenal of judges and provides a mechanism by which to resolve at least some of the normative conflicts (real or apparent), which may arise as a result of the lack of any complete and developed set of formal rules governing the precedence or hierarchy between norms in the international legal system.[110]

However, it is questionable whether the principle, and indeed the very language of *lex specialis*, is either appropriate or useful when discussing the complex issue of the relationship between international humanitarian law and international human rights law.

The very notion of a relationship between a general and a more specific rule presupposes that the rules are *ejusdem generis*. In other words, in order for the *lex specialis* principle even to be capable of application, the rules must be linked by a *genus/species* relationship, which—logically—cannot exist between rules which belong to different, and unlinked, bodies of law. It is accordingly of the essence of the *lex specialis derogat legi generali* rule that the antinomy between rules which requires resolution—or at least a situation of redundancy—must arise between rules existing broadly within the same branch of law.

Of course, despite certain broad similarities of aim, international humanitarian law and international human rights law are fundamentally distinct and different, such that articulation of their interaction through giving primacy to one of them as *lex specialis* is simply not possible from the point of view of legal reasoning.[111] For that reason alone, the language of *lex specialis* is arguably inapt to describe the relationship.

The use of the language of *lex specialis* to characterize international humanitarian law is also inappropriate, however, insofar as the term necessarily and unavoidably evokes the maxim *lex specialis derogat legi generali*, and consequently suggests, at least by implication, that international humanitarian law prevails. This serves to muddy the waters, and lends itself to continued efforts (in particular, on the part of the States confronted with challenges to their conduct in armed conflict) to argue that the protections of international human rights law should give way to international humanitarian law.

In the light of those considerations, although, as discussed above, it is tolerably clear that in using those words the intention was not to refer to the maxim *lex specialis derogat legi generali* as a mechanism of coordination between the two

---

[110]Lindroos (2005), p. 28.

[111]Cf. Lindroos (2005), p. 66.

bodies of law, the use by the ICJ in its *Nuclear Weapons* Advisory Opinion of the words "*lex specialis*" in relation to international humanitarian law was unfortunate. It has confused matters,[112] whilst at the same time opening the door to instrumental arguments by some States.

The correct articulation of the two bodies of law would appear to be better understood as one essentially akin to systemic interpretation of the norms of international human rights law in the specific context of armed conflict and in light of the applicable rules of international humanitarian law.

Such an approach is clearly permissible, and indeed required, under the general rules of interpretation under the law of treaties. However, such systemic interpretation is subject to certain limits, most notably that the "ordinary meaning" of the words of the relevant provision may not permit a result which reconciles the conflicting rules, and that a harmonious interpretation may well be inconsistent with the "object and purpose" of the treaty.

Even if not used to denote a relationship in which international humanitarian law prevails in case of conflict, but rather a relationship based on interpretation of international human rights law in the light of relevant rules of international humanitarian law, use of the terminology of *lex specialis* is liable to create a bias in favor of the conclusion that international humanitarian law must prevail insofar as interpretation of international human rights law cannot produce a solution which resolves the conflict. One may speculate that, although no express reference was made to the term in its reasoning, the overtones of the *lex specialis* character of international humanitarian law were a contributing factor in the decision in *Hassan* in effect to disapply the clear letter of Article 5(1) of the ECHR.

As such, it would be preferable if the tag *lex specialis* were abandoned altogether in the specific context of the discussion of the relationship between international humanitarian law and international human rights law, and the relationship were rather to be understood as one in which international humanitarian law is to be regarded as simply one of the "relevant rules of international law applicable in the relationship between the parties"[113] which are to be taken into account when interpreting international human rights law.

Whilst international human rights law is applicable in peacetime *and* in war, and international humanitarian law is only applicable in armed conflict, there is no reason why, taken as a whole, international humanitarian law should always and necessarily be seen as more "special" than international humanitarian law in situations of armed conflict. In many cases, the two bodies of law complement each other and can be combined in order to offer greater protection for individuals, whilst allowing courts and tribunals applying international human rights law to take into account the specificities of the situation where the two bodies of rules

---

[112]Including by leading some commentators to suggest that the ICJ in fact intended to make reference to the principle *lex specialis derogat lex generali*; see, e.g., Abresch (2005), p. 744.

[113]Article 31(3)(c) of the VCLT.

provide for different standards.[114] The principle of systemic interpretation allows the interpreter sufficient latitude to pursue this result.

Nevertheless, there will inevitably be some situations where the letter of the law does not permit such harmonious interpretation. The *lex specialis* principle, for all of the reasons outlined above, is not suitable to provide a solution to this type of situation.

In this regard, it is suggested that the better (and more principled) view is that which acknowledges, on the one hand, that, inevitably, situations may arise in which a harmonizing approach through interpretation is not possible, and, on the other, that, as a result, there may be situations in which conduct which is "lawful under international humanitarian law can at the same time constitute a violation by the State in question of some other international obligation incumbent upon it".[115]

However, States need not necessarily end up facing the dilemma of which set of obligations to respect. First, it is difficult to imagine situations in which international humanitarian law would positively *require* States to take action which would violate their obligations under international human rights law. Insofar as the rules of international humanitarian law are prescriptive in terms of the treatment to be accorded to individuals, the conduct which is prohibited or required will normally a fortiori also be prohibited or required under international human rights law. Conversely, to the extent that the rules of international humanitarian law are permissive, for instance with regard to detention or killings in armed conflict, the State is free not to carry out the relevant conduct insofar as it would violate its international human rights law obligations.

Such an approach, although sustainable from a purely theoretical perspective, is bound to be labeled as idealistic and out of touch with the realities of armed conflict.

Second, and by way of response to such an objection, it should be noted that international human rights law itself is not blind to the exigencies faced by States engaged in armed conflict. All of the principal international human rights treaties contain provisions which permit States to derogate from certain aspects of their obligations in time of war or other public emergency.[116] As such, and notwithstanding the decision of the Grand Chamber in *Hassan*, where States engage in military operations which may involve them acting in a manner which, whilst permitted under international humanitarian law, may be inconsistent with their (derogable) human rights obligations, by far the better solution would be to require them to enter an appropriate derogation. This would require prior consideration of potential human rights issues, ensure at least a degree of legal certainty and transparency, as well as ensuring a minimum of *ex ante* domestic and international

---

[114]For a nuanced assessment of the impact of international human rights law on military operations, see Sari (2014).

[115]*Croatian Genocide*, para. 474.

[116]See, e.g., Article 4 of the ICCPR; Article 15 of the ECHR; Article 27 of the ACHR. The only notable exception is the ACHPR, which does not make any provision for derogation in states of emergency. For an insightful discussion of the availability of derogation in relation to the extraterritorial conduct of a State, see Milanovic (2014a).

scrutiny of the measures States propose to take. For States which are prepared to take the politically difficult decision of becoming involved in military operations abroad, and profess to be serious about their human rights commitments, such an approach is the least which can be expected.

References

Abresch, William. 2005. A Human Rights Law of Internal Armed Conflict: the European Court of Human Rights in Chechnya. *European Journal of International Law* 16/4: 741-767.

Arnold, Roberta, and Noëlle Quénivet (eds). 2008. *International Humanitarian Law and Human Rights Law*. Leiden: Martinus Nijhoff.

Bethlehem, Daniel. 2013. The Relationship between International Humanitarian Law and International Human Rights Law in Situations of Armed Conflict. *Cambridge Journal of International and Comparative Law* 2/2: 180-195

Bothe, Michael, Karl J. Partsch, and Waldemar A. Solf. 1982. *New Rules for Victims of Armed Conflicts: Commentary on the two 1977 Protocols Addition to the Geneva Conventions of 1949*. The Hague: Martinus Nijhoff

Bowring, Bill. 2009. Fragmentation, *lex specialis* and the Tensions in the Jurisprudence of the European Court of Human Rights. *Journal of Conflict and Security Law* 14: 485-498.

Cheng, Bin. 1953. *General Principles of Law as Applied by International Courts and Tribunals*. London: Stevens & Sons.

Doswald-Beck, Louise, and Sylvain Vité. 1993. International Humanitarian Law and Human Rights Law. *International Review of the Red Cross* 33: 94-119.

ILC Study Group on Fragmentation. 2006a. Report of the Study Group on the Fragmentation of International Law, finalized by Martti Koskenniemi, UN Doc. A/CN.4/L.682, 13 April 2006.

ILC Study Group on Fragmentation. 2006b. Conclusions of the work of the Study Group on the Fragmentation of International Law: Difficulties arising from the Diversification and Expansion of International Law, ILC Report 2006, UN Doc. A/61/10.

Koskenniemi, Martti. 2004. Study on the Function and Scope of the *lex specialis* Rule and the Question of "Self-Contained Regimes". UN Doc. ILC(LVI)/SG/FIL/CRD.1/Add.1 (2004).

Lindroos, Anja. 2005. Addressing Norm Conflicts in a Fragmented Legal System: The Doctrine of *lex specialis*. *Nordic Journal of International Law* 74/1: 27-66.

Matz-Lück, Nele. 2010. Treaties, Conflicts between. In *Max Planck Encyclopedia of Public International Law*. http://opil.ouplaw.com.

Milanovic, Marko. 2014a. Extraterritorial Derogations from Human Rights Treaties in Armed Conflict. Forthcoming in *Collected Courses of the Academy of European Law*, ed. Nehal Bhuta. Oxford: Oxford University Press. http://ssrn.com/abstract=2447183.

Milanovic, Marko. 2014b. The Lost Origins of *lex specialis*: Rethinking the Relationship between Human Rights and International Humanitarian Law. Forthcoming in *Theoretical Boundaries of Armed Conflict and Human Rights*, ed. Jens D. Ohlin. Cambridge: Cambridge University Press. http://ssrn.com/abstract=2463957.

Moir, Lindsay. 2003. Decommissioned? International Humanitarian Law and the Inter-American Human Rights System. *Human Rights Quarterly* 25/1: 182-212.

Orakelashvili, Alexander. 2008. The Interaction between Human Rights and Humanitarian Law: Fragmentation, Conflict, Parallelism, or Convergence?. *European Journal of International Law* 19: 161-182.

Pellet, Alain. 2012. Article 38. In *The Statute of the International Court of Justice: A Commentary*, eds. Andreas Zimmerman, Christian Tomuschat, Karin Oellers-Frahm and Christian J Tams, 731-870. II ed. Oxford: Oxford University Press.

Prud'homme, Nancie. 2007. *Lex specialis*: Oversimplifying a More Complex and Multifaceted Relationship?. *Israel Law Review* 40/2: 355-395.

Sari, Aurel. 2014. The Juridification of the British Armed Forces and the European Convention on Human Rights: 'Because It's Judgment that Defeats Us'. http://ssrn.com/abstract=2411070.

Sassòli, Marco and Laura M. Olson. 2008. The Relationship between International Humanitarian and Human Rights Law Where It Matters: Admissible Killing and Internment of Fighters in Non-International Armed Conflicts. *International Review of the Red Cross*, 90: 599-627.

Van den Herik, Larissa, and Helen Duffy. 2014. Human Rights Bodies and International Humanitarian Law: Common But Differentiated Approaches. Forthcoming in *The Harmonisation of Human Rights Law,* eds. Carla Buckley, Philip Leach and Alice Donald. Leiden: Brill /Martinus Nijhoff. http://ssrn.com/abstract=2448146.

Wolfrum, Rudiger. 2011. Sources of International Law. In *Max Planck Encyclopedia of Public International Law*. http://opil.ouplaw.com.

Zegveld, Liesbeth. 1998. The Inter-American Commission on Human Rights and International Humanitarian Law: A Comment on the Tablada Case. *International Review of the Red Cross* 38: 505-511.

Zorzetto, Silvia. 2013. The *Lex Specialis* Principle and its Uses in Legal Argumentation. An Analytical Inquiry. *Eunomía. Revista en Cultura de la Legalidad* 3: 61-87.

Discrimination for Sexual Orientation in Poland: The Role of the Judiciary

Katarzyna Girdwoyń

Abstract Discrimination is considered to be one of the main challenges in the process of strengthening human rights. This chapter explores whether, despite significant conservatism of the Polish society, even slow social changes are reflected in the adjudicating practices of Polish courts and, if they are, what is the main reason for these changes to take place. After a short description of the legal status of homosexuals in Poland and the principle of autonomy of courts in interpreting legal provisions, the attention focuses on Polish jurisprudence. This analysis leads to the conclusion that Polish courts, particularly of higher instances, have started to interpret the law and to fill the gaps brought about by statutory regulations in compliance with the Polish Constitution and the Convention for the Protection of Human Rights and Fundamental Freedoms as well as with the guidelines issued by the European Union and the Council of Europe.

1 Introduction

Currently in Poland one can see some signs of social changes, which have had an impact both on the way the law is legislated and how it is applied. Many controversial questions, such as: the right to abortion for reasons other than medical or as a result of a crime, in vitro procedures or the right to euthanasia, are still being the focus of more or less intense debate, which confirms their social importance. Yet, those problems do not pertain only to human rights, but also to questions of morality and religion, which means that passing a law that touches on those questions is not a simple task. Against this background, it seems relatively clear-cut and obvious, either from a moral or religious point of view, to legally oppose any discrimination

K. Girdwoyń (✉)
Assistant Professor of Criminal Law, University of Warsaw, Warsaw, Poland
e-mail: k.girdwoyn@uw.edu.pl

© Springer International Publishing Switzerland 2015
L. Pineschi (ed.), *General Principles of Law - The Role of the Judiciary*,
Ius Gentium: Comparative Perspectives on Law and Justice 46,
DOI 10.1007/978-3-319-19180-5_14

in any of its aspects. Discrimination is considered to be one of the main challenges in the process of strengthening human rights.[1]

Unfortunately, at present there are many situations in Poland where discrimination takes place, especially in the area of labour law, i.e., employment status or payment for women's work. The signs of such discrimination, as well as examples of violation of the existing regulations can be found in questions women are asked by potential employers concerning their private life, e.g., if they have or are planning to have children. Another example is the termination of women's employment contracts after they return to work from maternity leave. However, when such a case goes to court, the judgment is unequivocally in favour of the woman.[2]

Another important problem, also in the sphere of social life, is manifested in the cases of relatively frequently occurring discrimination of ethnic minorities. One example is a case when Roma people were refused to be served at a restaurant due to their ethnic origin. Another case of ethnic discrimination occurred when a Polish citizen of Palestinian origin was refused permission to work as a volunteer at the European Soccer Cup in 2012 held in Poland. Polish media have reported both cases in detail and non-governmental organizations involved in human rights protection, such as the Helsinki Foundation for Human Rights, have shown their interest in them.

On many buildings in Poland one can still find anti-Semitic graffiti which, taking into account Polish history and the World War II, is particularly hard to comprehend. But due to relative uniformity of the Polish society in terms of religion and ethnicity, and also because of the lack of separatist tendencies resulting from such uniformity, the trouble with ethnic minorities does not present itself as an important issue to the public, and only few of such cases go to court. Thus it is difficult to discuss this area in terms of traditional lines of judicial decisions.

There are also some cases of discrimination against people with disabilities. There were two cases that made the headlines because blind persons with guide dogs were not allowed into a restaurant and a shop. The courts ruled that persons treated in such a way should get compensation. However, the fundamental problem with respect to the disabled is not the lack of regulation or the application of law by the courts—it is the simple issue of making it possible for them to move in the public space, use public transport or cross the street.

There are many reasons why people suffer discrimination. Yet it is worth noticing that the need to treat people equally irrespective of their sex, age, ethnic origin or disability in a democratic State does not bring up any serious doubts in Poland. While the issue of equal rights for homosexuals has continuously been a bone of contention among the Polish society, the legal status of homosexual persons

---

[1]Jabłońska and Knut (2012), p. 21.

[2]There is also another factor that may play a role in the Polish legal system: the profession of a judge, similarly to that of a public prosecutor, is considered to be mainly represented by women: 6,353 out of 9,933 judges in total are women. See: http://www.gazetaprawna.pl/707048. On 30 April 2014, the first woman ever was appointed the First President of the Supreme Court.

causes serious controversies, not only, as it would seem, in the Polish society.[3] The Secretary-General of the Council of Europe, Mr Thorburn Jagland, has said that the discrimination of Lesbian, Gay, Bisexual and Transsexual (LGBT) persons is "one of the longest and most difficult to fight forms of discrimination".[4]

There are several arguments that make the discrimination against homosexuals a relevant question. It is quite alarming that 24 % of the students of the first year of one of Polish medical universities consider homosexuality to be an illness and that this opinion is shared by 22 % of the last year students. This shows that education in this area is not very effective.[5] Moreover, the legal status of sexual minorities, which I will discuss later in this chapter, is much worse than that of other minorities exposed to discrimination. Therefore it is the courts that can fill the gap brought about by lack of appropriate regulations.

The goal of this chapter is to attempt to show whether, despite significant conservatism of the Polish society, even slow social changes are reflected in the adjudicating practices of Polish courts and if they are, what is the main reason for these changes to take place.

2 Legal Status of Homosexuals in Poland

It is hard not to agree with the statement that:

Many would assert that a fundamental purpose of law today is to promote a more dynamic social order, designed to ensure that society is not locked into historic structures which sustain inequality, but is based on principles on equality and the prevention of social exclusion.[6]

The Polish Constitution guarantees equality of all persons before the law and prohibits discrimination. Article 32(1) of the Constitution stipulates:

All persons shall be equal before the law. All persons shall have the right to equal treatment by public authorities. No one shall be discriminated against in political, social or economic life for any reason whatsoever.[7]

In the commentary to the Constitution one can read that there are no exceptions to or departures from the principle of equality and that discrimination must not be justified by any legal provisions or reasons.[8] Despite the fact that it has been

---

[3]See the judgment of the case C-147/08 *Jürgen Römer v. Freie und Hansestadt Hamburg* [GC] [2011] ECR I-3591; *Vejdeland and Others v. Sweden* (App. no. 1813/07), ECHtR, judgment of 9 February 2012.

[4]Jabłońska and Knut (2012), p. 15.

[5]*Raport o dyskryminacji osób LGBT w Polsce dla Europejskiej Komisji Przeciwko Rasizmowi i Nietolerancji*, Warsaw, 2014, p. 5.

[6]Partington (2006), p. 34.

[7]See: http://www.sejm.gov.pl/prawo/konst/angielski/kon1.htm.

[8]Skrzydło (2011), p. 145.

seventeen years since the Constitution was adopted, and twenty-one years since the ratification by Poland of the Convention for the Protection of Human Rights and Fundamental Freedoms (ECHR), still until today Poland has not managed to regulate in full the legal status of homosexual persons. Before 2002, the Polish law did not acknowledge the issue of homosexual minorities in Poland at all. Until that time expressions such as sexual orientation or sexual minority had not been used in any domestic legal act.[9] The real division on the issues relating to this group, which is perhaps exposed more to discrimination by the Polish society than any other minority, has been obviously reflected in the divisions in the Polish parliament. Those divisions were the reason for the rejection in January 2013 again, after extremely hostile and homophobic discussions,[10] of three different bills on registered partnership, including one presented by the government. The opponents of such regulations, the former Ministers of Justice, among others, have cited the provision of the Constitution of the Republic of Poland stipulating that:

> Marriage, being a union of a man and a woman, as well as the family, motherhood and parenthood shall be placed under the protection and care of the Republic of Poland (Article 18).[11]

It is worth mentioning that none of the provisions contained in those three proposed bills dealt with the issues of same-sex marriages or child adoption by such marriages.

Due to lack of political majority and strong right-wing objections, Poland is not party to the Protocol no. 12 to the ECHR, which forbids discrimination in all spheres. Although several regulations introduced into the Polish legal system aim at preventing and oppose discrimination in all spheres of life, so far as sexual minorities are concerned, those regulations address only labour-law-related issues. Moreover, as a consequence of these objections Poland has implemented European standards only partially. One example is the Act of 3 December 2010 on the implementation of some regulations of the European Union regarding equal treatment, drafted with the purpose to determine ways to prevent violation of the equal-rights principle due to sex, race, ethnic origin, nationality, religion, denomination, belief, disability, age or sexual orientation (Article 8).[12] However this statute, referred to as "law of equality"[13] was heavily criticized for the fact that:

> The least protected ground is sexual orientation, which enjoys the right to equality only in the sphere of employment, whilst the grounds of race, ethnic origin and nationality (and gender to a lesser degree) are protected in all spheres of life.[14]

---

[9]Biedroń (2008), p. 12.

[10]*Raport o dyskryminacji osób LGBT w Polsce dla Europejskiej Komisji Przeciwko Rasizmowi i Nietolerancji* cit.

[11]See: http://www.sejm.gov.pl/prawo/konst/angielski/kon1.htm.

[12]See: http://www.brpo.gov.pl/en/content/act-3rd-december-2010-implementation-some-regulations-european-union-regarding-equal.

[13]Wieczorek and Bogatko (2013), p. 78.

[14]*Raport o dyskryminacji osób LGBT w Polsce dla Europejskiej Komisji Przeciwko Rasizmowi i Nietolerancji* cit., p. 19.

The regulations on preventing discrimination on the grounds of sexual orientation were implemented literally only in the sphere of employment. In 2004 the Polish Labour Code was amended to include regulations which imposed equal treatment of employees in the process in hiring them, terminating their employment, allowing them access to training courses to advance their professional qualifications irrespective of their sex, age, disability, race, religion, nationality, political convictions, trade union membership, ethnicity, denomination, sexual orientation, and also due to employment for definite or indefinite term, full time or part time (Article 18(3)(a)). Also the Act of 20 April 2004 on the promotion of employment and the employment market, which determines the role of the State in promoting employment, reducing the effects of unemployment and occupational activization, contains provisions designed to protect the equal treatment of people in their access to the services of employment market and other instruments of that market irrespective of, among other reasons, sexual orientation.

In terms of legal consequences for the violation of the prohibition of discrimination, apart from the Labour Code, "the law of equality" envisages regulation, which will grant the right to compensation to anyone with respect to whom the principle of equal treatment has been breached. However, according to the Ministry of Justice's statistics, in 2011 only thirty cases were brought to courts and seventeen of them were resolved with a court's decision (out of which nine claims were dismissed, in six cases the suit was remanded to the complainant, one was rejected and in one case the proceedings were discontinued) while thirteen cases were left to be heard in 2012.[15] Even though the government tried to pass a bill amending the regulation to penalise the discriminatory behaviour towards sexual minorities, and in spite of intense activities of the organizations defending the right of the minorities, the law was not amended.[16] The Polish Criminal Code, apart from offences against peace and humanity and war crimes, also envisages criminal protection of persons from hate speech and other bias-motivated crimes in Poland, sometimes referred to as "criminal discrimination".[17] Article 256 states that, whoever publicly promotes a fascist or other totalitarian State system or incites hatred based on national, ethnic, racial or religious differences or for reason of lack of any religious denomination, shall be subject to a fine, the penalty of restriction of liberty or the penalty of deprivation of liberty for up to two years. Whereas, who publicly insults a group within the population or a particular person because of his national, ethnic, racial or religious affiliation or because of his lack of any religious denomination or for these reasons, breaches the personal inviolability of another individual, shall be subject to the penalty of deprivation of liberty for up to three years (Article 257).

While the legal status of homosexuals in the sphere of employment could be viewed as satisfactory, still there has not been any political will to regulate the

---

[15]See http://www.orka2.sejm.gov.pl/IZ7.nsf/main/6009A444.

[16]*Raport o dyskryminacji osób LGBT w Polsce dla Europejskiej Komisji Przeciwko Rasizmowi i Nietolerancji,* p. 17.

[17]Ibid., p. 18.

rights of this minority group in terms of right to statutory succession, or rights with respect to court procedures. Due to the fact that there is no such law, the role of courts that interpret civil, criminal, labour or tax law with respect to situations involving homosexual persons is absolutely paramount.

3 The Autonomy of Courts in Interpreting Legal Provisions

Article 178(1) of the Polish Constitution, which expresses the principle of the independence of the judiciary, also states that judges are subject only to the Constitution and statutes. The legislative power when enacting or amending laws may thus exert an influence on the work of judges.[18] Because of that, it has been acknowledged that the principle of the independence of judges is not an absolute feature. A judge's duty is to decide cases within the frames of law and in this way to guard the interest and guidelines they are supposed to serve, irrespective of the fact whether legal provisions are in compliance with their personal views and beliefs, or not. This means that judges are bound to a certain degree by the political system of the Country in which they implement the administration of justice.[19] Another provision of the Constitution stipulates that the Constitution is the supreme law of the Republic of Poland whose provisions shall apply directly unless the Constitution provides otherwise (Article 8). A controversial question both raised in the Supreme Court case law and academic writing is whether judges—other than those of the Constitutional Tribunal—may ignore statutory provisions and base their judgment solely on the provision of the supreme law— the Constitution. However, there is no doubt that judges make use of constitutional norms, particularly its principles in order to establish the correct line of interpretation of statutory provisions.[20]

Having said that, let me stress that although judges cannot refuse to apply the mandatory law, we should not forget that in the course of the decision-making process they should take into account not only their experience and common sense, but also the customs and practices that are observed by the society at large.[21] As a result it should be pointed out that the contents of the principle of the independence of judges comprises also the readiness to defy their own assessments based on their own experience, stereotypes and prejudices.[22] In the Polish legal literature it is emphasized that one of the fundamental components of their independence is their autonomy in adjudicating all factual doubts in the case, as well as the

---

[18]Skrzydło (2011), p. 246.

[19]Murzynowski (1994), p. 226.

[20]Garlicki (1997), p. 12.

[21]Gapska (2010), p. 165.

[22]Constitutional Tribunal, K 11/93, 9 November 1993, no. 2, item 37.

autonomy in the interpretation of the law.[23] However, the Polish legislation provides for certain significant exceptions to the rule, namely, that judges should interpret legal provisions independently.

The basic exception is presented in the Constitution itself. According to Article 193, any court may refer a question of law to the Constitutional Tribunal as to the conformity of a normative act to the Constitution, ratified international agreements or statute, if the answer to such question of law will determine an issue currently before such Court. According to Article 190(1) of the Constitution, judgments of the Constitutional Tribunal shall be of universally binding application and shall be final, which means that the requirement to take them into account is binding not only for the legislator but also for legal organs, including courts and the public prosecution.[24] Therefore the role of the Tribunal in a nutshell is to strike out unconstitutional provisions from the legal system.[25] As has been recognized by the Constitutional Tribunal itself, its role is not to perform the interpretation of legal provisions in order for them to be applied by the courts. Moreover, the tribunal is not appointed to assess whether the interpretation of provisions done by the courts or other legal organs is correct.[26]

However, due to the fact that the real contents of many provisions are being construed in the course of their application, the Constitutional Tribunal helps to determine if the interpretation of a provision conforms to the Constitution and if that interpretation is stable and unequivocal.[27] In one of its judgments, the Tribunal pointed out that if:

[A]n interpretation of a given provision has been expressed unequivocally and authoritatively in the judicature of the Supreme Court or of the Supreme Administrative Court, then it should be recognized that the rule has acquired such contents that was approved by the courts of highest instance.[28]

As the Constitutional Tribunal is considered to be the court whose duty is to guard that the Constitution is observed in the law-making area, it is the function of the European Court of Human Rights (ECtHR) in Strasbourg to ensure that the decisions of courts are compatible with the ECHR. Ratifying the European Convention in 1992, Poland recognized the jurisdiction of the Convention's control organs. Therefore the Polish Constitutional Tribunal has consistently emphasized that the Polish law must be interpreted in a way that is consistent with international obligations.[29] This standpoint of the Polish Tribunal was expressed for the first time in 1997. In its judgment concerning the equality of rights of women and men, the Tribunal underlined that:

---

[23]Wiliński (2011), p. 42.

[24]Ibid.

[25]Safjan (2006), p. 10.

[26]Constitutional Tribunal, SK 1/04, OTK-A 2004, 27 October 2004, no. 9, item 96.

[27]Constitutional Tribunal, K 10/08, OTK-A 2010, 27 October 2010, no. 8, item 81.

[28]Constitutional Tribunal, SK 17/07, OTK-A 2008, 10 June 2008, no. 5, item 81.

[29]Wiliński (2011), p. 33.

The consequence of the obligation to ensure compatibility of the law with the Constitution, which is borne by the parliament and government, is the obligation to ensure that the mandatory legislature is construed in such a way that will guarantee this compatibility most thoroughly.[30]

Apart from the Constitutional Tribunal, in Poland there are two courts, decisions of which have a significant effect on judgments of common and administrative courts, namely the Supreme Court and the Supreme Administrative Court. The Polish Constitution states that the Supreme Court shall exercise supervision over common and military courts regarding judgments (Article 183). Article 1 of the Supreme Court Act[31] states the Supreme Court shall be a judicial body appointed, among others, to administer justice by means of ensuring, as part of its supervisory duties, the compliance with the law and uniformity of judicial decisions of common and military courts by hearing cassations as well as adopting resolutions to adjudicate questions of law. Until 1989 the Supreme Court was authorised to adopt guidelines concerning the interpretation of law and to explain legal provisions and resolve legal questions, which gave rise to doubts; the guidelines were formally binding for all courts. The current regulation introduces only one exception to judges' autonomy in the interpretation of law. The provisions of the civil procedure as well as of the criminal procedure authorize solely the courts of second instance to refer to the Supreme Court a legal question requiring a substantial interpretation of the law. However this resolution ties the judges solely in a given particular case.

The other legal bases for the Supreme Court to render resolutions regarding legal questions are the provisions of the Supreme Court Act. According to Article 60, where should there be discrepancies between the decisions of common courts, military courts or the Supreme Court, the First President of the Supreme Court (and other entities) may request their adjudication by the Supreme Court. If the Supreme Court bench decides that the submitted question requires clarification, and that the revealed discrepancies need to be adjudicated, it shall adopt a resolution (Article 61). Upon their adoption, the resolutions of the entire Supreme Court bench, a bench of joint chambers or a bench of the entire chamber, shall become legal principles. A bench of seven justices may grant a resolution the power of a legal principle. In fact, unlike in the common law system, the decisions rendered by the Supreme Court are not mandatory for all courts acting in Poland.[32] In practice, both the resolutions of the Supreme Court entered in the code of legal principles as well as other rulings issued by this Court are treated as peculiar source of the law by the lower level courts.[33] There are many cases where the judges cite

---

[30]Constititional Tribunal, K 15/97, OTK 1997, 27 September 1997, nos. 3–4, item 37.

[31]*Ustawa z dnia 23 Listopada 2002 r. o Sądzie Najwyższym* (Act of 23 November 2002 on the Supreme Court). Available at: http://www.sn.pl/en/about/SiteAssets/Lists/Status_prawny_EN/EditForm/consolidated_text_of_the_Act_on_the_Supreme_Court.pdf.

[32]Zbrojewska (2013), p. 9.

[33]Murzynowski (1994), p. 231.

previous judgments of the courts of higher level to minimise the risk of having their judgments quashed or amended in case of appeal or cassation. [34]

It is worth adding that the Polish law envisages one more possibility when the court, which tries a case is tied by other court's decision. According to Article 442 of the Criminal Procedure Code in a case of reversal by the second instance court the judgment rendered by the first instance court and remanding the case for re-examination, the legal opinions and directions of the second instance court with respect to the further course of the proceedings shall be binding upon the court to which the case has been remanded for re-examination. Similar provision with respect to the civil proceedings is envisaged in Article 386.

The Supreme Administrative Court has a similar position to the Supreme Court. The former is empowered to adopt resolutions in specific administrative cases as well as resolutions aimed at clarifying law provisions, whose application caused discrepancies in the way the law was interpreted by the administrative courts, which is referred to as "abstract resolution".[35] In Poland as of January 2004 a two-instance administrative court proceedings have been functioning and the Supreme Administrative Court is the body supervising the activity of *voivodship* administrative courts in the area of adjudicating. Yet the essential difference between the abstract resolutions of the Supreme Court and those of the Supreme Administrative Court is the fact that the latter are formally binding for all administrative courts (Article 269(1)).[36]

4 Legal Status of Homosexual Persons in the Light of the Jurisprudence of the Polish Courts

According to the Constitutional Tribunal, the principle of equal rights can be expressed in a formula which would envisage that it is forbidden to create a law that would differentiate the legal status of those entities whose real situation is the same.[37] Yet as it would seem, taking into account the legal status of homosexual persons in Poland, the Polish society's view on this issue is translated into the decisions of politicians representing them. It is worth examining if this observation has an impact on the judges who are supposed to apply the decisions of the Constitutional Tribunal in practice.

In 2011 the Polish Society of Anti-discrimination Law conducted a survey on the attitudes of judges of the common courts of law towards discrimination as such. The result of this survey cannot be considered as representative because only

---

[34]Łętowska (2010), p. 8.

[35]Bojanowski (2008), p. 138.

[36]Dąbek (2008), p. 198.

[37]Constitutional Tribunal, P 4/03, OTK-A 2004, 7 June 2004, no 6, Item 55.

fifty-four judges answered the questionnaire.[38] Yet in my opinion the survey's result may give us a general view on the way the Polish judges think.

The survey showed that sexual minorities are a group which is exposed to discrimination to the greatest extent. Such an answer was given by 14 % of judges, while 10 % of the respondents answered that it is the ethnic minorities who are mostly discriminated. Religious minorities were mentioned only by 2 % of the respondents. The fact that some persons are given worse treatment because of their sexual orientation was confirmed also by the research carried out by the Polish government. In that research almost half of the respondents answered that the reasons for bad treatment of minorities are sexual orientation or mental illness.[39] The most often mentioned spheres of life where discrimination takes place are: difficulties in finding and keeping a job (20 %), rejection or verbal aggression (16 %), intolerance (18 %). The probable reason for this is the fact that labour law covers only the area of employment in which the question of equal treatment also of homosexual persons is clearly articulated. Hence the majority of cases in the courts is dealing with the results of discrimination related to employment; most of the requests for help directed to the Polish Society of Anti-discrimination Law are also related with the same problems.[40]

As the most frequent reasons for discrimination, the judges indicated: stereotypes and social prejudices—54 %; individual negative attitude towards representatives of social groups—37 %, and culture, tradition and history—22 %. It is a meaningful fact that as much as 20 % of the respondents indicated that the reasons for discrimination are behaviours and attitudes of minorities themselves.[41] The respondents pointed out that a demonstrative way of manifesting one's sexual orientation is considered to be a provocation, which to some degree justifies explains discriminating treatment.[42]

As to the assessment of the Polish legal provisions concerning the prevention of discrimination, 80 % of the respondents have stated that Poland has a sufficient number of instruments to fight discrimination, 9 % said that the number is insufficient, while 11 % answered "hard to say". The protuberant questions that, according to the judges, have not been resolved so far are: parental rights, inheritance and tax rights, as well as increasing the protection against discrimination due to sexual orientation.[43]

However, it is quite alarming that in reply to the question whether discrimination is an important social problem as many as 22 % of the respondent judges said "no", while 13 % said "hard to say". The respondents explained that only a small number of such cases were brought to courts.[44]

---

[38]Wieczorek and Bogatko (2013), p. 107.

[39]Górniak (2013), p. 41.

[40]Wieczorek and Bogatko (2013), p. 129.

[41]Ibid., p. 113.

[42]Ibid., p. 151.

[43]Ibid., pp. 155, 166.

[44]Ibid., p. 129.

It is interesting to compare the opinions of the judges with judgments of the Supreme Court and Supreme Administrative Court in cases dealing with the legal status of a homosexual person. Let me begin with criminal law, as its provisions regulate in detail the issue of the rights of next of kin of the accused. First of all, in some cases their will is crucial for the decision whether the proceedings are instituted or not. In Poland the great majority of offences are prosecuted *ex officio*, i.e., the authorities responsible for the prosecution of an offence have an obligation to institute and conduct preparatory proceedings if there is a good reason to suspect that an offence has been committed. Yet there are some cases where the consent of the injured party, i.e., the victim, is absolutely required to authorise the prosecutor or the police to prosecute an offence. Good examples of such acts are all offences against property (such as theft, burglary, causing criminal damage, fraud against next of kin), illegal threat, exposing another person to HIV infection, or unintentional causing bodily harm in a car accident. In those cases there is no option to prosecute the offence against the injured party's will. The main purpose of those provisions is the need to protect the good of the family.[45] Moreover, the next of kin of the accused is authorised to refuse to testify in a case against the accused relative. According to Article 182(1) of the Polish Criminal Procedure Code, the next of kin to the accused may refuse to testify. Such a person does not have to give reasons for his or her refusal,[46] and his/her decision is binding on the court. Hence to invoke this right it is sufficient to file an appropriate statement by the authorised person prior to his or her questioning. This provision is supplemented by Article 185, according to which, a person having a particularly close relationship to the accused may be exempted from the obligation to give testimony, if such a person applies for such exemption. However, the person so applying has to lend credence to the fact of having a particularly close relationship to the accused,[47] while an exemption from the obligation of giving testimony is decided by the court.[48] It is worth adding here, that the Criminal Procedure Code determines that the next of kin of the injured party also has some rights within the course of the proceedings, e.g., in the event of death of the injured party, his/her rights may be exercised by his/her next of kin, which means that he/she may file a civil complaint against the accused in order to litigate, within the framework of the criminal proceedings, for his/her property claims directly resulting from the offence. Such a person, when death of his/her next of kin was caused by a criminal offence, is authorised to bring indictment and support charges even when the public prosecutor has acknowledged that the proceedings have failed to disclose grounds sufficient to justify the preparation of an indictment. Therefore it is absolutely relevant to define what the term "next of kin" really means.

The legal definition of this term is included in Article 115(11) of the Polish Criminal Code, which states that a next of kin is a spouse, an ascendant, descendant, brother or

---

[45]Grzegorczyk (1987), p. 236.

[46]Supreme Court, I KR 329/80, OSNKW 1981, 20 January 1981, no. 6, item 37.

[47]Grzegorczyk (2003), p. 345.

[48]Ibid., p. 346.

sister, relative by marriage in the same line or degree, a person being an adopted relation, as well as his/her spouse, and also a person actually living in co-habitation. It is worth noticing on a footnote, that till 1964, a person living in co-habitation was not considered to be next of kin to the accused and the Criminal Code was then amended to change this situation. The amendment was a consequence of the Supreme Court's interpretation of law laid down in the judgment of 8 October 1959.[49] At the time of the judgment, the binding law gave the discussed rights only to the spouse of the accused.

However, how to understand the term of "person actually living in co-habitation?". Since this term does not have an established meaning in the legal vocabulary, the question was left to be decided by the judicature. The Supreme Court for the first time voiced their opinion as early as in 1975 under the rule of the previous Criminal Procedure Code of 1969. In the judgment of 12 November 1975,[50] the Supreme Court stressed that the relevant and indispensable features of living in co-habitation should be as follows: shared physical and psychological co-habitation, economic ties and stability of the union in question. Those features could indicate that between two persons of different sex there is a union, which differs from a marriage only by the fact that it lacks the legal sanction of a real marriage.[51] Similarly, in 2004, the Supreme Court, issuing its judgment, recognized also that the term "living in co-habitation" should be applied solely to common-law marriage, in particular to the union of persons of different sex,[52] equivalent in fact to the marital relationship, which according to Article 18 of the Polish Constitution denotes only a union between persons of different sex.[53] The legal position established by the Supreme Court[54] was changed only in 2013. In its judgment the Supreme Court stated that the term "living in co-habitation" incorporates persons who, irrespective of their sex and age, lived together by which we assume that they share and run their household and (as it may seem) are connected by definite psychological ties.[55] Yet it is worth noticing that—due to the fact that the actual facts of the case being dealt with by the Supreme Court did not refer to homosexual persons living in co-habitation—the Supreme Court did not address the issue directly. However since the term "living in co-habitation" refers to the persons who share and run their household, irrespective of their sex, we can expect that this will constitute a premise for the courts of law to stop treating this term in its traditional scope.

---

[49]VI KO 88/59, Nowe Prawo 1960, no. 5, p. 877.

[50]KR 203/75, OSP 1976, vol. 10, item 187.

[51]Ibid.

[52]It is worth underlining that the Supreme Court itself, denying homosexual persons the use of the priviledges of the heterosexual couples, indicated the possible occurence of a situation where one of the participants of criminal proceedings could be a homosexual person who had legally married or entered into a legally registered partnership in a State where it is possible to do so. See Supreme Court, IV KK 63/03, OSNwSK 1/2003, 27 May 2003, item 1132.

[53]II KK 176/04, LEX no. 121668.

[54]Appeal Court in Cracow, II Ka 226/97, OSN PiPr 1998, 11 December 1997, no. 10, item 23; Appeal Court in Cracow, II Aka 135/02, KZS 2002, 27 June 2002, nos. 7–8, item 52.

[55]Supreme Court, III KK 268/12, LEX no. 1311768, 12 March 2013.

Yet the first judgment, that pointed out that homosexual partners should be treated in the same way as heterosexual couples, was rendered in a civil case. In 2007 the Appeal Court stressed that:

> There is no reason to apply different rules when reconciling the assets of a homosexual common-law marriage than those which are applied in heterosexual common-law marriage.[56]

This judgment however was binding only in this particular case. In 2012 the Supreme Court reaffirmed[57] that the person who is/was actually living with the tenant of the same sex is entitled to succeed the tenant in lieu of the one who died. In its substantiation of the judgment the Court invoked not only Article 32 of the Constitution, establishing the obligation of equal treatment and the respective prohibition of discrimination, for reasons of, among others, one's gender or sexual orientation. It is worth adding that the Court supported a postulate expressed by another panel of this Court in the substantiation of another judgment that:

> [F]acing lack of explicit regulations regarding the same sex couples, substantial law should be construed to close the gap by taking into account justified interests of those persons.[58]

The reasoning of the judgment of 2012 also indicates that for the resolution of the analysed matter the judgment rendered by the ECtHR on 2 March 2010 in *Kozak v. Poland*[59] is of material, however supplementary importance. In *Kozak v. Poland* the European Court stressed that sexual orientation as one of the most intimate aspects of personal life is protected by Article 8 of the ECHR. It is worth adding, that the latter judgment was also taken into account by the Appeal Court in Warsaw while passing its judgment of 26 June 2014, which concludes that there are no convincing juridical reasons, nor are there any of sociological of psychological nature, that would support the differentiation of legal consequences of co-habitation of heterosexual and homosexual couples. On the contrary, emotional, physical and economic bonds that are established in the course of such co-habitation are in both cases the same, and can form just as strong a relationship. The Court also referred to the contents of Article 32 of the Polish Constitution. However, as it was mentioned before, judgments of the appeal courts are not binding upon other courts, and on the other hand, the standpoint of the Supreme Court has not so far been translated into other civil entitlements of homosexual couples. Same-sex partners have no right to refuse to testify in civil cases. Furthermore, those small, however positive changes, introduced by the ruling of the Supreme Court in civil and criminal law through the interpretation of the term "living in co-habitation" in the spirit of equality of homosexual couples, did not bring about any further changes within other branches of law. The Supreme Administrative Court in its judgment of 20 March 2012[60] refused the persons of the same sex being in a steady relationship

---

[56]Appeal Court in Białystok, I ACa 590/06, LEX no. 965765, 23 February 1997.

[57]Supreme Court, III CZP 65/12, LexisNexis no. 4134116, 28 November 2012.

[58]Supreme Court, IV CSK 301/07, OSNC 2009, 6 December 2007, no. 2, item 29.

[59]*Kozak v. Poland* (App. no. 131202/02), ECtHR, judgment of 2 March 2010.

[60]II FSK 1704/10, LEX no. 1066917.

the right to be exempted from the tax on the deed of gift to which exemption next of kin would be entitled. According to this judgment, homosexuals have no right to apply preferential rules of annual tax return settlements as married couples. It is very difficult to understand why homosexual partners have different legal status and, respectively different treatment depending on a branch of law.

The last judgment worth mentioning does not concern the rights of homosexual persons, but deals with the issue of discrimination of homosexual minority as a group. In October 2011[61] the Circuit Court in Warsaw issued a very controversial decision upon the motion of the political party *Narodowe Odrodzenie Polski* (National Rebirth of Poland) to enter in the register their additional graphic symbols. Apart from such emblems as the Celtic Cross, the party applied to the Court to enter one more graphic sign, namely *"zakaz pedałowania"* (which could mean in Polish—both "cycling forbidden" as "pedalling forbidden" and "gays forbidden", since in Polish gay people are often offensively referred to as "pedals", meaning "faggots", which is an offensive derogatory term and should not be used).

However the Court has approved the petition basing its decision on the opinion of two experts who stated that:

> The contents of the sign using the structure and symbol of a prohibitive road sign, conveys the message that homosexual intercourse is forbidden in public places, which is consistent with generally accepted custom and any attempt to interpret it otherwise is a proof of being oversensitive.[62]

Consequently, the Court stated that although this sign is obscene, yet it does not promote any message of fascism, Nazism or hate-speech. Appeal against this ruling was brought by the public prosecutor and by the Ombudsman. In January 2012 the Appeal Court[63] reversed the decision subject to review, ordering the Circuit Court to re-assess if the implicit message of the sign can be considered compliant with the Constitution.

The Court of second instance also emphasized that open disapproval of homosexual persons, expressed in this symbol seems to be clear for any viewer and the compliance of this symbol with public legal order does not require an expert opinion. After re-examination of the case and taking into account the legal opinion and directions of the Appeal Court, the Circuit Court refused to officially register the sign of *Narodowe Odrodzenie Polski*. The Court however did not examine the question of compatibility of this sign with the Polish legal order, as specified by the Polish Constitution and the ECHR, but refused the motion on formal grounds saying that according to the Appeal Court a political party is not permitted to have more than one graphic symbol.

---

[61]The order of the Circuit Court in Warsaw, VII Ns Rej Ew Pzm 77/09 (unpublished).

[62]See: http://www.nop.org.pl/wp-content/uploads/2011/11/ekspertyza-sadowa-dot-znakow-NOP.pdf?6949c1.

[63]The order of the Appeal Court in Warsaw, I Aca 1387/11, 13 January 2013, available at: http://www.rpo.gov.pl/sites/default/files/13288838550.pdf.

5 Conclusion

Although the interference of the law with socially or morally controversial issues happens on three levels of legal order, legislation, application and interpretation of the law, sometimes it is the judicature that ensures that the law catches up with social, economic and political changes.[64] However it may seem that divisions within the Polish society and parliament with respect to the most controversial social issues are also reflected in the judgments of the Polish courts. Arguments raised in the public debate both in favour and against the regulation of legal position of homosexual couples, namely Articles 32 and 18 of the Polish Constitution, are also reflected in the reasons for judgments, including the ones of the Supreme Court, which then understandingly translates into the decisions of the courts of lower instances.

> Conflicts between different legal principles and rights and freedoms of citizens are a judge's daily bread, and at times one is caught in a position where one must make choices that should have been made by the legislator.[65]

This of course raises yet another question—whether the judges impose their own personal set of values, or whether it is the system encompassed in the Constitution which undergoes some evolution alongside the changing society.[66]

It seems that the Polish courts, particularly of higher instances, have started to interpret the law and fill the gaps brought about by statutory regulations in compliance with the Polish Constitution and the ECHR as well as the guidelines issued by the European Union and the Council of Europe, which will be reflected in the decisions of the courts of lower instances. Analysing the reasons of their judgments it is difficult to ascertain which factors had the most bearing on their decisions—the above-mentioned legal acts or the jurisprudence of the ECtHR. It must also be remembered that it would be irrational to claim that the present-day codified Constitution of a democratic State comprises clear-cut provisions that are indifferent and inert *vis-à-vis* a dynamic set of values, or that it is universal and granted for eternity.[67]

References

Banaszak, Bogusław, and Michał Bednarczyk. 2012. *Aktywizm sędziowski we wpółczesnym państwie demokratycznym*. Warsaw: Wydawnictwo Sejmowe.

Biedroń, Robert. 2008. Wprowadzenie do problematyki przeciwdziałania nietolerancji i dyskryminacji ze względu na orientację seksualną w zatrudnieniu. In *Rola związków zawodowych w przeciwdziałaniu nietolerancji i dyskryminacji ze względu na orientację seksualną w zatrudnieniu*, eds. Tomasz Szypuła and Krzysztof Śmiszek, 9-23. Warsaw: Kampania Przeciw Homofobii.

---

[64]Koncewicz (2010), p. 191.

[65]Morawski (2009), p. 67.

[66]Banaszak and Bednarczyk (2012), p. 26.

[67]Ibid., p. 256.

Bojanowski, Eugeniusz. 2008. Uchwałodawcza działalność Naczelnego Sądu Administracyjnego i jej znaczenie w systemie prawa. In *Orzecznictwo w systemie prawa*, eds. Tomasz Bąkowski, Krzysztof Grajewski and Jarosław Warylewski, 135-145. Warsaw: Wolters Kluwer Polska.

Dąbek, Dorota. 2008. Między precedensem a źródłem prawa. In *Orzecznictwo w systemie prawa*, eds. Tomasz Bąkowski, Krzysztof Grajewski and Jarosław Warylewski, 193-207. Warsaw: Wolters Kluwer Polska.

Gapska, Edyta. 2010. *Czynności decyzyjne sądów w postępowaniu cywilnym*. Warsaw: Wolters Kluwer Polska.

Garlicki, Leszek. 1997 *Konstytucja Rzeczpospolitej Polskiej. Komentarz*. Vol. III. Warsaw: Wydawnictwo Sejmowe.

Grzegorczyk, Tomasz. 1987. *Wnioskowy tryb ścigania przestępstw*. Warsaw: Acta Universitatis Lodziensis.

Grzegorczyk, Tomasz. 2003. *Kodeks postępowania karnego. Komentarz*. Warsaw: Zakamycze

Górniak, Jarosław. 2013. Równe traktowanie standardem dobrego rządzenia – raport z badań sondażowych. In *Prawo antydyskryminacyjne w praktyce polskich sądów powszechnych. Raport z monitoringu*, eds. Monika Wieczorek and Katarzyna Bogatko. 91-61. Warsaw: Polskie Towarzystwo Prawa Antydyskryminacyjnego.

Jabłońska, Zofia, and Knut Paweł. 2012. *Prawa osób LGBT w Polsce. Raport z badań nad wdrażaniem Zalecenia CM/Rec (2010) Komitetu Ministrów Rady Europy dla Państw Członkowskich w zakresie środków zwalczania dyskryminacji opartej na orientacji seksualnej lub tożsamości płciowej*. Warsaw: Kampania Przeciwko Homofobii.

Koncewicz, Tomasz. 2010. Unijna ścieżka precedensu. Nie "czy", ale "jak". In *Precedens w polskim systemie prawa*, eds. Anna Śledzińska-Simon and Mirosław Wyrzykowski, 187-228. Warsaw: Zakład Graficzny UW.

Łętowska, Ewa. 2010. Czy w Polsce możemy mówić o prawie precedensowym? In *Precedens w polskim systemie prawa*, eds. Anna Śledzińska-Simon and Mirosław Wyrzykowski, 9-14. Warsaw: Zakład Graficzny UW.

Morawski, Lech. 2009. Zasada trójpodziału *władzy. Trybunał Konstytucyjny i aktywizm sędziowski. Przegląd Sejmowy 4 (93): 59-74*.

Murzynowski. Andrzej. 1994. *Istota i zasady procesu karnego*. Warsaw: Wydawnictwo Naukowe PWN.

Partington, Martin. 2006. *Introduction to the English Legal System*. Oxford: Oxford University Press.

Safjan, Marek. 2006. Niezależność Trybunału Konstytucyjnego i suwerenność konstytucyjna RP. *Państwo i Prawo* 6: 3-7

Skrzydło, Wiesław. 2011. *Konstytucja Rzeczpospolitej Polskiej. Komentarz*. Warsaw: Zakamycze.

Wieczorek, Monika, and Katarzyna Bogatko (eds.). 2013. *Prawo antydyskryminacyjne w praktyce polskich sądów powszechnych. Raport z monitoringu*. Warsaw: Polskie Towarzystwo Prawa Antydyskrymacyjnego.

Wiliński, Paweł. 2011. *Proces karny w świetle Konstytucji*. Warsaw: Wolters Kluwer Polska.

Zbrojewska, Monika. 2013. *Rola i stanowisko prawne Sądu Najwyższego w procesie karnym*. Warsaw: Ekonomik.

Principle of Legality and Role of the Judiciary in Criminal Law: The Influence of the ECtHR Case Law on the Italian Legal System

Francesco Mazzacuva

Abstract This chapter focuses on the interpretation of the term "law" given by the European Court of Human Rights and on the subsequent overview of judicial law-making. This approach has had an important influence on the scholarly discussion about the problematic consequences of judicial overruling. In some recent judgments, this phenomenon has been compared to changes in the law, although this conclusion encountered the strong opposition of the Italian Constitutional Court.

1 The Interpretation of the Word "Law" in the Case Law of the European Court of Human Rights

One of the most important features which characterizes the system of protection of fundamental rights established by the Convention for the Protection of Human Rights and Fundamental Freedoms (ECHR) is the creation of a jurisdictional body entrusted with the ascertainment of violations. Furthermore, the European Court of Human Rights (ECtHR) has, over time, not limited itself to verifying the respect of the guarantees laid down in the ECHR, but has frequently provided an "evolutive" interpretation of these guarantees,[1] especially giving an "autonomous" definition of certain provisions.[2] In the scope of such development of the European system of protection of human rights, the inclusion of *judicial law* under the concept of "law" has undoubtedly been one of the points with the highest cultural impact on civil law systems.

---

[1]See Valticos (2000), p. 1472 and Prebensen (2000), p. 1132.
[2]See Ganshof van der Meersch (1988), p. 201 ff.; Ost (1989), 440 ff.

F. Mazzacuva (✉)
Research Fellow in Criminal Law, Researcher in University of Parma, Parma, Italy
e-mail: francesco.mazzacuva@unipr.it

© Springer International Publishing Switzerland 2015   311
L. Pineschi (ed.), *General Principles of Law - The Role of the Judiciary*,
Ius Gentium: Comparative Perspectives on Law and Justice 46,
DOI 10.1007/978-3-319-19180-5_15

This theoretical approach was developed beginning with the judgment *Sunday Times v. United Kingdom* of 26 April 1979, in which the ECtHR observed that the word "law" in the expression "prescribed by law"[3] must cover not only *statutory law* but also *unwritten law.*[4] On that occasion, the European Court was asked to establish whether the prohibition to publish certain articles in order to prevent the commission of the offence of contempt of court had a legal basis in the English system. In fact, the offence was not covered by any *statutory definition*, as it was rather the results of a long-term elaboration of the *common law*, in which the contempt of court was recognized in a vast and heterogeneous series of hypotheses. Faced with this problem, the ECtHR decided that the offence should nonetheless be considered as "prescribed by law". The reasons leading to the Court's conclusion were essentially twofold.

First of all, the ECtHR observed that:

> [I]t would be contrary to the intention of the drafters of the Convention to hold that a restriction imposed by virtue of the common law is not "prescribed by law" on the sole ground that it is not enunciated in legislation: this would deprive a common-law State which is Party to the Convention of the protection of Article 10 (*and of others*) and strike at the very roots of that State's legal system.

Then, the European Court observed that the core of the principle of legality is well summarized by the requirements of "accessibility" and "foreseeability" of law.[5] From this point of view, both statutory definitions and judicial interpretation have to be taken into consideration and, what is more, the Court remarked that absolute precision in statutory provisions cannot be attained and might also entail excessive rigidity, while "the law must be able to keep pace with changing circumstances".[6] Therefore, even if a statute providing incrimination or any other limitation of a fundamental right is in force, its foreseeability relies essentially upon the way it is interpreted and applied by the courts.

---

[3]The existence of a *law provision* is notably a requirement which has to be satisfied by every kind of public limitation of fundamental rights provided for by the ECHR. For instance, this requirement is established by Article 5 with regard to deprivation of liberty (which may be ordered "in accordance with a procedure prescribed by law") and by Articles 8, 9, 10 and 11 with regard to the right to respect of private and family life, to the freedom of thought, conscience and religion, to the freedom of expression and to the freedom of assembly and association. Moreover, the existence of a law provision is notably the core of the principle of legality in criminal law (*nullum crimen, nulla poena sine lege*) laid down in Article 7 of the ECHR.

[4]On this topic, see Matscher (1996), p. 272 ff.; Delmas-Marty (1989), p. 153 ff.; Cremona (1990), p. 190 ff.

[5]The requirement of "predictability" of law is probably the main feature of the "formal" conceptions of the rule of law, notably pointed out in Dicey (1959); Cass (1995), p. 954 ff.; Raz (1977), p. 198 ff. On this topic, see also Craig (1997), p. 467.

[6]*Sunday Times v. The United Kingdom* (App. no. 6538/74), ECtHR, judgment of 26 April 1979, para. 49; *Kokkinakis v. Greece* (App. no. 14307/88), ECtHR, 25 May 1993, para. 40.

This kind of approach was also employed with regard to the principle of legality in criminal law, enshrined in Article 7 of the ECHR.[7] In fact, starting from *Kokkinakis v. Greece* of 24 March 1993, the ECtHR has established that any assessment based upon Article 7 of the European Convention cannot be limited to the wording of relevant statutory provisions and that their judicial interpretation has to be taken into consideration also.

In *Kokkinakis*, the applicant argued that, on the basis of the textual formulation of the relevant Greek statutory provision, it would have been impossible to foresee his conviction for the offence of proselytism. According to the claimant, the lack of predictability was due to the overly general legal definition of the offence and to the expansive and contradictory interpretation rendered by the national courts. The ECtHR recognised that the Criminal Code provision incriminating proselytism was, to a certain extent, vague. Consistently with the conclusion reached in the *Sunday Times* case, however, the Court also dwelt on the interpretation of the offence given by the Greek Supreme Court: in this respect, the European Court deemed the case law on that point sufficiently settled and coherent and dismissed the application.

The judgment is also well known because the ECtHR, for the very first time, stated that Article 7 of the European Convention is not confined to prohibiting the retrospective application of the criminal law to an accused's disadvantage, but it also embodies the principle that only the law can define a crime and prescribe its penalty. The decision also established the principle that criminal law must not be extensively construed to an accused's detriment employing means such as analogical reasoning. Even if such prohibition of extensive and analogical interpretation could be understood as a contradictory claim of the prevalence of statutory law on judicial law,[8] in the Court's view it actually entails that any interpretation must be reasonably foreseeable in the light of statutory provisions and, above all, of judicial precedents.[9]

In the light of foregoing premises, in the case of *Pessino v. France* of 10 October 2006, the ECtHR for the first time found a violation of Article 7 of the ECHR because of lack of *accessibility* and *foreseeability* in criminal law. The main reason which led the Court to this conclusion was represented by the uncertainty of judge-made law. In particular, the ECtHR observed that the French government had been unable to indicate any judicial precedent from the Court of

---

[7]See Harris et al. (2009), p. 333 ff.; Emmerson et al. (2007), p. 380; van Dijk et al. (2006), p. 653 ff.; Rolland (1999), p. 294 ff. In the Italian scholarship see Bernardi (2001), p. 260 ff.; Zagrebelsky (2011), p. 74 ff.; Manes (2012); Nicosia (2006), p. 57 ff.

[8]The contradiction between prohibition of extensive interpretation and recognition of the evolutive role of judicial lawmaking is remarked by Sudre (2001), p. 354, and, before, by Chiavario (1969), p. 105 ff.

[9]This point is underlined by Bernardi (2001), p. 263, and, more recently, by Di Giovine (2011), p. 2238.

Cassation in which that offence had previously been interpreted in the extensive manner which led to the conviction of the applicant.[10]

In conclusion, the European Court on the one hand recognises the fundamental importance of the *law in action*. Even if simultaneous contrasting interpretations have been deemed to be contrary to the principle of fair trial established in Article 6(1) of the ECHR,[11] judicial law-making has nonetheless always been recognised as an important factor of evolution of each legal system. Moreover, the ECtHR has repeatedly stated that its institutional role is not concerned with assessing the correct interpretation of national legislation. However, should a new interpretation result as unfavourable to the defendant, the Court would consider its retrospective application as being contrary to Article 7 of the ECHR. In other words, the ECtHR seems to adopt the logic of the adjudicative technique known as *prospective overruling*. This means of adjudication has been initially developed in the United States and it prescribes that, in certain cases, new interpretation can merely be stated, while it will be applied only to future conducts.

Finally, it is important to remark that the European Court in the last years seems to have abandoned its self-restraint, as evidenced by the recent judgments *Dragotoniu and Militaru-Pidhorni v. Romania*,[12] *Liivik v. Estonia*[13] and, most recently, *Del Rio Prada v. Spain*,[14] in which violations of Article 7 of the ECHR were caused precisely by a retroactive application of a judicial overruling.

The two historical decisions about marital rape, in which the ECtHR held that an unfavourable overruling could be considered predictable even in light of changes in the socio-cultural context and of the "evil" nature of the prohibited

---

[10]*Pessino v. France* (App. no. 40403/02), ECtHR, judgment of 10 October 2006.

[11]*Beian v. Romania* (App. no. 30658/05), ECtHR, judgment of 6 December 2007, in which the Court criticized the contradictory case law of the Romanian High Court, with these terms: "The practice which developed within the country's highest judicial authority is in itself contrary to the principle of legal certainty, a principle which is implicit in all the Articles of the Convention and constitutes one of the basic elements of the rule of law .... Instead of fulfilling its task of establishing the interpretation to be followed, the HCCJ itself became a source of legal uncertainty, thereby undermining public confidence in the judicial system". Similar observations appear in later judgments, such as *Iordanov v. Bulgaria* (App. no. 56856/00), ECtHR, judgment of 2 July 2009. On this topic, see Cadoppi (2014a), p. 15; Cerqua (2011).

[12]*Dragotoniu and Militaru-Pidhorni v. Romania* (App. nos. 77193/01 and 77196/01), ECtHR, judgment of 24 May 2007, in which the Court observed that the qualification of bank employees as public officers could not be foreseen at the time of the bribery, being the result of a subsequent evolutive interpretation.

[13]*Liivik v. Estonia* (App. no. 12157/05), ECtHR, judgment of 25 June 2009, in which the conviction for the offence of "misuse of official position" on the basis of a wide interpretation of the concept of "economical prejudice" was considered as unpredictable for the accused.

[14]*Del Rio Prada v. Spain* (App. no. 42750/09), ECtHR [GC], judgment of 21 October 2013, in which the Grand Chamber confirmed that the new interpretation given by the *Tribunal Supremo* (so-called "*doctrina Parot*") on sentence adjustments and remissions which entailed a retrospective lengthening of the applicant's imprisonment constituted a violation of Article 7 of the ECHR.

conduct, remained rather isolated.[15] Notably, the applicants complained of being the first convicted in the United Kingdom for the offence of marital rape by reason of the repeal of the common law principle of the "marital exemption" (stated by Sir Matthew Hale in 1736). According to this now-repealed principle, marital rape would not be punishable because of the implied consent to sexual intercourse given by the wife upon entering into marriage. The European Court, however, acknowledged that:

> [T]he essentially debasing character of rape is so manifest that the result of the decisions of the Court of Appeal and the House of Lords – that the applicant could be convicted of attempted rape, irrespective of his relationship with the victim – cannot be said to be at variance with the object and purpose of Article 7.

For understandable reasons, this reasoning was criticized not only by civil lawyers,[16] but also by English ones.[17]

2 A Comparison with the Italian System

In the Italian criminal law, the problem of judicial overruling has traditionally been related to the principle of culpability (*principio di colpevolezza*) rather than to the principle of legality. In particular, with the famous judgment no. 364 of 1988, the Constitutional Court affirmed for the first time the constitutional value of the principle of culpability and, therefore, the necessary existence of the defence of *unavoidable ignorance of law*.[18] Exemplifying cases of such unavoidable ignorance, the Constitutional Court dwelt specifically on the problem of unsettled case law and sudden changes in interpretation, which may be detrimental for the accused.

Comparing the point of view of the ECtHR with the position of the Italian Constitutional Court, two aspects can be observed.

Firstly, it is clear that the principle of legality intended as *foreseeability* of the criminal law—or "recognisability", using the words of the Italian Constitutional Court—is closely connected to the principle of culpability. The latter is intended by Italian scholars, following the German model, as a principle upon which the individual must be considered blameworthy for the offence committed in order to

---

[15]*S.W. v. United Kingdom* and *C.R. v. United Kingdom* (App. nos. 20166/92 and 20190/92), ECtHR, judgment of 22 November 1995.

[16]Van Drooghenbroeck (1996), p. 473, who observes that the Court seems to make confusion between principle of legality and justification of criminalization policies. For similar observations, see Sudre (2001), p. 355, and Roets (2007), p. 127.

[17]See Osborne (1996), p. 406; Ashworth and Horder (2013), p. 59 ff. The judgments are agreed instead by Simester et al. (2013), p. 24 ff.

[18]The Constitutional Court notably adopted the position expressed by Pulitanò (1976), p. 545 ff., and Bricola (1973), p. 56 ff.

be punishable.[19] This means that he must have had at least the opportunity to understand the negative value of his behaviour and, subsequently, to act differently. Very briefly, freedom of self-determination serves as the common basis both for the requirement of offender's *mens rea* (and, more in general, of his *culpability*)[20] and for the requirement of "predictability" of criminal law.[21]

This link between principle of legality and principle of culpability can be clearly observed both in the case law of the Italian Constitutional Court and in the judgments of the ECtHR.

In the judgment no. 364 of 1988, in fact, the Constitutional Court stated in an extremely significant manner that:

> [T]he mandatory nature of law would be worthless if the a person would be held accountable for a conduct which he cannot prevent or whose proscription he cannot, without the slightest fault on his own part, understand. The principle of culpability, in this sense, does not only complete the principle of legality but rather it constitutes its second aspect, recognised in any system based on the Rule of law.[22]

In a very similar way, in the important *Sud Fondi* judgment, the ECtHR affirmed that strict liability would be incoherent with the requirements of accessibility and predictability of criminal law and that, therefore, Article 7 of the ECHR implies that intention or negligence have to be ascertained along with the *actus reus*.[23]

The second aspect which needs to be noted is that, notwithstanding analogous points of view on the principle of foreseeability of criminal law, the diverse conception of judicial law has brought the two Courts to different overviews of the problem of judicial overruling in the *element analysis* of criminal liability.

In fact, civil lawyers usually do not include case law under the concept of "law",[24] due to the cultural heritage represented by the clear separation between legislative and judiciary powers. Subsequently, a new interpretation is not

---

[19]In the German scholarship, see Kaufmann (1967), p. 533 ff.; Achenbach (1974); Roxin (1987), p. 356 ff., in which he finally accepted a "liberal" foundation of the principle of culpability. The liberal approach is also widespread among Italian criminal lawyers: see Fiandaca (1987), p. 855 ff. and Padovani (1987), p. 819 ff.

[20]See Roxin (1987); Bartoli (2005); Donini (2004), p. 70 ff. In the English scholarship, on the connections between *mens rea* and freedom of self-determination, see Ashorth and Horder (2013), p. 155. The idea that for every offence there should be both an *actus reus* element and a *mens rea* element which relates to that *actus reus* is also sometimes referred to the so-called "correspondence principle", described by Lord Kenyon in *Fowler v. Padget* (1789) as "a principle of natural justice that the *actus non facit reum nisi mens sit rea*". On this topic, see Spencer and Pedain (2005), p. 237; Simester et al. (2013), p. 196 ff.

[21]The connection between self-determination and principle of legality is plainly recognized at least since the statements made by Jeremy Bentham and Cesare Beccaria during the eighteen century.

[22]Constitutional Court, judgment no. 364 of 1988, para. 8.

[23]*Sud Fondi Srl and others v. Italy* (App. no. 75909/01), ECtHR, judgment of 20 September 2009, para. 116.

[24]See Vogliotti (2003), p. 334 ff.

considered as a new "law" whose retrospective application (if detrimental) is prohibited by the principle of legality, but rather as a lack of the subjective element of crime (*mens rea*) by virtue of the specific defence provided by Article 5 of the Italian Criminal Code (as "amended" by the Constitutional Court judgment no. 364 of 1988).[25]

In the opinion of the ECtHR, instead, such new interpretation entails the very absence of the *objective element* of the offence (*actus reus, tipicità* in Italian, *Tabtestand* in German) because of the lack of any legal basis of the offence. As precisely underlined by the former Italian judge of the European Court, Vladimiro Zagrebelsky:

> What at national level is reason of exclusion of guilt, in the scope of the Convention is a reason of exclusion of the very existence of a "law" provision.[26]

Now, like many scholars underline, the "Italian style" solution guarantees a certain balance between opposing needs. On the one hand, it aims to preserve the clear separation between parliamentary legislation and judicial law-making (prohibited, at least in theory). On the other hand, it still permits the acquittal of the accused in the event that a particular change of interpretation is not effectively predictable.[27]

However, some criminal lawyers point out today that the consideration of the problem of judicial overruling in the field of *mens rea* is basically artificial. It is true, in fact, that the need for predictability of criminal law is linked to the principle of culpability, but not every guarantee connected to that principle must be taken into account when ascertaining *mens rea*. At a closer look, an unfavourable overruling constitutes an aberration of the legal system and not a lack of comprehension of the unlawful nature of the behaviour due to individual's deficiencies. Consequently, the defendant's acquittal should be justified not by a presumed absence of *mens rea*, but rather by the non-existence of any provision of "law" (in a wider and "substantial" meaning) capable of guiding the individual's behaviour.[28]

It is precisely for this reason that even in Italian scholarship, at least in the modern reconstructions of the principle of legality which emphasises the importance of the "law in action", the aforementioned "prospective overruling" is

---

[25]This kind of solution is also agreed by the largest part of Italian criminal lawyers: see Fiandaca and Musco (2009), p. 390; Marinucci and Dolcini (2009), p. 293 ff.; Pulitanò (1976), p. 177 ff. and 512 ff.; Donini (1991), p. 493 ff., and Donini (1996), p. 272 ff.; Viganò, (2000), p. 258 ff. In the German legal system, the same solution surfaces in the important judgment of the *Bundesgerichtshof* of 18 March 1952 and in the Criminal Code of 1975; see also Welzel (1952), and Jescheck (1988), p. 188 ff.

[26]See Zagrebelsky (2011), p. 100.

[27]See Romano (2004), p. 47.

[28]See Grande (1990), p. 417 ff.; Vogliotti (2003), p. 348; Cadoppi (2014b), p. 319 ff., and recently, Donini (2011), p. 95 ff. and Valentini (2012), p. 150 ff.

increasingly referenced as a possible remedy, since it promises to provide more reliable solutions to the problem of unfavourable judicial overruling than the defence laid down in Article 5 of the Criminal Code.[29]

3 The Signs of a Paradigm Shift in the Italian Case Law and the "Answer" of the Constitutional Court

The contrast between the two different conceptions of judicial law-making and judicial overruling has clearly emerged in some recent decisions adopted by the Italian courts, especially since the *Beschi* judgment of the United Chambers (*Sezioni Unite*) of the Court of Cassation.[30]

The mentioned decision arose from a request for pardon, pursuant to a Convention in force between the two States, submitted by an Italian citizen convicted in the United Kingdom and subsequently transferred to Italy for the execution of the penalty. A first request had been previously rejected pursuant to a widespread interpretation of the Convention according to which the pardon could only be granted to persons convicted by an Italian court. However, after some time, the United Chambers of the Court of Cassation overruled that conclusion, establishing that the pardon could also be granted to those who had been convicted abroad and then transferred to Italy for execution of the penalty and, for this reason, the convicted person submitted the mentioned second request of pardon. The issue, however, was that Article 666 of the Criminal Procedure Code determines a second request for pardon similar to a previous one as being admissible only in cases where changes have occurred in the factual situation or in the legal framework.

Accordingly, in determining the second request for pardon to be admissible, in the *Beschi* judgment the Court of Cassation affirms in an extremely significant way that the United Chambers' adoption of a different interpretation must be compared to a change of "law". This conclusion was supported by underlining the fact that the United Chambers are a jurisdictional body appointed to resolve contrasting interpretations with decisions, which, although not formally binding, have a great persuasive capacity to guide future decisions. Furthermore, the judgment refers precisely to the case law of the ECtHR, according to which judge-made law must be considered as a component of the concept of "law".

---

[29]See Cadoppi (2014b), p. 321 ff. On the remedy of prospectivity of overrulings, see also Riondato (2000), p. 239 ff.; Donini (2004), p. 2202 ff.; Balsamo (2007); Scoletta (2013). In the German Scholarship, see Naucke (1968), p. 2321 ff.; Neumann (1991), p. 331 ff.; Schmitz (2011), p. 33 ff., and Hassemer and Kargl (2010), p. 51 ff. It has been observed, however, that even in the United States this technique is not adopted often, being preferred even in that system the *mistake of law* defence in order to conform to the declaratory nature of precedents: see Grande (1996), p. 469 ff., and Pomorski (1975), p. 192 ff.

[30]Court of Cassation, United Chambers, judgment no. 18288 of 2010.

The *Beschi* decision shows that the point of view of the European Court has been accepted with respect to the relation between written law and judicial law-making. This is especially true when the Court of Cassation recognises "a *concurring relationship* between legislative and judicial powers" as well as "a limited creative nature of the interpretation". Therefore, judicial overrulings are qualified as "new law" (*ius novum*) and not merely as a "different factual situation" having originated from a newly emerged "legal reasoning" (which was the alternative solution proposed in order to declare the second instance admissible).

In the wake of the *Beschi* judgment, some authors argued that courts should be empowered to overturn final *convictions* (*res iudicata*) as a result of favourable changes in the case law as well, at least in cases of "*judicial decriminalisation*" (i.e. new interpretation according to which certain behaviours are not considered as punishable anymore), also considering the progressive recognition of the principle of the retrospective application of the more lenient law (*lex mitior*) as a fundamental right.[31] The problem arises because Article 2 of the Italian Criminal Code and Article 673 of the Criminal Procedure Code provide for the overturn of definitive convictions (and the subsequent release of the convicted person) only in cases of "formal" legislative decriminalisation.

For this reason, the Turin Trial Court (*Tribunale di Torino*) petitioned the Constitutional Court to declare Article 673 of the Criminal Procedure Code to be unconstitutional for not providing for this remedy in cases of favourable overrulings of the United Chambers entailing a "substantial" decriminalization. In a nutshell, the Constitutional Court was requested to make an "additive" decision, intended as a decision aimed to introduce a new rule in the system as mandated by principles of the Constitution.[32]

More specifically, the case originated in the context of the illegal entry and the stay of a non-European citizen within the territory of Italy. The case resulted in a conviction for failure to exhibit personal identification documents and residence permits (provided for by Article 6(3), of the legislative decree no. 286/1998). However, a few months after the conviction became final (*res iudicata*), the United Chambers of the Court of Cassation ruled that such an offence is to be interpreted as applying only to non-EU citizens who were *regularly* present on the State's territory. At the same time, considering that illegal immigrants clearly cannot possess

---

[31]In the case law of the Constitutional Court, the constitutional rank of that principle has been recognised since the judgments no. 393/2006 and 304/2006, which made reference also to the judgment of the European Court of Justice, joined cases C-387/02 *Silvio Berlusconi*, C-391/02 *Sergio Adelchi*, C-403/02 *Marcello Dell'Utri and others* [2005] ECR I-3565, and to the wording of Article 49 of the Charter of Fundamental Rights of the European Union. Finally, the ECtHR in the judgment *Scoppola v. Italy* has stated that "a consensus has gradually emerged in Europe and internationally around the view that application of a criminal law providing for a more lenient penalty, even one enacted after the commission of the offence, has become a fundamental principle of criminal law". See *Scoppola v. Italy* (App. no. 10249/03), ECtHR, judgment of 17 September 2009, para. 106.

[32]Tribunale di Torino, 27 June 2011. http://www.penalecontemporaneo.com (26 July 2011).

a residence permit to produce, their conduct was already covered by the separate offence of *illegal immigration* (the consequence of which is deportation as opposed to imprisonment).[33]

As a result, the defendant petitioned the court to see his conviction overturned as per Article 673 of the Criminal Procedure Code. However, the Turin Trial Court refused to give an extensive interpretation of the provision to include judicial decriminalisation (even if this interpretation would have been more consistent with the case law of the ECtHR and decided to petition the Constitutional Court. It is significant, furthermore, that the Court of Turin also claimed that there had been a violation of Article 117 of the Constitution, namely the provision by which the binding force of the judgments of the ECtHR is recognised in the Italian system (and which subsequently allows for the declaration of unconstitutionality of national statutes in contrast with the Strasbourg case law).

The Constitutional Court, however, dismissed the petition.

Firstly, it was observed that, despite the fact that the European Court adopts a "wider" notion of law, so far this approach has never been "linked" to the principle of the retrospective application of the "more favourable" law to the purpose of recognising a right to the application of the new favourable interpretation. Furthermore, the Constitutional Court remarked that the same principle, even after the *Scoppola* judgment of the ECtHR, cannot be considered as an absolute principle, but rather one that can be balanced with other overriding interests.

Finally, the Constitutional Court stated that even if statutory decriminalisation may have retroactive effect and allow for the overturning of a final conviction, in case of favourable overruling an exception to the principle of the retrospective application of the more lenient law must be allowed because of the clear distinction between *statutory* and *judicial* law. This distinction derives from the fact that in the Italian system precedents have no binding effects. Therefore, the reasoning of the Court of Turin would paradoxically lead to the solution that, faced with a favourable overruling, all previous convictions ruled in similar cases should be overturned but, at the same time, each court could adopt the previous interpretation and convict other persons accused for the same conduct.

The strongest argument in the reasoning of the Constitutional Court is though represented by the assertion according to which, ultimately, each comparison between statutory law and judge-made law (and then also any form of binding nature of precedents) would be contrary to the principle which reserves to the parliament the legislative power in criminal matters (Article 25 of the Constitution) and to the principle of separation of powers according to which the only binding law is the statutory law enacted by the parliament (Article 101 of the Constitution).[34]

---

[33]Court of Cassation, United Chambers, judgment no. 16453 of 2011.

[34]This kind of approach can be found notably in Guastini (1998), p. 467 ff., and it has been recently recalled, in a commentary on the instance made by the Court of Turin, by Gambardella (2012).

Even in light of the peremptory nature of the latter argument, the judgment of the Constitutional Court encountered various criticisms in the wake of its announcement.

From the point of view of criminal lawyers, a solution that keeps a defendant imprisoned even if his conviction relied on an interpretation later disowned by the United Chambers is to be rejected out of hand. In fact, a problem of equality of treatment with regard to individuals prosecuted for a similar contemporary behaviour arises. Particularly, if these individuals were to be sentenced after the favourable overruling, they would fully benefit from the new interpretation, while the first class of defendants would not. In the light of such an unreasonable discrimination, it has been stressed that the penalty hardly would be compliant with constitutional principles, with particular reference to its "re-educational" purpose, enshrined in Article 27 of the Constitution.[35]

It is probably also for these reasons that another component of the Court of Turin facing a similar case decided, while the petition filed with the Constitutional Court was still pending, that a conviction could already be overturned by following a broad and consistent interpretation of Article 673 of the Criminal Procedure Code.

More generally, the exclusion of any binding effect of judicial precedents has been contested, observing that this effect could be recognised at least with regard to the decisions of the United Chambers, given their importance in the Italian legal system in guiding lower courts and the Court of Cassation itself.[36]In particular, the adoption of such a strict definition of the term "law", so starkly in contrast with the one conceived by the ECtHR, was criticized by some public lawyers, among which one significantly compared the attitude of the Constitutional Court to that of Penelope in the Odyssey, weaving a web during the day (when affirming the binding nature of the European Court's judgments) and unravelling it at night (when constitutional "counter-interests" are invoked in order to neutralize the value of those judgments).[37]

It should however be noted that, when the Constitutional Court points out that the absence of binding nature of precedents could lead a court to discard the interpretation of the United Chambers and adopt once again the unfavourable interpretation, this kind overruling might be applied non-retrospectively. In this assertion one could glimpse an implicit acceptance of the requirements of accessibility and predictability of judicial law-making theorised by the ECtHR beyond the "artificial" solution represented by the defence of mistake of law.[38]

---

[35]See Cadoppi (2012), p. 262 ff.

[36]See Cadoppi (2014b), p. 330 ff.

[37]See Ruggeri (2012a, b).

[38]See Manes (2012), p. 3481, who observes that the reasoning of the Constitutional Court in judgment no. 230 of 2012 should not be referred to the different problem of detrimental changes of interpretation.

4 Conclusion

The reasoning of the Constitutional Court shows the difficulties that Italian lawyers encounter when facing the new paradigm represented by the wide concept of "law" developed by the ECtHR. However, it is extremely significant to note that criticism towards the theory of the "declaratory nature" of judicial interpretation and the recognition of the "activism paradigm"[39] are gradually surfacing in legal scholarship as well as in the case law of the Court of Cassation.

The acceptance of judicial law-making, moreover, does not necessarily impinge upon parliamentary prerogatives because, even if the rejection of the declaratory paradigm blurs the distinction between the adjudicatory and legislative function, the latter maintains its power mostly intact.[40] On the other hand, this kind of approach would undoubtedly strengthen the liberal ideals expressed in the principle of legality, chiefly the right of individuals to predict the consequences of their actions (especially those with punitive purposes). In particular, this could be achieved by subordinating overrulings to the prohibition of retrospective effects.[41]

References

Achenbach, Hans. 1974. *Historische und dogmatische Grundlagen der strafrechtssystematischen Schuldlehre*. Berlin: J. Schweitzer Verlag.

Ashworth, Andrew, and Jeremy Horder. 2013. *Principles of Criminal Law*. Oxford: Oxford University Press.

Balsamo, Antonio. 2007. La dimensione garantistica del principio di irretroattività e la nuova interpretazione giurisprudenziale "imprevedibile": una "nuova frontiera" del processo di "europeizzazione" del diritto penale. *Cassazione penale* 47: 2202-2212.

Bartoli, Roberto. 2005. *Colpevolezza: tra personalismo e prevenzione*. Torino: Giappichelli.

Bernardi, Alessandro. 2001. Articolo 7. Nessuna pena senza legge. In *Commentario alla Convenzione europea per la tutela dei diritti dell'uomo e delle libertà fondamentali*, eds. Sergio Bartole, Benedetto Conforti and Giuseppe Raimondi, 249-306. Padova: Cedam.

Bricola, Franco. 1973. Teoria generale del reato. *Novissimo digesto italiano* XIX: 7-93.

Cadoppi, Alberto. 2012. *Il principio di irretroattività*. In *Introduzione al sistema penale*, eds. Gaetano Insolera, Nicola Mazzacuva, Massimo Pavarini and Marco Zanotti, 243-282. Torino: Giappichelli.

Cadoppi, Alberto. 2014. Giudice penale e giudice civile di fronte al precedente. *L'indice penale* 17: 11-34.

Cadoppi, Alberto. 2014. *Il valore del precedente nel diritto penale. Uno studio sulla dimensione in action della legalità*. Torino: Giappichelli.

Cass, Ronald A. 1995. Judging: Norms and Incentives of Retrospective Decision-making. *Boston University Law Review* 75: 941-996.

---

[39]One the contrast between declaratory paradigm and activism paradigm, see Sampford (2006), p. 165 ff.

[40]Ibid., p. 168.

[41]On the strict relationship between rejection of the declaratory paradigm and prospectivity of overrulings, see Charnock (2009), p. 415 ff.

Cerqua, Luigi D. 2011. Il valore del precedente nell'ordinamento giuridico italiano. *Il giudice di pace* 15: 189-192.

Charnock, Ross H. 2009. Overruling as a Speech Act: Performativity and Normative Discourse. *Journal of Pragmatics* 41: 401-426.

Chiavario, Mario. 1969. *La Convenzione europea dei diritti dell'uomo nel sistema delle fonti normative in materia penale*. Milano: Giuffré.

Craig, Paul P. 1997. Formal and Substantive Conceptions of the Rule of Law: An Analytical Framework. *Public law* 21: 467-487.

Cremona, John J. 1990. The Interpretation of the Word "Law" in the Jurisprudence of the European Court of Human Rights. In *Selected Papers 1946-1989*, ed. John J. Cremona, 187-194. Marsa, Malta: Publishers Enterprisers Group.

Delmas-Marty, Mireille. 1989. Légalité pénale et prééminence du droit selon la Convention européenne de sauvegarde des droits de l'homme et des libertés fondamentales. In *Droit pénal contemporain. Mélanges en l'honneur d'André Vitu*, 151-167. Paris: Editions Cujas.

Dicey, Albert V. 1959. *Introduction to the Study of the Law of the Constitution*. London: Macmillan; New York: St. Martin's Press.

Di Giovine, Ombretta. 2011. Il principio di legalità tra diritto nazionale e diritto convenzionale. In *Studi in onore di Mario Romano*. Napoli: Jovene.

Donini, Massimo. 1991. *Illecito e colpevolezza nell'imputazione del reato*. Milano: Giuffré.

Donini, Massimo. 1996. *Teoria del reato*. Padova: Cedam.

Donini, Massimo. 2004. *Il volto attuale dell'illecito penale*. Milano: Giuffré.

Donini, Massimo. 2011. *Europeismo giudiziario e scienza penale*. Milano: Giuffré.

Emmerson, Ben, Andrew Ashworth, and Alison MacDonald A. (eds.). 2007. *Human Rights and Criminal Justice*. London: Sweet & Maxwell.

Fiandaca, Giovanni. 1987. Considerazioni su colpevolezza e prevenzione. *Rivista italiana di diritto e procedura penale* 30: 836-880.

Fiandaca, Giovanni, and Enzo Musco. 2009. *Diritto penale. Parte generale*. Bologna: Zanichelli.

Gambardella, Marco. 2012. *Eius est abrogare cuius est condere*. http://www.penalecontemporaneo.com.

Ganshof van der Meersch, Walter J. 1988. Le caractère "autonome" des termes et la "marge d'appreciation" des gouvernements dans l'interprétation de la Convention européenne des droits de l'homme. In *Protection des droits de l'homme: la dimension européenne. Mélanges en l'honneur de Gérard J. Wiarda*, eds. Franz Matscher, Herbert Petzold and Gérard Wiarda, 201-220. Köln: Heymanns.

Grande, Elisabetta. 1990. La sentenza n. 364/1988 della Corte costituzionale e l'esperienza di "common law": alcuni possibili significati di una pronuncia in tema di errore di diritto. *Foro italiano* 113: 415-427.

Grande, Elisabetta. 1996. Principio di legalità e diritto giurisprudenziale: un'antinomia?. *Politica del diritto* 27: 469-484.

Guastini, Riccardo. 1998. *Teoria e dogmatica delle fonti*. Milano: Giuffré.

Harris, David J., Michael O'Boyle, and Colin Warbrick (eds.). 2009. *Law of the European Convention on Human Rights*. II ed. Oxford, New York: Oxford University Press.

Hassemer, Winfried, and Walter Kargl. 2010. § 1 StGB. In *Strafgesetzbuch*, eds. Urs Kindhäuser, Ulfrid Neumann and Hans-Ullrich Paeffgen, 160-208. III ed. Baden-Baden: Nomos.

Jescheck, Hans-Heinrich. 1988. L'errore di diritto nel diritto penale tedesco e italiano. *L'indice penale* 22: 185-204.

Kaufmann, Arthur. 1967. Dogmatische und kriminalpolitische Aspekte des Schuldgedankens im Strafrecht. *Juristenzeitung* 22: 554-560.

Manes, Vittorio. 2012. Commento all'art. 7. In *Commentario breve alla Convenzione europea di diritti dell'uomo*, eds. Sergio Bartole, Pasquale de Sena e Vladimiro Zagrebelsky, 258-288. Padova: Cedam.

Manes, Vittorio. 2012. Prometeo alla Consulta: una lettura dei limiti costituzionali all'equiparazione tra "diritto giurisprudenziale" e "legge". *Giurisprudenza costituzionale* 57: 3474-3482.

Marinucci, Giorgio, and Emilio Dolcini. 2009. *Manuale di diritto penale. Parte generale*. III ed. Milano: Giuffrè.

Matscher, Franz. 1996. Il concetto di legge secondo la recente giurisprudenza della Corte di Strasburgo. In *Scritti in onore di Guido Gerin*, 265-281. Padova: Cedam.

Naucke, Wolfgang. 1968. Rückwirkende Senkung der Promillegrenze und Rückwirkungsverbot (Art. 103 Abs. 2 GG). *Neue Juristische Wochenschrift* 21: 2321-2324.

Neumann, Ulfrid. 1991. Rückwirkungsverbot bei belastenden Rechtsprechungsänderungen der Strafgerichte? *Zeitschrift für die gesamte Strafrechtswissenschaft* 103: 331-356.

Nicosia, Emanuele. 2006. *Convenzione europea dei diritti dell'uomo e diritto penale*. Torino: Giappichelli.

Osborne, Craig. 1996. Does the End Justify the Means? Retrospectivity, Article 7, and the Marital Rape Exemption. *European Human Rights Law Review* 4: 406-416.

Ost, François. 1989. Originalité des méthodes d'interprétation de la CEDH. In *Raisonner la raison d'État*, ed. Mireille Delmas-Marty, 404-463. Paris: Presses universitaires de France.

Padovani, Tullio. 1987. Teoria della colpevolezza e scopi della pena. *Rivista italiana di diritto e procedura penale* 30: 798-835.

Pomorski, Stanislaw. 1975. *American Common Law and the Principle nullum crimen sine lege*. The Hague: Mouton.

Prebensen, Søren C. 2000. Evolutive Interpretation of the European Convention of Human Rights. In *Protection des droits de l'homme: la perspective européenne. Mélanges à la mémoire de R. Ryssdal*, eds. Paul Mahoney, Franz Matscher, Herbert Petzold and Luzius Wildhaber, 1123-1137. Berlin: Carl Heynemans Verlag KG.

Pulitanò, Domenico. 1976. *L'errore di diritto nella teoria del reato*. Milano: Giuffrè.

Raz, Joseph. 1977. The Rule of Law and its Virtue. *Law Quarterly Review* 93: 195-211.

Riondato, Silvio. 2000. Retroattività del mutamento penale giurisprudenziale sfavorevole, tra legalità e ragionevolezza. In *Diritto e clinica per l'analisi della decisione del caso*, ed. Umberto Vincenti, 241-257. Padova: Cedam.

Roets, Damien. 2007. La non-rétroactivité de la jurisprudence pénale in malam partem consacrée par la CEDH. *Recueil Dalloz* 183: 124-128.

Rolland, Patrice. 1999. Article 7. In *La Convention européenne des droits de l'homme. Commentaire article par article*, eds. Louis Edmond Pettiti, Emmanuel Decaux and Pierre Henri Imbert, 293-303. II ed. Paris: Economica.

Romano, Mario. 2004. *Commentario sistematico del codice penale*. III ed. Milano: Giuffrè.

Roxin, Claus. 1987. Was bleibt von der Schuld im Strafrecht übrig?. *Schweizerische Zeitung für Strafrecht* 104: 356-377.

Ruggeri, Antonio. 2012. Ancora a margine di Corte cost. n. 230 del 2012, post scriptum. *Consulta online*: 1-5.

Ruggeri, Antonio. 2012. Penelope alla Consulta: tesse e sfila la tela dei suoi rapporti con la Corte EDU, con significativi richiami ai tratti identificativi della struttura dell'ordine interno e distintivi rispetto alla struttura dell'ordine convenzionale. *Consulta online*: 1-8.

Sampford, Charles. 2006. *Retrospectivity and the Rule of Law*. Oxford: Oxford University Press.

Schmitz, Roland. 2011. § 1 StGB. In *Münchner Kommentar zum StGB*, ed. Wolgang Joecks, Klaus Miebach, 41-76. II. ed. Munich: Verlag C.H. Beck.

Scoletta, Marco. 2013. La legalità penale nel sistema europeo dei diritti fondamentali. In *Europa e diritto penale*, eds. Carlo Enrico Paliero and Francesco Viganò, 195-283. Milano: Giuffrè.

Simester, Andrew P., John R. Spencer, Robert Sullivan, and Graham J. Virgo (eds.). 2013. *Simester and Sullivan's Criminal Law. Theory and Doctrine*. V ed. Oxford: Hart.

Spencer, John R., and Antje Pedain. 2005. Approaches to Strict and Constructive Liability in Continental Criminal Law. In *Appraising Strict Liability*, ed. Andrew P. Simester, 237-283. Oxford: Oxford University Press.

Sudre, François. 2001. Le principe de la légalité et la jurisprudence de la Cour européenne des droits de l'homme. *Revue pénitentiaire et de droit pénal* 4: 335-356.

Valentini, Vico. 2012. *Diritto penale intertemporale*. Milano: Giuffrè.

Valticos, Nicolas. 2000. Interprétation juridique et idéologies. In *Protection des droits de l'homme: la perspective européenne. Mélanges à la mémoire de R. Ryssdal*, eds. Paul Mahoney, Franz Matscher, Herbert Petzold and Luzius Wildhaber, 1471-1482. Berlin: Carl Heynemans Verlag KG.

Van Dijk, Pieter, Fried Van Hoof, Arjen van Rijn, and Leo Zwaak (eds.). 2006. *Theory and Practice of the European Convention on Human Rights*. IV ed. Antwerp: Intersentia.

Van Drooghenbroeck, Sébastien. 1996. Interprétation jurisprudentielle et non-retroactivité de la loi pénale. *Revue trimestrielle des droits de l'homme* 27: 459-479.

Viganò, Francesco. 2000. *Stato di necessità e conflitto di doveri*. Milano: Giuffrè.

Vogliotti, Massimo. 2003. Penser l'impensable: le principe de la non-rétroactivité du jugement pénal in malam partem. La perspective italienne, *Diritto & questioni pubbliche* 3: 331-378.

Welzel, Hans. 1952. Il nuovo volto del sistema penale. *Jus* 3: 31-76.

Zagrebelsky, Vladimiro. 2011. La Convenzione europea dei diritti dell'uomo e il principio di legalità nella materia penale. In *La Convenzione europea dei diritti dell'uomo nell'ordinamento penale italiano*, eds. Vittorio Manes and Vladimiro Zagrebelsky, 69-107. Milano: Giuffrè.

CPSIA information can be obtained at www.ICGtesting.com
Printed in the USA
BVOW06*1206050715

407444BV00003B/15/P

9 783319 191799